Ezra Pound in London and Paris
(1908–1925)

Ezra Pound in 1909. (American Literature Collection, Beinecke Rare Book and Manuscript Library, Yale University)

EZRA POUND IN LONDON AND PARIS

1908 · 1925

J. J. Wilhelm

The Pennsylvania State University Press
University Park and London

Other Books on Ezra Pound by J. J. Wilhelm

Dante and Pound: The Epic of Judgement
The Later Cantos of Ezra Pound
Il Miglior Fabbro: The Cult of the Difficult in Daniel, Dante, and Pound
The American Roots of Ezra Pound

Library of Congress Cataloging-in-Publication Data

Wilhelm, James J.
    Ezra Pound in London and Paris (1908–1925) / J.J. Wilhelm.
    p. cm.
    Includes bibliographical references.
    ISBN 978-0-271-02798-2
    1. Pound, Ezra, 1885–1972—Homes and haunts—England—London.
2. Pound, Ezra, 1885–1972—Homes and haunts—France—Paris.
3. Poets, American—20th century—Homes and haunts. I. Title.
PS3531.O82Z893   1990
811'.52—dc20
[B]   89–16149

Copyright © 1990 The Pennsylvania State University
All rights reserved
Printed in the United States of America

It is the policy of The Pennsylvania State University Press to use acid-free paper for the first printing of all clothbound books. Publications on uncoated stock satisfy the minimum requirements of American National Standard for Information Sciences—Permanence of Paper for Printed Library Materials, ANSI Z39.48–1984.

Gerrit Lansing
dreitz om, bos trobaire

Contents

Preface	ix
Acknowledgments	xi
A Chronology of Pound's Early Life	xiii
List of Abbreviations	xv

I. THE CONQUEST OF LONDON

1. The World of Elkin Mathews (August 1908–January 1909) — 3
2. The Triumphs of 1909: The Shakespears and Ford (January–April 1909) — 14
3. A Time of Exultations: Hulme and Yeats (April–October 1909) — 30
4. Romance, Medieval and Modern: Bride and Dorothy (October 1909–June 1910) — 44
5. The Brief Return of 1910 (June 1910–February 1911) — 57
6. From Rummel in Paris to Ford in Giessen (February–August 1911) — 67
7. The Road to Imagism: Some Editors (August 1911–February 1912) — 76
8. "The Aldingtons" and Miss Monroe (February–December 1912) — 91
9. More Potential Imagists: Frost, Fletcher, Lowell (January–August 1913) — 108
10. Art and the Orient: Gaudier-Brzeska and Fenollosa (August 1913–January 1914) — 126
11. Toward Amy's *Ism* and Wyndham's Blasts (January–August 1914) — 140

II. WAR, DISILLUSION, AND DEPARTURE

12. The Delights of Mr. Eliot/The Horrors of War (September 1914–June 1915) — 167
13. The Quest for the *Cantos* (July 1915–December 1916) — 178
14. *The Little Review* and La Belle Iseult (1917) — 193
15. Peace and Major Douglas (1918) — 204
16. Propertius and the Roads of France (1919) — 222
17. Mauberley (and Pound) Say Goodbye (1920) — 239

III. THE PARIS INTERLUDE (1921–1925)

18. The Constellations of Paris — 259

19 A Paris Diary	297
20 "The Fortieth Year of My Life..." (1925)	346
Bibliography	355
I. Works Cited in Text	355
II. Other Sources, Largely Biographical	359
III. Chronology of Pound's Major Books to 1926	362
General Index	365
Index of References to the *Cantos*	384

Preface

Although this book can be read as a separate entity, it is also a sequel to my earlier *American Roots of Ezra Pound* (Garland, 1985). To assist those who have not read the earlier volume, I have supplied at the start a chronology of Pound's early years, emphasizing significant events. Whenever characters from those years appear in this volume, I have tried to identify them properly.

The writing of this book entailed the help of many librarians, especially those at the Humanities Research Center at the University of Texas, Austin; the Lilly Library of Indiana University, and the Burke Library of Hamilton College. Special thanks are also rendered to the staff of the Beinecke Library of Yale, including Patricia Willis, formerly of the Rosenbach Museum. I would also like to mention Nancy Shawcross, formerly with the Lincoln Center for the Performing Arts and now with the Van Pelt Library of the University of Pennsylvania; Louisa Berger of the Youngstown Public Library; and Joseph Consoli of the Alexander Library, Rutgers.

Numerous others assisted me in special areas: Peter Griffin and Carlos Baker on Hemingway; A. Walton Litz and James Longenbach on Yeats; Donald Gallup on Eliot; James Generoso on Major Douglas and Social Credit; Timothy Materer on vorticism; Gerrit Lansing on imagism; Fred Rudge on the Youngstown history of his family; and Pierre L. Ullman and Drusilla Lodge on Margaret Cravens and Eugene Paul Ullman.

I would never have had the courage to progress to this volume without the encouragement of Carroll F. Terrell, Stuart Y. McDougal, Marjorie Perloff, and Wendy Stallard Flory. Hugh Kenner spent an afternoon with me discussing the strategy of procedure. I was also assisted greatly by Pound's daughter, Mary de Rachewiltz, whom I visited at Brunnenburg in May of 1987, and Olga Rudge, whom I interviewed twice: during the misty Venetian winter of 1986 and the bright summer of 1987. I could never have assembled the many photographs in this work without the invaluable help of a former student, William Harper, who supplied me with reproductions of manuscripts and copies of photos, especially those of Paris, before his untimely death at the age of 32 on February 16, 1989 . . . *too quickly taken.*

Acknowledgments

I would like to thank the Estate of Ezra Pound, New Directions Publishing Corporation (New York), and Faber and Faber Ltd. (London) for permission to quote from the works of Ezra Pound listed in the Bibliography; beyond the right of fair usage, I must specifically cite *Personae*, Copyright 1926 by Ezra Pound; *The Cantos of Ezra Pound*, Copyright © 1934, 1937, 1940, 1948, 1956, 1959, 1962, 1963, 1966, 1968, and 1972 by the Estate of Ezra Pound; *Collected Early Poems*, Copyright © 1976 by the Trustees of the Ezra Pound Literary Property Trust, all rights reserved; *Selected Letters*, Copyright 1950 by Ezra Pound and Copyright © 1971 by New Directions; and *Ezra Pound: Translations*, Copyright © 1926, 1954, 1957, 1958, 1960, 1962, and 1963 by Ezra Pound.

I would also like to thank the Trustees of the Ezra Pound Literary Property Trust and the following libraries for permission to quote from unpublished materials in their archives: the American Literature Collection of the Beinecke Rare Book and Manuscript Library of the Yale University Library for materials in the collections of Pound and Evelyn Bride Scratton; the Lilly Library of Indiana University for materials in the collections of Pound and Nancy Cunard; the Harry Ransom Humanities Research Center at the University of Texas, Austin, for Pound materials.

Gracious thanks are also owed to the following:

To John Hemingway and the John F. Kennedy Library for permission to quote from the letters of Ernest Hemingway.

To A. R. A. Hobson, the heirs of Nancy Cunard, and the Lilly Library of Indiana to quote from Cunard's letters to Pound.

To the Macmillan Publishing Company to quote from the works of William Butler Yeats.

To the Rare Books and Manuscript Division of the New York Public Library, Astor, Lenox and Tilden Foundations, to quote from the Ezra Pound–John Quinn correspondence, as well as to Oxford University Press and B. L. Reid to quote from Reid's book *The Man from New York: John Quinn*.

To the © Trustees of the Wyndham Lewis Memorial Trust and to Omar Pound for permission to quote from Wyndham Lewis's *Blasting and Bombardiering* and his letters; as well as to the Estate of Mrs. G.

A. Wyndham Lewis for the use of photographs of Lewis and his art work.

To Omar Pound for granting me the permission to quote from the correspondence of Olivia and Dorothy Shakespear contained in *Ezra Pound and Dorothy Shakespear: Their Letters 1909–1914*, © Omar Pound.

To New Directions Publishing Corporation for permission to quote from Hilda Doolittle's *End to Torment*, © 1979.

A Chronology of Pound's Early Life

October 30, 1885: Born in Hailey, Idaho, to Homer and Isabel Weston Pound; his father was in charge of the Federal Land Office, supervising local mining.

Winter 1887: The Pounds abandon Idaho to live with Isabel's protective uncle Ezra Brown Weston and his wife Frances (Aunt Frank) in their boardinghouse at 24 East 47th Street, Manhattan.

1888: Baby Ezra and his family journey to Chippewa Falls to visit his paternal grandfather, Thaddeus C. Pound, a former lumbering executive and retired congressman from Wisconsin.

1889: Homer Pound accepts a job as an assistant assayer in the United States Mint at Philadelphia, where he works until his retirement in 1928.

1890: The Pounds move to the northern suburb of Jenkintown.

1892: They settle finally into their long-term residence at 166 Fernbrook Avenue, Wyncote. Pound enrolls in the Chelton Hills School nearby.

1894: Uncle Ezra, Pound's namesake, dies in New York; young Ezra attends Florence Ridpath's private school near his house.

1895: Ezra is enrolled in the Wyncote Public School. He transfers to the Cheltenham Military Academy in 1897, when he also professes his faith in Christianity at the Calvary Presbyterian Church; this remained his formal religion until his death, when he was buried in the Protestant section of the island cemetery of San Michele, Venice (1972).

1898: Aunt Frank Weston takes him and his mother on a grand tour of Europe, especially Italy.

1901: He enters the University of Pennsylvania, where he later meets William Carlos Williams, a medical student two years ahead of him. Socially, he also meets Hilda Doolittle (the future H.D.), whose father teaches astronomy at Penn. Another friend is a tubercular artist named William Brooke Smith.

1902: The Pounds and Aunt Frank take Ezra on his second tour of Europe.

1903: Because of poor marks, Pound transfers to Hamilton College in Clinton, New York, where he studies Provençal with William Pierce Shepard and Anglo-Saxon with Joseph D. Ibbotson, as well as numerous other languages.

1905: He receives his bachelor's degree with great improvement in his record, and he dreams of writing a world epic somewhat in the nature of Dante's *Divine Comedy*. He meets a traveling pianist who performs in nearby Utica named Katherine Ruth Heyman, or "Kitty," who also introduces him in time to the pianist Walter Morse Rummel.

Fall 1905: He enrolls again at Penn, studying Romance languages under Hugo Rennert and receiving an M.A. in the spring of 1906.

Summer, Fall 1906: On a fellowship from Penn, he studies Spanish literature in Madrid, and then returns to do poorly in coursework with such professors as Felix Schelling, whom he annoys with iconoclastic remarks. His fellowship is not renewed. Aunt Frank marries Dr. James Beyea and sells her boardinghouse to open a large hotel called the New Weston, which bankrupts her in 1909.

Summer 1907: Pound falls in love with Mary Moore of Trenton (to whom he will dedicate *Personae*) and miraculously finds a teaching job at Wabash College in Crawfordsville, Indiana.

September–February 1907–8: Pound has a disastrous experience trying to lead a one-man Department of Romance Languages in this puritanical school in a provincial town. He is accused by his two spinster landladies of harboring an actress overnight in his room and is fired (with full pay). His most important friend here was Fred Vance, a painter who had studied art in Montparnasse, Paris.

March–August 1908: Jobless in mid-year, Ezra persuades his father to give him some money (with the helpful recommendation of Witter Bynner) to go off to Europe. He settles in Venice for the summer, doing publicity work for Kitty Heyman; he also publishes his first book of poems, *A Lume Spento*, at his own expense, dedicating it to the sickly Smith, who died after his departure. As the summer draws to an end, Pound decides to head north to London to establish his career as a writer.

List of Abbreviations

Pound's works are cited in the most available recent editions; first editions are listed in the Chronology of Pound's Major Works in the Bibliography.

ABCR: *ABC of Reading.* New York: New Directions Paper, 1960.
Cantos: *The Cantos of Ezra Pound.* New York: New Directions, 1972.
CC: *Companion to the "Cantos of Ezra Pound,"* ed. C. F. Terrell, 2 vols. Berkeley: University of California Press, 1980, 1984.
CEP: *Collected Early Poems of Ezra Pound,* ed. M. J. King; introduction by L. Martz. New York: New Directions, 1976.
EPDS: *Ezra Pound and Dorothy Shakespear: Their Letters 1909–1914.* ed. Omar Pound and A. Walton Litz. New York: New Directions, 1984.
EPMC: *Ezra Pound and Margaret Cravens: A Tragic Friendship, 1910—1912,* ed. Omar Pound and Robert Spoo. Durham: Duke, 1988.
FLMS: Fletcher, John Gould. *Life Is My Song.* New York: Farrar and Rinehart, 1937.
FSL: Frost, Robert. *Selected Letters,* ed. L. Thompson. New York: Holt, Rinehart, 1964.
GBM: *Gaudier-Brzeska: A Memoir.* New York: New Directions, 1970.
GK: *Guide to Kulchur.* New York: New Directions, 1970.
HSL: Hemingway, Ernest. *Selected Letters,* ed. Carlos Baker. New York: Charles Scribner's Sons, 1981.
LBB: Lewis, Wyndham. *Blasting and Bombardiering.* London: Eyre and Spottiswoode, 1937.
LE: *Literary Essays of Ezra Pound,* ed. T. S. Eliot. New York: New Directions Paper, 1968.
LL: Lawrence, D. H. *Letters,* ed. J. T. Boulton. Vol. I: Cambridge: Cambridge University Press, 1979.
MPL: Monroe, Harriet. *A Poet's Life: Seventy Years in a Changing World.* New York: Macmillan, 1938.
PC: Paige Carbons: Letters by Ezra Pound, largely to his parents; American Literature Collection, Beinecke Library, Yale University.

PD:	*Pavannes and Divagations.* New York: New Directions, 1958.
Pers.:	*Personae: Collected Poems.* New York: New Directions, 1926, 1949.
PF:	*Pound/Ford: The Story of a Literary Friendship.* New York: New Directions, 1982.
PJ:	*Pound/Joyce: Letters*, ed. Forrest Read. New York: New Directions, 1970.
PL:	*Pound/Lewis: Correspondence*, ed. Timothy Materer. New York: New Directions, 1985.
PR:	*Paris Review.*
RJQ:	Reid, B. L. *The Man From New York: John Quinn and His Friends.* New York: Oxford, 1968.
SL:	*Selected Letters 1907–1941 of Ezra Pound*, ed. D. D. Paige. New York: New Directions Paper, 1971.
SP:	*Selected Prose 1909–1965 of Ezra Pound*, ed. William Cookson. New York: New Directions, 1973.
SR:	*Spirit of Romance.* New York: New Directions Paper, 1968.
TEP:	*Translations of Ezra Pound*, intro. Hugh Kenner. London: Faber and Faber, 1953.
TSEL:	*Letters of T. S. Eliot.* Vol. I (1898–1922), ed. Valerie Eliot. San Diego: Harcourt Brace Jovanovich, 1988.
YCP:	Yeats, William Butler. *Collected Poems.* New York: Macmillan, 1956.
YL:	Yeats, William Butler. *Letters*, ed. A. Wade. London: Hart-Davis, 1954.

I

THE CONQUEST OF LONDON

1

The World of Elkin Mathews (August 1908–January 1909)

Ezra Pound arrived in London on August 14, 1908, prepared to assault the literary scene, and, as we know, he did this with great success. In Letter 53 to Mary Moore, Pound says that he traveled from Venice to London in a seventy-two-hour jaunt by train ("sans bunk"). He spent one night in Paris with a friend named Walter Morse Rummel, a handsome, blond pianist who was the grandson of the inventor of the telegraph and the Morse Code, and who had inherited enough money to locate himself in Paris for the rest of his life. Rummel had arranged some music for Pound's pianist friend Kitty Heyman back in the states in 1906 and was known in America for his concerts.

In a one-page essay titled "How I Began," which appeared in *T. P.'s Weekly* on June 6, 1913, Pound said: "I came to London with £3 knowing no one" (707). This is not quite accurate. During his fellowship visit of 1906, the poet had met Mrs. Ann Withey (whom everyone called "Miss"), and he now revisited her comfortable rooming house at 8 Duchess St. near Portland Place. She endorsed the card that enabled him to use the British Museum Library, which was not far away. In the already-mentioned letter to Miss Moore, Pound said that he was going to Steinway Hall to arrange some musical affairs for a woman—either Kitty, who would join him after her Venetian concert on September 2, or a friend of hers, a Scottish soprano named Elizabeth Granger Kerr, who also endorsed his card and loaned him ten shillings until money could arrive from home. Called affectionately "Meg," Miss Kerr remained a friend during Pound's London years; her recitals of Hebridean and other folk songs were of special interest to the Celtic circle gathered around the poet Yeats, who had long been Pound's idol during his college years.

After a short time, it was clear that Pound could not afford Miss Withey's establishment, and so he took a dreary room in the northeastern suburb of Islington. There he pawned a few of his copies of his first book, *A Lume Spento*, to bring in some money until a subsidy from his father could arrive. Five years later, in the *New Age* of January 23, he said: "During the prelude of my London existence . . . before people began to let me into their drawing-rooms—I was permitted, even forced, to notice some of the viscera of the metaphorical beast . . . the implacable dullness of Suburbia—often a healthy dullness . . . boarding-houses, complete with billiard table (no cushions), bath (out of order), hot and cold water (geyser not working), pink, frilly paper decorations, complete board and lodging, 12s. 6d. per week. . . . Foods, unthinkable and unimaginable, odours, etc.! And I haven't been anywhere near the bottom. I've been far enough."

At last four pounds arrived, and he wrote home on September 27: "I move back to a respectable part of London tomorrow. . . . The Duchess St. was over high." He then took up quarters at 48 Langham Street, not far from the Withey place; this was near Great Titchfield Street and across the alley from one of the Yorkshire Grey pubs. Up in his garret room, Pound could hear the conversations of the lower-middle-class clientele as they emerged from the pub at closing time. He recalled one of these in Canto 80/502:

> "Jolly woman" said the resplendent head waiter
> 20 years after i.e. after old Kait'
> had puffed in, stewing with rage
> concerning the landlady's *doings*
>   with a lodger unnamed
> az waz near Gt Ti[t]chfield St. next door to the pub
> "married wumman, you couldn't fool *her*"

In the 1930s, Pound published some satiric verses under the name of Alfred Venison, the Poet of Titchfield Street (see Pound's modern *Personae*, 257ff.).

From the start, Pound's problem was a lack of money. As he said in "How I Began," "during the first five years . . . I had exactly one brief poem accepted by one American magazine," and the net result of his activities was "in cash, five dollars." Concerning his books published in England, he claimed that he had not received "a brass farthing." In other words, despite his literary triumphs to come, he never reaped any financial profit to speak of. This constant inability to support himself without some assistance from his family helps to explain why the subject of economics looms so large in his work.

As soon as he was settled, Pound devised ways of marketing his already published book. Very perceptively, he sought out the famous bookseller and publisher Elkin Mathews (1851–1921), who ran a Dickensianly congenial shop in a little bent lane called Vigo Street, off bustling Regent Street. Mathews was well known to Pound because he had published *The Wind Among the Reeds*, a book by Pound's idol Yeats, in 1899. He and John Lane, who ran a shop across the way from 6B Vigo Street, had been partners in publishing back in the 1890s, when they issued *The Yellow Book*. Splitting away, Mathews continued to publish that work for a time with Aubrey Beardsley as the well-known illustrator. Under his own name, he also published such writers as Lionel Johnson, John Masefield, and J. M. Synge. One year before Pound's arrival, he had issued a slim volume of poems titled *Chamber Music*, written by an exiled Irishman named James Joyce; but Pound would not be aware of this man until Yeats mentioned him four years after this time.

Both Mathews and his former partner agreed to distribute some copies of *A Lume Spento* in their shops. Of the two men, Mathews seemed to Pound to be the easier one to deal with. *Punch Magazine* once described Elkin as being monkish and medieval-looking. Photographs show that he had a gentle, rounded face, with balding hair and soft, watery eyes. He was very sympathetic to the impoverished young American, and his friendship proved to be invaluable, because his shop was a favorite meeting place for writers to gather during the late afternoons, where they might sip tea and talk about things literary. Pound's attitude toward Mathews changed somewhat in the 1910s, when the *Selected Letters* show him describing the publisher as stupid, insensitive, and too afraid of blue-nosed censorship—but this is typical of the kind of antagonism one often finds between authors and their publishers. After Mathews died in 1921, Ezra wrote his widow a very moving letter in which he stressed his awareness that it was Mathews who first believed in him enough to accept his work, and who launched him on the literary scene.

By October the name of Ezra Pound could be heard around town among circles who were interested in poetry. On October 21, Ezra wrote his old friend William Carlos Williams from Penn a long letter in which he defended *A Lume Spento* against Williams's charges that much of it was didactic or dull. Pound very pointedly remarked that Williams did not seem aware that he was using a poetic intermediary to voice various sentiments, and that these opinions were not necessarily those of the poet himself. Then, in a way that anticipated some of the beliefs of imagism, Pound listed what he felt were the four most important objectives in his work:

1. To paint the thing as I see it.
2. Beauty.
3. Freedom from didacticism.
4. It is only good manners if you repeat a few other men. . . . Utter originality is of course out of the question. (*SL*, 6)*

When Pound was not spending mornings at the Museum reading in his announced course of study, the Latin humanists of the Renaissance, he was often in the little shop on Vigo Street meeting the fascinating men of letters who assembled there. Some of these were young, but in the main the types that Pound found most appealing were the older men, of the sort that he described very beautifully in "I Vecchii" (*Pers.*, 181):

> They will come no more,
> The old men with beautiful manners . . .
>
> Old men with beautiful manners,
> Sitting in the Row of a morning;
> Walking on the Chelsea Embankment.

Among the older men whom he met through Mathews were Selwyn Image, who made a strong first impression, Victor Plarr, Laurence Binyon, and Ernest Rhys—all of whom had vivid memories of a well-established literary past.

Selwyn Image, who was born in Avignon, France, in 1849, was both a writer and an artist. In Paris, he had known the French poet Verlaine, and in London he had moved earlier in a circle around John Ruskin and the pre-Raphaelite painters (see Canto 89/601). He had maintained a studio for a time in a house at 20 Fitzroy Street, where Lionel Johnson, Yeats's alcoholic friend, and others painted, and where the musician Arnold Dolmetsch gave clavichord recitals. After

---

*See Abbreviations on pages xv–xvi and Works Cited in Text on pages 355–59 when authors or titles are given.

1910 the "serene Image," as Ernest Rhys called him in *Everyman Remembers* (97–98), became the Slade Professor of Poetry at Oxford. He died in 1930.

Victor Gustave Plarr (1863–1929) was a transplanted Alsatian from Strasbourg who was the Librarian of the Royal College of Surgeons. He was a former member of the Rhymers' Club (with Yeats, Johnson, and Ernest Dowson) who liked to recount to Pound at Sunday dinners stories about the Franco-Prussian War, especially the charge of Galliffet, which is narrated in his version in Canto 16/70. Plarr is also the Monsieur Verog of the "Siena Mi Fé" section of *Hugh Selwyn Mauberley:*

> Among the pickled foetuses and bottled bones,
> Engaged in perfecting the catalogue,
> I found the last scion of the
> Senatorial families of Strasbourg, Monsieur Verog.
>
> For two hours he talked of Gallif[f]et;
> Of Dowson; of the Rhymers' Club;
> Told me how Johnson (Lionel) died
> By falling from a high stool in a pub . . .
>
> M. Verog, out of step with the decade,
> Detached from his contemporaries,
> Neglected by the young,
> Because of these reveries.
>
> (*Pers.*, 193)

Ezra was not, however, one of the young who neglected Plarr.

Laurence Binyon (1869–1943) was a writer, art expert, and finally Keeper of Prints and Drawings at the British Museum. In 1907 he had finished a four-volume catalogue of English drawings in the Museum, and he was publishing in 1908 an important book called *Painting in the Far East.* He was also a poet, and became especially close to Pound in the 1930s, when "BinBin" (as Ezra soon called him) was translating Dante's *Divine Comedy* into a workable English terza rima, with Ezra at his shoulder. When they first met, Pound described Binyon as a modern Wordsworth or Matthew Arnold (PC 98). He respected Binyon's judgment in many ways, especially the advice that he once gave to Yeats: "Slowness is beauty" (Canto 87/572).

During his incarceration at Pisa, Pound recalled these idyllic days when he spent the mornings studying at the Museum and then took lunch with Binyon and his followers. Often they went to the Vienna Café, which had a glass ceiling on the ground floor and rich fare, with cheaper food upstairs. The waiters in the Oxford Street establishment were almost entirely Austrian. Binyon would usually eat there with his protégés, such as Arthur Schloss, who changed his German name to Waley when World War I came. Waley would one day be considered a rival of Pound's when it came to Chinese translation:

> Mr Binyon's young prodigies
> pronounced the word: Penthesilea
> There were mysterious figures
> that emerged from recondite recesses
> and ate at the WIENER CAFÉ
> which died into banking, Jozefff may have followed
> his emperor.
>
> (80/506)

Josef was an Austrian waiter who went home at the outbreak of World War I, while the restaurant became a bank. Penthesília (not -éa) was an Amazon Queen, a character in Binyon's two poems "The Coming of the Amazons" and "The Battle."

Of all the older men, none was more valuable at this time than Ernest Rhys (1859–1946), a doughty Welsh-Englishman who had long since earned an excellent reputation as the editor of the Camelot and Everyman series of classics. In 1908 he still had very strong ties with the publisher J. M. Dent of Everyman fame, and it was because of his praise that they would publish Pound's *Spirit of Romance* in 1910. Yet despite this aid, Rhys also helped perpetrate one of the less flattering portraits of Ezra. In *Everyman Remembers* (244), Rhys tells how at a poetry session held at his house in Hermitage Lane, Hampstead, Pound became bored with somebody's reading and started to munch on a bouquet of red tulips.

This questionable episode has been much quoted, but there are also others who claimed that Pound was acting in a very Bohemian manner during his early days in London. The half-American novelist Phyllis Bottome, whose relatives attended Penn, said in *From the Life* (71): "When I first met Ezra at a tea-party given by May Sinclair in pre-war London, he made the impression on me of an electric eel," since he was a "tall, slight, nervous young fellow, with the face of a scholarly satyr, red-gold hair, and a pointed beard of the same colour." She added that he "endangered every chair he sat on," anticipating the objection of Gertrude Stein in the 1920s.

Another older man of letters to befriend Pound was the jewel-collector Edgar Jepson (1863–1938), a "lover of jade" as he is affectionately called in Canto 74/433. Jepson said in his memoirs that when he first met Ezra, not long after the poet's arrival, at a meeting of the

Square Club, the young visitor was "crowned with a mass of bright fair hair and often bearded; wearing a velvet coat and one turquoise ear-ring, he was the most picturesque of Pennsylvanians, and how the much dingier Square Club writers did hate that picturesqueness! . . . I always saw him, not so much as a poet, as the warrior of the arts" (152f.). Jepson also noted that women "ran after him with commendable pertinacity." Clearly there were many different opinions about Pound's eccentric behavior and dress—as many as there had been at staid Wabash College. Obviously Pound took risks at times, but they were calculated risks, and they were not openly offensive to most people. To the more solid members of the older generation (Mathews, Plarr, Binyon, and Rhys), this young man from the States was a welcomed breath of fresh air in the stuffy drawing rooms of "polite" Edwardian society. Whatever sins Ezra Pound might be guilty of, boredom was not one of them.

Shortly after his arrival, Pound made another move that had important ramifications for the future. Acting on the suggestion given in Philadelphia by a ticket seller named Smith to look up a certain Sullivan, who was connected with the Covent Garden Market, Pound did find the man and learned through him that because of the death of one Churton Collins, there was now an opening for a lecturer at the London Polytechnic Institute. Armed with his master's degree, Pound went intrepidly to the school, which was not far from Miss Withey's place. There he was delighted to learn that he would indeed be hired to deliver some lectures from January 21 to February 25 on the subject: "The Development of Literature in Southern Europe." This uplifting news made him once again entertain a glimmer of hope that he might be able to support himself in the future in some academic position.

From his little room on Langham Street, Pound wrote to Mary Moore that he was assembling a new book of about fifteen poems to appear before Christmas, to be titled *A Quinzaine for This Yule* (Moore Letter 56). The poems would attack the sacrosanct "Mrs. Grundy" mentality that he found so prevalent among the British. In December, precisely on target, the book appeared, published by Pollock and Company and dedicated to "The Aube of the West Dawn," who was Kitty Heyman. She was now in London between engagements. Letter 57 to Mary Moore, written the day before Christmas, mentions that Kitty will soon be off to Berlin to play the piano with the Philharmonic Orchestra, and she will not be back in England until March.

Letter 60 to Mary, written on March 23 of 1909 (the anniversary of his landing in Gibraltar), said that the pianist was due back soon from her tour, but the two were conducting themselves with "frigid

The "Kitty-mama," who helped Pound make his London Conquest. (American Literature Collection, Beinecke Rare Book and Manuscript Library, Yale University)

politeness." It appears that Miss Heyman's successes abroad and her rather strong views on women's rights had created a certain friction, and very soon "Her Highness" vanishes from the scene. We shall encounter her again on Pound's return to New York in 1910. Pound also told Mary in his pre-Christmas letter that he had received about seventy poems from home, and that he was putting together another book to be called *Personae;* this would be dedicated to her.

Meanwhile, the one hundred copies of *A Quinzaine* published by Pollock sold out, and Elkin Mathews, like Santa Claus, quickly decided to issue a second run for post-Christmas sales. This he did, and Pound would soon have two Mathews volumes in print. Culled largely from his San Trovaso Notebook of the previous summer in Venice, *A Quinzaine* opened with a dreamily sentimental epigraph written by one Weston St. Llemys (Loomis), who, of course, was none other than Pound himself. It moved through several poems written for or about Kitty Heyman. The finest poem, and the only one to make its way into later collections of Pound's lyrics, was the strangely compelling "Night Litany," which calls on the "God of the night" to purify the heart of the person praying.

In "How I Began," Pound spoke of the mystical spell of this poem: "I know that for days the 'Night Litany' seemed a thing so little my own that I could not bring myself to sign it." The remainder of the poems in this volume are reminiscent of the sensual, often archaic style of Swinburne. Pound at this time was eager to meet the aged and sickly poet, but that was not to be. Swinburne died on April 10, 1909, from pneumonia, without ever encountering the newcomer. Pound lamented this setback in his Conquest of London in Canto 82/523:

> Swinburne my only miss
> and I didn't know he'd been to see Landor
> >   *and* they told me this that an' tother
> and when old Mathews went he saw the three teacups
> >   two for Watts Dunton who liked to let his tea cool,
> So old Elkin had only one glory
> >   He did carry Algernon's suit case *once*
> when he, Elkin, first came to London.
> >   But given what I know now I'd have
> >   got thru it somehow . . .

Theodore Watts-Dunton was Swinburne's friend and caretaker, who lived with him in the end. The events described here probably took place in the 1880s, when Mathews was new in town from Exeter.

As 1909 came on, Pound seemed to be gaining some control over his situation. Taking the poems for a third collection to the messy but comfortable rear office in Mathews' bookshop, Ezra asked the elderly editor if he would be willing to publish his new book of verse, *Personae*. Mathews looked over the manuscript, and, after a time, said, according to "How I Began":

Mr. E.M.: "Ah, eh, do you care to contribute to the costs of publishing?"
Mr. E.P.: "I've got a shilling in my clothes, if that's any use to you."
Mr. E.M.: "Oh well, I rather want to publish 'em anyhow."

Mathews then gave the novice the same generous terms that he had given the popular romantic novelist Maurice Hewlett, but, as was already reported, no royalties were ever paid.

By January 7, Pound announced to his father that Mathews had arranged for him to meet a very interesting younger poet named James Griffyth Fairfax, who had been born in Australia in 1886 and was now studying at New College, Oxford. Fairfax was a member of a group of younger poets that included Frederic Manning, who had been born in 1882, the son of a mayor of Sydney, Australia. He had been brought to England in 1897 to be educated by one Reverend Arthur Galton. Pound became friendly with the two younger poets, and he even reviewed Manning's first book of poetry, *The Vigil of Brunhild* (1907), in the *Book News Monthly* of Philadelphia in April of 1909. For a time he was also close to Fairfax, who later reviewed him favorably in Australia, but as that young man drifted further and further into conventional Oxonian circles, he removed himself from Ezra's ken until he died in 1976. Manning, however, remained a friend for many years until his death in 1935. It was he who introduced Ezra to a wealthy socialite whom everyone called "Aunt Eva" in the middle of January of 1909.

Eva Fowler (1871–1921) was an American citizen through her father Paul Neumann, a naturalized American of Prussian origins, but she had married a successful British steam-plow manufacturer named Alfred "Taffy" Fowler (1860–1933). This very sociable couple held numerous teas and parties in their town quarters in Knightsbridge, across from Hyde Park, as well as in their country house in Kent, known as Daisy Meadow. Taffy is mentioned in Canto 18, where he is called "Hamish." His hard work and ingenuity in selling his products abroad are contrasted with the double-dealing exploits of the infamous munitions salesman "Zenos Metevsky" (true name: Sir Basil Zaharoff). Eva, who was partial toward Americans, was instantly fond of this newcomer from Philadelphia, and she promised that she would do her best to escort him into her own quarter in the London social-literary world. It was through her and Manning that Pound met Olivia Shakespear ("undoubtedly the most charming woman in London"; Paige Carbon, 96*) and her daughter Dorothy, whom he would marry in 1914.

---

*These are carbons made by D. D. Paige of Pound's letters, especially to his parents, which are essential for any early biography of Pound. They are housed in the Beinecke Library at Yale and are currently being edited by Pound's daughter, Mary de Rachewiltz; hereafter they are abbreviated as *PC*.

2

The Triumphs of 1909: The Shakespears and Ford (January–April 1909)

The Shakespears lived in a comfortable house at 12 Brunswick Gardens in Kensington, where more and more of Pound's friends would live. Henry Hope Shakespear (1849–1923) was a typical lawyer: cautious, punctilious, and not at all anxious to have his daughter consort with a poor poet. His wife Olivia was a lovely, dark-haired, dramatic-looking woman who was well-known as a novelist. In 1909 she was working on *Uncle Hilary*, the story of an older man who eventually marries a younger woman who has been betrayed by her husband in India, where Olivia had family ties. Uncle Hilary was also the name of a small statue of Buddha that sat in the Shakespears' living room, a parlor "full of white magic," as Ezra described it to Mary Moore (Letter 59). Mr. Shakespear's family, which was not related to the famous William, had been ropemakers in the 1600s who later became involved in business and the civil service in India, where Henry Hope had been born. As a result, both he and Olivia, as well as their daughter, had an interest in things Oriental.

Olivia had been born on the Isle of Wight, the younger daughter of Major General Henry Tod Tucker, who had served in the Orient; her birth date is usually given as 1863, but 1864 seems more correct (see

Olivia Shakespear as she appeared in the *Literary Year-Book* of 1897. Yeats likened her profile to that on a Sicilian coin in a letter to her on December 6, 1926.

Paideuma 15, 240). Her father was related to a famous Virginia family that included the jurist St. George Tucker. One of her cousins was the poet Lionel Johnson, the alcoholic friend of Yeats who had introduced her to the Irishman back in 1894, igniting an affair that lasted for about two years and was resumed in 1903. In 1909 Yeats was back in the company of his old tormentor, the beautiful actress and revolutionary Maud Gonne, who was treating him more kindly now. But the friendship between Yeats and Olivia went on undiminished; known to the poet as Diana Vernon or D.V. in his notes and diary, Olivia remained sympathetic to him until her death in 1938, even when others were skeptical of his forays into the occult. This interest in the mysterious was a tie that bound Yeats to the two Shakespear women—although it was quite common in upper-middle-class circles of the time. Even when she was close to her death in 1973, Dorothy would often speak about "vibrations" and extrasensory perceptions in a serious way.

Dorothy was a bright, pert, pretty English girl with a winning smile and twinkling eyes, although some people found her cold. Born in London on September 14, 1886 (just one year after Ezra), she had been educated at fashionable schools in England and Geneva, where she had mastered French, albeit in the Swiss manner. In school she had become fond of painting, and her letters to Ezra—edited by Omar Pound and A. Walton Litz—are interspersed with sketches and drawings, just as his often contain calligraphic designs, especially after his interest in Chinese. Dorothy's penchant for art came in handy when Ezra needed to introduce some Chinese characters into his work, since she could freely supply these. She was enormously helpful to Ezra during the coming vorticist period when Pound was close to Wyndham Lewis and other painters.

Dorothy was already twenty-two when Ezra entered her life, and she was a rather advanced twenty-seven when they married. After her return from Switzerland, she had been living the confined life foisted upon single upper-middle-class girls at the time. Perhaps this explains why the sudden appearance of this eccentric young poet from the States excited her so much. Dorothy wrote the following impassioned words in her private notebook for February 16 of that year:

> "Ezra."
> Listen to it—Ezra! Ezra!—And a third time—Ezra! He has a wonderful, beautiful face, a high forehead . . . prominent over the eyes; a long, delicate nose, with little, red nostrils; a strange mouth, never still, & quite elusive; a square chin, slightly cleft in the middle—the whole face pale; the eyes gray-blue; the hair golden-brown, and curling in soft wavy crinkles. Large hands, with long, well-shaped, fingers, and beautiful nails.
>
> Some people have complained of untidy boots . . . how could they look at his boots, when there is his . . . moving, beautiful face to watch? Oh! fools, fools! . . . I do not think he knows he is beautiful. . . .
>
> Oh! Ezra! how beautiful you are! With your pale face and hair! I wonder—are you a genius? or are you only an artist in Life? (*EPDS*, 3)

As the passage shows, Dorothy fell in love with the American at first sight. This "different" poet clearly seemed to be the person who might free her from the rather humdrum life she was living. Throughout her notebook Dorothy writes about Ezra as if he were Keith Rickman, the hero of May Sinclair's popular novel *The Divine Fire*, an artist who inflamed women. In her entry for November 4–5 of this year, Dorothy quotes a letter from Fred Manning: "He (Ezra) is not as other men are—He has seen the Beatific Vision Which is an extenuating circumstance" (*EPDS*, 9). Dorothy retained this strong feeling for him to her dying day, as Hugh Kenner has let us know in his sensitive portrait "D.P. Remembered"—even in her old age when she was spending her winters alone in Rapallo at the Hotel Grande Italia e Lido, and he was living up on the hill in the house of Olga Rudge, his lover from the 1920s onward.

On Ezra's side, one does not feel passion so much as affectionate warmth. He calls her "Coz" (Cousin, one of the family) rather than "darling." He writes in a sprightly, jocular vein that does not have the smoldering intensity that one feels in his letters to Mary Moore. Still, it is clear that he felt a love for this young woman; he spent a great deal of time after January of 1909 at teas with the Shakespear ladies and in accompanying them on vacations. From the start, Ezra was also fascinated by Mrs. Shakespear. It is almost as if he were a Tristan (one of his favorite personas) who has gone away to a foreign land to be cured by an older woman, but who ends up by marrying her daughter—both with the name of Isolde.

Some people have foolishly suggested that Ezra never did love Dorothy. But he had no social or financial gain from their eventual marriage five years later. By that time, he had fully ingratiated himself into the Shakespear world, and Dorothy's income was enough to support only herself. Even when other women did appear—Bride Scratton, Iseult Gonne, Nancy Cunard, and others—he never abandoned the sprightly Dorothy. He was truly one of the family—much closer to the women than to old Henry Hope Shakespear, who, on learning that his wife might leave him for another man, seemed more concerned about the loss of his social position than of his wife—and so Yeats and Olivia decided it was kinder to simply deceive him than to totally abandon him.

Hugh Kenner has judged the matter fairly in his sketch of Dorothy in *Paideuma* (2, 493):

> Ezra Pound's story is inextricable from hers. "She can be alarmingly aloof," said a man who knew her well. He thought that perhaps the bond with that aloofness helped shape, for

better or worse, the way Ezra's psyche set during the first War. On the other hand, would Gaudier, or would Lewis, have come to count for so much in Ezra's mind had Dorothy not lived through her eyes, and had her mother Olivia not purchased Lewises and Gaudiers? His alliance with Miss Rudge was with a musician, as though to redress some balance of the senses: an ear-world. For years he loved both women.

Sometimes knowing the end of a story impedes us from understanding the beginning.

Although Pound could now meet Yeats at almost any point he wished, that still was not possible because the Irish poet was tied up in business in Dublin; they would not meet until May. And so, postponing the main objective in his London mission, Ezra turned to the serious business of delivering his lectures at the Polytechnic. There were six of them, and they covered the following areas, all of which had been prepared by his work at Hamilton and Penn:

1. Introduction, with criticism from Plato to Yeats
2. The major troubadours
3. Religion in the Middle Ages: St. Francis of Assisi
4. Portuguese poetry
5. Latin lyricists of the Renaissance
6. Books and Their Makers in the Middle Ages—which was based largely on a book with the same name by George H. Putnam, which he had studied at Hamilton

Most of the time he wrote out his lectures in advance, except for the first two, which he delivered in a semi-impromptu manner, blending rough notes with spot readings. He did not have a particularly stunning effect on his audiences, which were held to a minimum because of the dire January weather. Most of the time the building was enveloped in a dense fog that cut down on the turnouts, and since his pay depended on the number of his listeners, he was not exactly enriching himself.

By the end of January, however, Pound was sought after by many people other than the Shakespears. In a letter written to Mother Isabel on January 31, where Ezra mentions the charming Mrs. Shakespear for the first time, he runs through his busy agenda for the week:

Monday: lunch with Eva Fowler.
Tuesday: to Lady Russell's house to see a parlor play featuring Miss Schletter, with lunch following.

Wednesday: Manning in town from Reverend Galton's place at Edenham in Lincolnshire for lunch at Eva's, along with young Fairfax down from Oxford.
Thursday: lecture day; lunch with Miss Aimée Lowther.

His life was rich, but his wallet was poor. Still, he could crow to "Bill" Williams in a letter of February 3: "Am by way of falling into the crowd that does things here. London, deah old London is the place for poesy" (*SL*, 7).

It might be useful to give a rundown of some of the people whom Pound encountered at this time, including those already mentioned, with dates taken from the Paige Carbons of letters to his parents (when the dates are included):

January 31: Manning to present him to Laurence Binyon
February 6: Mathews to present him to Selwyn Image, Binyon
February 10: Delightful meeting with Binyon
Paige Carbon 101: Supper at Ernest Rhys's with Fairfax
February 21: Meets with Selwyn Image, who talks about Verlaine; tea with the Shakespears; May Sinclair takes him to dinner at the Lyceum Club
Paige Carbon 103: Disappointing visit to the Poets' Club to hear George Bernard Shaw, Hilaire Belloc and Maurice Hewlett carrying on in a pompous way (his adulation of Shaw, whom he had idolized at Penn, now having vanished)
Paige Carbon 108: Victor Plarr, "most congenial."

With this success, it is easy to understand why he moaned in his letter home on March 15: "I seem to fit better here in London than any where else, if I can only guess wot's the answer to the problem of sustinence."

The meeting with May Sinclair, which was arranged by the always accommodating Mathews (in lieu of royalties), was important for a variety of reasons. First of all, May was an ardent feminist who was immediately drawn to the iconoclastic American; she fed him at clubs and restaurants like Pagani's, where the Italian cuisine reminded him of Italy; she defended him constantly from attacks (especially in 1912 in her book *Feminism* and later); and she in turn introduced him to her own circle of friends, including one Ford Madox Hueffer, who would change his last name to Ford in 1919.

At first Ezra was a bit suspicious of May, suspecting that she was perhaps sizing him up as the model for another character in a book like *The Divine Fire*, but soon he discarded this distrust and became her devoted follower, even feeling free to stop in on her whenever he chose. In *End to Torment*, Hilda Doolittle describes how she was taken to May's studio in Edwardes Square after her arrival in London:

> Richard [Aldington] and Ezra and I were walking together in Kensington that morning when Ezra said, "We'll look in on May." Miss Sinclair opened the studio apartment door. Her somewhat Queen Mary bang or fringe was done up in curl papers. I tugged at Richard's sleeve to suggest that we go home, but Ezra had already swung on into the studio. May Sinclair made no reference to her early morning appearance. She was as Norman Douglas once said, "a rare thing nowadays, my dear, a gentlewoman." (10)

Hilda goes on to mention visiting May during the twenties, when the once-vigorous woman (who had been born near Liverpool in 1863) was now in decline, constantly attended by a grim nurse. Then May suffered through years of collapse. Before her death in 1946, she remembered her three young visitors and left them each small sums of money and books from her library. Ironically, this was at a time when both Hilda and Ezra were now institutionalized—she at a clinic in Lausanne and he in St. Elizabeth's in Washington.

We do not know exactly when in 1909 Pound first met Ford, but some time in early March is a good guess, because Pound mentions Ford's journal shortly afterward in his letters (PC 103). May Sinclair took him to South Lodge for a literary-game party, according to Ford's best biographer, Arthur Mizener (173), but the young earringed poet did not carry off the first prize of bay leaves. There is no doubt that, of all of Pound's many friends, "Fordie" was one of the truest. We need only go to the *Cantos* to see the high esteem that Pound attached to the man. In the following passage, Pound presents Ford as a masterful expresser of things (*res*), not mere words (*verba*), in comparison with William Yeats:

> and for all that old Ford's conversation was better,
> consisting in *res* non *verba*,
> despite William's anecdotes, in that Fordie
> never dented an idea for a phrase's sake
> and had more humanitas [Chinese character] jen
> (Canto 82/525)

Even stronger is the tribute that Pound wrote on Ford's death in France in 1939:

There passed from us this June a very gallant combatant for those things of the mind and of letters which have been in our time too little prized.... For the ten years before I got to England there would seem to have been no one but Ford who held that French clarity and simplicity in the writing of English verse and prose were of immense importance as in contrast to the use of a stilted traditional dialect, a "language of verse" unused in the actual talk of the people....

In 1908 London was full of "gargoyles," of poets, that is, with high reputation, most of whose work has gone since into the discard. At that time, and in the few years preceding, there appeared without notice various fasciculae which one can still, surprisingly, read, and they were not designed for mouthing, for the "rolling out" of "ohs."...

I did not in those days care about prose. If "prose" meant anything to me, it meant Tacitus..., a damned dangerous model for a young man.... Start with Tacitus and be cured by Flaubert *viâ* Ford, or start with Ford or Maupassant and be girt up with Tacitus.... (*PF,* 171, 173)

Ford's *English Review* had appeared for the first time in December of 1908, and Pound noted proudly that Ford published people like Thomas Hardy, Henry James, W. H. Hudson, Joseph Conrad, Anatole France, Arnold Bennett, H. G. Wells, and John Galsworthy—all within the brief space of about a year. Ford says in *Thus To Revisit* (58 n.) that he and Arthur Marwood founded the review in order to print Hardy's "A Sunday Morning Tragedy," which nobody else would touch. Pound regarded this journal as one of the finest of the century. It was also the first serious review to publish his poetry.

Looking like a quintessential German and acting like a quintessential English gentleman (or so he imagined), Ford was described as follows by his part-time editorial assistant Douglas Goldring in his early reminiscence *South Lodge:* "My first impressions of Ford are of a tall thin man with fair hair and a blonde moustache which imperfectly concealed defective front teeth. He wore a grey-blue swallow-tail coat of uncertain cut, carried a leather despatch case of the kind the French call a *serviette* and had an 'important' manner which in some ways suggested an Under-Secretary of State" (15). Less kind commentators, like the hypercritical Wyndham Lewis, described him as "a lemonish pink giant ... with his mouth hanging open like a big silly fish" in his appropriately named *Rude Assignment* (161). Even Ford's young friend David Garnett, the son of Edward (Keeper of the Books at the British Museum) and Constance (the well-known translator from Russian), could not resist mentioning Ford's "rabbit teeth in his shark's mouth" in his *Golden Echo* (I, 188).

Ford's father, Francis Hueffer, had been a critic of music (especially Wagner) who had left his native Germany to come to London to work for the *Times*. He was the author of a book that was known to Pound from his Hamilton days: *The Troubadours, a History of Provençal Life and Literature in the Middle Ages*. He also edited the works of the troubadour Cabestan and wrote an opera called *The Troubadour* based on Cabestan's life (see Pound's Canto 4). Mr. Hueffer, whose first name was originally Franz, soon became a British citizen, and he married the youngest daughter of the well-known Victorian artist Ford Madox Brown. Born in 1873, "Fordie" grew up in a society of pre-Raphaelite painters, musicians, and writers, like the Rossettis, and he very early learned the power and importance of words—especially English words. In another of his many memoirs, *Return to Yesterday*, Ford describes his youthful friendships in Kent near the Channel with Henry James, Stephen Crane, and especially the Polish writer Joseph Conrad, whose works he helped to "English." Being in some sense a foreigner himself (because he always felt the German part of his roots strongly), he was obviously amenable to meeting all foreigners, especially Americans.

In 1909, when Pound first met him, Ford was living and working at 84 Holland Park Avenue, not far from 10 Church Walk, where Pound would move in September. The first time that Wyndham Lewis visited the office, the editor was not to be found in the largish, L-shaped room on the second floor above a rather smelly poultry-fish-and-cheese store on the ground level (Ford's living quarters were on the third floor). Hearing a noise, Lewis went upstairs and opened a door—only to find the editor, like a startled walrus, sitting in two feet of hot water scrubbing himself. Unperturbed, young Lewis asked if he might read the renowned editor his latest story, and the surprised Ford had little choice but to sit through a reading of "The Pole" while he continued his ablution. When the reading was finished, the editor told the novice to deposit the manuscript on his desk—it had been accepted—and he bade the young genius adieu. The story was later published. No one ever knew if this anecdote was true—since Ford was full of similar tales and Lewis vehemently denied it—but such stories made for lively conversation. A natural, vital language of the people—that was what Ford (like Dante) was after, and he was haranguing Pound on this subject from the start, as we know from Pound's letters (*SL*, 49 n.)

Although Ford had married one Elsie Martindale back in 1894, he was not usually with her; she had a place in the country, where her health forced her to stay. Ford meanwhile had fallen in love with a novelist named Violet Hunt, who wrote fantastic stories like "The Coach" (which Ford also published) and other works that had attracted the attention even of the discerning Henry James, who was a friend of both. Born in 1866, Violet was the daughter of a popular painter named Alfred William Hunt, while her mother was a novelist with whom she sometimes still collaborated. She had known Ford in her youth, although she was seven years older than he was. An ardent feminist like her friend May Sinclair, Violet had turned her home, which she shared with her aging mother, into a literary and social center. The address of South Lodge, as it was called, was 80 Campden Hill in Kensington, and it was near to both Church Walk and Holland Park Avenue, although Ford would soon vacate the latter address to lodge with "Mrs. Alfred Hunt." A plaque on the house, which became his residence from 1910 until after World War I, honors Ford over the women. Violet, who was called by some "the Colette of London" because of the brilliance of her salon, was described by David Garnett as "a thin viperish-looking beauty with a long pointed chin and deep-set, burning brown eyes under hooded lids" (I, 183). Some people said that she would skewer any friend for the sake of an epigram, but she would simply say in response that this behavior was expected of her. She was immediately fond of Ezra Pound, although she had certain reservations about his outlandish dress and recklessness with her expensive furniture. She and Ford welcomed him into her social set, where he met many pretty young artists like Amber (Amélie) Rives, whose death in 1945 is memorialized in Canto 74/434.

In his early *South Lodge*, Douglas Goldring (who was not so kind in his later account of Ford's life, *The Last Pre-Raphaelite*) described Ezra Pound's appearance on the scene in this way:

> The transformation of South Lodge from a rather stuffy and conventional Campden Hill villa, into a stamping ground for *les jeunes* was brought about far more by Ezra Pound than by Ford. Ezra's irreverence towards Eminent Literary Figures was a much needed corrective to Ford's excessive veneration for those of them he elected to admire. From his room in a lodging house ... Ezra sallied forth in his sombrero with all the arrogance of a young, revolutionary poet who had complete confidence in his own genius. He not only subjugated Ford by his American exuberance, but quickly established himself at South Lodge as a kind of social master of the ceremonies. Opposite the house there was a communal garden containing tennis courts.... Ezra immediately grasped its pos-

sibilities and having a liking for tennis which, with his long reach and lithe, wiry figure, he played excellently, insisted that the tennis courts should be made available. Ford and Violet, both of whom adored every form of entertaining and loved to be surrounded by crowds of friends, were delighted. The garden was taken over and every afternoon a motley collection of people, in the oddest costumes, invaded it at Ezra's instigation, and afterwards repaired to South Lodge—or to 84 Holland Park Avenue—to discuss *vers libre*, the prosody of Arnaut Daniel and, as Ford records, "the villainy of contributors to the front page of the *Times Literary Supplement*." (47)

Although most people remember Ford today largely for *The Good Soldier*, which is popularly called the best French or Flaubertian novel written in English, and the tetralogy called *Parade's End*, Ford had written at least twenty-four books and monographs by the time he met Pound in 1909. Important as these were, Pound always remembered him most fondly for his conversation. Ford was a master of words, and he impressed the importance of these on his young charge: "And as Ford said: get a dictionary / and learn the meaning of words" (Canto 96/689). Although the full importance of this statement had not settled in on Ezra yet—that would wait for his visit to Giessen in 1911—he was still very receptive to most things that "Fordie" said. Both Ford and Violet were extremely hospitable toward him, even when they themselves were on shaky financial ground.

At the start of 1910, Ford would lose his bankrupt review when Violet persuaded a wealthy friend named Alfred Mond (later Sir Melchett), whose money came from chemical concerns, to purchase it. Mond then replaced Ford with Austin Harrison as his chief editor and installed Norman Douglas as a sub-editor as he tried to convert the literary magazine into a liberal political tool—an act that Pound always considered dastardly: "Mond killed the English Review / and Ford went to Paris (an interval)" (Canto 104/744).

A lisping brother of Mond, whose name was Robert, is quoted pejoratively in Canto 80/497: "It will not take uth twenty yearth / to cwuth Mutholini / and the economic war has begun."

Also in January of 1910, Ford would go to jail for non-support of his family (enacted in defiance of a court order that was denying him a divorce), and he would then make the incredibly foolish move of going to Germany in an attempt to get free of his wife by becoming a German citizen. But that tragicomedy can wait. Suffice it to say that Ezra Pound remained close to the couple during all these coming

South Lodge, the home of Violet Hunt and her mother. A plaque on the wall behind the tree to the right proclaims it a sometime residence of Ford Madox Ford. Pound's favorite tennis courts were directly across the street. (Kenneth Alcock)

tribulations, and Violet thanked him in her autobiography *Flurried Years* (1926) and elsewhere.

In *Return to Yesterday* (1931), Ford painted a vivid picture of the young American's emergence on the London scene:

> Then came Ezra, led in by Miss Sinclair. His Odyssey would take twelve books in itself. In a very short time he had taken charge of me, the review and finally of London.... When I first knew him his Philadelphian accent was comprehensible if disconcerting; his beard and flowing locks were auburn and luxuriant; he was astonishingly meagre and agile. He threw himself alarmingly into frail chairs, devoured enormous quantities of your pastry, fixed his pince-nez firmly on his nose, drew out a manuscript from his pocket, threw his head back, closed his eyes to the point of invisibility and looking down his nose would chuckle like Mephistopheles and read you a translation from Arnaut Daniel. The only part of the *albade* that you would understand would be the refrain:
>
> "Ah me, the darn, the darn it comes toe sune!" (388)

Contrary to what Ford said, the last line is not from Arnaut Daniel; it is from an anonymous Provençal alba known as *En un vergier* that Pound translated first as "Alba Innominata," appearing that fall in *Exultations* (*CEP*, 125), and later as "Vergier" (*Pers.*, 177).

A letter written in March to Homer Pound (PC 103) said that Ezra had just received proofs from the *English Review* for his famous poem "Sestina: Altaforte," in which he adopts the voice of the manly troubadour Bertran de Born:

> Damn it all! all this our South stinks peace.
> You whoreson dog, Papiols, come! Let's to music!
> I have no life save when the swords clash.
> But ah! when I see the standards gold, vair, purple, opposing
> And the broad fields beneath them turn crimson,
> Then howl I my heart nigh mad with rejoicing.
>
> (*Pers.*, 28)

This much-admired poem was in many ways artificial, as Pound himself admitted in "How I Began." It was a Browningesque experiment in trying to recreate a voice and a genre from another culture. A sestina is a poem consisting of six stanzas each with six lines, in which the six end-words recur in differing patterns from stanza to stanza. It is obviously a tour de force that depends on the vigor of the end-words for its success. Ford published the poem in his June issue.

In "How I Began," Pound tells how the sestina came into being. It was "written in the British Museum reading-room. I had De Born on my mind. I had found him untranslatable. Then it occurred to me that I might present him in this manner. I wanted the curious involution and recurrence of the sestina. . . . I wrote the first strophe and then went to the Museum to make sure of the right order of permutations, for I was then living in Langham Street, next to the 'pub,' and had hardly any books with me. I did the rest of the poem at a sitting. Technically it is one of my best, though a poem on such a theme could never be very important." Still, it is a standard anthology piece.

In his October issue, Ford published the poem that established Ezra Pound's literary reputation: "The Ballad of the Goodly Fere." Even while he was writing it, Pound told his father, he was aware of the poem's significance to his career: "I have this morning written a Ballad of Simon Zelotes, which is probably the strongest thing in English since 'Reading Gaol', and a thing that any one can understand." This letter, Paige Carbon 107, was written sometime in April. The poem is probably Pound's best-known lyric work:

> Ha' we lost the goodliest fere o' all
> For the priests and the gallows tree?
> Aye lover he was of brawny men,
> O' ships and the open sea . . .
>
> I ha' seen him cow a thousand men
> On the hills o' Galilee,
> They whined as he walked out calm between,
> Wi' his eyes like the grey o' the sea . . .
>
> A master of men was the Goodly Fere,
> A mate of the wind and sea,
> If they think they ha' slain our Goodly Fere
> They are fools eternally.
>
> I ha' seen him eat o' the honey-comb
> Sin' they nailed him to the tree.
>
> (*Pers.*, 33–34)

Pound also discussed the composition of this vigorous poem in "How I Began":

> In the case of the "Goodly Fere" I was not excited until some hours after I had written it. I had been the evening before in the "Turkish Coffee" café in Soho. I had been made very angry by a certain sort of cheap irreverence that was new to me. I had lain awake most of the night. I got up rather late in the morning and started for the Museum with the first four lines in my head. I wrote the rest of the poem at a sitting, on the left side of the reading-room, with scarcely any erasures. I lunched at the Vienna Café, and later in the afternoon being unable to study, I peddled the poem about Fleet Street, for I began to realise that for the first time in my life I had written something that "everyone could understand," and I wanted it to go to the people.
>
> The poem was not accepted. I think the "Evening Standard" was the only office where it was even considered. Mr. Ford Madox Hueffer first printed the poem in his review some three months afterwards.

Meanwhile, on April 16 appeared the *Personae* of 1909 (not to be confused with the more famous and complete *Personae* of 1926, which the abbreviation *Pers.* in this work indicates; the latter is Pound's definitive collection, still in print with some later additions). Both *Personaes* were dedicated to Mary Moore, who did not even notice the first homage until it was pointed out to her. Although the 1909 volume was full of various poems that were completely new to many Britons, the majority of the poems had already appeared in *A Lume Spento;* but that book had experienced a very limited printing and distribution. The few truly new poems that appeared here included "Xenia," "An Idyl for Glaucus," and "In Durance." Most of the works dealt with themes and tones that Pound had experimented with much earlier at college, but to an England that was still not fully aware of his existence, his work seemed exciting and fresh.

An unsigned reviewer in the *Daily Telegraph* of April 23 (assumed to be W. L. Courtney) said: "It is more or less inevitable that we should on being touched by a new writer, seek to 'place' him by comparison with the old. Mr. Ezra Pound then suggests such incompatibilities as a troubadour of old Provence and—Walt Whitman. He has much of the sense of beauty of things and of words . . . of the one, much of the vigorous individuality of the other." F. S. Flint, who had met Pound earlier in April, said on May 27 in A. R. Orage's *New Age:* "Mr. Pound is a poet with a distinct personality. Essentially he is a rebel against all conventions except sanity; there is something robustly impish and elfish about him. He writes with fresh beauty and vigour . . . revolting against a crepuscular spirit in modern poetry."

The most stunning reviews were two written by a red-haired Welsh journalist named Edward Thomas in the *Daily Chronicle* of June 7 and in Ford's *English Review* of June. The impact of Thomas's adulation on the literary establishment has been chronicled by Edgar Jepson, the "lover of jade," in his memoir: "I shall never forget the meeting of the Square Club a few days after that monstrous action: the pale, shocked, contorted faces of the poet-makers . . . the nervous leaping into corners; the choked whispers; the jerky gestures; even between the courses the harsh sound of grinding teeth. Poor Edward Thomas! He did look so hot and bothered. . . . How *could* he have liked the verse of a man whom none of them had discovered, much less made? . . . The Club rocked on its foundations and so did English literature!" (140). Mr. Thomas recanted shortly thereafter, however, as we shall see.

Not all was praise, though. The *Nation* of London on August 28 ran a highly critical anonymous review, saying that Pound's experiments with language—like using "ellum" for "elm" and calling Apollo Phoebus " 'Pollo Phoibee, old tin pan"—were not only irritating but also ludicrous. To some extent this attack on archaisms and awkward neologisms was justified, but to see only a "lively din" in Pound's work was inexcusable. Rupert Brooke, the so-called "golden boy of Edwardian letters" (he was then twenty-two), wrote a very mixed review in the *Cambridge Review* of December 2, but he closed with a strongly positive statement: "Mr. Pound has great talents. When he has passed through stammering to speech, and when he has more clearly recognized the nature of poetry, he may be a great poet. It is important to remember his name; and we shall be made to recognize it when he turns from prose, admirable prose as it sometimes is, to confine himself to the form in which he wrote 'Camraderie.' " Later in 1912 Brooke would attack Pound bitterly in the *Poetry Review* for some adverse criticism of his friend Lascelles Abercrombie, another promising poet, but Abercrombie in no way lived up to people's expectations, and Brooke's untimely death in World War I cut his career short.

Clearly Ezra was in his ascendance. The reject from Wabash College and outcast from Philadelphia had at last found a home—at the top of the literary set in the center of the English-speaking world. Perhaps his greatest accolade came from the comic *Punch*, which said in its usual whimsical way in its issue of June 23:

> Mr. Welkin Mark [Elkin Mathews] . . . begs to announce that he has secured for the English market the palpitating works of the new Montana (U.S.A.) poet, Mr. Ezekiel Ton, who is the most remarkable thing in poetry since Robert Browning. . . . He has succeeded where all others have failed, in evolving a blend of the imagery of the unfettered West, the vocabulary of Wardour Street, and the sinister abandon of Borgiac Italy.

These tongue-in-cheek words demonstrated that Ezra Pound, still not twenty-four years old, had arrived.

3

A Time of Exultations: Hulme and Yeats (April–October 1909)

Six days after the publication of *Personae* on April 16, Pound attended the restaurant meeting of a new club that had no name, except perhaps the Secession Club. This group was an offshoot of the stodgy Poets' Club, which had been founded by an energetic young man-of-letters named T. E. Hulme. The Poets' Club had consisted of such venerable members as Selwyn Image, Lady Margaret Sackville, and a chivalric gentleman named Francis W. Tancred, who traced his roots to the Tancreds of medieval crusading fame.

The older club had published some of its members' work for the Christmas season of 1908, and had been severely criticized by a young reviewer named F. S. Flint, writing in the newly reconstituted *New Age* of February 11. The mercurial Mr. Hulme was inclined to agree with the brash attacker, and so he suddenly abandoned the more established circle and decided to form a new one with the outspoken Flint.

Frank Stewart Flint (1885–1960) was a rising figure at this time. He had been born to very poor parents who were unable to provide him with a decent college education. As a result, he began working in his teens, but at night he pursued his studies in languages, perfecting his

Latin and French, and even experimenting with more exotic tongues like Japanese. It was later said (by Hilda Doolittle, for one) that Flint was capable of handling nine or ten foreign tongues, while his Cockney wife was scarcely capable of dealing with one. In 1904, at the age of nineteen, Flint had joined the Civil Service, and over the years he became the chief of the Overseas Section of the Ministry of Labour. He was essentially a shy man, always rather embarrassed by his untutored wife and extremely susceptible to the influences of the more dominant men around him, although he was also capable of turning on them, as we shall see.

In his February assault, Flint had dismissed the Poets' Club as a typical English clique that was more interested in wining and dining than in the serious craft of poetry (charges that Pound himself was leveling at this time). Flint contrasted the contemporary Britishers with the very vital poets in France, such as Mallarmé, who were making daring experiments in verse and opening up new modes of expression. He praised Lady Sackville's verse (perhaps a bit ironically), but had little good to say about most of the others, except for a few pieces like Hulme's little poem "Autumn," which was built around a "quaint conceit." (Later Flint would hail this creation as the Argo of modern poetry.) This little poem tended to loom as more and important with the passage of time. Three years later it would be published in the *New Age* issue of January 25, 1912, as part of a small group whimsically titled "The Complete Poetical Works of T. E. Hulme." Pound even played a role in continuing this jest in his *Ripostes* of that year, when he included "Autumn" with four other short pieces under the same title. Even today, in the modern *Personae*, one can find "Autumn" tucked away on page 252:

> A touch of cold in the Autumn night—
> I walked abroad,
> And saw the ruddy moon lean over a hedge
> Like a red-faced farmer.
> I did not stop to speak, but nodded,
> And round about were the wistful stars
> With white faces like town children.

When Pound joined the " 'School of Images,' which may or may not have existed" (as he playfully remarked in his 1912 *Ripostes*), he was simply checking up on this new group and the extravagant Mr. Hulme. At his first encounter, when the group was dining at a well-known artists' restaurant called The Eiffel Tower (or, as Pound more correctly called it, La Tour Eiffel), the young American read his still unpublished "Sestina" in such an exuberant manner that the waiters screened off the area so that the other guests would not be annoyed. Pound was supposedly dressed in his best "Italianate" manner—which may simply mean that he was avoiding the drab browns affected by the other men.

We are not sure who took him there. Later Flint guessed it was Florence Farr (1860–1917), a good friend of Olivia Shakespear and Yeats. Florence was a well-known actress who had married an actor named Edward Emery in 1884, but she had divorced him later, going on to have affairs or friendships with a variety of famous writers, even Yeats and Shaw. She was one of the so-called "transitional" women of the day, being active in suffragette causes and also deeply interested in theosophy and the occult. Florence was popular among poets because she had perfected a new way of reading poetry by half-intoning it to the music of a psaltery. This lyre-like instrument of the past had been especially designed for her by the famous instrument-maker Arnold Dolmetsch.

According to Fergus FitzGerald, the son and editor of the Irish patriot Desmond FitzGerald, his father, who was also a poet at this time, told him that he and Florence were the two who introduced the young American to their circle, although Selwyn Image and Ernest Rhys might also have been involved. Desmond FitzGerald (1888–1947) was one of the masterminds of the Easter Uprising in Dublin in 1916, when many of the Irish entertained the false notion that the warring Germans were going to help them throw off the yoke of English servitude. Although he had been born in London, Desmond was fiercely Celtic by blood and sympathy. He idolized Yeats, whose other Irish poet friends, such as Joseph Campbell, also supported the new club.

Pound later became a strong admirer of FitzGerald as a patriot and doer, as is shown in Canto 95/644:

> And damn it there were men even in my time
> Nicoletti, Ramperti, Desmond Fitzgerald
>   (the one alive in 1919)

Here the Irishman is linked with the Italian prefect at Lake Garda whom Pound was to meet shortly (see Canto 74/427) and Marco Ramperti, a tough-minded Italian journalist. There is also a reference to Desmond in Canto 92/618:

And honour?
Fitzgerald: "I was."
When he freed a man
who had not been at the Post Office
(Oireland 1916) . . .

It was very important for every "true" Irishman after 1916 to have been at the Post Office, the center of the military activity during the uprising. Desmond, who "was" there, is here described as freeing a weakling or pretender. His actions during this period are documented in his *Memoirs:* he was arrested by the British and not freed until 1919. When Ireland finally won its independence in the 1920s, FitzGerald served as the Minister of External Affairs and then as the Minister of Defense. Although Pound was not directly interested in Irish politics, he says often in essays in the *New Age* that he sympathized with them as underdogs against an insensitive Empire. The last important regular member of the new poets' group was an experimenter named Edward Storer.

In a cranky essay called "The History of Imagism," which appeared years later in the May 1, 1915, issue of the *Egoist* (when Flint had become estranged from Pound through the intervention of Amy Lowell), the government clerk and Symbolist expert told the story of the club in this way:

> Somewhere in the gloom of the year 1908, Mr. T. E. Hulme, now in the trenches of Ypres, . . . proposed to a companion that they should found a Poets' Club. . . . At the end of the year they published a small plaquette . . . called "For Christmas MDCCCCVIII."
>
> In November of the same year, Edward Storer, author already of "Inclinations," much of which is in the "Imagist" manner, published his "Mirrors of Illusion," the first book of "Imagist" poems, with an essay at the end attacking poetic conventions. The first poem in the book was called "Image," here it is:
>
> Forsaken lovers,
> Burning to a chaste white moon,
> Upon strange pyres of loneliness and drought.
>
> Mr. Storer, who has recanted much since, was in favour then of a poetry which I described in reference to his book, as "a form of expression, like the Japanese, in which an image is the resonant heart of an exquisite moment. . . ."

Flint then describes how he attacked the Poets' Club, and how he and Hulme formed the new group, which met for the first time on Thursday, March 25, 1909. He emphasizes their search for inventiveness. Joseph Campbell was imitating certain Hebraic poetry forms, while Flint himself was promoting the Japanese *tanka* and *haiku*. All were interested in promoting free verse.

Flint stressed that in all the activities the "ringleader" was Hulme, who "insisted too on absolutely accurate presentation and no verbiage." Flint says that Hulme and Tancred spent hour after hour searching for the right phrase. As for Ezra Pound, Flint treated him in the most dismissive manner possible:

> On April 22, 7907 [*sic*], Ezra Pound . . . joined the group . . . he could not be made to believe that there was any French poetry after Ronsard. He was very full of his *troubadours;* but I do not remember that he did more than attempt to illustrate (or refute) our theories occasionally with their example. The group died a lingering death at the end of its second winter.

The last statement tells the whole sad, inflated story. No one will argue that such a group existed and that it was interested in reforming the poetry of the period, or that a few of its members were writing verse that was ahead of its time (after all, Yeats and Ford and Hopkins had done the same); but Flint, who was extremely jealous of Pound in 1915, was absolutely determined (with the formidable force of Amy Lowell behind him) to claim that he and Hulme had invented the movement that she was then successfully promoting. The fact remains that, without the Ezra Pound of 1912 between 1909 and 1915, there would not have been any movement at all. A few colorful songbirds and some fragmentary tunes do not constitute a spring.

Pound himself was never niggardly in his naming of people who had helped or influenced him. The fact that he later included Hulme's slim corpus of poems among his own is a tribute in itself. In his prefatory note to *Ripostes*, Pound even called his own group "the descendants of the forgotten school of 1909." But the word "forgotten" stands out. If Edward Storer was indeed writing imagist-like poems in 1908, he later changed his style completely, and went on to publish traditional and verbose translations of Sappho. Hulme himself never added anything to his collected works, and hence the "School of Images" passed into silence—except insofar as Ezra Pound kept its hidden messages alive. Yet, as Flint suggested later, the Ezra Pound of 1909 was not quite ready to effect a poetic revolution. That would have to wait for the more forceful message of Ford Madox Ford in 1911 and later developments.*

Hulme's inflated reputation as "the founder of imagism" stems largely from this essay of Flint and the work of his editor, Sir Herbert Read, as well as Alun R. Jones's *Life and Opinions of T. E. Hulme*. Jones would like to persuade his readers that Pound soon fell under the spell of the hypnotic Hulme, who was two years older and better established as a local figure. But there are three objections against asserting this influence. First, Pound never speaks of Hulme's impact on him in the same way that he openly speaks of Ford's. Second, Pound's poetry does not change when he is close to Hulme; no change is effected until after the 1911 visit by Pound to Ford in Germany; Ford's admonitions at Giessen were always cited by Pound as most responsible for his transformation. Finally, Hulme espoused at this time the philosophy of Henri Bergson, who believed that language was never fully able to capture reality in the way that an imagist would try to capture it. Bergson leads more logically to a stream of consciousness or the impressionism of a Marcel Proust than to the hard realism of Ezra Pound, which captures moments in time like an efficient camera. In a very penetrating analysis of Bergson and Hulme (who are usually dismissed by professional philosophers for being too impressionistic), Herbert N. Schneidau concludes quite logically in *The Image and the Real* that: "Pound's poetics suggests the possibility of a 'poetry of reality,' whereas Hulme's leads only to a subjective, self-assertive toying with unsatisfactory, untrustworthy words" (56).

Personally, Hulme (1883–1917) did not have the kind of social grace that Pound admired in men like Yeats or Ford. The tall, brawny man from northern Staffordshire spoke with a distressing nasal twang and tended to act in a rather bull-like fashion. Of course, the two young men were rivals in a city that could not afford too many rebels, and Hulme clearly had a head start. By 1909 Hulme was far more conversant with modern French culture than was Pound, who still had not penetrated the major works of Flaubert, Baudelaire, and Théophile Gautier—although Ford was talking about them, and they would be constantly mentioned by Flint, who would soon be Ezra's friend.

The greatest difference between the two primary instigators was that Pound was a poet and Hulme a conceptual thinker. Hulme often did not even bother to put his best ideas on paper. He had an independent income from a cousin of his mother, and as a result did not have to eke out a living the way Pound did. Hulme was preaching a return

---

*See the January 30 entry for 1921 in chapter 19 for still another twist by Flint.

to classicism from romanticism, and Pound was also interested in this, but not for the same reason. Hulme saw romanticism as a later form of lax Renaissance humanism, a further falling-away from religion and a denial of Original Sin, which Hulme felt was necessary in all serious thinking. After leaving Hamilton, Pound could never share any of this theocentric thinking. He never believed in the "sex and sin guilt racket," and he was appalled by the Thomistic bent that swept over Hulme during the coming years. The philosopher saw World War I (which destroyed him) as the noble act of a Christian state that had risen to totalitarian grandeur to express its deep courage. Pound found the war revolting. In the thirties, of course, Pound would also be drawn to admire totalitarianism, but as a reaction against diffidence and inertia—never with the late-medieval spirit of crusading that Hulme espoused.

There is no doubt too that Hulme's brutish behavior was repellent to Pound. Ford's young friend David Garnett in his *Golden Echo* described the philosopher as "a big, rather overbearing man . . . who looked like a farmer at a fair" (I, 237). Hulme was known to suddenly abandon friends at a restaurant for a few minutes, and then rush back, complaining loudly that it was damned hard to fornicate with a woman on the stairwell of a London subway. He sometimes urinated openly in the streets, and when a bobby threatened to arrest him one time, Hulme warded the man away with the huffy statement: "Do you know that you are addressing a member of the middle classes?" He had been ejected from St. Johns College, Cambridge, for some unspeakable crime during the arrival of the king on the campus, and he was reinstated only in 1912, after he had published his translation of Bergson's *Introduction to Metaphysics*. These anecdotes (related by the admiring Mr. Jones and David Garnett) do not describe the kind of person that Pound found congenial. Pound could be extroverted, but was seldom vulgar; his sense of "troubadour ethic" would never allow him to treat women in the brutish fashion described above. We shall pick up on Mr. Hulme again in 1911.

The much-desired meeting with Yeats is believed to have taken place in early May. The Irish poet had already received a copy of Pound's first book, and he was aware of the American's presence because of Olivia, who took Ezra to the Woburn Buildings around May 9. This tenuous dating is based on a letter to William Carlos Williams (*SL*, 7), in which Ezra brags that he has been praised by the greatest living poet. But although Pound also mentions attending some of Yeats's home poetry readings in a letter dated only "1909" (PC 108), there does not seem to have been any meaningful commerce between the two writers until October—largely because Yeats, still troubled by the death of Synge and Abbey Theater problems and his own nervous condition, spent most of that summer in Paris or at Coole Park, not returning to London until after October 12 (YL, 528ff.).

With the astonishing success of *Personae* came some unexpected benefits. Despite the lackluster reception of his previous course, the Polytechnic discussed the addition of a much longer course that coming fall and winter, on the subject of Romance literatures in the Middle Ages, and by the fall this course was established. The congenial Ernest Rhys also persuaded Dent and Sons to issue a book by Pound covering the same ground as the lectures. This led to the signing of a contract for *The Spirit of Romance*. Pound was especially happy, since he saw the book as a way of expressing his creative talents through translation and also as a possible credential for gaining future academic work. For many years he dreamed about a job as a professor. His financial situation in London continued to be shaky, and he constantly had to keep writing home, asking for money. If Homer Pound had not been such a caring father, the whole course of modern literature might have been different. But with the money came appeals from Isabel to come home. Why should he be starving in London when he could be living comfortably at home in Philadelphia?

Because of this endless persuasion, Pound did indeed try to win another fellowship from the University of Pennsylvania, even though he knew that he did not have the slightest chance in the world. His debacle at Wabash College had ended all that. But to please his parents, he investigated a possible position at Hobart College and elsewhere.

Vaguely promising that he would "drift home" the following spring, Pound asked his parents that summer to please forward more of his books, including his Moore edition of Dante, his Provençal anthologies by Carl Appel and Gaston Paris, and his *Cid* and *Aucassin and Nicolette*—clearly showing that he saw his future lying in a medieval direction (PC 110, 113). By September 9, he was promising Homer that *Spirit of Romance* was "really going to be good."

Then, at the beginning of September, he made a move to Hammersmith, a western suburb, possibly on the advice of Ford, whose mother lived there; but soon he found the area depressing, and so he finally moved to Kensington to be near his friends. The place he selected was a small room without a private toilet in a cozy mews off a walk that wound around in a church graveyard, which one entered at Kensington High Street; the walk bent around the back entrance of St. Mary Abbots and led to Holland Street. The Old Library and Town Hall of Kensington at this time stood at the entrance; today most of the graves have been cleared from the cemetery. Pound rented the top

10 Church Walk, the far house on the left. Pound usually lived on the top floor, where he unfortunately could pick up the tolling of the bells of St. Mary Abbots, which was located in the foreground. (Kenneth Alcock)

floor of 10 Church Walk from Sam Langley, a grocer with the old Anglo-Saxon virtues (so Ezra told Patricia Hutchins: *Ezra Pound's Kensington*, 68) for 8s. a week with an option on taking meals cooked by Mrs. Langley. He wrote to Isabel that he was "luxuriating in a more sizable room" (PC 117), although many visitors found the space cramped. The room was rather spartanly furnished, with an iron bedstead, a mahogany washstand, an open table that served as a desk, and a small bathtub that slid under the bed for concealment. On the walls were some watercolors by Violet's father, Alfred William Hunt. The annoying thing about the place was that the bells of St. Mary Abbots had the nasty habit of pealing at ungodly hours, and the peals set up terrible vibrations in the room. At those moments, Pound would sometimes send imprecations over the deserted graveyard. He also took to penning some very abrupt notes to Reverend Pennefeather, but to no avail; the bells tolled on. Years later in Olga Rudge's little house above Rapallo, he would appreciate the distant peal of the sexton of San Pantaleo playing operatic arias on the soft Mediterranean air (see the Addendum for Canto 100/800).

In that same letter to his mother announcing his new quarters, Pound lamented the nervous breakdown of Arthur Symons, the friend of Yeats who had taught Yeats most of what he knew about French symbolism; but Pound noted that Symons was recovering. All that September, he was writing "narrative stuff" for his lectures and future book, although he made it clear that he had dispensed with the idea of ever writing any prose except as a stop-gap measure to make money. He had begun a novel while he was living on Langham Street, but had subsequently abandoned it.

In October a variety of happy events occurred. "The Ballad" appeared in Ford's review, and then on October 25, Mathews unveiled his new book, *Exultations*, which contained that already famous poem and the sestina. *Exultations*, which was dedicated to his old friend from Wyncote chess days, Reverend Carlos Tracy Chester, did not fare quite as well with reviewers as its predecessor had. The greatest defector was Edward Thomas, who, in a review in the *Daily Chronicle* of November 23, complained first about Pound's needless obscurities and his forced attempts to be suave or learned, concluding: "having allowed the turbulent opacity of his peculiarities to sink down, we believe that we see very nearly nothing at all." That was quite a change from his earlier praise.

An unsigned review in the *Spectator* of December 11 said: "Mr. Ezra Pound is that rare thing among modern poets, a scholar. He is not only cultivated, but learned.... We feel that this writer has in him the capacity for remarkable poetic achievement, but we also feel that at present he is somewhat weighted by his learning." Yet an anonymous review in the *Observer* (December 26) welcomed the new book as a second offering from one who had achieved remarkable success so quickly, and found numerous lines, as in "Piere Vidal Old" and "The Ballad," hauntingly beautiful. F. S. Flint, who was now a friend, said in Orage's *New Age* on January 6, 1910: "there is in Mr. Pound's new book a gift of real, though vague, beauty, impalpable gold."

Although many poems in *Exultations* had appeared earlier, there were still some important new additions. The "Alba Innominata" mentioned by Ford was there, along with Pound's translation of Bertran de Born's elegy on the death of Prince Henry, a son of Henry II of England: "Planh for the Young English King." The long monologue "Piere Vidal Old" told how the troubadour ran mad under a wolfskin for the love of Loba of Penautier. It dramatically tries to summon up the spirit of this rather wild poet who consorted with the forces of nature. Surely Bertran's derisive cry to the twelfth century: "O Age gone lax!" was also Ezra Pound's cry to the twentieth.

But the most beautiful poem in *Exultations* was undoubtedly "Francesca," a simple, direct work that speaks to the reader without any annoying allusions or forced effects. It was certainly Pound's most controlled performance to date, and is still one of the most beautiful love poems of the century:

> You came in out of the night
> And there were flowers in your hands,

> Now you will come out of a confusion of people,
> Out of a turmoil of speech about you.
>
> I who have seen you amid the primal things
> Was angry when they spoke your name
> In ordinary places.
> I would that the cool waves might flow over my mind,
> And that the world should dry as a dead leaf,
> Or as a dandelion seed-pod and be swept away,
> So that I might find you again,
> Alone.
>
> (Pers., 36)

The simple "rightness" of this poem makes one wonder why it took Pound so long before he could bring himself around to writing in this vein. But there were still many artifacts of the nineteenth century cluttering his mind and his verse style; it would not be until two years later that he would start expressing himself, as here, in a manner that can be called modern.

Again in early October he met Yeats. He wrote at that time between October 7 and 11 to his father: "Yeats has at last arrived and I had about five hours of him yesterday." Those five hours were purchased through the kind intervention of Olivia Shakespear. Yeats had come at this point in his life to a crossroad. Behind him lay his great late-romantic achievements, the world of Irish fays and heroes who people the universe of his Celtic twilight, as well as the world of direct political action, where he and his friends believed that they could convert the little island nation into a major cultural force in Europe. In *Estrangement*, which he wrote that year, Yeats said in Section 53: "There is a dying-out of national feeling very simple in its origin. You cannot keep the idea of a nation alive when there are no national institutions to reverence, no national success to admire, without a model of it in the mind of the people." In *The Death of Synge*, which commemorated the death of the Irish dramatist that had taken place on March 24 of this year, Yeats could perhaps see the death of his own Celtic dreams.

When he returned to London from Dublin and Coole in late September, Yeats was beginning to embark on the next great period of his life, involving experiments with spiritualism and psychic phenomena and showing a new interest in a poetry that was based on universal archetypes—stemming from places like Byzantium or Japan. Olivia Shakespear, his former lover and still devoted friend, was of importance here, since she had long been interested in the occult. Pound was also drawn into this activity, despite the usual pragmatic bent of his mind. He soon wrote home to his mother, asking for the hour of his birth so that he could have an accurate astrological chart constructed (PC 152). She told him that he had been born at 3:00 p.m. (although one wonders about the accuracy of the hour); as a result, he was a Scorpio with Aries rising (but close to Pisces), with Moon in Leo and Venus in Sagittarius. An analysis of his chart indicates an extremely strong personality (at times overbearing), with great prophetic powers and a pioneering sensibility, capable of great warmth and caring or of rabid hostility; a promise of genius is blended with a hint of grave tragedy.

Yeats, who had earlier roomed with Arthur Symons, had been living since 1895 in the Woburn Buildings, which were located on what is now Woburn Walk in the Borough of Camden. The poet had deliberately chosen this unfashionable part of London to live in because he wanted to be closer to "the people," although the many guests at his Monday night social gatherings often felt uneasy in the neighborhood. In *South Lodge*, Douglas Goldring has given us a picture of what those famous nightly meetings were like:

> I shall never forget my surprise, when Ezra took me for the first time to one of Yeats's "Mondays," at the way in which he dominated the room, distributed Yeats's cigarettes and Chianti, and laid down the law about poetry. Poor golden-bearded Sturge Moore, who sat in a corner with a large musical instrument by his side . . . endeavoured to join in the discussion on prosody, a subject on which he believed himself not entirely ignorant, but Ezra promptly reduced him to a glum silence. . . . I was sitting next to Yeats on a settle when a young Indian woman in a *sari* came and squatted at his feet and asked him to sing "Innisfree," saying that she was certain he had composed it to an Irish air. Yeats was anxious to comply with this request but, unfortunately, like so many poets, he was completely unmusical, indeed almost tone deaf. He compromised by a sort of dirgelike incantation, calculated to send any unhappy giggler into hysterics. I bore it as long as I could, but at last the back of the settle began to shake and I received the impact of one of the poet's nasty glances from behind the pince-nez. (49)

Goldring never became a select member of the crowd; Pound paid his dues and reaped his reward, becoming both a disciple and a friend of the older man.

To begin with, Yeats was somewhat suspicious of Ezra. He wrote to Lady Gregory on December 10 of 1909 about "this queer creature

Ezra Pound, who has become really a great authority on the troubadours" and who "has I think got closer to the right sort of music for poetry than Mrs. Emery—it is more definitely music with strongly marked time and yet it is effective speech. However he can't sing as he has no voice" (YL, 543). Mrs. Emery was the already mentioned actress Florence Farr.

Very soon though, at Olivia's urgings, Yeats began to see Ezra as someone to take seriously. Ezra, in turn, began to promote the poetry of "Uncle William" to Ford, who had great difficulty stomaching the self-conscious, ethnically limited Celtic sensibility. (Ford considered himself too continental to be interested in things Irish.) Ezra's two older friends were never cordial to each other, despite the young American's efforts to bring them together. As Pound said years later, he soon realized that it was wiser to keep them apart, and this he did.

Pound's own description of a soirée at Yeats's place occurs in Canto 82/524, which mentions the performance of a well-known Polish medium named Stanislawa T. Tomczyk, who was married to Everard Fielding:

> Miss Tomczyk, the medium
> baffling the society for metaphysical research
>   and the idea that CONversation . . . . . .
>   should not utterly wither
> even I can remember
>   at 18 Woburn Buildings
> said Mr. Tancred
>   of the Jerusalem and Sicily Tancreds, to Yeats,
> "If you would read us one of your own choice
>   and
>   perfect
>   lyrics"
> and more's the pity that Dickens died twice
> with the disappearance of Tancred

There is no point entering here on a meaningless debate about poetic influences. We are concerned here only with the beginning of a long friendship, and in any friendship there is a reciprocity. Pound seemed to bring out of Yeats much of the mischief, daring, and love of adventure that was latent in him, while Yeats seemed able to tone the younger man down, to supply him with an image of paternal control. Pound always stood in awe of sensitive older men, from his father to the Irishman, while Yeats probably was feeling the need for a son or at least a young disciple who was intelligent and faithful. In any case,

Yeats was the last of the Grand Old Men who befriended the penniless Pound. The others—Mathews, Rhys, Plarr—gave him physical gifts like contracts and dinners; Yeats gave him the far more important gifts of the mind and spirit.

4

Romance, Medieval and Modern: Bride and Dorothy (October 1909–June 1910)

The new lecture series began at the Polytechnic on Monday evening, October 11, and continued into mid-March, when the last lecture was canceled because March 28 was a bank holiday. Two subscribers for the entire series were the Shakespear ladies, who attended religiously, even though the lecturer was often desultory or distracted, showing very little awareness that he was frequently talking over the heads of his audience. Pound labored all that winter on those lectures, interrupting his prose-writing only to pen an occasional "Canzone" or long poem (the title but not the spirit of these compositions, which led to the book *Canzoni*, was Dantesque). Three of these canzoni were purchased by Ford (who was now very low on money) and appeared in the January 1910 issue of his *English Review*. Since the lectures were published in June of the coming year as *Spirit of Romance*, with numerous changes, we can more or less determine their contents from that later volume.

The current *Spirit of Romance*, published by New Directions, is not at all identical with the book issued by J. M. Dent in 1910. For example, many notes were added in 1929 and 1932, and chapter 5, "Psychology and Troubadours," was not present then; according to a note on page

87, this chapter appeared in G. R. S. Mead's journal *The Quest* "about 1916," although there is reason to believe that it was delivered as a lecture in 1912. The chapter is clearly an aberration from the rest of the book, which is an original and straightforward attempt to place the roots of medieval "romance" with the Romans (as the etymology of the word indicates), and to connect the various literatures of medieval Europe in a comprehensible way. Chapter 5, on the other hand, makes the following extravagant claim: "That the spirit was, in Provence, Hellenic is seen readily enough by anyone who will compare the *Greek Anthology* with the work of the troubadours" (90). This is not very apparent to many people, whether one compares the Greek and Provençal languages, the stanzaic patterns (wherever stanzas exist), the metrical constructions, the images, the rhetorical conceits, or even the "ideas," insofar as these exist. It is possible to say that the troubadours celebrated Amor, and this reconstructed god has some similarities with Greek Eros, but Amor is far more spiritual, more Christian, than Eros ever thought of being. In Canto 4, Pound attempts to make the correlation poetically, and this works, because Greek myths like the devouring of Itys can be related to the troubadour legend of the eating of the heart of Cabestan by his beloved at the conniving of her jealous husband—but that kind of similarity dissolves when one tries to analyze it conceptually or prove it historically.

As for the rest of the book, the idea that romance is universal (not an invention of twelfth-century France, as C. S. Lewis and scores of French scholars seemed to believe) is perfectly valid. But clearly the main reason for writing this book (which was an extreme labor, as we know from his letters home) was that it gave Pound a chance to be a cicerone in the museum of medieval literary beauties. Vast stretches of the book are translations, and they certainly help a reader who does not know the many original languages to enjoy these treasures of the past. The title, however, is somewhat curious, because "romance" is never really defined (if indeed it can be defined). Instead of focusing on romance or romanticism, we soon see that its opposite, classical precision, is really the subject that interests Pound more. When he is discussing Arnaut Daniel in chapter 2, Pound cannot keep from linking him to the later Dante and seeing both poets as striving to express a "vivid and accurate description of the emotion" (28). Instead of seeing Arnaut primarily as a defiant romantic (as in the bold lines "I am Arnaut, who hoards the wind / And chases the rabbit with the ox / And swims against the rising tide"), Pound tends to see him more as a precise hewer of words.

Chapter 3, "Proença," is really little more than a quick tour through the main poems of the troubadour tradition that appealed to Pound and to Dante. Chapter 4 focuses on *The Cid*, and the shift from lyrics to a narrative poem is somewhat jarring. Chapter 6 (the old chapter 5) discusses the philosophical nature of the early Italian lyric in very intelligent terms (Pound is keenly aware of the *differences* in poetry, unlike many other scholars, who use terms like "courtly love" or modern structuralist approaches to make everything blur together); the chapter shows Pound's increasing interest in Dante's best friend, Guido Cavalcanti. Chapter 7 stresses Dante's *Divine Comedy*, and here Pound shines, for his love of that work is readily apparent. The last four chapters deal with François Villon, whose rugged realism Pound could appreciate fully; Lope de Vega, who still interested the poet from his study with Rennert at Penn; the Portuguese Camoëns; and the Latin poets of the Renaissance.

The book was clearly quite an accomplishment for a young man of twenty-five, and it holds up well on reading today, largely because of the fervor behind the writing. The men thanked at the start of the book are Dr. Shepard of Hamilton, Padre José Maria de Elizondo from Madrid days, and Ernest Rhys. Good as the work was, it was still not good enough for the University of Pennsylvania to acknowledge it as a substitute for a dissertation or for Pound to use it in order to get a fulltime appointment as a teacher somewhere. An anonymous review in the *Nation* of New York saw the work as unscholarly and poorly laid out, with ineffectual translations. Edward Thomas, writing in the *Morning Post* of August 1, 1910, did still another flip-flop, and once again praised Pound for having written an informative book with the accent on humanity rather than scholarship; he added: "but on the whole we had rather he confined himself to translation and the severest exposition." Mr. Thomas actually met Pound in late September of 1909 at the revered Square Club, under the aegis of Edgar Jepson, where Pound also encountered G. K. Chesterton and John Masefield, neither of whom he admired as writers. That meeting might explain Thomas's regained appreciation later.

During 1909 Pound also met two young men whom he did not immediately become fond of: Wyndham Lewis (1882–1957) and D. H. Lawrence (1885–1930); in the case of Lewis, of course, there would be a warming trend about four years later. Pound explains their unfriendly meeting (shortly after Lewis had been "discovered" by Ford) in Canto 80/507, indicating that Laurence Binyon, who considered Pound his "bulldog," took him from the British Museum to lunch at the Vienna Café, where the young painter was eating with Yeats's old poet friend, Sturge Moore:

So it is to Mr Binyon that I owe, initially,
Mr Lewis, Mr P. Wyndham Lewis. His bull-dog, me,
   as it were against old Sturge M's bull-dog, Mr T. Sturge Moore's
   bull-dog, . . .

The two protégés merely glowered at one another.

In October of that year another Ford discovery appeared on the scene: D. H. Lawrence, a coal miner's son who was at this time teaching school in Croydon, South London. That summer, a young lady friend named Jessie Chambers had sent a batch of Lawrence's poems to Ford in the hope that he might publish them, and Ford had at once recognized their merit. For a brief time that fall, Lawrence was drawn into the orbit of South Lodge, even though his lower-middle-class background and distrustful ways clashed with those of the luminaries there. For example, one day in late November, Lawrence and Miss Chambers were invited to Violet's place on Campden Hill, where they encountered Pound, who proceeded to make them both uncomfortable. According to their report, Pound attempted to show them how to eat an apple in the American way. He then noisily chopped up a piece of the fruit and wolfed it down. Then he allegedly went on to make several disparaging comments about working-class manners that did not delight his fellow guests.

It is clear that D. H. Lawrence and Ezra Pound were not meant to be close friends. Both of them grasped this immediately, thereby saving themselves a great deal of wasted time. Pound admired the tough, tensile quality of much of Lawrence's work, but the novelist's mind with its realistic bent was not the sort that interested the poet greatly. Pound could see that Lawrence's obsession with sex and sensuality was necessary for breaking free from a repressive culture, but after one broke free, what came next? During that autumn, the two men met for an "at-home" party sponsored by Violet Hunt at the Reform Club, and Pound even treated the poorer Lawrence to a dinner at his beloved Pagani's in Great Portland Street. Shortly after November 20, Lawrence wrote to his friend Louisa Burrows that Pound was a "jolly nice" fellow and was "a good bit of a genius, and with not the least self consciousness" (LL, 145). The provincial Lawrence was impressed by the American's ability to meet "all the Swells" like Yeats and Ford, and yet Lawrence saw a clear-cut distinction between the two: Pound worshiped the goddess Beauty (the *to kalòn* of *Hugh Selwyn Mauberley*), while *he* worshiped Life. Who could have named the differences more succinctly or more exactly?

The two young men, both destined for greatness, tended to stay in touch for a while (almost as if they could sense each other's importance). Lawrence even spent at least one night in Pound's room on Church Walk when he missed a train and had to suffer the bells, but an eventual drifting apart took place (LL, 147). Lawrence was actually afraid of both Ford and Pound, as he revealed in later letters; he feared that these two extremely dynamic personalities might overpower him, and he would become an impotent wraith in their grasp. Of course he was always willing to be present if there was some major event or if there was a good review in the offing (such as Pound gave to his poetry; see *Literary Essays*, 387–88), but the two men had the extremely good sense to see from the start that they were moving in separate directions.

It was at one of Yeats's Monday night soirées during that winter that Ezra Pound met Bride Scratton (1882–1964), who was one of the great loves of his life. Bride, the bored wife of a dull businessman, yearned for a life of excitement and literary expression. She was slightly older than Ezra—and in many ways just as outspoken, for she possessed her own mind in a day when women were just coming to express themselves openly. Although Pound did not approve of feminism per se, he seems to have been drawn to feminists like Bride, Violet, and May. In 1923 in Paris, he was able to help publish a little book of Bride's titled *England*, which was issued under her maiden name, B. M. G[oold]-Adams. This was also the year in which Bride finally was free from her husband after he sued her in a proceeding in which Ezra Pound was named as the co-respondent (Scratton versus Scratton and Pound).

During the spring of 1910, when William Carlos Williams stopped in on Ezra on his way back from postdoctoral medical studies in Germany, he noted in his *Autobiography* (116) that Ezra kept a candle lighted in front of the photograph of a beautiful, unknown young woman. Since Williams had met Dorothy Shakespear, he knew that it was not she who was receiving this worship. Ezra apparently never divulged the woman's name, and since he and "Bill" had had long intimate talks about girls back in Philadelphia, one wonders why this particular affair was shrouded in such mystery. The best explanation may be that the woman was Bride, and that Pound did not want to discuss the difficulties inherent in the love of a married woman, with all of its frustrations. Or possibly Pound was simply carrying on the great troubadour tradition of never revealing the true identity of one's beloved.

In any case, there was a correspondence between Bride and Ezra, some of which is available at the Beinecke Library at Yale. Unfortunately most of the early letters are missing, possibly because of her

Bride Scratton (also known by her pen name of B. M. G.-Adams) loved Ezra Pound passionately for more than a decade and was involved with him in a divorce case in 1923. (American Literature Collection, Beinecke Rare Book and Manuscript Library, Yale University)

jealous (but equally untrue) husband. The first extant letter from Ezra (undated) begins with an affectionate "Cara mia" and says that the poet feels like a dog with a foot trapped in coil wiring because he is not in the presence of his beloved. Another undated letter (the donor, Bride's son Michael, guessed anywhere between 1909 to 1916) says that Bride's letters are a great consolation, but Ezra still feels hideous because he cannot have her by him. He then complains that she seems to be "diddle dancing" on the rim of a crater, obviously because she does not have the courage to abandon her husband. There is another undated piece of paper with some simple words scratched upon it, as if they were a line from the *Cantos* describing the ideal city of Dioce: "To build a dream over the world." Even as late as January 19, 1931, when Pound was living in Rapallo with Dorothy and had his long-time lover Olga above on the hill, he still told Bride, who was now living in Cambridge and acting as a guide to the University, that he had dreamed about her the night before. It was, indeed, a passionate affair.

Who was this woman who maintained a long subterranean affair with the poet and involved him in her disastrous divorce and subsequent disgrace? Bride says in some imaginary letters to a fictional lover (who is actually Ezra) that she feels as if she has the scarlet letter A engraved on her forehead. The grounds for her divorce were "adultery," and that charge, as well as divorce itself, was not considered the common thing that it is today. Evelyn St. Bride Scratton was the daughter of an army captain named Francis Goold-Adams, who was killed by the tragic explosion of a shell in a peacetime accident in 1885, the year of Pound's birth. Bride had been born three years earlier to the handsome captain and his ill-tempered, frigid wife, Evelyn, who quickly married another man with money after the funeral. Bride then grew up in their house as an unloved stepchild. After she finished basic schooling, she went off to St. Andrews in Scotland (a good hunting-ground for husbands, she says in her papers at Yale). There she met a dashing young golfer named Ned Scratton, who worked for his rich, dipsomanic father, who had an estate first in Ogwell, Severn, and then in Hawksfold, Norfolk. Ned and she contrived to spend a lot of time in South Kensington after they were married there in 1905. A retarded daughter was born to them the very next year, so that when Bride met the young American poet, she already had one child, who had been committed to a home. She would have three more, including Michael, whose handwritten memoirs at Yale supply us with most of these facts that do not come from Bride herself. Michael was born in 1914, the year that Pound finally married Dorothy Shakespear after a protracted courtship.

It was obvious from the start that Ned and Bride were not suited for each other (the same story that one can observe with the Shakespears, the Patmores, and many others), but in this pre-divorce world, couples were trapped together, especially when children appeared on the scene. Because the husband maintained two living quarters (in Norfolk and London), it was easy for Bride to slip free of him; then when World War I came, he was away for a long stretch in the service. It was only after the war that Ned (who was philandering widely, and who remarried quickly after the divorce) found out that his wife was regularly seeing the American poet. We shall pick up that part of the story in 1922, when Bride (under the secret name of "Thiy," an ancient Egyptian queen) was with Ezra in Verona—along with T. S. Eliot. Even in the 1930s, Pound addresses Bride often in letters as Thiy or Thij, just as he kept the Dryad name alive for Hilda Doolittle.

Pound's affair with Bride Scratton is a constant undercurrent in these early years. Wendy Stallard Flory was probably right when she said in *Ezra Pound and the "The Cantos"* (206, 217) that when Pound refers to the eyes of three women haunting him in the *Pisan Cantos* (78/482–83; 81/520 et al.), he was adding Bride to Dorothy and Olga. Others would try to keep this reference vague, since it is based on Dante's allegorical line "Three ladies circling around my mind" (*Tre donne intorno alla mia mente;* 78/483), but Pound himself is never fully allegorical; from imagism onward, he grounded his imagery in reality and experience.

If we ask why he did not try to marry this woman whom he loved so much, economics is once again the answer. Bride was comfortably married to a man of means who could support her and her children well; Pound, as we know, was always a poor, struggling poet with no visible means of support. Then too, there was the stigma attached by a repressive society to a divorced woman, plus the indignities heaped upon the children. At the end of the twentieth century, we tend to forget the progress that has been made in social liberalism. It seems that Bride herself held back most strongly, for in the imaginary letters that she writes to a lover, she pleads that she cannot possibly run away and join him in Paris because she is too afraid of the future, too grounded in her comfortable present (although in the later twenties, her life was not comfortable until her husband died and she got custody of two of the children, with a stipend to rear them). For a stretch after the divorce, she was miserably poor. Ultimately Bride was a coward; she did not have the kind of courage that the violinist-artist Olga Rudge always displayed during her life. Bride allowed bourgeois morality to destroy her dream, and in the long run, it was she who suffered the most.

4 Bride and Dorothy

As December waned, Yeats left town again (he was in and out of London on his way to Paris or Dublin during much of this period), and his young admirer wrote to his mother in Wyncote: "He is the only living man whose work has anything more than a most temporary interest—possible exceptions on the continent" (PC 143). On December 20, Pound was received in triumph by sixty members of the Poets' Club, including the Irishman Joseph Campbell, who delivered "The Ballad of the Goodly Fere" in full sonorous grandeur clad in bardic robes. Pound himself celebrated the event (which included his election to the club) by reading from chapter 2 of the forthcoming *Spirit* on Arnaut Daniel. Meanwhile, his social life whirled along: Sunday dinners with Victor Plarr, Monday nights with Yeats, constant luncheons with Fordie and Violet (although these would diminish as Ford's tenure at the *English Review* ended and he was replaced by Mond's puppet), constant teas with the Shakespear ladies, and a variety of dinner engagements with Aunt Eva and Taffy Fowler, May Sinclair, Ernest Rhys, Lady Anne Penelope Low, and numerous others. When William Carlos Williams joined him around March 6 of 1910, Pound took him on a whirlwind tour of galleries (largely to see the paintings of Turner) and introduced him to Dorothy, Olivia, and "Uncle William" Yeats, who called out after Ezra following a reading at his place—an act that should have seemed impressive to the doctor from Rutherford. But in his *Autobiography* (114), Williams lets us know that he was not quite as impressed as Ezra thought he was.

Still, the specter of poverty was constantly dogging Pound's movements. Without numerous four-pound doles from Homer, he simply could not have survived. The lectures were not really pulling in people from the streets, and so he was supplementing his income by some lucrative private tutoring. In order to scrounge up some cash, Pound tried unsuccessfully to get some reviewing jobs, and he also tried to peddle some articles written during the previous year. He translated some French and Italian songs for the singer Mrs. Derwent Wood (born Florence Schmidt), and although these poems, largely by Verlaine, were performed on March 1 at Bechstein Hall, he received very little for his service. Then in the middle of March he was paid £15 for the three canzoni that Ford had published back in January (one of Ford's last acts as editor of the *English Review*), and Ezra was prepared to flee to Italy.

On March 23 he lunched with Violet Hunt, had tea with the Shakespears (who promised to join him soon in the South), and then grabbed an 8:45 express for Paris, where he stayed for two days with his pianist friend, Walter Morse Rummel. At this time he met a charming but strange young woman from Madison, Indiana, by the name of

October 1909–June 1910   53

Margaret Lanier Cravens (distantly related to the poet Sidney Lanier), who studied piano with Maurice Ravel and was believed to be having an affair with Rummel. Supported by a wealthy but domineering aunt back in Indiana, Margaret admired Pound's poetic powers and vagabond love of life, since she was the opposite: introverted and "neurasthenic," as they called it in those days. Immediately and in a way that Pound himself found almost incredible, she began to send him sums of money—as much as $1,000 a year—which was clearly more than she could afford. They began a rather bland correspondence (almost none of her letters survive), as Pound suddenly reveled in the notion that he had a patron.

He went first to Bergamo and Verona, and then moved quickly on to Lake Garda. When Homer Pound had the temerity to ask him why on earth anyone would want to visit Verona, Ezra answered indignantly in early April that it was "perhaps the most beautiful city in North Italy" (PC 167). He said in *Spirit* (22) that its Church of San Zeno was to architecture what Arnaut Daniel was to lyric poetry in the High Middle Ages. Yet he was drawn inexorably to the nearby lake. Getting off the train at Desenzano, he then backtracked about eight miles to Sirmione, a little town that perches on a narrow spit that projects into the azure Lake Garda and contains the ruins of the Villa of Catullus. Pound was aware, from his Penn days, of Catullus' famous salute to his villa and lake on his return from government duty in Asia Minor: "Laugh! splash loud laughter, my inland sea!" But he was not prepared for the great beauty that awaited him. With no trouble at all, he found a room for about five shillings in an establishment called the Hotel Eden, which became engraved on his consciousness as a place of paradisal bliss. His quarters were neat and clean, and he had a magnificent view of the towers of Brescia off to the west. Due north over miles of azure water lay Salò, the town where a doomed Mussolini would try to piece together the last shards of his lost Imperium. Just behind the Eden lay the crenellated castle of the Scaliger family, whose Can Grande was one of the strongest protectors of the exiled Dante; it had been constructed to control the single passageway leading in from the mainland, and its mighty walls slipped downward into the limpid waters of the lake, whose colors Pound described in the soon-to-be-published "Blandula, Tenulla, Vagula" (*Pers.*, 39) as clear sapphire, cobalt, cyanine, and triune azure—more or less exhausting the words for "blue."

He bathed often in the lake's waters and even tried out a spa where hot sulphur springs gushed forth; he also spent hours musing over the ruins of the Roman poet's once proud villa above the much-visited Grottoes of Catullus. The whole peninsula was swarming with springtime flowers, and the smells from the fruit trees blending with the aromatic herbs of the area made the air seem purer and sweeter than anything he had ever breathed before. These aromas, combined with the breathtaking view, carved an indelible trace in his mind so that years later at Pisa he would write in Canto 76/458 (adding a famous Japanese mountain to take the place of a nameless one in the Italian Alps):

>   this wind out of Carrara
>   is soft as *un terzo cielo*   [a third heaven]
>   said the Prefetto
>   as the cat walked the porch rail at Gardone
>   the lake flowing away from that side
>   was still as is never in Sirmio
>   with Fujiyama above it: "La donna ..." ["Woman"]
>   said the Prefect, in the silence

Or again in Canto 74/427:

>   as Fujiyama at Gardone
>   when the cat walked the top bar of the railing
>   and the water was still on the West side
>   flowing toward the Villa Catullo
>   where with sound ever moving
>   in diminutive poluphloisboios
>   in the stillness outlasting all wars
>   "La Donna" said Nicoletti
>   "la donna,
>   la donna!"

The word "poluphloisboios" is the ancient Homer's onomatopoetic invention for the sound made by the babbling sea, and Prefect Nicoletti has already been mentioned in connection with Desmond FitzGerald.

Pound spent much of his time relaxing, but he also corrected the proofs for *Spirit*, sent three more poems to the new staff at the *English Review*, and received payment for two which had appeared in the April issue: "Canzon: Of Incense" and "Thersites: on the Surviving Zeus." Meanwhile, he heard the good news that his name was now spreading around the world. James Griffyth Fairfax reviewed *Personae* and *Exultations* favorably in the Melbourne *Book Lover*, and the New York *Literary Digest* also reviewed Pound's work, albeit unfavorably. Up to this time, Homer had zealously promoted his son in Phila-

The best-known photograph of the young Dorothy
Shakespear Pound. (Omar Pound)

delphia and both the *Bulletin* and the *Book News Monthly* had taken cognizance of his work. But in Sirmione, Pound lay back in the vernal sun and dreamed about the time of Guido Cavalcanti and Dante, when poets were protected by strong patrons like the Scaligers, and they did not have to eke out a living as best they could.

Late in April Dorothy and her mother arrived, bringing the news from London that Yeats was now saying very kind things about him. Dorothy immediately fell in love with Sirmione and Italy, which she had never seen before. Later she would describe this visit as the event that opened her eyes to visual splendors she had never been aware of before. As an artist, she was delighted by the chance to sketch watercolors of the views. In short, she found the "eyetalian peninsula"

(Canto 80/510) as spiritually moving as Pound did, and it is easy to see why in the future, when they were both tired of London and worn down by Paris, they would select Italy as their home.

Surely this was one of the happiest periods in Pound's life. And just as surely this was the time when he was most infatuated with Dorothy, finding it delightful to see the delight in her face and eyes as he uncovered all of the miracles of the land he knew so well—especially in Venice, where they moved next on May 6. There he escorted the two Shakespear ladies—the bright-eyed young girl and the older, suaver beauty—up and down the canals and over the little bridges into remote corners to see a finely carved stone portal or a hidden painting or a house that looked just right in a certain slanting of light at some point in the late afternoon. Dorothy and Ezra were both amused when they overheard some Italians wondering aloud whether they were brother and sister or lovers. Certainly this trip helped to make their already close friendship even closer, so that Pound was now clearly a part of the family, despite what Henry Hope might think or say.

Pound returned to Sirmione a few days later and visited Verona and Vicenza to work for a time alone. Finally, in early June he said farewell to northern Italy and was off by train for Paris, where he stopped briefly to become better acquainted with his new and secret patron, Margaret Cravens. They attended a melodrama called *La Vierge Folle*, in which a female character shoots herself to death—a morbidly premonitory event for the "neurasthenic" Miss Cravens, whose piano career and amatory quests were not going well.

Pound then left for London, where he gave up his room, and went off to Liverpool to board the *Lusitania* on June 18 for America. According to a letter from D. H. Lawrence to one of his female friends, written on June 24 (LL, 166), Pound and he had discussed the future very seriously, and Ezra had rather dejectedly concluded that he had to return to the States, since his father could no longer support him. Pound had decided to sell boots if necessary, and was considering exploring the "other hemisphere," almost certainly as a booking agent for Kitty Heyman. When Lawrence suggested that Ezra should look into the promising new world of the movies, Pound frowned. He was not at all looking forward to returning to the land of his birth.

5

The Brief Return of 1910
(June 1910–February 1911)

Arriving in New York in late June, Pound spent a short time there and then took the train to Philadelphia on June 25. His family, deeply involved in their Christian Endeavor work, had sublet their house in Wyncote (which would not be theirs again until 1912), and were living on Mount Vernon St. near the Mint or, for that summer, in a rented house in suburban Swarthmore. Pound was obviously dislocated by being in this strange house in an unfamiliar suburb, far from his cozy tower room and his books. But he was happy to see Hilda again, to whom he had written in May, extolling the virtues of Sirmione (where the jobless Ford was now vacationing) and trying to persuade her to make the leap to Europe. Now they seemed grounded forever in their inimical native city. But Pound was not one to suffer captivity easily. He soon persuaded his parents that his taste of big-city life in London had convinced him that he could survive only in a metropolis and so, with their consent, he moved back to New York around August 8, subletting quarters first on Waverly Place near Washington Square and then on Fourth Avenue (now Park Avenue South), with a view of the towers around Gramercy Park.

Hilda had a difficult time persuading her choleric father, who still deeply mistrusted Pound, that she should go to the metropolis to find some literary work, but at last he yielded. In October she joined a kindly old woman named Julia Wells, who had fed Pound and given him some free lodging in Venice back in 1908. Wells lived at 4 Patchin Place in Greenwich Village—a charming mews that would be made famous later by such occupants as Djuna Barnes and Pound's close friend E. E. Cummings. At this time a conspicuous occupant was a painter named Warren Dahler, whom Pound calls "the Chris Columbus of Patchin" in Canto 80/508.

Hilda was never really happy in New York. She visited all of the literary employment agencies, as well as editorial offices, but could find no suitable work. She was also quite disappointed with her former lover, because he was so wrapped up in his social life and writing and a prospective business deal that he did not seem to be paying much attention to her. It was apparent to Ezra that whatever love had flamed between the two had become now merely a strong friendship—but Hilda resisted making this recognition. For quite a while she would go on thinking that Ezra Pound would be her future husband, even though at this time she was also experimenting with her first lesbian relationship, with a Philadelphia girl named Frances Gregg. It hurt Hilda's pride to be ignored, and so after a relatively brief time, she decided to return to the comforts of her family, although she steadfastly promised Ezra that she would join him in not too long a time in Europe. Pound never discussed any of his London amours with her; in fact, Hilda would be deeply shocked when she learned later that Dorothy Shakespear was being groomed to be the future Mrs. Pound. Although Hilda's biographers tend to view Pound at this point as a deceiver, it is also possible to see him as a gentleman who did not want to destroy the very worthwhile friendship that had sustained them for so long.

Meanwhile, Pound kept up his cordial relations with two of his other youthful loves: Viola Baxter of Utica, who would soon marry a man named Jordan, and Mary Moore of Trenton, who had not even noticed that *Personae* had been dedicated to her. Viola was still beautiful but infuriatingly chaste (as William Carlos Williams saw her), while Mary was still involved with her many beaux from Princeton. Pound thrilled both young women with tales about his conquest of London, and Mary especially vowed that she would join him there some day soon—and in fact, she would keep this promise in 1912. During this visit, she would enjoy herself immensely, but her heart was in America, and on returning to her native Trenton, she would marry an advertising executive named James Frederick Cross (that "cross" you have to bear, Pound would remind her endlessly). They would see each other later in Rapallo, but then the friendship would lie fallow until Pound's St. Elizabeth years, when Mary stood quite firmly beside her longtime friend. Viola Baxter also lost touch with Pound for a while, but during his time of trial, she likewise reappeared from the shadows and wrote him reams of letters—about afternoon soap operas and Broadway shows and the baking of chocolate cakes, the kind of everyday banalities that help one keep some sense of "normalcy" in a world of nightmare. Yet a passionate love for any of these three old flames—given Dorothy and Bride—was now out of the question.

Pound also renewed his acquaintance with the formerly protective Kitty Heyman, who was still basking in the success of her latest winter tour in Europe. She had played in His Majesty's Theatre in London and had been hosted there by two friends from Russia, the Prince and Princess Lydia Bariatinsky; the latter, who will be mentioned later in a context involving Henry James, acted professionally under the sobriquet Madame Gavorskaia. Kitty was staying at the Judson Hotel on Washington Square South (an elegant address long since gone). Unquestionably the idea of acting as her agent was still on Pound's mind, but although Kitty received him kindly, nothing came of it. "Her Highness" was now entertaining the likes of Prokofiev, and she was deeply engrossed in a study of Buddhism, which the Confucius-oriented Pound did not fully appreciate. Doubtlessly she was a bit jealous of the way he had forged his own path in London society, putting her to the side. In any case, a lacuna developed in their friendship. We have to jump to 1914 to find her mentioned again: Hilda took her some books when Kitty was visiting London (PC 329). There is then a broader leap to Letter 74 to Mary Moore (written in the St. Elizabeth's years) in which Pound regrets that he did not look Kitty up on his whirlwind visit of 1939. She died two years later of natural causes near her home in Connecticut. Pound told Mary that he was sorry that he lost touch with the gifted pianist, who had always protected him with maternal warmth.

Another old friend whom he saw often was "Bill" or "Bull" Williams, who was now practicing medicine in the Jersey Meadowlands at Rutherford. Pound and Hilda visited the Williamses that fall, and they had a good time until Bill introduced them to his fiancée, Flossie (Florence) Herman. Hilda, who was always something of a Philadelphia Main Line snob, found the artless Flossie insensitive, drab, and lower-middle-class Teutonic, just as she snubbed the Jewish Kitty, and then later F. S. Flint and his Cockney wife. Flossie's opinion of the two poets was also mixed. Old Mr. Williams, if we can trust his son's memory (*Selected Essays*, 7–8), is believed to have made a much-quoted critique of Pound's poetry at this time, saying, in effect, "don't say 'jewels' when you mean 'books' "—although Pound never fully recalled this event. After Hilda left, Pound spent Thanksgiving Day with the Williamses, and he visited them again shortly before leaving the States that following February.

One of the first people whom Pound looked up on his settling in New York was Yeats's artist father, John B., who was living in a boardinghouse at 317 West 29th Street, which was run by the Petitpas sisters from France. The elder Yeats then introduced Ezra to his good friend and patron, the lawyer John Quinn. Quinn was a handsome, dapper Irish-American from Ohio who was spending much of his lucrative salary on satsifying his taste for beautiful art. He had met the elder Yeats in Ireland and had bought some of J.B.'s finest productions. Their friendship eventually encouraged the poet's father to move to America, where he would end his days in 1922. The introduction of Pound to Quinn was extremely important for many other people, because the lawyer was on his way to becoming the Maecenas of the twentieth century, with a great deal of literary help from Pound. Already Quinn had moved into a large, fashionable apartment on Central Park West, which he would soon be stocking with Matisses, Van Goghs, Picassos, Epsteins, and the like.

The introduction, however, did not have an immediate effect. Pound said that Quinn angered him at that first meeting because of the lawyer's imperious manner (PC 455). But Quinn was sufficiently impressed with Ezra to keep in touch with his work over the next five years, even when the poet had returned to London. Suddenly, in the winter of 1915, Quinn was shocked on reading an article by Pound on Jacob Epstein in the *New Age* of January 21 to find that Ezra was satirizing art patrons who stock up on old masters and do not invest in contemporary art (RJQ, 197ff.). Believing that it was he whom Ezra was attacking, Quinn wrote the poet a friendly but indignant reply. He ran down a list of his recent acquisitions, pointing out that the majority of them were quite contemporary. Ezra felt duly chastened; he wrote back a polite apology and then went on to reminisce about a certain hot August evening back in 1910 that they had spent together on Coney Island. From that time on, there was a strong bond between the two men until Quinn's sicknesses led to his early death in 1924 at the age of fifty-four.

The Pound-Quinn friendship would lead the lawyer to start subsidizing writers as well as artists, and to begin acquiring important manuscripts, such as Joyce's *Ulysses* and Eliot's *Waste Land*. Later Pound put Quinn into Canto 12 under the alias of "Jim X," who relates the "Tale of the Honest Sailor," an obscene story about a sodomitic merchant seaman who gives birth to a child. This tale, recited before a boring meeting of prissy bankers, is meant to point up the wit of the lively Irishman, who was as distinguished for his humor as for his taste in art.

The hot August night that Pound later remembered involved a visit by Quinn, Yeats senior, Pound, the painter John Sloan, his wife Dolly, and a friend named King to the famous amusement park. Five years later, Pound could vividly recall the bright lights of the steeplechase against the sultry, star-strewn sky and the exciting motor ride back home, since a car ride in these days was also an adventure. Pound later remembered the face of old J. B. Yeats smiling beatifically like an Old Testament prophet as he rode upon an elephant. He also recalled the sure-eyed, lanky Mr. Quinn poised like a boyish sharpshooter in a shooting gallery. This is the way he phrased the memory, writing from the hellhole of Pisa many years later:

... his, William's, old "da" at Coney Island perched on an elephant beaming like the prophet Isaiah
    and J. Q. as it were aged 8 (Mr John Quinn)
at the target.

(Canto 80/507)

On February 11, shortly before Pound left New York to return to Europe, the elder Yeats wrote to his son: "Carlton Glidden, an artist of talent who has a lot to learn, but who is a very nice fellow indeed, told me today that Ezra Pound was at his studio a few days ago and talked a lot about you, quoting quantities of your verse, which he had by heart, placing you very high, and as the best poet for the last century and more. I tell you this as he is going in a few days to Europe to stay in Paris, etc. Quinn met and liked him very much. The Americans, young literary men, whom I know found him surly, supercilious and grumpy. I liked him myself very much, that is, I liked his look and air, and the few things he said, for tho' I was a good while in his company he said very little."

In early September the pianist Walter Morse Rummel, who had been engaged in a long summer tour that included Stockbridge in July and Chicago in mid-August, joined Pound for a two-week vacation in the rented house in Swarthmore. There the Pounds entertained him with parties and musicales, which Rummel himself participated in. At this time Pound introduced the handsome blond man to Hilda, who was immediately impressed by him, as she recounts in *End to Torment* (17). In October, back in Paris, Walter wrote that a female admirer from Swarthmore was one of many who had written him warm "fan" letters recently. During that hot period, Rummel and Pound had lengthy conversations about music, the future, poetry, and philosophy; Rummel, in fact, was keeping a diary about his visit and jotting down meditations (see the literary portrait of him in chapter 18).

After the Philadelphia visit, Rummel accompanied Pound back to New York, and even stayed with him in the place that he was subletting from "a mad lady from Colorado," as Pound wrote to the faithful Dorothy (*EPDS*, 38). The elegant pianist, who was accustomed to deluxe accommodations, felt very uneasy sleeping in the bed of a lady whom he had never met, and he was even more embarrassed when her private undergarments kept appearing in improbable places. Before he sailed from Boston to Liverpool on the *Saxonia* on September 13, Rummel invited Pound to stay with him in Paris, where they could work on setting some troubadour translations to music and also on creating some new musical accompaniments for some of Pound's poems. This was a dangerous invitation to extend to a young man who was already restless and discontented. Homer and Isabel were desperately trying to hold their son in his native land, and they were probably quite happy to see Mr. Rummel depart. In a letter of September 16, written on *Saxonia* stationery, Walter asks: "When is your epic coming out! Do you see light there?!" This is probably the earliest recorded mention of the *Cantos*, and shows the depth of the Rummel-Pound communication.

Before Pound himself left New York, he definitely tried to give the city a chance. Near his place on Fourth Avenue was the well-known Little Book Shop Around the Corner, run by an educated Englishman named Laurence J. Gomme. This was New York's answer to Elkin Mathews' place on Vigo Street, and it attracted writers like Joyce Kilmer, Harry Kemp, and others, who were the best that New York had to offer, although, as Yeats père indicated, Pound did not get along with any of them. Ezra certainly availed himself of the many cultural opportunities of the metropolis: the Broadway theater, the Metropolitan Opera (where he heard *Carmen*), and the Metropolitan Museum of Art (where he admired a Goya).

For some time that fall, he was busily engaged in what he termed a business "game" (PC 178), which was almost certainly the establishment of a magazine, although Williams suggested in his *Autobiography* (92) that Pound was trying to promote an antisyphilitic drug called "606" produced by Paul Ehrlich. He tried to touch up relatives, and renewed his acquaintance with a rather questionable entrepreneur named Francis S. ("Baldy") Bacon, whom he had met back in "the good old days" of Aunt Frank's boardinghouse on East 47th Street. This establishment had been torn down as Frances Weston had tried to run a new hotel further up on Madison Avenue called The

New Weston—and had disastrously failed. Baldy at this time was engaged in a printing scheme, and so he was a logical person to contact if one wanted to establish a magazine or a printing house. Pound mentions him prominently in Canto 12/53:

> Baldy's interest
> Was in money business.
> "No interest in any other kind uv bisnis,"
> Said Baldy.

Baldy had begun his career by operating a money racket in Cuba, and had then

> Returned to Manhattan, ultimately to Manhattan.
> 24 E. 47th, when I met him,
> Doing job printing, i.e., agent,
> going to his old acquaintances,
> His office in Nassau St. . . .

Baldy's ambition was to "eat up the whole'r Wall St." He lived for a time with a fellow named "Mons Quade who wore a monocle on a wide sable ribbon." Apparently Pound could not reach an agreement with either man, although he did keep in touch with them. When Wyndham Lewis wanted some addresses during his settling in America in 1939, Pound told him to look up Baldy at 80 Maiden Lane near Wall Street, as well as "That ass Quade" in Washington (PL, 216).

It was certainly with the idea of getting some capital that Pound went in October to Plainfield, New Jersey, in order to have dinner with the rich and kindly stockbroker William Baldwin Wadsworth, a relative of his mother. After listening to the family bragging about their sports cars and stocks, Pound finally touched up old William for a loan, and he got it—although it was not enough money to start a new magazine or any other venture. As for the more literary Charles David Wadsworth, Pound visited his elegant townhouse on Central Park South in November and spent a delightful evening in which Charles himself acted very "decorative" while "Madame" Vera, his wife, was quite cordial, and their son William spoke about being bored by law (PC 185). But the literary talk was largely about their mutual relative Henry Wadsworth Longfellow—not Yeats and contemporaries—and so Pound felt that he was not intellectually close to them.

After a great deal of searching, finally in early November Pound found his beloved Aunt Frank, who was lying low after her debacle with her overly large hotel. She was often staying out in Belmar, New

Jersey, with Cousin Sadie Wessells, where she would die in 1913. Poor Aunt Frank was just a vestige of her old ebullient self. Since she no longer had a job to occupy her time, she did not know quite what to do with her life. She seems to have had a strained relationship with her current husband, Dr. James Beyea, who had taken a house on the Upper West Side of New York City near Alexander Hamilton's Grange. Although the two would retain their marriage to the end, when Aunt Frank died on July 29, 1913, she was laid to rest with her great beloved, Pound's namesake, Ezra Brown Weston, in Cypress Hills Cemetery in Queens.

In late October, Pound renewed his friendship with Witter Bynner, who had helped him go to Europe back in 1908 when Bynner had written a supportive letter about Pound's poetry to Homer Pound. It was Bynner who had introduced the poet to Small, Maynard and Company Publishers of Boston, and that firm published Pound's first American collection of verse, *Provença*, on November 22 of this year. *Provença* was simply a selection of "the best of the two volumes, *Personae* and *Exultations*," along with some longer poems that would appear in *Canzoni* the following year. In 1912, they would also publish Pound's *Sonnets and Ballate of Guido Cavalcanti*, on which he was feverishly working all that fall. Cavalcanti and his tight, spare poetry were very much on Ezra Pound's mind during this year and for the next thirty years or more.

Despite some pleasant experiences, the visit of 1910 seems to have been doomed from the start. Pound was not in any way insensitive to the beauty of New York. At night he found the skyline incomparably dazzling. He wrote a short lyric in honor of the city, called "N.Y.," which was published later in *Ripostes:*

> My City, my beloved, my white! Ah, slender,
> Listen! Listen to me, and I will breathe into thee a soul.
> Delicately upon the reed, attend me! . . .
>
> My City, my beloved,
> Thou art a maid with no breasts,
> Thou art slender as a silver reed.
> Listen to me, attend me!
> And I will breathe into thee a soul,
> And thou shalt live for ever.
>
> (*CEP*, 185)

But the halcyon world of his childhood seemed to have vanished. In its place was a busy, monumental world that seemed not only hectic but hostile. He did admire the Caracallan splendor of the now destroyed Pennsylvania Railroad Station (whose massive columns lie immersed in the Jersey swamps) and the glistening spire of the Metropolitan Life Insurance Company, which was next door to Dr. Parkhurst's gem of a church, which he still dutifully attended. But the spire's beauty was flawed by a clock that projected too far outward, and the train station's steps were too narrow. The new New York Public Library should have been a thing of beauty, but there was "another example of botch, of false construction" because "They have tried to conceal a third floor behind the balustrade" and "the third floor shows like an undershirt projecting beyond a man's cuff." From his window facing Gramercy Square, he could see a lovely apartment house, but the marble splendor of the façade was ruined because the building was crowned by an ugly water-tank. In short, everything seemed flawed.

Many of the preceding observations were voiced in letters to Margaret Cravens and others, but they appeared as quoted in A. R. Orage's *New Age* from 1912 to 1913, and were finally gathered together in a book called *Patria Mia*, which did not appear until 1950. That book most eloquently conveys Pound's extremely ambivalent feelings toward his native land. There was a great deal of beauty in America, but there were also vulgarity and commercialism, which always threatened to stifle the aesthetically pleasing. Pound also felt a great sense of alienation as he walked the city's streets in New York. Years before, as he traveled around with Aunt Frank and Uncle Ezry, he had felt that the city belonged to them. But now, suddenly, there were floods of immigrants from Eastern and Southern Europe who were displacing the old-line White Anglo-Saxon Protestants from whom he was largely descended. Even when he received the great honor in January of 1911 of being elected a member of the prestigious Barnard Club, and when he attended one of the inaugural meetings of the Poetry Society of America, he did not feel uplifted. His heart was abroad.

Finally, after much arguing with his family and an attack of jaundice that struck him at the start of the new year (and went on for a good six months), Pound persuaded his reluctant parents to give him enough money to return to Europe. Pound later told Quinn in 1915 that during his entire stay in America he earned only £14—enough for a return ticket to Europe. He wrote his parents that Elkin Mathews was "ready to blaze away" on *Canzoni*, and Walter Rummel was anxiously waiting to collaborate with him in Paris (PC 192). The Pounds really had no choice; they could see that Ezra had not enjoyed any of the success in New York that he had had in London, and so, since in many ways they were living vicariously through him, they gave in.

5 The Brief Return of 1910

After a last-minute visit with the Williamses and a final note to Hilda, begging her to join him abroad, Pound boarded the famous *Mauretania* on February 22 and was once again at sea. He would not come home for almost thirty years.

6

From Rummel in Paris to Ford in Giessen (February–August 1911)

On his return to London in late February, Pound might have been expected to linger for some time in the city, but instead he simply looked a few people up—Yeats, Plarr, Ford, May Sinclair, and Lady How—and was then off by train to Paris (PC 199). He was anxious to get to work on collaborating with Walter Rummel, but the pianist was occupied and did not join Ezra until March 18. In the interim, Pound took a room in a pension on the Left Bank by the Odéon and was captivated once again by the city. In a letter home in early March (PC 202), he tells Isabel that he was indeed very wise in selecting Paris as a place to work in, since London was too hectic. The Bibliothèque Nationale contained valuable manuscripts of troubadour poems and vidas which he was using in his study of Arnaut Daniel. He was seeing a lot of Walter's brother, Frank, an artist and cellist who was showing him around (PC 212). More privately, he was also paying court to his patron, Miss Cravens, whose identity he kept concealed from almost everyone. Despite an urgent invitation to serve as a secretary to Ford, who was dying of boredom in Giessen, Pound was content in Paris, and his memory of this happiness would lure him here in the future.

Pound's editing and translating of Arnaut Daniel were now proceeding smoothly, and his collaboration with Rummel was also working well. This would culminate with the publication that September of *Three Songs of Ezra Pound for a Voice with Instrumental Accompaniment* by Rummel in London. The lyrics for two of the songs, "Madrigale" and "Aria," were dedicated to an unnamed "Weaver of Beauty"—a secret name for Margaret Cravens, who did not want any public association with any production. These two and "Au bal masqué" would all appear in *Canzoni*. In March of 1913 Pound and Rummel would also issue *Hesternae Rosae: Serta II* (Yesterday's Roses: Garland II), which was a collection of nine troubadour songs for piano and voice, with English translations by Pound and music by the composer. Two songs of Arnaut Daniel were included in this volume. Clearly, Pound and Rummel worked well together, and their association would go on for many years.

Pound informed his parents that he had finished his Parisian work on Arnaut by mid-May. Earlier, he had bumped into the Mapel sisters (Adah and Ida), whom he had met in Spain in his fellowship year of 1906 (PC 208); these redoubtable ladies would surprisingly reappear in his life, especially during his St. Elizabeth's years, offering him consolation and happy memories of the past. Yeats also appeared nearby in Versailles for a rest, and the two "dawdled" around Notre Dame together (Canto 83/528); once again Pound extravagantly praised him to Homer (PC 210). In that same letter in May, Pound mentions meeting Arnold Bennett, the successful novelist much admired by Ford. But Pound said bluntly that this man did not interest him, largely because of his forced sense of humor. He later wrote one of his most acid (and brilliant) poems about Bennett under the title "Mr. Nixon," a sequence in *Hugh Selwyn Mauberley:*

> In the cream gilded cabin of his steam yacht
> Mr. Nixon advised me kindly, to advance with fewer
> Dangers of delay. "Consider
>   "Carefully the reviewer . . .
>
> "I never mentioned a man but with the view
> Of selling my own works.
> The tip's a good one, as for literature
> It gives no man a sinecure.
>
> "And no one knows, at sight, a masterpiece.
> And give up verse, my boy,
> There's nothing in it . . ."
>
>   (*Pers.*, 194)

Unknown to Pound then, Bennett was deeply engrossed in a study of modern French literature, especially Rémy de Gourmont, and could have opened some vistas for the poet. In 1946, in retrospect, Pound said to Wyndham Lewis about Bennett: "We understeemed him."

Through Rummel and the visiting Yeats, Pound met several French poets, but he found most of them "gutless" (PC 210). He studied the paintings of Matisse and found only one that interested him; he also was rather dispassionate about Cézanne. He listened to the music of Claude Debussy, Rummel's idol, but found anything "impressionistic" murky and ill-defined. Then he had his portrait painted by an American named Eugene Paul Ullman (1877–1953). Actually, the decision was engineered and subsidized by Margaret Cravens, who was a good friend of both Ullman and his wife, the "liberal" novelist Alice Woods, who also hailed from Indiana.

Margaret likewise had her portrait painted by Ullman, who was quite fond of this troubled girl who would become even more troubled when she learned later that her father committed suicide that year on April 22. Neither the painter nor his wife was fond of Pound; and Alice deplored the amount of time he spent in Margaret's apartment on the Rue du Colisée. Ullman at this time was in his florescence, establishing a reputation for painting sensitive portraits with highlights. He was the wealthy son of a German immigrant to America named Sigmund Ullman, who had made a fortune with his Ullman (later National) Printing Ink Corporation. These facts help to explain the otherwise cryptic line in Canto 80/505: "and the ink's heir painting high lights." During this time Pound finished his first Cavalcanti book in Margaret's apartment, which she shared with two girls from America.

After editing twelve of the then-accepted fifteen cansos of Arnaut Daniel, Pound checked the proofs of *Canzoni* and then dashed off by train to his beloved Hotel Eden in Sirmione by July. Unfortunately, *Canzoni* is not considered one of his greater books. Still, a number of the poems made their way into the 1926 edition of *Personae* (38–53). Although Ford would severely criticize this volume for being too Swinburnian and Oxonian, it is possible that he and later generations did not quite appreciate what Pound was doing here. Pound wrote to Dorothy something that has not usually been stated about this work: "Artistically speaking it[']s supposed to be a sort of chronological table of emotions: Provence; Tuscany, the Renaissance, the XVIII, the XIX, centuries, external modernity (cut out) subjective modernity. finis. . . . I don[']t suppose any body'll see it—the table of contents—in this light but when my biographers unearth this missive it will be recorded as an astounding proof of my genius" (*EPDS*, 37–38).

Pound was trying to begin with imitations of the cansos of Provence and the canzoni of Italy and then move forward in time. The opening piece, "Canzon: The Yearly Slain," which was written in reply to Fred Manning's "Korè," follows an elaborate and intricate troubadour form. It is headed by an epigraph from Dante's *De vulgari eloquio* 2.10, where Dante says in Latin: "The form of this stanza was used in almost all the cansos of Arnaut Daniel, and we have followed it"; Pound in turn follows them. The first stanza sets the pattern for six more (with envoi) which duplicate the rhyme scheme of the first:

> Ah! red-leafed time hath driven out the rose
> And crimson dew is fallen on the leaf
> Ere ever yet the cold white wheat be sown
> That hideth all earth's green and sere and red;
> The Moon-flower's fallen and the branch is bare,
> Holding no honey for the starry bees;
> The Maiden turns to her dark lord's demesne.
>   (*CEP*, 133)

The rhyme words in the first lines of the next stanzas are "sows, blows, goes, gloze, glows." Forgetting the stiff and archaic diction, it is a masterful tour de force. After Pound gives the troubadours their due, he translates or imitates Cavalcanti and Dante, some Renaissance Latin, Italian, and French writers, and then jumps to Leopardi and the Victorian period. He has a tribute to Rummel called "Maestro di Toc[c]ar," which is reminiscent of his tributes to Kitty Heyman. The book ends with Heine translations and the *Und Drang* sequence, which is at times quite modern, as in Section V:

> How our modernity,
> Nerve-wracked and broken, turns
> Against time's way and all the way of things,
> Crying with weak and egoistic cries!
>   (*CEP*, 169)

There is a feeling of T. S. Eliot's *Waste Land* in this lengthy poem. But since nobody at the time perceived the synchronic progression in the work, it was badly reviewed (see, however, the article by James Longenbach in *Paideuma, 13:* 389ff.).

Pound also altered the form of *Canzoni* by cutting out some poems, especially a long one called "Redondillas, or Something of That Sort." This seemed to him too formless, but it contained some rather powerful lines:

I am that terrible thing,
                the product of American culture,
Or rather that product improved
                by considerable care and attention.
I am really quite modern, you know,
                despite my affecting the ancients.
                                    (*CEP,* 220)

Another poem that was cut was titled "To Hulme (T.E.) and Fitzgerald (A Certain)"; it is written in a Northlands dialect such as Hulme spoke, and is the kind of dialect poem that Desmond FitzGerald could read with an Irish brogue (*CEP,* 214–15). Pound also parodied the style of A. E. Housman:

O woe, woe,
People are born and die,
We also shall be dead pretty soon
Therefore let us act as if we were
                dead already ...
            (*CEP,* 163–64)

But *Canzoni* was not a success. It was most warmly received by the two people to whom it was dedicated, Olivia and Dorothy Shakespear, and it may be safely said that, more than any other work, it belonged to Dorothy, who shared in its production, as her correspondence with Ezra makes clear.

Toward the end of July, Pound decided to leave Sirmione. But before that, he went down to Mantua to meet Edgar Williams ("Bill's" brother), an architect, and together they examined churches and palaces in the area, including nearby Goito (Sordello's home town), and then Verona (PC 217). In the latter city, they visited the church of San Zeno (so extravagantly praised in the chapter on Arnaut Daniel in *Spirit of Romance*), and they especially noticed a magnificent hand-carved pillar on which the sculptor had engraved his name:

                ADAMINUS
            DE   SCO
                GEORG
            IO   ME
                FECIT

"Adam of St. George made me." The pride of the artist shone through just as Arnaut proudly signed the envois of many of his verses. Edgar's comment on the difference between medieval and modern procedures in sculpture appears in Canto 77/480:

> So he said, looking at the signed columns in San Zeno
> "how the hell can we get any architecture
>   when we order our columns by the gross?"

Pound moved on to the Hotel Belle Venise in Milan, in order to inspect Manuscript R 71 Superiore in the Ambrosian Library, whose director, Achille Ratti, would become Pope Pius XI (see Canto 80/502). This is the only manuscript containing any music of Arnaut (for *Lo ferm voler* and *Chansson do · il mot son plan e prim*). The musical notations delighted him, since they accorded perfectly with his own idea about the way that Arnaut's music should be written. Buoyed by this discovery, he made copies of the proper manuscript pages, and decided finally to go up to Germany—not just to visit Ford, but also to consult with the famous lexicographer Prof. Emil Lévy ("Lehvèè" he wrote the name in Paige Carbon 220), whom Professor Rennert of Penn considered the foremost authority on Provençal literature. Rennert also thought that the Frenchman Jean Beck was the best authority on troubadour music, and Pound was in correspondence with Beck too.

The visit to Lévy is memorably related in Canto 20:

> And so I went up to Freiburg,
> And the vacation was just beginning,
> The students getting off for the summer,
> Freiburg im Breisgau,
> And everything clean, seeming clean, after Italy.
>
> And I went to old Lévy, and it was by then 6.30
> in the evening, and he trailed half way across Freiburg
> before dinner, to see the two strips to copy,
>
> . . . .
> And he said: Now is there anything I can tell you?"
> And I said: I dunno sir, or
> "Yes, Doctor, what do they mean by *noigandres*?"
> And he said: Noigandres! NOIgandres!
> "You know for seex mon's of my life
> "Effery night when I go to bett, I say to myself:
> "Noigandres, eh, *noigandres*,
> "Now what the DEFFIL can that mean!"
>
>   (89–90)

The two men are debating a famous crux in Arnaut's poetry, which occurs in line 7 of *Er vei vermeills*. Pound then goes on to paint a paradisal nature scene in which he works the mystery word into his portrait, breaking it up into the units *d'enoi gandres*, which means "lacking all annoyance, displeasure" (ed. Wilhelm, 54). The picture ends with the image of a nude woman by candlelight, and the word *remir* (contemplate), which is taken from line 32 of *Doutz brais e critz* (*TEP*, 174). Pound is here trying to stress Arnaut's, Lévy's, and his own dedications to precision, as well as to suggest that the troubadours were worshipers of love, beauty, and nature:

> Sound: as of the nightingale too far off to be heard . . .
> The smell of that place—*d'enoi ganres*.
> Air moving under the boughs,
> The cedars there in the sun,
> Hay new cut on hill slope,
> And the water there in the cut
> Between the two lower meadows; sound,
> The sound, as I have said, a nightingale
> Too far off to be heard.
> And the light falls, *remir*,
> from her breast to thighs.
>
> (90)

He then journeyed by train to Frankfurt, and around August 5 arrived in nearby Giessen, which he called a "model town" (PC 220). However, he also expressed a negative attitude toward Germany to his parents that he often held during his lifetime: "I don't approve of it." Aside from German music, he had little regard for German culture in general. To Pound, Mussolini's fascism was never Hitler's Nazism; he saw the two as distinctly different developments, and he backed Hitler only when Italy could not support itself in World War II.

Ford at this time was living with Violet Hunt on Friedrichstrasse in the little university town which many people find rather pleasant. After his release from Brixton Jail for non-support in the winter of 1910, Ford had moved in with Violet at South Lodge, thereby adding to the general disgrace that he had already created for himself and her. Seeing that his wife Elsie would not grant him a divorce, he decided to capitalize on his German roots and use his relatives to enable him to gain citizenship in the Grand Duchy of Baden, where he could then obtain a German divorce (on the grounds of separation) that would enable him to rid himself of Elsie forever. For a year and a half, he and Violet had shuttled back and forth between Germany and

England, with stops in France and Belgium, and now they were stuck in this quiet college town. Eventually, without doing it, they would claim that they were legally married, and they would return to England in a pseudo-triumphal way that would lead to more disastrous results.

"The Hueffers," as they were soon to be known (the "Ford" change coming in 1919), received the always exuberant Ezra with proverbial open arms, since he was the perfect person to ruffle the calm of the town. They did their best to entertain their guest as they had in the old days. They took him up to the terraced convent of Schiffenberg, where he proclaimed his verses to the heavens on a shaky wooden platform that collapsed in the middle of his performance. They took him to several castles, which he thought all looked alike, and to the university, which is now an agricultural college, as well as to various taverns where the famous German *Gemütlichkeit* was sadly dissipated. Clearly, Giessen was neither Sirmione to Pound nor Kensington to "the Hueffers."

But one important event occurred that redeemed the whole trip and changed the course of modern literature. Pound made the unavoidable mistake of showing Ford his *Canzoni*. The older maestro read some of the verses carefully, then let out a howl, and started to roll on the floor. As Pound described it in the 1939 obituary, Ford

> ... felt the errors of contemporary style to the point of rolling (physically, and if you look at it as mere superficial snob, ridiculously) on the floor of his temporary quarters in Giessen when my third volume displayed me trapped, fly-papered, gummed and strapped down in a jejune provincial effort to learn, *mehercule*, the stilted language that then passed for 'good English' in the arthritic milieu that held control of the respected British critical circles, Newbolt, the backwash of Lionel Johnson, Fred Manning, the Quarterlies and the rest of 'em.
>
> And that roll saved me at least two years, perhaps more. It sent me back to my own proper effort, namely, toward using the living tongue (with younger men after me), though none of us has found a more natural language than Ford did. (*PF*, 172)

Anyone who doubts the sincerity of this statement should note that Pound again and again stressed the importance of Ford's influence (especially when he saw Hulme getting far too much credit for creating modern poetry). Ford's biographer Mizener has documented these tributes (216, 559). Pound pinpointed the actual date of this event in a letter to Ford in 1921: "say Aug 7th" (*PF*, 59). Although Pound liked to tease his friend later by addressing him in letters with such titles as "My dear ole Freiherr von Grumpus ZU and VON Bieberstein" (making fun of Ford's occasional pretensions to nobility), he always felt a deep and abiding respect for the man's intellect. If one were to seek a date to mark the beginning of modernism, August 7, 1911, would not be a bad nomination.

Of course things do not happen overnight. Pound did not sit down on August 8 to write "In a Station of the Metro" or any of the other famous imagist poems that were free of Victorian trappings. He left Giessen toward the end of that sweltering August, taking a long and thoughtful ride back to London, past the Cologne Cathedral by starlight and the towers of Brussels in the pale dawn (PC 220). As in that long journey from the debacle at Wabash College through the cornfields, he was thinking, thinking, thinking—about what he could do to transform his verse into the kind of expressive tool that Ford had indicated. And in the near future, that transformation would be effected.

7

The Road to Imagism: Some Editors (August 1911–February 1912)

When Pound finally returned to London in late August of 1911, he was somewhat adrift, since he had surrendered his place at 10 Church Walk, and would not get it back until November. In the interim he took a room with a Mrs. Worthington at 2A Granville Place, and then shared a house with the well-heeled Mr. Rummel at 39 Addison Road North. The pianist was shuttling back and forth between Paris and London, just as "the Hueffers" were enjoying a variety of spas and hotels on the Continent and in England. Pound's life becomes extremely complex at this point, and remains so until World War I. In recounting it, a biographer can only follow certain strands, neglecting others, but the reader should be aware that even if certain already familiar names are not mentioned directly, the personages are there.

Ford's words at Giessen weighed heavily on the poet's mind during that fall. But Pound refused to put the troubadours aside; he was too deeply immersed in Arnaut Daniel and medieval music. Therefore, almost as if he was following the advice of an adverse critic from the *Daily Mail*, he decided to translate Daniel exactly, rather than to play off him, as he had tried to do in *Canzoni*. This move, which might have seemed anachronistic and contra-Ford, actually turned out to be a salvation, because, as Dante perceived in his *De vulgari eloquio*, Arnaut has a hard and tight command of language with a colloquial ring:

> *Anc ieu non l'aic, mas ella m'a*
> *totztemps en son poder Amors* . . .
>
> I never had her, but she has me
> Forever in her power—Love . . .
> (ed. and trans. J. J. Wilhelm, 26–27)

Arnaut consistently throws the Book of Poetic Clichés out the window and pens daring lines like the following:

> *En breu brisaral temps braus,*
> *Eill bisa busina els brancs* . . .
>
> Briefly bursteth season brisk,
> Blasty north breeze racketh branch . . .
> (*TEP,* 168–69)

Pound's "Portrait d'une Femme" would be rejected by a magazine because it had too many "r's" in the opening line.

Arnaut also shows an intricate mastery of meter, never allowing the monotonous beat of the metronome to control what he is saying, unlike Swinburne, who is frequently carried away by his rhythm and the sheer "glamor" of his words. The following "song" shows an enormously skillful blending of words to rhythm (the music is unfortunately lost):

> *L'aura amara*
> *Fals bruoills brancutz*
> *Clarzir*
> *Quel doutz espeissa ab fuoills,*
> *Els letz*
> *Becs*
> *Dels auzels ramencs*
> *Ten balps e mutz,*
> *Pars*
> *E non-pars* . . .
>
> The bitter air
> Strips panoply
> From trees

>   Where softer winds set leaves,
>   And glad
>   Beaks
>   Now in brakes are coy,
>   Scarce peep the wee
>   Mates
>   And un-mates.
>   (*TEP*, 160–61)

Finally the very "modern" medieval poet could conjure up a beautiful image of a sensual nature that would linger in the reader's mind (and be put to his own use by Pound in Canto 20):

> *Dieus lo chauzitz, . . .*
> *Voilla, sil platz, qu'ieu e midonz jassam*
> *En la chambra on amdui nos mandem*
> *Uns rics convens don tan gran joi atendi,*
> *Quel seu bel cors baisan rizen descobra*
> *E quel remir contral lum de la lampa.*
>
> God . . .
> . . . grant that we two shall lie
> Within one room, and seal therein our pact,
> Yes, that she kiss me in the half-light, leaning
> To me, and laugh and strip and stand forth in the lustre
> Where lamp-light with light limb but half engages.
>   (*TEP*, 172ff.)

The tone, the feel, and the pictorial sign are definitely *not* Victorian. Just as T. E. Hulme at this time, attending an Aristotelian Society meeting in Bologna, was overwhelmed by the gold Ravenna mosaics, seeing a geometric symmetry there that had been lost through the centuries and that tied in with the work of Epstein and Gaudier-Brzeska (who was now coming onto the scene), so Pound rightly saw that one can learn from the past, that being contemporary for the sake of contemporaneity has little meaning; after all, newspapers do that daily.

If we compare these Arnaut translations with a typical version of Cavalcanti that would appear, through the time lag, in the spring of 1912, we can see a distinct difference:

>   This most lief lady, where doth Love display him
>   So full of valour and so vestured bright,

> Bids thy heart "Out!" He goes and none gainsay him;
> And he takes life with her in long delight.
> (Sonnet XVI, ed. Anderson, 69)

The language is somewhat abstract, the meter regular and boring, the diction archaic. This is what Ford was arguing against. Pound, however, would not perfect his style overnight. The translations of Arnaut Daniel that he published in the *New Age* that winter were still old-fashioned and often uncertain. The explosive "En breu brisaral temps braus" begins rather tamely: "Soon will the harsh time break upon us," and other translations were in prose. But for the next decade, the modern *miglior fabbro* ("better craftsman," as Eliot was to call Pound later) was trying to master the secrets of his medieval predecessor.

During that fall Pound met an editor who would be very useful to him in the future: G. R. S. Mead (1863–1933) of the *Quest*, a famous occultist and associate of Yeats. Mead asked Pound to write a talk on "Troubadour Psychology" (which later became chapter 5 of *Spirit*). Pound said about this topic to his mother: "whatever the dooce that is" (PC 223), and his confusion is apparent in the lecture, which was published in October. This was not the proper time to be mixing Yeats's mysticism with Ford's precision, and even today chapter 5 of *Spirit of Romance* seems out of touch with Pound's present and his future, as was already stated in chapter 4.

Although Pound's first attempt at translating Cavalcanti was flawed, he returned to the poet often later, drawn to him by Dante's respect and by Pound's own recognition of genius there. In his essay "Cavalcanti," published in 1934 but worked over for decades, Pound describes his fascination with the Italian and his attempt to promote him:

> When the late T. E. Hulme was trying to be a philosopher in that milieu, and fussing about Sorel and Bergson and getting them translated into English, I spoke to him one day of the difference between Guido's precise interpretive metaphor, and the Petrarchan fustian and ornament, pointing out that Guido thought in accurate terms; that the phrases correspond to definite sensations undergone; in fact very much what I had said in my early preface to the Sonnets and Ballate.
>
> Hulme took some time over it in silence, and then finally said: 'That is very interesting'; and after a pause: 'That is more interesting than anything I have ever seen in a book.' (*LE*, 162)

Back from the Bologna conference with a new interest in art, Hulme fell in with the talented sculptor Jacob Epstein. He invited many artists to join the writers who assembled at his evening salons on Tuesdays at the Venetian-palace home of Mrs. Ethel Kibblewhite at 67 Frith Street (it had formerly been the residence of the Venetian Embassy in London). Hulme was using this place as his business address. In his *Autobiography*, Sir Jacob Epstein (later knighted) reports that he saw clear-cut signs of animosity between the two competing intellectuals (59–60). Hulme allegedly told the sculptor that he was merely tolerating Pound for the time, but would "kick him downstairs" when the proper moment arrived. Yet Hulme was hardly invincible. Wyndham Lewis tells how Henry Slonimsky, Pound's old student-friend from Penn who had done extensive work on the pre-Socratic philosophers, attended one of these meetings, and the talk got around to Immanuel Kant, the German philosopher whom Hulme professed to know almost by heart; when Slonimsky tried to pinpoint his host on certain details, Hulme "floundered like an ungainly fish" (LBB, 106).

Dorothy Shakespear also attended some discussions and was quite unimpressed, as she shows in her letter of December 5 (*EPDS*, 80). Pound himself described Hulme's talks on Bergson to his mother only as "rather good" (PC 232), and Hilda Doolittle, who arrived shortly, thought that it was better to study Latin and Greek than listen to philosophic abstractions. Possibly the best thing that Hulme did for Pound at this time was to introduce him to A. R. Orage, the great editor who would publish the poet extensively. Hulme seems to have won this honor (PC 238), and by November of 1911, Pound told his parents that he would probably be writing a column regularly in the *New Age* (PC 229).

Hilda did indeed arrive in London that fall, after a harried trip with her lover Frances Gregg and Frances's jealous mother, who kept berating Hilda for trying to take her daughter away from her. They had toured France together, but without any joy. William Carlos Williams mentions in his *Autobiography* (90) how he went down to the pier in New York to see Hilda and her friends off on the *Floride* in July, along with old Mr. Doolittle, who was abandoning his chair of astronomy at Penn. Father Doolittle was perfectly well aware that his daughter was going abroad to see Ezra Pound—not to be touring French castles. Williams recalls how the old man sat disconsolately and silently as the *Floride* disappeared.

The unhappy trio went first to Paris, where they heard Rummel play, toured the countryside, and then moved over to London, where they were eagerly awaiting Pound's introduction to his friends. Pound did indeed introduce the two younger women, especially to Dorothy and May. In late October the two Greggs got ready to return to Philadelphia, and Hilda had to make a choice. Despite the ardent persuasions of Frances, she bravely decided to remain in London with Ezra, knowing full well that this decision would infuriate her parents. But she had come into a stipend of £200 a year, and she was sure that she could subsist on this. And so, to the consternation of Frances but the delight of Mrs. Gregg, Hilda valiantly bid them farewell. When Frances got home, she broke off her affair with Hilda, but she would appear the following year—with a handsome husband.

Although Ezra was happy to see Hilda again, he had long before decided that if he was going to marry anyone, it would be Dorothy, who had been unwaveringly true to him in his absence and had corresponded regularly. Finally he arranged a confrontation with her venerable father, who wanted to be certain that the poet had the resources to support her. Pound tried to persuade Henry Hope that he had a guaranteed income of £200 or more per year, with a chance to earn much more through royalties, but he did not dare to mention his secret patron, Margaret Cravens. When Mr. Shakespear investigated, he found that the main source of Pound's income was his father. Even Homer's strong letter in support of his son did little to convince the lawyer, and so the marriage was postponed. This was extremely depressing to Dorothy and especially Olivia, who was deeply concerned that her daughter was becoming hopelessly tied to a man whom she could never marry, while at the same time Dorothy showed no interest in anyone else. Again, economics was the villain.

Meanwhile that fall gossip about an "engagement" between Dorothy and Ezra reached Hilda, who first stayed out in Hampstead near Ernest Rhys, but finally moved into 6 Church Walk, just across "the piazza" (as Pound called the open mews) from Ezra. Hilda recounts in *End to Torment* how crushed she felt when she first heard the news that Ezra was engaged to the British girl. In this account, the informant seems to have been the ubiquitous Mr. Rummel; the questioner is a psychiatrist:

> "What did you feel when this—this Walter told you that?"
> "Look—it's impossible to say. I felt bleak, a chasm opened—."
> "But you said that you had loved this American girl, this Frances—and you were going around with Richard—." "I don't know what I felt. I had met Walter years before, in America, in a house the Pounds had for the summer...."
> "You mean, Ezra told people that you were engaged to him?"
> "I don't know—only Walter said, 'I think I ought to tell you,

though I promised Mrs. Shakespear not to,—don't let her know or anyone. But there is an understanding. Ezra is to marry Dorothy Shakespear.'" (17–18)

This was quite a blow to a young woman who had just cut her ties—close Moravian ties—with her possessive family. And if she could not have Ezra, then whom could she have? The answer to that would wait for the following year. Pound did not in any sense abandon her; he was still across the mews, and he introduced her to all the people who were likely to befriend her, especially May Sinclair and Brigit Patmore. The comfort that Hilda found in these women was premonitory of her future.

During Christmas of 1911, Pound left Hilda to her female friends and accepted an invitation to go to the country around Salisbury to visit the writer of historical romances Maurice Hewlett (1861–1923) and his nearby friend, the old-fashioned poet Henry Newbolt (1862–1938), both of whom are conspicuously mentioned in Canto 74/433. The trip made an indelible impression on Pound because of a sight he had of some pigs running alongside his car (like the pigs outside the camp at Pisa) and because of memories of Hewlett's romantic novel *The Queen's Quair* (1903), which dealt with the stabbing of Mary Stuart's Secretary of State and lover, David Rizzio, by her husband and friends:

> beyond the eastern barbed wire
>   a sow with nine boneen
> matronly as any duchess at Claridge's
>
> and for that Christmas at Maurie Hewlett's
> Going out from Southampton
> they passed the car by the dozen
>   who would not have shown weight on a scale
>   riding, riding
>   for Noel the green holly
>   Noel, Noel, the green holly
> A dark night for the holly
>
> That would have been Salisbury plain, and I have not thought of
>   the Lady Anne [Blunt] for this twelve years
>   Nor of Le Portel
> How tiny the panelled room where they stabbed him
>   In her lap, almost, La Stuarda
>
>   (Canto 80/515)

The coming year 1912 would be a momentous one in the life of Ezra Pound, in that he would cultivate three editors besides Mead who opened their journals to him: A. R. Orage of the *New Age*, Harold Monro of the *Poetry Review*, and Harriet Monroe of *Poetry*. We shall leave Miss Monroe for later, since she did not appear until August. As was said before, Pound met Orage through Hulme during November of 1911, when the *New Age* began to publish his twelve-part series called "I Gather the Limbs of Osiris" (abridged in *Selected Prose*, 21ff.), but it seems that he did not really know the editor until January. He also met Harold Monro around November, since Hilda speaks of Ezra's inviting her to tea with him in early December.

Alfred Richard Orage (the name is pronounced by Americans to rhyme with "mirage," although Britishers rhyme it with "porridge") was born in 1873 from humble stock. His mother, an orphan, was believed to be Irish, while his farmer father descended from French Huguenots who had transplanted themselves in Yorkshire. Orage began his career by teaching school, but he soon became bored by that. Moving to Leeds, he fell in with a group of Fabian Society members who were trying to reform society, largely through socialist ideas. At the same time he was developing his private interests in philosophy (especially Nietzsche), the occult (especially theosophy), and literature (especially Hindu).

Finally moving to London, Orage met many prominent Fabians, such as George Bernard Shaw, who in 1907 loaned him and a partner, Holbrook Jackson, enough money to buy a moribund paper called the *New Age* to transform it into a socialist tool that would also further the arts. Although Orage himself was deeply imbued with socialist ideas, especially Guild Socialism, he never allowed the paper to descend into one narrow arena, except for one brief period. He maintained it for all liberal causes, including the arts. Considering himself an eclectic socialist, Orage very much feared the kind of monolithic state that many of his friends desired. Over the various years, he published several self-proclaimed socialists like Shaw and H. G. Wells, as well as such literary figures as Hulme, Katherine Mansfield, John Middleton Murry, Herbert Read, and Edwin Muir. He also published those with opposing political and aesthetic views. Indeed, it is obvious that a left-wing editor who liked Hindu epics had to be extremely liberal in order to publish a writer like Pound, who was always rightist in his politics and who would soon be a prime spokesman for Chinese literature, although Hindu and Bengali literature were at this time still interesting to him.

Paul Selver, a translator from Slavic languages who met Pound for the first time in the *New Age* office, said in his tribute to Orage: "With his clipped beard, his semi-Shakespearean profile and his velveteen apparel, Ezra flaunted his aestheticism in a manner which jarred upon some of the less aesthetic *New Age*-ites" (33). Selver went on to become friendly with Pound and to attend his first sessions with the imagists, but he eventually withdrew from the circle, feeling out of place. Selver insists that Orage never fully approved of Pound's free-verse techniques or many of his aesthetic beliefs, but he admired the young American's rebelliousness and forthrightness, and therefore was more than delighted to give him space in his journal. It was only during the Rapallo years, when Pound was clearly moving toward fascism, that Orage had some negative feelings toward him.

Orage's greatness lay in his ability to tolerate people of all beliefs. Shaw called him the greatest editor of the twentieth century, and Pound's devotion to him was almost like that of a disciple, if we may believe Selver. For it was Orage who would eventually make the aesthetic Mr. Pound political-minded, through the help of his friend Major C. H. Douglas, who appears on the scene later. For now we can quote one of the many passages in the *Cantos* where Orage's name is praised over writers who had no firm social and political beliefs (in Pound's eyes):

> But the lot of 'em, Yeats, Possum and Wyndham
>   had no ground beneath 'em.
>
> Orage had.
>   (Canto 98/685)

Possum is, of course, T. S. Eliot, the author of *Old Possum's Book of Practical Cats*.

Orage was a tall, well-knit, dark-haired man with bright, kindly eyes, who always looked far younger than he was (he was 38 in 1911), and who dressed in simple, somewhat crumpled clothes. He was a charismatic personality who was bound to attract admirers and disciples. Orage held forth in an office that bore the address of 38 Cursitor Street (in the business part of London where Mr. Shakespear had his law office); but to gain access, one actually had to bend around Chancery Lane into a cul-de-sac known as Tooks Court. On climbing a narrow stone staircase, where there was the perennial smell of printer's ink and the sound of stompings of the presses, one encountered a formidable secretary who tried to keep the editor from being overrun by his many visitors. Actually, Orage liked to conduct a great deal of his business across Chancery Lane in a chain outlet ABC Restaurant—often in the basement, where he would talk for hours with old cronies like Shaw or Wells or G. K. Chesterton (one of his

A. R. Orage in a drawing made in 1909 by F. E. Jackson.

favorite adversaries) or with Pound's younger crowd. There or in the nearby Kardomah-chain restaurant, Pound met such newcomers as Allen Upward (whose *Divine Mystery* he reviewed favorably), John Middleton Murry, and the Powys brothers, who would soon become intimate friends of Frances Gregg.

Usually genial with people, though severe toward ideas, Orage tried to dream up ways of helping poor artists like Pound, even though he was never very rich himself. Usually he paid people like Selver, who had a teaching job, nothing; but for Pound and his cohorts, Orage could often scrape up a few shillings or even a pound. Therefore, when he commissioned a twelve-part series, he was truly subsidizing the poet. In 1917, Ezra began to work for Orage regularly as a music critic, under the name of William Atheling, and then as an art critic, under the name of B. H. Dias.

The first part of "I Gather the Limbs of Osiris," which appeared on November 30, 1911, and is not reprinted in *Selected Prose*, was the famous translation of the Anglo-Saxon poem "The Seafarer," while other parts included translations of Arnaut Daniel. "The Seafarer" caused such a hubbub among academicians when it appeared that many people tended to overlook the vigor and the power of its language. This song of a voyager begins in Pound's version this way:

> May I for my own self song's truth reckon,
> Journey's jargon, how I in harsh days
> Hardship endured oft.
> Bitter breast-cares have I abided,
> Known on my keel many a care's hold,
> And dire sea-surge, and there I oft spent
> Narrow nightwatch nigh the ship's head
> While she tossed close to cliffs. Coldly afflicted,
> My feet were by frost benumbed....
>
> (*TEP*, 207)

Scholars pointed to such howlers as Pound's rendering *eorthan rice* as "earthen riches" rather than "kingdom of the earth" (is there a real difference here?) and to many other supposed mistakes; but Fred C. Robinson has written a brilliant explanation of Pound's translation technique in the *Yale Review* (Winter, 1982) that should quiet forever the notion that Pound was totally ignorant of Anglo-Saxon. Pound had studied Old English with Joseph Ibbotson at Hamilton, and he used the Sweet edition, which many of his criticizers did not possess (at least in his edition), and which sanctifies many of his readings. In addition, seeing that every translator has to be to some degree an editor unless he is blessed with that rare thing, a perfect text, Pound made some emendations and changes on his own—sometimes ill-advisedly. Almost without exception, Pound's future translations—Propertius, Cavalcanti, and the Confucian Odes—would face this same flat-footed, pedantic criticism that does not acknowledge the translator as a secondary creator, as Pound envisaged his being. In any case, the Arnaut Daniel translations that followed in the series were not subjected to such merciless berating—largely because so few people understood Provençal. These translations were almost uniformly magnificent, but they would not appear as a book until they were included in *Instigations* (1920) and the *Translations of Ezra Pound* (1953). Pound tried to publish the Daniel separately in 1915 in Chicago and in 1917 in Cleveland on the press of one Reverend C. C. Bubb, but the latter project was apparently torpedoed by German submarines.

The third editor whom Pound met at this time was Harold Monro, a Cambridge graduate who had been born in Belgium in 1879 but was of British stock. In the latter part of 1911, Monro had agreed to publish a periodical for the stuffy Poetry Society, but at the same time he used their *Gazette* to subsidize his own *Poetry Review*, which he combined with it. The first issue appeared in January of 1912, when Pound told his parents that he was taking Monro to one of Yeats's Monday night poetry readings (PC 237). At this time, Monro had an office in Chancery Lane, a stone's throw from Orage's *New Age*. Monro and Pound, however, were not spiritually akin. Monro was too conservative, never wanting to alienate the Georgian crowd of Rupert Brooke, Edward Marsh, and Lascelles Abercrombie; but he was still broad-minded enough to want to include Pound and his growing circle in his enterprises.

The February 12 issue of Monro's *Poetry Review* published Pound's much-quoted "Credo" in an essay called "Prolegomena" (it can now be found in "A Retrospect" in the *Literary Essays*, 9ff.). This concise statement of beliefs includes the following four points:

1. absolute rhythm (something that corresponds to the emotions)
2. the natural object as the perfect symbol
3. "technique as the test of a man's sincerity"
4. symmetrical forms (like the sonnet) are limited in their applications to certain subjects (and therefore a freer form is needed).

In short, much of the groundwork for imagism was already being laid. Monro also published that August a very important review of contemporary French poetry by F. S. Flint, which was to make many people, Pound included, aware of a number of figures who had previously eluded them.

Because Monro did have certain standards (though never a precise overall philosophy), he eventually had a complete falling out with the fusty Poetry Society, and in 1913 founded his own magazine, *Poetry and Drama*. This journal appeared in eight quarterly numbers from March 1913 to December 1914, until World War I effectively shut it down. It was published from Monro's much-visited Poetry Bookshop, which was located at 35 Devonshire (now Boswell) Street near the British Museum. This magazine offered a forum not only for Pound and his followers but also their opponents, because Monro seldom took sides. He published both the conservative *Georgian Poetry* volumes and Pound's *Des Imagistes* anthology—the latter of which lost money. Perhaps one of Monro's greatest achievements was that he opened the second floor of his shop to poetry readings for poets of all persuasions, from Yeats to Brooke to Pound. On the top floor of this elegant Georgian townhouse, which was surrounded by slum tenements, lived for a time the famous sculptor Epstein. Although Monro never touted Pound to the degree that he promoted some others, he nevertheless spoke promisingly of the poet's future in his final assessment of the scene, *Some Contemporary Poets*, written in 1920. Monroe died in 1932, no longer close in any way to the American, who was then living in Italy.

In February of 1912, Pound at last met one of his idols, Henry James (1843–1916). He reports in three almost successive letters to his parents (PC 238, 241, 242) that he first met the famous expatriate novelist at someone's house (Violet Hunt's?) and they "glared" at each other across the parlor. Then he met the man again and started to like him; and finally, James was "delightful." Apparently the stiff person whom some imagine James to have been very soon became the warm person that Ford and Violet knew him to be, as he appears in Leon Edel's massive biography. But James could be very straitlaced at times; he dropped his two adulterous friends summarily when their scandal became public.

Pound had known James's work from the start. He always saw James as the man who had tried to give America a sense of its past and a sense of values, yet who had been disregarded—in short, someone like himself. After James's death, Pound wrote a fine tribute that appeared in the *Little Review* (August, 1918) and is reprinted in *Literary Essays* (295ff.). In this essay, Pound describes how James appeared to him at one of his meetings. He begins by emphasizing James's "wonderful conversation," aligning him with Ford, and then he describes some specific traits:

> The massive head, the slow uplift of the hand, *gli occhi onesti e tardi* [the eyes noble and slow-moving; from Dante] the long sentences piling themselves up in elaborate phrase after phrase, the lightning incision, the pauses, the slightly shaking admonitory gesture with its 'wu-a-wait a little, wait a little, something will come'; blague and benignity and the weight of so many

years' careful, incessant labour of minute observation always there to enrich the talk. I had heard it but seldom, yet it is all unforgettable.

The man had this curious power of founding affection in those who had scarcely seen him and even in many who had not, who but knew him at second hand. (*LE*, 295)

This prose was transformed into poetry in Canto 7/24, where James is placed in a Flaubertian world of things, which is precisely the world that Pound was working toward in 1912:

> And the great domed head, *con gli occhi onesti e tardi*
> Moves before me, phantom with weighted motion,
> *Grave incessu*, drinking the tone of things,
> And the old voice lifts itself
>   weaving an endless sentence.

In his later years, Pound would think back reflectively to a scene in which the novelist appeared with his housekeeper:

> Mr James shielding himself with Mrs Hawkesby
> as it were a bowl shielding itself with a walking stick
> as he maneuvered his way toward the door
>   (Canto 74/433)

Then in Canto 79/488, Pound recalls a scene at a garden party where the Russian princess and actress Lydia Bariatinsky (who entertained Kitty Heyman frequently) accosts the formidable American writer:

>   ...her holding dear H. J.
> (Mr. James, Henry) literally by the button-hole...
> in those so consecrated surroundings
>   (a garden in the Temple, no less)
>   and saying, *for once,* the right thing
> namely: "Cher maître"
> to his checqued waistcoat, the Princess Bariatinsky,

It is no accident that Hugh Kenner began *The Pound Era* with a passage on James, because the American represented to Pound the finest characteristics of the older generation, combining the attention for detail of Flaubert with a sense of compassion and a regard for liberty that were not apparent to many of his critics.

In the essay "Rémy de Gourmont," which follows the one on James in *Literary Essays*, Pound opens by contrasting the Frenchman with the then naturalized British citizen: "The mind of Rémy de Gourmont was less like the mind of Henry James than any contemporary mind I can think of. James' drawing of *moeurs contemporaines* was so circumstantial, so concerned with the setting, with detail, nuance, social aroma, that his transcripts were 'out of date' almost before his books had gone into the second edition...." Pound goes on to say that "On no occasion would any man of my generation have broached an intimate idea to H.J.... or even to Mr Yeats with any feeling that the said idea was likely to be received, grasped, comprehended.... You could, on the other hand, have said to Gourmont anything that came into your head..." (339). In the only letter from James to Pound at Yale, the older man on September 5, 1913, graciously declined to submit anything to the *Freewoman*.

Another kind of barrier seems to have existed with W. H. Hudson (1841–1922), the author of *Green Mansions* and other novels that convey a strong feeling for nature. According to Walter Baumann's note in *Paideuma, 15* (123), Hudson made a remark about nature that clung to Pound's mind in his book *British Birds* (reprinted 1923): "Birds... are not automata" (Canto 97/678). Pound met Hudson through Ford that February at South Lodge, and he liked the man a great deal. At Ford's persuasion, he also tried to admire Hudson's "straight" prose, but he told Ford later that, after examination, this prose did not seem very straight at all (*PF*, 59). In short, once again there was a gap between *les jeunes* and the old that only Ford Madox Ford seemed able to bridge—and even he only tenuously. As a result, nothing more came of the meetings with Hudson and James. There was no visit to Lamb House, but Pound's great respect for James continued, since both T. S. Eliot and Pound were vitally aware of the importance of a literary tradition. "Artists are the antennae of the race," says Pound in *ABC of Reading* (73). The artist transmits some sense of moral values that keeps civilization together. Without him, things fall apart. The tragedy, Pound could already see at the time of World War I, was that the artists were scarcely listened to, and that was why the world was crumbling.

Then at some point during the late winter, Pound met the third person of the triumvirate that would serve as the core for the oncoming imagist movement, Richard Aldington.

8

"The Aldingtons" and Miss Monroe (February–December 1912)

> *To break the pentameter, that was the first heave*
> —*Canto 81/518*

Richard Aldington (1892–1962) first appeared to Hilda and then to Ezra at teas that were arranged by the sociable Brigit Patmore (1882–1965). Brigit was the extremely beautiful, unhappy wife of a dull insurance executive named John Deighton Patmore, who was a grandson of Coventry Patmore, a writer of the Victorian generation whom Pound and his circle detested. The Patmores lived near Holland Park in Kensington—and later in a large house that now belonged to illustrator Edmund Dulac, who was soon to be friendly with Pound through Yeats; they sold the second house in 1924 when the husband went broke through poor investments in Baltic shipping. Since Brigit and Deighton were never kindred spirits, she had taken to immersing herself in the Kensington literary world that focused around Violet Hunt, who had introduced her to Pound in 1909 before his American visit. It was Ezra who asked Brigit to invite the lonely Hilda to tea one day early in 1912. Brigit tells in *My Friends When Young* how, at her club in Piccadilly, the shy Dryad told the red-haired Irish beauty (whom John Cournos would call the most beautiful woman in London) that in America only maids were called Brigit. Unoffended, Mrs. Patmore laughed and said, "Well, here we give it to saints" (65). She was immediately fond of this somewhat awkward, inward-turning young woman, who looked as if she had just stepped down from a Grecian urn; in fact, it was even rumored broadly that the two were lovers, although this was vehemently denied by Brigit.

Always on the go, Brigit had met young Aldington a bit earlier through his brothers. She was constantly intrigued by Richard, even after he and Hilda were married, although she adamantly denied any liaison with him before 1928, when the two began a decade-long relationship together. In 1912 Richard was supporting himself by writing sports items for newspapers. Born to a middle-class lawyer and a countrified mother, Aldington was a tall, blond, blustery fellow who tended to attract or repel strangers on sight. When Virginia Woolf first met him, she described him in her diary on December 21, 1924, as a "bluff, powerful, rather greasy-eyed, nice downright man, who will make his way in the world, which I don't much like people to do." Others were less kind. Still, from the start, it has to be remembered that Aldington was a good six or seven years younger than most of his close friends, and he often tended to act that way.

Whatever flaws Richard had, he impressed both Hilda and Ezra from the start because of his interest in the Greek language and culture, which he had been developing at University College London, and because of his devotion to poetry. Aldington unquestionably fell in love with Hilda at once, and he deeply resented Pound's presence. This resentment colors his whole acquaintance with Pound, culminating in his uncomplimentary memoirs. In order to be nearer Hilda, Richard moved to her house at 6 Church Walk, but took a room two flights up from hers. As a result, by the spring of 1912, the three leaders of the new movement were forming a cozy microcosm (or so Pound thought). In his autobiographical *Life for Life's Sake* (published in 1941), Aldington says in retrospect Hilda was the real genius of the group, far "more distinguished" than Ezra (111). But back in 1912, he was saying no such thing, since he was relying on Ezra for introductions and support.

Richard says in his memoir that the trio usually spent their mornings at the British Museum and their late afternoons over tea, either in the shop at the Museum or at a variety of "fashionable and expensive tea-shops . . . Thus it came about that most of our meetings took place in the rather prissy milieu of some infernal bun-shop full of English spinsters. Naturally, then, the Imagist *mouvemong* was born in a tea-shop—in the Royal Borough of Kensington" (134). The word *mouvemong* is Richard's parody of Ezra's pronunciation of the French word for "movement."

Later, in "A Retrospect," Pound says quite simply:

> In the spring or early summer of 1912, 'H. D.,' Richard Aldington and myself decided that we were agreed upon the three principles following:
> 1. Direct treatment of the 'thing' whether subjective or objective.
> 2. To use absolutely no word that does not contribute to the presentation.
> 3. As regarding rhythm: to compose in the sequence of the musical phrase, not in sequence of a metronome. (*LE*, 3)

Pound told Harriet Monroe that the place where the major part of this event transpired was "certainly in Church Walk" (PC 354), although by that he might have simply meant Kensington.

Hilda told the story in still a different way in *End to Torment:*

> "But Dryad," (in the Museum tea room), "this is poetry." He slashed with a pencil. "Cut this out, shorten this line. 'Hermes of the Ways' is a good title. I'll send this to Harriet Monroe of *Poetry*. Have you a copy? Yes? Then we can send this, or I'll type it when I get back. Will this do?" And he scrawled "H. D. Imagiste" at the bottom of the page. (18)

The other poem he sent was titled "Priapus." Clearly this episode was in the fall (after Miss Monroe had appeared on the scene); it is also mentioned by Aldington, who tells how Pound kept "butting in on our studies and poetic productions, with alternate encouragements and the reverse" until Ezra read Hilda's poems and "removed his pince-nez and informed us that we were Imagists."

It seems probable that two separate events are conflated here. In April, before all three took off for Paris and the continent, they enunciated certain basic principles of writing in the Kensington milieu. Then, on returning from the continent at the end of summer, the event in the Museum took place. Pound had clearly formulated the term "imagist" (or French *imagiste*) by late April, when he was working over the proofs of *Ripostes*, since he uses it in his introduction to the five poems of Hulme that he appended to his own work.

In March, before they left, the extravagant Italian futurist Filippo Tommaso Marinetti directed a large exhibition at the Sackville Gallery. Although Pound himself was strongly opposed at this time to the gimmick-ridden futurists with their odes to automobiles and desire to sweep away all existing art, he still saw through them that the time was right for an artistic rebellion. If they could get away with their wild parodies, then something saner might succeed. Later, when he was living in Italy, Pound would appreciate Marinetti and his attempts at art much more deeply. Also in March, Ezra made another plea to Henry Hope Shakespear for the hand of his daughter. The poet triumphantly showed the lawyer a new contract with Swift and Company of London to issue the British edition of his Cavalcanti and his next collection, *Ripostes*, along with a firm commitment for the future (*EPDS*, 88). But again Mr. Shakespear was unimpressed with the poet's solvency, and the marriage was once more postponed.

Then on April 3 an unfortunate event occurred that triggered the outbreak of the scandal that had long threatened. On that day, an obscure literary-promotional journal called the *Throne* ran an announcement for a new romance called *The Governess*, which was being published by Chatto and Windus. In the promotional material, the joint authoresses were named as "Mrs. Alfred Hunt, one of the popular novelists of the old days, and her daughter, Miss Violet Hunt (now Mrs. Ford Madox Hueffer) one of the successful of the modern school." Immediately the real Mrs. Hueffer, Elsie, went into a rage. She had earlier challenged the *Daily Mirror* about usurping her legal title as Ford's wife and had won a retraction; now she initiated a lawsuit, demanding the full and sole legal rights to her name. Unfortunately for the nerves of all, the trial was not immediately scheduled, and would not in fact take place until February of 1913. In the interim, the couple were shunned by many people like Henry James and were forced to remain invisible for a time. Secretly, Ford sank into a nervous collapse and did not see very many people for quite some time.

Toward the end of April, Mary Moore finally appeared on the scene. Pound squired her around for a short time, seeing that she was entertained by his female friends (especially Dorothy), and then he left for Paris. He was too busy with the promising future to be concerned with the past. In Paris he stayed in Rummel's fashionable studio, with a balcony view of the Eiffel Tower, at 92 Rue Raynouard on the Right Bank. This was not far from the Rue de Ranelagh, where Olga Rudge frequently lived after her mother abandoned Olga's native Youngstown for New York, London, and Paris. Rummel and Pound worked on their joint ventures, and Ezra read the proofs of *Ripostes*, which would appear that October.

Socially Pound spent a lot of time with "the Aldingtons," if we may rush their marriage by a year or so. They were staying in the same hotel but in different rooms; this ruse fooled nobody except Pound, who steadfastly refused to acknowledge the fact that they were in love. This was obvious to everyone else, including Olivia Shakespear, who fondly called her daughter's rival Hamadryad instead of Dryad, working in the initials H. D. Richard was nicknamed the Faun (or sometimes Satyr).

The three poets, core of the Imagist Movement as one now proudly referred to it, continued to spend a great deal of time together—more than Richard liked. They looked up Henry Slonimsky, who had recently embarrassed Hulme with his knowledge. Slonimsky had just published the doctoral dissertation that he had completed at the University of Marburg in Germany, *Heraklit und Parmenides*, and was now an authority on pre-Socratic philosophy. He was an impassioned orator, and in Canto 77/469 Pound tried to capture the fervor of the tall, imposing scholar as he proclaimed in his Slavic accent:

"Haff you gno bolidigal basshunts? . . .
Demokritoos, Heragleitos" exclaimed Doktor Slonimsky 1912

It may seem strange now that Pound had no political passions in 1912, but at this time he was too immersed in things aesthetic. This would change with the coming war. Both Hilda and Richard were fascinated by anything Hellenic, and they spent one very memorable night with the scholar out-of-doors in the Luxembourg Gardens as he talked on and on about life on the Greek isles centuries ago under a bowl of stars.

The American edition of the Cavalcanti translations appeared that spring, but instead of being shipped to Homer, they wound up in the hands of Dorothy, who was checking Ezra's mail in his absence. She sent a copy to Margaret Cravens, who invited her to come over to Paris, and she also gave copies to Violet and Ford, who shared the dedication—but not with a bogus married name. Dorothy mentioned in a letter to Ezra that her father was surprised by one of Pound's last visits to their house because "I thought he was going abroad" (*EPDS*, 94). Clearly Dorothy wanted to be with Ezra in Paris, but she was tied to Brunswick Gardens—and not getting any younger. Pound, in the meantime, was preparing for a walking trip in southern France by studying the lives of the troubadours as they appear in the Bibliothèque Nationale manuscript of Miquel de la Tour, as he spelled the name. He went to 29 Rue du Colisée to say goodbye to Margaret Cravens on the day before her thirty-first birthday, May 26, and then headed for Poitou and the Limousin. We know from a note she sent three days later (*EPMC*, 111) that the meeting did not go well between them.

Then on June 1 the inevitable occurred. Margaret, whose grip on reality had never been very firm, shot herself to death in the heart. Everyone was shocked—especially Rummel, whom almost everyone blamed for the death because he had just announced his impending marriage to Thérèse Chaigneau, whose home in Passy Margaret had visited shortly before her final act. In self-retribution, Rummel blamed Pound, saying that Ezra's engagement to Dorothy had been leaked to Margaret (possibly through Hilda), and this was the cause of the suicide. In any case, Pound received word in Limoges from Dorothy and hurried back to Paris. There he received a short letter from Margaret informing him that she was "entering into God's Kingdom" (*EPMC*, 116–17). She also wrote a much longer letter to Rummel, calling him "the greatest influence in my life" (*EPMC*, 115).

Margaret's suicide had an especially depressing impact on Hilda. She described the episode this way in a book of tributes to Ezra issued in the 1930s:

> We were standing in the dark by an old bridge in Paris—that one I think that is just before the Ile de la Cité and the water was lapping underneath. We had just heard that a girl whom we all knew had very neatly shot herself through the heart. Ezra had been especially kind to her and she had told him of her neurosis and Ezra only of us knew that she slept with that beautiful little weapon under her pillow. None of us knew what to say: we were too shocked. She had been gay and kind and had wealth and opportunities and a beautiful apartment along the Tuileries, I think; anyhow chestnut blossoms, pink and white, were down the street when one leaned out of her high window. One of them said to me: "You had better go home." I had been especially unnerved as I had gone that afternoon expecting to have tea with her and the maid had said: "*Mademoiselle est morte*"—just like that. So I was saying goodbye, not knowing what else to say. But Ezra waved his affected stick somewhere towards it all in a vague helpless sort of manner.... He waved his somewhat Whistlerish stick towards the river, the bridge, the lights, ourselves, all of us, all that we were and wanted to be and the thing I wanted to say and couldn't say he said it before he dismissed me: "And the morning stars sang together in glory." (*Cantos of Ezra Pound: Some Testimonies*, 19)

Hilda's description of the "beautiful little weapon" reveals her own tangled feelings about survival.

Margaret's death occurred one year after the suicide of her father, Alexander Lanier Cravens (1851–1911), who was distantly related to the poet Sidney Lanier. After her death, the portraits of her and Ezra by Eugene Paul Ullman passed into the possession of her aunt, Drusilla Cravens, and then to Drusilla's niece, Drusilla Lodge of Madison, Indiana, where they seemed to disappear for a time. It is believed that Margaret's last act before shooting herself was to sit down at the piano and play one of the songs dedicated to her by Rummel and Pound. Pierre L. Ullman, a son of the painter, says that when his father cleaned out Margaret's apartment, which she shared with two other girls, he found a peremptory note from Pound from the South; he quietly disposed of it to avoid any further complications. The Ullmans tended to blame Ezra for her death—probably wrongly.

On June 18, writing from Rummel's apartment, Ezra told Dorothy that "M. is by now a small, fat, brown god sitting in a huge water-lily, splashing over the edge" (*EPDS*, 118). He also wrote a poem that was published two years later in *Blast No. 1* on the same subject:

> A brown, fat babe sitting in the lotus,
> And you were glad and laughing
>   With a laughter not of this world.
> It is good to splash in the water
> And laughter is the end of all things.

This is reprinted in the modern *Personae* with the title "Post Mortem Conspectu" (147).

Pound's obsession with Margaret continues to Canto 77/471, where she is mentioned with her relative Lanier and her maternal grandmother, the colorful "Rebel Rose" O'Neale Greenhow. The subject of romantic biographies by Ishbel Ross and Nash K. Burger, Rose was a Confederate spy; she was returning from England, weighted with British coins, on the blockade-running *Condor* when, on October 1, 1864, as a result of a storm and an attack, she went down in a small lifeboat that never made it to the North Carolina shore:

> O Margaret of the seven griefs
> who hast entered the lotus
>   "Trade, trade, trade . . ." sang Lanier
>   and they say the gold her grandmother carried under her
> skirts for Jeff Davis
>   drowned her when she slipped from the landing boat;
> doom of Atreus

After this distressing experience, Pound immediately headed south again, believing that the walking trip might be the best way to clear his mind. Yet his letters home to Dorothy express a constant world-weariness and even boredom at times. It was not easy to escape the ghost of Margaret.

On this second time out, Pound found a route that was based on *The Troubadours at Home*, a sentimental book by Justin H. Smith, a history professor from Dartmouth who at least tried to place the troubadours in their native environments. Pound returned to Poitiers and then went to Angoulême and Uzerche, which is near the ruined castle of Ventadorn (Ventadour), where the troubadour Bernart was born. He also visited Brive, Souillac, Sarlat, Gourdon (later loved by Nancy Cunard), and Cahors, which Dante had made infamous because of its practice of usury—a word that was still not a working part of Pound's vocabulary. He also saw the town of Le Puy with its pointed rock topped by a church, as well as La Chaise-Dieu (the Seat of God, which is mentioned in Cantos 23 and 107). In addition, he saw the town of Polignac, whose lord he would meet in Paris, and Rodez, where Sordello's beloved Guida had long ago ruled as Countess.

All of these cities had literary associations for him, since Miquel de la Tour had tied various troubadours to various places, where they seemed to function almost as the geniuses of the *loci:* Sarlat was the home of the wide-ranging Elias Cairels; the fat old guzzler Faidit had lived in Uzerche; Gourdon was the home of Lord Guilhem (a friend of Arnaut), just as the previously visited Poitiers was the home of the first troubadour, whom Pound calls Guillaume, Count of Peiteus; Périgueux had associations both with Arnaut and Bertran de Born. After Rodez, Pound visited Albi, where many medieval Manicheans lived and the Albigensian Crusade began. Averaging sometimes over twenty miles a day, he next arrived at the capital of the Southland, Toulouse. Then he climbed up into the Pyrenees to the airy castle of Foix (an Albigensian fortress), and back down to Carcassonne and Arles, with the beautiful cloister of St. Trophime; then he saw Nîmes, the home of Miquel, with its Roman theater (where a bloodless bullfight was staged), and the bustling market town of Beaucaire. Most of these places would be mentioned in the *Cantos*. He even sneaked in a quick trip to Italy, as we learn from "How I Began."

Finally worn out, he then headed in part by rail back to Le Puy and Clermont-Ferrand, and finally to Paris and home. He would make similar trips in the future with others, because the South of France, with its lost castles and dead traditions, had a haunting fascination for him. Old Provence was both eminently reachable and yet forever lost ("more remote than the Sumerians," Eliot said of the people who lived there).

Eventually the trip led to Pound's writing "Troubadours—Their Sorts and Conditions," which would be published in G. W. Prothero's stodgy *Quarterly Review* a year later, and is available in *Literary Essays* (94ff.). In this essay, Pound says: "a man may walk the hill roads and river roads from Limoges and Charente to Dordogne and Narbonne and learn a little, or more than a little, of what the country meant to the wandering singers; he may learn, or think he learns, why so many canzos open with speech of the weather; or why such a man made war on such and such castles" (95).

The same essay, in stressing the necessity of studying the troubadours as the initiators of modern poetry, mentions the Renaissance, which learned a great deal from them. Pound refers to Andreas Divus Justinopolitanus' translation of the *Odyssey* into Latin, which he translates into English in the opening lines of the *Cantos*. He had purchased Divus, as well as some of the authors mentioned in "Translators of Greek" (*LE*, 249ff.), from a Parisian bookseller at some point from 1906 to 1910, he says there. To Pound, the troubadours were anything but remote. He was even working on a long prose book about them and their countryside before he left Rummel's studio, and he added to it on the road. The manuscript lay for years unpublished, with the unofficial title "Gironde," but was due to appear deciphered by Richard Sieburth in his *Ezra Pound in France*. It is more a work about Languedoc landscape than about troubadour poetics.

A very tired poet returned to London in late August, hungry for conversation and anxious for rest. Almost in recompense for the trauma of the Cravens suicide, a letter arrived from an unknown woman in Chicago who said that she was founding an international magazine of poetry and she was asking him to contribute and participate in its formation. She was Harriet Monroe, and her magazine was called simply but appropriately *Poetry*.

Pound was exuberant. He immediately wrote her a long, enthusiastic letter (*SL*, 9–10) in which he praised her for her courage and warned her about the necessity of making the journal artistic and not exclusively American. He also confided that he himself had tried to found a magazine (almost certainly in 1910), but had failed. He enclosed two poems that she published later in 1917: "To Whistler, American" and "Middle-Aged" (*Pers.*, 235, 236).

We get an excellent picture of the relationship between these two very different people in Miss Monroe's autobiography, *A Poet's Life* (not well titled). She was a spinster (twenty-five years older than he, born in December of 1860) who had lived most of her life in the Midlands that he had fled in 1908. After the death of her wealthy lawyer father, who had squandered all of his money (shades of T. C. Pound, who was very ill now and would die penniless in her town two years later), she was forced to work as a teacher and then as a journalist, often as a reviewer, in New York. Returning to Chicago, she was appalled to find that wealthy city backing every form of the arts except poetry. As a result, she came up with her scheme, going to many affluent citizens and asking them to support her. Tough saleswoman that she was, she succeeded in getting the venture going.

Miss Monroe worked with an assistant named Alice Corbin Henderson, whom Pound published later and liked personally, but behind them was a formidable board of blue-nosed bankers and lawyers who wanted to veto anything that seemed the slightest bit extreme—and in 1912 in Chicago, that covered quite a bit of material. If some of her readers were shocked by Carl Sandburg's "hog-butcher of the world" or anything else that seemed to go beyond the lacy fringes of Victorian hymnology, then obviously they were appalled by the *Imagistes*. Harriet herself seems to have had a real penchant for writers like Vachel Lindsay, Rupert Brooke, and Joyce Kilmer, but she also appreciated the new movement. She had stumbled on Pound's poems in 1910 when she was passing through London on a daring trip around the world. Taken to Elkin Mathews's little shop by May Sinclair, she was handed Pound's work by the kindly proprietor. *Personae* and *Exultations* "beguiled the long Siberian journey with the strange and beautiful rhythms of this new poet, my self-exiled compatriot" (MPL, 223).

From the start, Pound saw the opportunity that he had been waiting for. After his initial reply, Miss Monroe offered him the job of foreign correspondent for her magazine, thus opening the door for foreign contributions, even French. On September 21, he replied:

> All right, you can put me down as "foreign correspondent" or foreign editor if you like, and pay me whatever or whenever is convenient. . . .
> You'll get whatever I do that is fit to print. (MPL, 260)

His third letter said that he was prying some poems out of Yeats "to set the tone." He succeeded in this, but then made the terrible mistake of changing a few words in three poems. This quite naturally upset the older, established poet, and he objected strenuously. But after he had made his point and regained his composure, Yeats rather strangely accepted either the exact changes or similar ones—mostly for the sake of precision or condensation. Pound was already showing in his editing that he was never purely arbitrary.

At this time, at Yeats's urging, he was soliciting the Bengali poet Rabindranath Tagore, whose poem *Gitanjali* was highly popular in London that autumn. Pound was even toying with the idea of learning Bengali in order to experience fully the flavor of the Indian's work, which Yeats touted for its sense of tranquility. Tagore, who was tall, impressive, bearded and usually robed in gray, left that winter to visit his son at the University of Illinois, and when he stopped in on Miss Monroe in nearby Chicago, he stalwartly defended Pound in various arguments. Unfortunately, Tagore's reputation began to fall away, especially as he ardently promoted Indian independence.

Pound's letter of October 9 to Harriet introduced Richard Aldington and the poem "Choricos," which appeared in the second issue of *Poetry*. This was Richard's first appearance outside of newspapers and fringe periodicals. During the month of October, Pound spent a great deal of time with his two primary colleagues, Richard and Hilda, across the "piazza" of Church Walk, along with the lovely and lonely Brigit Patmore, who clung to the trio and was reputed to have had an affair with each of the members at one point or another. Brigit was rapidly becoming a *femme fatale* who would allegedly begin the undermining of the Ford-Hunt affair even though she was one of Violet's closest friends. Finally, after the last letter, Pound sprang the newly baptized H.D. on the world, free of the name "Doolittle" that she had always detested:

> I've had luck again, and am sending you some *modern* stuff by an American, I say modern, for it is in the laconic speech of the Imagistes, even if the subject is classic. At least H.D. has lived with these things since childhood, and knew them before she had any book-knowledge of them....
>
> This is the sort of American stuff that I can show here and in Paris without its being ridiculed. Objective—no slither; direct—no excessive use of adjectives, no metaphors that won't permit examination. It's straight talk, straight as the Greek! And it was only by persistence that I got to see it at all. (MPL, 264)

He also enclosed some of his own poems from a set called "Contemporania," but he told Harriet not to publish them until she had published Aldington (November) and H.D. (January); his own followed in April, 1913. H.D. never pushed her poetry the way others did; she was therefore more than happy to see her old lover from Philadelphia suddenly accepting her as an equal and acting truly delighted with her work. Although her biographers tend to believe that H.D. did not start writing poetry until 1910, when Pound left her in America, there is every reason to believe, from the above statement, that she was writing it at the same time that he was composing *Hilda's Book*.

Speaking of *Hilda's Book*, that little treasury of early poems had fallen into the hands of Frances Gregg, who was suddenly back on the scene again in September. She had married a tall, stately, handsomely striking lecturer on Renaissance art named Louis Wilkinson. Passing through London on her honeymoon, Frances desperately tried to free H.D. from Ezra's clutches (totally ignoring Richard Aldington, whom she considered one step up from a hod-carrier). Frances went so far as to invite Hilda to accompany her and Louis to Venice, as if she already distrusted the marriage. Hilda wavered; clearly Pound was lost to her, and there were always uncertainties about the youthful Richard, whose attraction to Brigit even in the midst of their courtship had not gone unnoticed. But Ezra was furious. He told Hilda that if she went along on the Wilkinsons' honeymoon, she would destroy their marriage before it even began, and she would have that on her Moravian conscience for the rest of her life.

Still, Hilda went so far as to pack her bags and take a cab to Victoria Station to board the train. But at the last second Ezra intercepted her. After some furious denunciations, Hilda gave in and allowed the couple to travel alone (*Torment*, 8–9). Undaunted, the Wilkinsons then joined up with the good-looking, artistic Powys brothers, Llewelyn and John Cowper, who were old Cambridge chums of Louis. According to Kenneth Hopkins in *The Powys Brothers* (34), Frances was in love with the tubercular Llewelyn, but because of his fragile condition, she switched her allegiance to his brother. In any case, the *menage à quatre* proceeded to that refuge of all outcasts, Venice, where they carried on in the timeless manner of Englishmen emancipated from the restraints of their island. Frances took to appearing in public dressed like a boy, and the quadrangle was so outrageous that they were almost ejected bodily from the town. Later, settling in Italy because of Louis's interest in art, Frances kept *Hilda's Book* over the years (while H.D. totally forgot it), treasuring the volume even though it had been written by a rival. Both it and her diary survived the Nazi bombings of Plymouth in 1941, but Frances did not. *Hilda's Book* is now safely tucked away in the Harvard libraries. From Frances' diary, we learn that her first kiss came from the lips of Ezra Pound, and her first true lover was Miss Doolittle.

Pound was himself deeply involved in his own romantic troubles at this time. His relationship with Dorothy dragged on, despite the difficulties, but it was finally severely questioned in a sharp letter from Olivia Shakespear on September 13:

> You told me you were prepared to see less of Dorothy this winter. I don't know if you wd rather leave it to me to say I don't think it advisable she should see so much of you etc. or whether you wd rather do it in your own way—I suppose I cd trust you to do it? . . .
>
> I don't know if she still considers herself engaged to you—but as she obviously can't marry you, she must be made [to] realize that she can't go on as though you were her accepted lover—it's hardly *decent!*
>
> There's another point too—which is the personal inconvenience & bother to myself—I had all last winter, practically to keep 2 days a week for you to come & see her . . .
>
> She *must* marry—She & I can't possibly go on living this feminine life practically *à deux* for ever, & we haven't money enough to separate—& should have less than we have now if her father died . . .
>
> You *ought* to go away—Englishmen don't understand yr American ways, & any man who wanted to marry her wd be put off by the fact of yr friendship (or whatever you call it) with her.
>
> If you had £500 a year I should be delighted for *you* to marry her . . . (*EPDS*, 153–54)

This was an extremely tough letter from "the most charming lady in London." Yet both Ezra and Dorothy seem to have responded to it in a rather nonchalant way. He told her on September 14 that his visits to Brunswick Gardens had been cut to one a week, and she replied on September 15: "Once a week be hanged—which of many reasons that might be, is given?" Meanwhile most of his daylight time was spent at South Lodge for tennis and teas, while at night he was often engaged in reading to "Uncle William" Yeats, whom Dorothy called "The Eagle." Yeats's eyes were weak, and he found these readings helpful, while Pound always enjoyed the older man's conversation. During this period, as was already mentioned earlier, he kept Ford and Yeats strictly apart, since they could not stand each other. Meanwhile in his own place at 10 Church Walk, he began to hold Tuesday night poetry readings and discussions, usually attended by his young followers.

That autumn a certain amount of recognition came to Pound as the venerable anthologist Arthur Quiller-Couch asked him if he would like to be represented in the *Oxford Book of Victorian Verse*, even apologizing for the word *Victorian*. Pound was surprised and delighted to have this recognition, but when it came time to select the poems, Quiller-Couch chose two that Pound was suppressing, and that was the end of their agreement (MPL, 265). At the same time, the opposition was forming ranks too. The always jealous Rupert Brooke and his influential friend, Edward Marsh, who had become secretary to the First Lord of the Admiralty, a man named Winston Churchill, decided to publish their own selection of contemporary work to popularize poetry and to honor the reign of King George V, who had been crowned in 1911. Although Marsh respectfully requested two poems from Pound, Ezra and he could never agree on which two, and so after a visit from Marsh at Church Walk, the two men let the matter drop. As a result, Pound was omitted from the very visible collection that Harold Monro published then and in various volumes from 1915 to 1922.

A war was clearly brewing—an intellectual war—and Pound knew which side he was on. There was no point in trying to compromise with people who did not look at things in his way. Before long, it became apparent that his imagist school, as it was now known, did not really have a platform. As a result, in 1913, Pound asked F. S. Flint, who had joined the side that he thought was winning, to interview him and write up a general statement, which was then published in the March issue of *Poetry*. Flint copied down the three points already mentioned from "A Retrospect," but Pound himself then added some famous words of advice to writers in "A Few Don'ts":

> An 'Image' is that which presents an intellectual and emotional complex in an instant of time. . . .
>
> It . . . gives that sense of sudden liberation; that sense of freedom from time limits and space limits. . . .
>
> It is better to present one Image in a lifetime than to produce voluminous works. . . .
>
> Pay no attention to the criticism of men who have never themselves written a notable work. . . .
>
> Use no superfluous word, no adjective which does not reveal something. . . .
>
> Go in fear of abstractions.
>
> (*LE*, 4–5)

Given all these words of advice, the reader might well ask where Pound's own imagist productions were. The *Ripostes* published in October of 1912 (dedicated to William Carlos Williams) were clearly a step forward from the disastrous *Canzoni*, but the book did not contain those precise poems that would appear in the next collection, *Lustra* (1916). Of course there were many beauties: the now famous or infamous "Seafarer" adaptation; "Apparuit," which showed a brilliant control of Sapphic meter; and "The Return" (of the Gods), which impressed almost everyone because of its dramatic presentation (*CEP*, 182, 198). "Portrait d'une Femme" (whose subject was Florence Farr, Mrs. Emery) was written in a style that anticipates Eliot's "Portrait of a Lady." "Doria" (Δώρια; *CEP*, 193) is a splendid poem, but still the great imagist poems were lacking.

Here we have to take into account the well-known "time lag" between the creation of a work and its dissemination. Pound's most famous imagist poem, "In a Station of the Metro," was gestating in his mind. The scene that inspired this poem had been experienced the previous spring in Paris, as he explained in "How I Began," published in 1913:

> For well over a year I have been trying to make a poem of a very beautiful thing that befell me in the Paris Underground. I got out of a train at, I think, La Concorde and in the jostle I saw a beautiful face, and then, turning suddenly, another and another, and then a beautiful child's face, and then another beautiful face. All that day I tried to find words for what this made me feel. That night as I went home along the rue Raynouard I was still trying. I could get nothing but spots of colour. I remember thinking that if I had been a painter I might have started a wholly new school of painting. I tried to write the poem weeks afterwards in Italy, but found it useless. Then the other night, wondering how I should tell the adventure, it struck me that in Japan, where a work of art is not estimated by its acreage and where sixteen syllables are counted enough for a poem if you arrange and punctuate them properly, one might make a very little poem which would be translated about as follows:—
> The apparition of these faces in the crowd;
> Petals on a wet, black bough.

As we can see from this example, imagism was as much an exercise of the mind or a practice of the will (like Yoga) as it was an act of writing. Pound's rejections of the offers of Quiller-Couch and Marsh indicate clearly that he practiced what he preached.

A few weeks after *Ripostes* was published in October, Swift and Company went out of business as the manager absconded to Tangiers with some loot. As a result, a very important outlet for Pound was now closed, and so he had to go back to the patient Elkin Mathews, where he was accepted like an errant lamb. Pound did get some restitution from the liquidators of the firm, but when he toted up his earnings during that fall for his father, he had grossed about £65 (PC 274); this was not a grand sum (about $325), and certainly not enough to win Dorothy with, but it was better than he would make at other periods in his life.

In December, Pound wrote a longish report on the state of poetics in London for the January issue of *Poetry*. He again touted Yeats as "the only poet worthy of serious study" and "already a recognized classic." But he added that Ford's conversation was still the finest in London. He linked Yeats to Flaubert, whom he was now devouring, and he also saw the Irishman as a practitioner of precise speech. Of course he lauded the "youngest school here that has the nerve to call itself a school . . . the *Imagistes*." He said that a school sometimes consists of only two or three people, and he declined to spell out a platform, but he noted that Precision was a key word in what they were doing. After citing Aldington as an imagist, Pound mentioned some other poetic groups: the grand old men like Thomas Hardy, Robert Bridges, Sturge Moore, Henry Newbolt, Rhys, Plarr, and Wilfrid Scawen Blunt, "the last of the great Victorians"; and also his rivals, the young Georgians, led by Abercrombie and Brooke. That winter he was very active with Yeats and Tagore, as well as Tagore's pupil, Kali Mohan Ghose, with whom he collaborated on translations of the Hindi poet Kabir (1440–1518); these were published in the June 1913 issue of the *Modern Review* in Calcutta (*TEP*, 411ff.). The short phrase "saith Kabir," which occurs twice in Canto 77/474, is a memory of these happy times, when the campaigns were hot and the battlelines were forming, but the atmosphere was still gentlemanly. Outside of England, another war was forming, and that would not be so gentlemanly.

In December, a new imagist appeared, even though he was more of a novelist than a poet: an American named John Cournos, who had been born in Russia and had worked on the *Philadelphia Record*, which he had recently abandoned. A good friend of Henry Slonimsky, Cournos interviewed Pound for his old paper, writing a highly complimentary article. Pound then introduced Cournos around to his friends, and the good-natured newcomer soon became another member of his growing circle. Even Richard Aldington said good things about Cournos in his memoirs, as well as editing their letters. Cournos himself gave Pound one of the highest tributes he received from anyone, in his *Autobiography:* "Ezra, as I had cause later to find out, was one of the kindest men that ever lived. . . . It was written all over him, as the saying goes" (235).

When 1913 arrived, Pound was clearly enjoying one of his greatest periods of triumph. Cournos said: "Ezra knew almost every one worth knowing" (271). During 1912, Pound had been invited to speak at Cambridge, presumably to a meeting of an arts club called "The Gods," which Hulme attended; then in February of 1913 he addressed the Essay Society of St. John's College, Oxford, on Guido Cavalcanti. There he met William G. Lawrence (brother of the famous T.E.), who then visited Pound in London on June 2, where he met Tagore before William moved on to India. William saw that his more famous brother became familiar with Pound's work, as T.E.'s correspondence home shows.

Everywhere accolades seemed to be coming in Pound's direction. The great Yeats wrote to Lady Gregory on January 3 of 1913 that he valued the criticism of Ezra Pound more than that of his old friend Sturge Moore because Ezra's medievalism had taught him precision, and the older poet rated this highly; still, Yeats felt that Pound was often too experimental in his own verse and lacking in taste. But the highest praise came once again from *Punch*, which said in its issue of January 22:

> The bays that formerly old Dante crowned
> Are worn today by Ezra Loomis Pound.

They were no longer punning on his name; they now spelled it correctly. It is safe to say that every man of letters of any importance in England was now quite aware of the young American's identity.

9

More Potential Imagists: Frost, Fletcher, Lowell (January–August 1913)

During January of 1913, Pound was as busy socially and intellectually as he would ever be in his life. His days were spent in reading and writing, his nights in talking and dancing. The trendy spot that year was the so-called Cabaret Theater Club, whose official name was the Cave of the Golden Calf. It had been dreamed up by August Strindberg's second wife, an Austrian named Frida, who ran her racy establishment on little Heddon Street, just off Regent, not far from Elkin Mathews's bookshop.

The walls of the Cabaret had been painted by Wyndham Lewis; in her memoir (116), Violet Hunt described them as looking like hunks of "raw meat." Jacob Epstein had decorated the interior columns with the grotesque heads of various beasts. The effect of the art was to shock, while the entertainment—which included wild readings, dancing monkeys, impromptu comedy performances, and feverish dancing (either from patrons or paid artists)—was meant to provide staid London with some continental fun. The chalky-faced Madame Strindberg, usually swimming in furs, circulated among her guests with grandeur and charm, but always kept her eye cocked on the till since she was operating on a very small budget.

The Cabaret soon had the reputation of being the loosest and most entertaining place in town. Much later on April 1, 1955, the incarcerated Ezra wrote to young Ingrid Davies, a friend of Brigit Patmore, that the dances of these days were still the relatively innocent turkey trot and bunny hug—not the sensuous tango that Dorothy was then trying to learn; but these were still very far from the Viennese waltz. Madame Strindberg alternated gentility with bluntness. She was known to push away a wealthy client, saying in her heavy Mitteleuropa accent: "I don't haff to be polite to the people I sleep with!" She was usually most polite to Augustus John.

The year 1913 was the last fully happy one that anybody who survived the Great War would remember. All of Pound's friends would later speak with nostalgia about this period; and he himself:

> H.D. once said "serenitas"
>   (Atthis, etc.)
>   at Dieudonné's
>   in pre-history.
>   (113/787)

Although there was trouble on the international scene, Pound's letters are remarkably free of any mentions of it. He was all wrapped up in his work and his new position of power as foreign editor of *Poetry*, for which he was trying to recruit everyone conceivable, even the "detestable" D. H. Lawrence, who gave him "no particular pleasure" (*SL*, 17, 22); but Lawrence was off on the continent, courting his German wife-to-be, Frieda von Richthofen Weekley, whom he was luring away from his old French professor at Nottingham. They would return that summer.

The year 1913, however, was dreadful for "the Hueffers." Pound had spent the preceding Christmas with them in a remote cottage in Buckinghamshire that had once belonged to John Milton, and the ghost of that old Puritan, whom Pound always abjured, was hard to exorcise (*EPDS*, 170; misdated in *SL*, 28). Other guests for a time included the Compton Mackenzies. Faith Mackenzie in her memoir (271–72) said that Ezra talked everyone into submission with his nervousness. They were all fidgety because Elsie Hueffer's lawsuit was scheduled to be heard on February 7. When that day came, the case was speedily resolved in Elsie's favor. The effect on Violet and Ford was crushing; they decided to leave England until May, but the damage to their reputations and health had been done. Even their love affair was jeopardized by the scandal, as many friends began to flee from them—but never Ezra. All during this period of her "flurried years,"

Violet treasured the loyalty of Ezra Pound above all others, as she constantly made clear, along with Ford himself.

Meanwhile, one of Pound's letters written to Dorothy at this time (even though they were often only a few blocks apart) spoke about his dinners with old Victor Plarr, tea with Aunt Eva Fowler, readings at the recently opened Poetry Bookshop of Harold Monro, and, of course, his many nightly meetings with Yeats the Eagle (*EPDS*, 175). Yeats was now working on a series of short poems, "Upon a Dying Lady," in honor of the fatally stricken Mabel Beardsley, the lovely red-haired sister of the ill-fated Aubrey:

> La beauté, "Beauty is difficult, Yeats" said Aubrey Beardsley
> when Yeats asked why he drew horrors
> or at least not Burne-Jones
> and Beardsley knew he was dying and had to
> make his hit quickly
>
> hence no more B-J in his product.
>
> So very difficult, Yeats, beauty so difficult.
>
> (Canto 80/511)

Yeats was now asking for the younger poet's criticism, and was getting it, sometimes to his displeasure. When Ezra objected to some obvious details, such as the rhyming of "mother" and "brother," Yeats quietly removed the verses involved (*EPDS*, 180, 183, 186). Gradually—almost in spite of himself—the older man was listening to the younger.

The opening of Monro's bookstore brought a new face onto the London scene: the New England poet Robert Frost, whose first book, *A Boy's Will*, was being published as the poet was approaching his fortieth birthday (born March 26, 1874; died 1973). Frost had been extremely unsuccessful in the early part of his life, desultorily attending Dartmouth and Harvard, and finally settling down to live on a farm in New Hampshire. In 1912, he had decided that he truly wanted to be a poet, and he was willing to take any risks involved. Selling his farm, he transported his wife and four children to England, where he rented a country place in Buckinghamshire. On the cold afternoon of January 8, 1913, Frost was wandering the streets near the British Museum when he suddenly stumbled on Monro's place, where a sign informed him that there would be an opening party that evening. Frost immediately asked if he might attend, and was informed that the party was by invitation only, although he could certainly try to get one. Frost appeared that night, broke through the barriers, and suddenly felt very much at home among the many writers gathered in the shop, of whom Pound was not one. Out of a swirl of people, the person he liked the most was the unpretentious F. S. Flint. According to Lawrance Thompson's *Early Years* (410), Flint advised the newcomer to go to see Ezra Pound, since he controlled many important channels for publication. The rather shy Frost, feeling that Pound was probably too busy to approach directly, kept postponing calling on him, until Pound, who was aware of his presence through Flint, finally sent him a brief note: "At home, sometimes." Frost did not particularly appreciate the curtness, but he decided to go anyway.

Their first encounter at Church Walk was clearly successful. Even though Frost was not as learned or sophisticated as Pound might have liked, the older man had the strong Yankee bearing that the younger one could relate to his beloved Uncle Ezry Weston and his Massachusetts roots, and so the two got along tolerably well together. When Pound heard that Frost's book was just out, he insisted on accompanying the poet to the office of David Nutt, where he promptly usurped the sole remaining copy (so Frost, who always nurtured his injustices, grumbled years later).

Pound and he then returned to Kensington, where Ezra devoured the poems while the older man watched with curiosity and some suspense. With his inimitably quick and sure judgment, Pound immediately saw that this man had a gift for words and a distinctive voice. Even though Frost's New England bucolicism was not overly appealing to Ezra, his style was direct, forceful, and "natural" in a way that Ford could approve of. There was no nonsense in it. Pound then summarily dismissed his guest and dashed off a letter to *Poetry:* "Have just discovered another Amur'kn. VURRY Amur'k'un, with, I think, the seeds of grace. Have reviewed an advance copy of his book, but have run it out too long. Will send it as soon as I've tried to condense it. . . ." (*SL*, 14). The laudatory review appeared in *Poetry*'s May issue, but Frost was offended because Ezra attacked the American journals which had not published him; the New Englander believed that Ezra was trying to enlist him into his expatriate, imagist gang, and he wanted none of this (FSL, 97); as it turned out, he eventually felt more comfortable with their Georgian rivals. Ezra was a "generous person" (97), but he was pushy and too prone to regard Frost as an "untutored child" (84). Later in the *New Freewoman*, Pound praised Frost as if he were a member of the imagist party: "This man has the good sense to speak naturally and to paint the thing, the thing as he sees it" (*LE*, 382).

Pound tried to promote Frost's work as far as he could, not seeing that the older man might view this helping as "bullying" (FSL, 84). Miss Monroe, meanwhile, did not respond to Frost's poetry with any of the enthusiasm that Pound had expected. After a spring vacation, Ezra was once more pushing Frost in June (PC 281), having decided that "The Death of the Hired Man" was his finest production to date. Without asking for approval, he whisked it off to the *Smart Set* in New York (how the rural Frost hated that citified name!), whose editor, Willard Huntington Wright, had asked Pound to serve as an agent in London. Frost was infuriated by this move, which intensified their misunderstandings, leading ultimately to a cleft.

Pound reviewed Frost's second book, *North of Boston*, in a positive way ("Mr Frost's work is not 'accomplished,' but it is the work of a man who will make neither concessions nor pretences"; *LE*, 384–86), but an intimate friendship was impossible. When Ezra was in deep trouble in St. Elizabeth's and no one else could get him out, it would be old Robert Frost who would finally gird his loins and go down to Washington to "spring" the poet simply by insisting that he would not budge from the bureaucratic machine until Mr. Pound was let go. It worked. Although there were many who criticized Frost for his dilatoriness and lack of enthusiasm in the matter, Frost was not under the same obligation to Ezra that Eliot and others quite rightly felt. Yet by the late 1950s, Robert Frost had the kind of clout as an artist to set the beleaguered poet free—and, tardy or not, he did it, with the help of some others, of course.

During this busy spring, Pound promoted other friends like William Carlos Williams (whose *The Tempers* was issued by Elkin Mathews in 1913 at Pound's urging) and some new ones. Somehow, in the middle of all this activity, he managed to write some of his own poems in the new vein. The April issue of *Poetry* contained the little group called "Contemporania" that he had sent Harriet back in the fall. These poems clearly announced imagism as a movement in fact. Aside from the "Metro" poem, Pound also had two other classics. "The Garret" contains the following priceless simile, gleaned from his ballet-watching the year before:

> Dawn enters with little feet
>   like a gilded Pavlova,
> And I am near my desire.
>   (*Pers.*, 83)

It is contemporary verse, but harkens back to Homer in allusion and Sappho in emotion.

Another classic poem, "The Garden," portrays an upper-class British woman walking in the nearby gardens that Pound and Ford used to stroll in together; she is lonely and unable to communicate:

Like a skein of loose silk blown against a wall
She walks by the railing of a path in Kensington Gardens,
And she is dying piece-meal
    of a sort of emotional anaemia.

And round about there is a rabble
Of the filthy, sturdy, unkillable infants of the very poor.
They shall inherit the earth.

In her is the end of breeding.
Her boredom is exquisite and excessive.
She would like some one to speak to her,
And is almost afraid that I
    will commit that indiscretion.
                                        (Pers., 83)

In his much later *ABC of Reading* and elsewhere, Pound mentions that poetry is created through three methods: phanopoeia (image-making), melopoeia (sound or music-making), and logopoeia (literally, thought-making, although not in any rigid conceptual sense). This poem demonstrates the three modes in act. The woman is clearly depicted in her milieu, in a kinetic vein; the poem's sound structure is rich and controlled; and finally, in a way that far exceeds anything that the other imagists were producing at the time, the luminous cluster of detail works toward an idea; the woman is the British Empire, on the verge of collapse. Although written just a few years before the war truly begins, this poem is hauntingly premonitory, for World War I, although technically won by the British, was, in the last analysis, the beginning of the loss of their empire. But *we* put this idea upon the poem; the poem itself does not say it, does not crystallize into an idea. The important thing is that this poem shows clearly, in its movement and in its criticism of the society around him, two of the primary features of vorticism, which was already in the making. Pound outgrew imagism long before Amygism ousted him.

By the end of March, Pound was once more heading south, while Dorothy was touring Italy, largely Rome, with her mother and her young friend and relative Georgie Hyde-Lees, who would eventually marry the much older William Butler Yeats. En route to Italy, Pound stopped over briefly in Paris to see Rummel, and it is probably then, as his obituary for Rémy de Gourmont suggests in 1915 (*SP,* 416), that he "plunged into a meeting, a vortex of twenty men ... the group that centered about 'L'Effort Libre.' " This included Jules Romains, Charles Vildrac, Georges Duhamel, Georges Chennevière, and Jean Pierre Jouve—all of whom were in communication with the great editor of the *Mercure de France,* Gourmont. Pound enjoyed the Gallic wit of the group, who had just elected a railway inspector as their Prince of Thinkers—something that would scarcely be done in the top circles of sanctimonious England. He recalled this comic event early in Canto 27/129 and later in Canto 80/506:

> when they elected old Brisset Prince des Penseurs,
>   Romains, Vildrac and Chennevière and the rest of them
>   before the world was given over to wars

He did not meet the impressive Gourmont at this time, since that man, who suffered from the disfiguring disease of lupus, was very limited in his personal contacts; but Pound did meet one of Gourmont's good friends, an American expatriate from the Midwest named Natalie Barney, who would prove to be a close friend in the twenties (see a literary portrait of her in chapter 18).

By the middle of April, Pound was luxuriating once again in the Hotel Eden in Sirmione, swimming, reading, and writing poems and letters. Expecting to join Hilda and Richard in Venice in May, he reluctantly left Sirmione in order to keep his end of the appointment, and was most distressed to find "the Aldingtons" bogged down in Florence en route from Capri. Hilda had been in Italy for several months, having gone to Rome in the winter and then to Naples and Capri; she had been joined by Richard, who had an assignment from Orage to write articles for the *New Age.* The reason for her traveling was ostensibly to face her parents, since old Charles Leander, retired from Penn, was determined to bring his errant daughter home. When the snobbish parents arrived in Capri (which they didn't like) and met the peculiar Mr. Aldington (whom they liked even less), they decided to move on to Sicily and to hook up with their daughter later in Venice, hoping that by that time Mr. Aldington (whoever he was) would have disappeared. But unfortunately for them, Mr. Aldington was not about to disappear.

Pound encountered the distraught parents in Venice, and, much as they also disliked him, they seemed to welcome his presence, since the two Hellenophiles were nowhere to be seen. Pound wrote to Dorothy with forebodings that the Dryad and her cumbersome Faun would probably not like his magic city of water because they were so obsessed with Greek temples and statuary (which drove both him and the sculptor Gaudier-Brzeska wild because they found the latter too overtly erotic, too caressable). At last the stragglers appeared, and Hilda and Richard, true to form, were not unduly impressed by the place (*EPDS*, 226). This blindness to Byzantine splendor caused

Pound no end of anguish, but he managed to contain himself. The five tourists had some dinners together, but the meetings were tense, as old Mr. Doolittle was trying to determine which of the two men was the bigger threat to his daughter's chastity. Hilda herself seemed to be still wavering as to whether she truly wanted Richard or not, and obviously she was still wondering if by some miracle Pound might not suddenly ask for her hand. Pound told Dorothy that he did not think that Hilda truly loved Richard, but finally, in commenting on their giddy behavior, he said in exasperation: "I think they *must* be in love" (*EPDS*, 226). Pound clearly did not want to see the threat to his relationship with Hilda that the younger man posed. The confused Mr. Doolittle still was viewing Ezra as his primary nemesis, and he finally fled Venice in a rage, realizing that his daughter would never return to Upper Darby. He went home and foolishly burned whatever of Pound's valuable correspondence had survived to that date. Richard departed tactfully, without money, for London (Hilda's stipend would definitely help him through some lean times), while the two women went north to Innsbruck. Pound accompanied them to the lovely mountain town and then went on to Munich to examine the manuscripts of some German Minnesinger.

Then in mid-May, Ezra headed home, stopping in Paris, where he and Walter belatedly celebrated the appearance of *Hesternae Rosae* back in March. There on the terrace of a restaurant near the Luxembourg Gardens, he was introduced to two young American expatriates who would soon be loosely aligned with the burgeoning movement. They were Skipwith Cannell (accent on the second syllable), who was also from Philadelphia, and John Gould Fletcher, the son of a wealthy Arkansas banker, who had studied for a time at Harvard. Of the two, Cannell was the easier to get along with. Pound liked him and his vivacious wife, Kitty or Kathleen, who was a dancer and an excellent mimic (her imitations of Ezra delighted New York poets when the couple fled England at the outset of the war). The pair would soon follow Pound to England, and he would find a room for them on the second floor at 10 Church Walk. The serious-looking Cannell talked constantly about the Bible (which he praised for its free verse) and Edgar Allan Poe (whose imagery he adored), having read little else at the University of Virginia; as a result, his friendship with Pound would go nowhere (FLMS, 57–58).

John Gould Fletcher (1886–1950), on the other hand, promised at first to be a valuable intellectual asset to Pound's growing circle. But very soon his severe personality problems began to assert themselves. One needs only to read his memoir, *Life Is My Song*, to become aware of what a tormented, reclusive, distrusting person Fletcher was. His banker father's timely demise had freed him from uncongenial studies at Harvard, where Van Wyck Brooks in his *Scenes and Portraits* described Fletcher's "queer white skull-like face" and the aged-looking, "stiff-jointed" frame of this "most forlorn and hopeless individual" at the school (227). Even the usually kind Alfred Kreymborg described Fletcher, who was friendly to him, as "Gaunt, austere, gloomy . . . easily the loneliest among the many men" of London (395).

This hermitlike heir had decided to spend his life abroad, first in Rome and then in London, where he had taken an expensive apartment on Adelphi Terrace in Chelsea, close to the quarters of George Bernard Shaw; but he had not dared to speak to the playwright, even though he saw him frequently. Living for a few years in almost total reclusiveness, Fletcher finally dared to bring out, at his own expense, five volumes of his verse in a single year, and when he got the expected bad reviews, he was so crushed that he decided to remove himself to Paris. It was here that Pound met him, infused him with new hope about publication, and lured him back to London, where Fletcher would enjoy his first success. Yet, seldom thankful, Fletcher would brag instead that it was *he* who helped to make Pound by loaning him some valuable books of French writers whom Ezra was ignorant of—such as Gourmont, Tristan Corbière, Laurent Tailhade, Francis Jammes, Jean Pierre Jouve, Arthur Rimbaud, and André Spire, as well as Jules Romains and Charles Vildrac. Actually, as we have seen, Pound clearly knew many of these people from his recent contacts and from the lips of Symons, Flint, and Ford; he had, in fact, even reviewed Jouve's *Présences* in the February *Poetry* of 1913, and he would soon arrange for the publication of an English translation of Gourmont's *Horses of Diomedes* in the *New Freewoman* in the fall. He himself would write a series of articles (much resented by Fletcher) in the *New Age* that fall under the telling title "The Approach to Paris," showing that he was anything but ignorant of contemporary French literature at this point (FLMS, 73–74).

In any case, Fletcher meekly followed his new master back to the English capital, and there the two pretended for a time to like and respect each other. In *Life Is My Song*, Fletcher makes the following acerbic comment on Pound: "The more I studied him, the more I was convinced that he was a queer combination of an international Bohemian and of an American college professor out of a job" (71). To the elegant banker's son, "Bohemian" was a dirty word. Fletcher's estimation of Pound sank tremendously when he saw the unpretentious quarters on Church Walk, which other people found charming. Pound, seeing that the Arkansas millions could be put to good use, retaliated with kindness: he sent off some of Fletcher's newer and more digestible work to Harriet Monroe, and he got Hilda and Richard to try to persuade the cantankerous arrival to submit something to their forthcoming anthology, as yet unnamed. Fletcher, however, obstinately refused, resenting among other things Aldington's disparaging remarks about Walt Whitman, whom he revered. Fletcher's pride was even more wounded by Pound's blunt criticism when Ezra tried to put his "symbolist" poetry into some kind of order. One of Pound's main reasons for distrusting most symbolist verse was that the poets were undisciplined; they were willing to write down almost anything that came into their heads.

At this time Fletcher was very much under the spell of Arthur Rimbaud's theory of the colorations of vowels. He was writing "color poems" like the following:

Lacquered mandarin moments, palanquins swaying and balancing
Amid the vermilion pavilions, against the jade balustrades.
(Life Is My Song, 72)

Pound told Fletcher that these so-called "Irradiations" were far too labored; the internal rhymes (ver*mil*ion pa*vil*ions, *jade* balus*trades*) were obvious and cloying, and the images were rather nonsensical (what is a mandarin moment?). The wealthy Harvardian was deeply offended, as he makes clear. When Amy Lowell arrived on the scene in July, she pronounced these very same lines magnificent, even dubbing Mr. Fletcher a genius (91). It is no wonder then that when battle-lines were finally drawn for an artistic war, John Gould Fletcher would stand firmly on the side of Miss Lowell. Fletcher was the opposite of T. S. Eliot, who listened to Pound's criticism and profited from it. History has judged the difference.

At the end of this spring, Ezra engaged in a rather foolish confrontation with Lascelles Abercrombie, the friend of Rupert Brooke, who had gone on record saying that what poetry needed most was a return to the simplicity of Wordsworth. To Pound, who believed that Wordsworth cultivated the "simple" word over Flaubert's "just" word, this was blasphemy. And so he went into one of his periodic rages, sending off an angry note to the second-rate poet (who was soon a close friend of Robert Frost's) that challenged him to a duel. Poor Abercrombie, who knew even less about the art of fencing than the art of poetry, did not know how to react. According to John Cournos's memoir (236ff.), he was so disturbed by the affront that he went over to Yeats's place at Woburn Buildings for some advice and consolation. But when he knocked at the door, who should open it but Pound? Flabbergasted, Abercrombie turned on his heels and sped down the stairs, expecting epithets if not épées to be coming after him. Then, recalling that Pound had given him the choice of weapons, Abercrombie rather brilliantly suggested that they pelt each other with unsold copies of their books. Pound dissolved in laughter, as did everyone else, and fortunately the whole thing ended in good humor—except for the ill-tempered Fletcher, who seized on this comic encounter in his autobiography (72) to point out still another example of Pound's unstable behavior and his constant affront to the proper mores of the country he had adopted. Humor was never one of the banker's son's virtues. In a letter to Mabel Beardsley in November, Yeats dated this event in the fall.

Early that summer, both good and bad news came to the poet in London. On the bad side, he learned that on July 29, his beloved Aunt Frank had died in New Jersey, and of course he was unable to attend the funeral. He did not mention this very sad event to Dorothy until August 9, when he said: "She was a picturesque old monument" (*EPDS*, 241). Yet good news came earlier in June, as he was offered the job of literary editor on a new version of an existing periodical. It was a women's suffragette magazine that had originally been called the *Freewoman*, but had been rechristened the *New Freewoman* as its first issue appeared that month. The magazine had a long history of unsuccessful attachment to various women's groups in America and England, and it had at last fallen under the business control of a wealthy, shy, enormously kind Quaker woman named Harriet Shaw Weaver (1876–1961). She was collaborating with the magazine's founder, her longtime companion Dora Marsden, an ardent feminist editor who was deeply interested in philosophy and linguistics, albeit in a rather fuzzy-headed manner. Also working with them at the time was the young Rebecca West, whose attention had been called to Pound by their mutual friends, Violet and Ford.

In June a meeting was arranged between the relevant people at South Lodge, and they got along well together. Miss Weaver, who had an excellent eye for talent, saw Pound's genius immediately, but her comrade was jealous and reluctant, fearing that Ezra would advance from the one page allotted him to taking over the whole magazine (which is precisely what he set out to do). One of the secrets of Pound's success with the ladies was that he persuaded the tightfisted Fletcher to part with some of his cash to finance the literary side (*EPDS*, 238), and since the magazine was losing money badly at the time, this investment was extremely important. Eventually in November, they would change the name to the *Egoist*, in deference to Harriet's love of Whitman's "Song of Myself" and on Dora's side to her firm notion that until women developed their egos, they would continue to allow men to dominate them. Even with the new title and Pound's contributions, the magazine continued to flounder, being kept alive by strong-willed women like Amy Lowell and May Sinclair, who freely donated money to the cause.

At last Pound was fully in charge of his own part of a journal. Fortunately the ladies tended to leave him alone; Dora disliked creative literature, and Harriet was determined not to be nosy, but she did read what he published, and she particularly approved of the work of James Joyce when it started to appear the following year. Harriet immediately felt a kinship with Joyce and his terrible problems in getting his work published. Wealthy herself through inheritance from her physician father, she had great compassion for the talented but poor, and was determined to help them in any way she could. Despite many legal and printing problems, she allowed *Portrait of the Artist As a Young Man* to run between her covers, and she even branched into book publishing in order to issue *Portrait* in that form; she also published Wyndham Lewis' *Tarr* and Pound's *Dialogues of Fontenelle*, the last one proving to be a financial disaster. Her extraordinary kindness (so opposite the conduct of Fletcher) would manifest itself especially in 1919, when, in the midst of serializing *Ulysses*, she inherited even more money and then generously gave Joyce a grant of £5000 worth of War Loan bonds (anonymously, only finally owning up to her action at his insistence); this enabled the beleaguered writer, with further help from John Quinn and others, to live most of the rest of his life in comfort.

But that is rushing things. Back in the summer of 1913, as Pound assumed literary control of the *New Freewoman*, he immediately exercised his powers to the full. In September he ran his own reviews of the poetry books of Lawrence, De la Mare, and Frost, as well as two books by Fletcher (which the irate American did not especially welcome, since he had stipulated in giving Pound the money that he wanted no formal or informal attachment to the magazine). The first of three installments of "The Serious Artist" appeared in October, as well as the famous "Religio, or, The Child's Guide to Knowledge" in unsigned form. The former article is a defense of poetry-writing as an art, not the casual avocation that so many British gentlemen considered it to be; in it, Pound says: "It is occasionally suggested by the wise that poets should acquire the graces of prose" (*LE*, 51). In the latter article, which was reprinted often later, especially in response to T. S. Eliot's famous question "What does Mr. Pound believe?" Pound essentially wrote a modern pagan catechism:

> What is a god?
> A god is an eternal state of mind.
> What is a faun?
> A faun is an elemental creature . . .
> When is a god manifest?
> When the states of mind take form.
> When does a man become a god?
> When he enters one of these states of mind . . .
> By what characteristic may we know the divine forms?
> By beauty.
>
> (*SP,* 47)

This was rather powerful propaganda; it is easy to see why the *New Freewoman* was considered daring, and was sometimes close to having scrapes with the law.

In November appeared Pound's review of Allen Upward's recently issued *Divine Mystery*, which the reviewer called "the most fascinating book on folk-lore that I have ever opened" (*SP,* 403). He felt that Upward, a lawyer who had lived for a time in Nigeria, offered an excellent account of the growth of religion from crass superstition to messiah worship to a level where it might have some applicability to modern science. Pound always regarded Upward, who had now joined his circle unofficially, with the greatest respect. Born of Welsh parentage in England in 1863, Upward became an outstanding barrister and a rather powerful liberal politician in Wales, although his curiosity constantly impelled him into exotic places. In 1897, while acting for Greece on Corfu, he purchased a jewel (later turned into a seal-ring) that had a John Barleycorn-like figure upon it scattering grain. Upward (or Pound) identified this as Sitalkas, a grain-god manifestation of Apollo of Delphi, who was also the subject of an early poem by Hilda Doolittle.

Then in 1901, Upward went to Africa, where he acquired much of the anthropological expertise needed for writing *The Divine Mystery*. His mind was always concerned with religious and philosophical thoughts. An earlier book, *The New Word*, dealt to a great degree with Plato, Roger Bacon, and the development of idealism. This had been issued in 1907, when Alfred Orage was beginning to publish his *New Age*. The socialist editor soon asked his equally liberal friend to contribute some articles on current thinking, and Upward criticized Nietzsche, whom Orage happened to like. The two men also differed in other important ways, since Orage was drawn to Hindu thought and Upward to Chinese, especially Confucius.

At the turn of the century, Upward and his partner Lancelot Byng had acquired a small printing firm on Fleet Street and published the Wisdom of the East Series. Upward offered *The Sayings of Confucius* (1904), while Byng contributed translations of the Confucian *Odes*. Most of this information comes from Upward's biography, *Some Personalities* (1921), which the eccentric genius published without ever using his real name—simply the sobriquet "20/1631," a number that had been assigned to him by the Board of Education.

In his far-ranging experience and reading, Upward had amassed a wealth of information of many kinds, which Pound clearly revered. In *The Divine Mystery* Upward praised those who were true geniuses, although he also noted that they often wound up being sacrificial victims, rather than the leaders or priests of the mysteries, which they should have been. In a playful autobiographical poem, "The Discarded Imagist," which he published in the *Egoist* when imagism had splintered into camps, Upward said of his career:

I withstood the savages of the Niger with a revolver;
I withstood the savages of the Thames with a printing-press . . .

Pound worked these lines from memory into Canto 74/437, where he aligned Upward (who committed suicide in 1926) with the Predappio-born Mussolini (who was brutally treated as a sacrificial victim by the very society that had once adored him):

if on the forge at Predappio? sd/ old Upward:
   "not the priest but the victim"
   his seal Sitalkas, sd/ the old combattant: "victim,
withstood them by Thames and by Niger with pistol by Niger
with a printing press by the Thomas bank"
until I end my song
         and shot himself;

In a very perceptive article on Upward that appeared in the Pound journal *Paideuma*, A. D. Moody showed the impact that Upward had on Pound. To the young poet, this polymathic personality seemed to be in touch with all the mysteries that he had tried so hard to define: Upward perceived them as loose but coherent ideograms or idea-pictures, rather than as hardened concepts. Although Richard and Hilda somewhat resented Upward's presence, considering him an old lawyer who had wrongly strayed into the company of young poets, Pound appreciated the man's intellect. Upward's mind, like Orage's, ranged far and wide (from China to Africa to Greece): there was no nonsense in his thought, as there was in that of many of the quacks who flocked to Mead's Quest Society or who gathered around the now spiritualistic Yeats. Many of the passages in the *Cantos* that concern the Eleusinian Mysteries probably owe something to the whimsical Welshman, who (despite the skeptical Richard and Hilda) had indeed studied poetry deeply and also wrote it. Pound would include one of Upward's works in the first issue of his imagist anthology; he was never bound to any *ism* in the face of genius. It was precisely their mutual admiration of courage and independence that made both him and Upward friends—and ultimately, despite their wishes, victims of the societies around them. Perhaps some half-suspected intuition of their future tragedies was what really brought the two together.

Suddenly in the middle of that summer came stirrings from a new quarter: the Boston millionairess Amy Lowell (1874–1925). In 1912 in her late thirties, Amy had published her first book of poems: a late-Romantic volume entitled *A Dome of Many-Coloured Glass*. In January of this year, she then discovered H.D.'s poems in *Poetry*, along with the news that there was a rising school in London under the direction of Ezra Pound, whose reputation she was already well aware of. After reading Hilda's poems very carefully, a perception dawned on her: "Why, I must be an Imagiste too!" She then dashed off a note to Harriet Monroe, whom she was promising to subsidize to a degree, firmly requesting a letter of introduction to her enterprising foreign editor.

Miss Monroe had been rather slow to realize exactly who Miss Lowell was: from the Boston Lowells, with two famous brothers— Abbot Lawrence Lowell, a President of Harvard, and Percival, an astronomer in Arizona who was determinedly searching for those canals on Mars that he was sure existed. But as soon as Harriet recognized the true identity of her subscriber, she was quick to capitalize on the affiliation, and so she obligingly sent Amy the address of Mr. Pound, even though she had some slight misgivings about the potential outcome of this meeting. Almost immediately Amy purchased a ticket for England, and on July 8 she was off, prepared to assault the bastion of Mr. Pound.

Miss Lowell arrived in London in full grandeur, with scores of suitcases and a private, liveried car. She stayed in her favorite quarters, a five-room penthouse atop the Berkeley Hotel, which offered a panoramic view of Green Park and the lamplighted vista of Piccadilly, with its perennially busy horse and motor traffic. Immediately she invited Ezra Pound to join her there for dinner, and he was quick to comply. During that first encounter he made every effort to be cordial, seeing her as an important ally for the future. He did his best to overlook her overblown appearance, which made her so sensitive that she often draped the mirrors in her rooms so that she would not have to see herself.

In a report back to Harriet, Amy was ecstatic because Ezra had selected one of her poems ("In a Garden") to publish in the *New Freewoman*, which he was secretly hoping that she would underwrite; this poem would also appear in his future anthology. Pound also offered to introduce her to Yeats and Ford, and Amy very much appreciated this gesture. At the same time she cautioned Harriet that he was surely "no flatterer." She described Ezra to Miss Monroe, who had still not met him, as "a young man, arrayed as 'poet' and yet making the costume agreeable by his personal charm; . . . the violence of his writings giving way to show a very thin-skinned and sensitive personality opening out like a flower in a sympathetic circle, and I should imagine shutting up like a clam in an alien atmosphere" (MPL, 276). She even took him on a motorcar-ride to Oxford, and he felt windblown for days (*EPDS*, 245).

During this time Amy was also courting John Gould Fletcher. She invited him for a private party in her elegant suite, too, and there they savored magnificent food catered by special servants and each other's poetry. Amy sat enraptured while the Arkansan intoned his "Irradiations," and then she made her unforgettable proclamation of him as a genius. Many people felt that Amy was romantically interested in Fletcher, despite the rather ludicrous combination of her portliness and his scrawniness, but Fletcher was now involved in an affair with a married woman and did not respond to her advances. As a result, Amy abandoned these plans, if indeed she ever had them, and when she appeared in London the following year, she was accompanied by her friend for life, Ada Dwyer Russell, who inherited her estate Sevenels (for 7 Lowells) and much of her money on her death in 1925.

The first encounter between Pound and Lowell seemed, in short, to have gone well. Ezra told Robert Frost that summer that when he was finished with the "old girl," she would think that she had been born spouting free verse. But this was only round one. Round two, which would take place the following summer, would produce the famous confrontation that would split imagism forever and send Pound, who was already moving away from it, deeper on his own quest for a poetry that moves as well as presents—the cinema against the snapshot.

In early August Pound put the finishing touches on *Lustra*, which contains his finest "imagist" work; but because that volume was cursed—it would not appear until 1916—the time lag would distort the proper sense of his intellectual development. By 1916 Ezra Pound was a very different man. On August 3 of 1913, Ezra informed Dorothy that he had already "typed" *Lustra* (*EPDS*, 237), and the addition of the machine certainly expedited his future output. In 1914 he would buy a new machine with a £40 prize that he garnered from *Poetry* through the kindness of Yeats, who wanted the money passed on to someone more needy. Later Pound would attack typewriters with such bravado that he was forced to keep two on hand. He would manipulate the typewriter exactly as if it were a musical instrument, always careful to mark pauses and balances in his typing and to arrange things in a way that suggests calligraphy. The appearance of the text was meaningful. Pampered as we are today by machines of every variety, we forget those simple joys of the 1910s when a motorcar ride to Oxford was a great event; when Amy Lowell gave D. H. Lawrence a typewriter the following year, he was eternally grateful to her.

By the end of that summer, Pound had the material for an imagist anthology, but as yet no publisher. John Cournos had told him about a friend in New York, Alfred Kreymborg, who with the painter and photographer Man Ray and others was starting a journal called *Glebe*. Kreymborg was one of those kindly artistic types like Cournos who believed in the perpetuation of the arts above all material values. He and Ray had been eking out an existence in a shack on the Hudson Palisades overlooking the Jersey swamps, and so they named their journal in honor of Williams's "bloody loam" of the Meadowlands: *glaeba* in Latin means "clod of soil." In his autobiographical *Troubadour*, Kreymborg said of Pound: "In a world where most people slavishly coddled their own egos, here was a fellow with a heart and intelligence at the service of other contemporaries" (204). On receiving Pound's offer, Kreymborg and his associates quickly decided to make the anthology their first issue, but problems arose and it appeared in February of 1914 as Issue 2, under the title *Des Imagistes, An Anthology*. Richard Aldington said that the title was ungrammatical, and should have been *Quelques Imagistes* (137).

Pound enclosed six of his own poems in the collection, including four Chinese adaptations that he made from the scholar H. A. Giles' *History of Chinese Literature* (published in 1901); these have all been printed on page 108 of *Personae*. One of Giles' ten-line translations was reduced to the following three lines by Pound in a severe act of concision:

> O fan of white silk
>   clear as frost on the grass-blade,
> You also are laid aside.

By a strange turn of fate, Mary Fenollosa, the widow of a scholar of philosophy and Oriental art who had lived and taught in Japan, was searching for someone to edit and promulgate her husband's unpublished notebooks. She saw those poems, as well as some of Pound's other works, through some friends from India, and she asked if she might meet the young man. Pound also published ten poems of Aldington in *Des Imagistes*, seven of H.D., five of Flint, and one each of Cannell, Williams, Ford, Upward, Lowell, and Cournos—quite a mixed bag. At the last moment in December, following a suggestion by Yeats, he added a poem titled "I Hear An Army Charging" by an Irish exile living in Trieste, with the name of James Joyce.

10

Art and the Orient: Gaudier-Brzeska and Fenollosa (August 1913–January 1914)

...it must be pointed out that Pound is the inventor of Chinese poetry for our time.

—*T. S. Eliot (1928)*

In music, the year 1913 was a memorable one, for in the spring in Paris, Igor Stravinsky shocked the staid ballet-goers who had come to hear another delightful *Petrouchka* by offering them his bitonal *Rite of Spring*, which first assaulted their ears and then sent them screaming into the streets. Modernism had arrived. Stravinsky's juxtaposition of rhythmic patterns, backed by a cacophony of horns which expostulated in brass, told people that art had changed. No longer should one expect the soothing allegorical fantasies of a Burne-Jones in art, the lullabies of a Liszt, or the euphoric declamations of a Rudyard Kipling or an Alfred (Lawn, Joyce called him) Tennyson. What Stravinsky did with music, Pound would soon be doing with words. Pound's *Cantos* would become his *Rite of Spring*, and they were already well in the mind, if not quite on the drawing board. Still, Pound's most important contacts in 1913 were with artists, not musicians—and especially with a man who had a half-French, half-Polish unpronounceable name.

In July Pound quite literally bumped into the sculptor Henri Gaudier-Brzeska (*EPDS*, 237). In his later memoir of the dead artist, Pound recounted how their meeting took place. He was viewing an Allied Artists' exhibition at the Albert Hall with Olivia Shakespear when suddenly a young man began to course along with them "like a well-made young wolf or some soft-moving, bright-eyed wild thing" (*GBM*, 44). The young man was fascinated by the fact that they were primarily interested in modern art. On the ground floor of the hall, they paused before a muscular figure *(The Wrestler)* sculpted in green clay. Pound turned to his catalog and tried to pronounce the name of the creator, which had an "appalling assemblage of consonants." When he failed three times to get it right, the stalker emerged from behind the pedestal and said (in French): "You simply say Jaersh-ka. I'm the one who sculpted these things." Then he shot away like "a Greek god in a vision."

Pound was intrigued by this apparition; he sent a dinner invitation to the man's studio, but the artist did not respond. Then, later, Pound received a card addressed to "Madame," inviting him to come to the artist's workroom, which was in the arches under a railway line in Putney. This was hardly an elegant location, since the sounds of the trains' screeching whistles came at ten-minute intervals and the floor sometimes filled up with water, requiring the sculptor to cut his stone in hip-boots. As it turned out, Henri knew Jacob Epstein quite well and also John Cournos, and soon a meeting was arranged, which led to a fast and firm friendship. Pound was then introduced to the sculptor's "sister," Sophie, with whom he was living when she was not out in the country working as a governess or teacher. Pound and Sophie did not especially get along well together—indeed, the neurotic Polish woman tended to like very few of Henri's friends, and so her absences were not missed, especially since she professed to be a novelist and wanted Pound to promote her work. Pound immediately introduced Henri by himself to all of his important friends, trying to drum up some trade. The two also socialized often together, having late drinks at the popular Café Royal or dinners at the Eiffel Tower or dancing sessions at Madame Strindberg's Cabaret.

Henri's story was as strange as his name. He was the son of a carpenter named Gaudier, born in 1891 in the Loire Valley. Because he had very early shown a talent for drawing and languages, he won scholarships and work opportunities that took him to Orléans, Bristol, Nuremberg, Munich, and Paris. It was in the last city that he met the strange Polish woman named Sophie Brzeska, who would soon become an integral part of his life. Sophie's story was quite pathetic: she was one of nine children born to a neurotic family that had treated her very badly. As a result, she had moved to Cracow, Paris, and New York, supporting herself by working for wealthy families either as a maid or a governess. Eventually she wound up back in Paris, where she was trying to increase her store of languages and was also contemplating suicide.

These two lonely individuals met at the St. Genevieve Library on the Left Bank, and were immediately taken with each other. Because Sophie was about twenty years older than Henri, she insisted that a love affair between them would be indecent. As a result, they began to live together as a brother and sister, and Henri even absorbed her name as part of his to make it look legitimate. H. S. Ede detailed their lives in his fascinating *Savage Messiah* (a nickname given to Henri by his fellow artists in London), chronicling their misadventures in Paris and then London, leading up to the encounter with Pound. He tells how, when Katherine Mansfield heard Sophie recite the litany of her illnesses and bouts with poverty and squalor, the English novelist was so repelled by her "Polish tale" of violence that she refused to ever see the woman again (136). This infuriated Henri, who was working on a head of her lover, John Middleton Murry, and so he first cursed Mansfield and then destroyed the head by pelting it with stones.

Ede does not categorically say that the couple's affair was platonic, but it was so billed, and they usually clung to this story, except when it seemed advantageous to appear to be lovers. Jacob Epstein, who seemed to be somewhat jealous of the young Frenchman (claiming that Henri liked to "change his style from week to week"), recounts in his *Autobiography* that when Ezra and Henri visited his studio in 1913, observing him at work on his *Rock-Drill* (a title subsumed by Pound for some of his later cantos), Pound was babbling away excitedly, when Henri abruptly shouted: "Shut up, you know nothing!" (56). But that was not Henri's usual attitude toward the American. He admired Pound's poetry and felt deeply appreciative of Pound's efforts to help him financially, as for example when Olivia purchased from him one of the torsos of a woman modeled by Nina Hamnett.

Gaudier-Brzeska said often that he felt a strong, indefinable affinity between his work and the poetry of Ezra Pound, yet he hesitated to be specific. One might say that there is a clear correlation between the sculptor's classically cut *Fawn*, which is precise and lifelike, and the imagist poems being written at this period by Pound. As Ezra felt the imagist movement slipping away into mediocrity and stasis, Gaudier-Brzeska would become ever more important to him, since the sculptor, both in his own catlike movements and in the flow of the masses in his creations, clearly grasped the importance of kinesis in art. Henri and Ezra, along with Wyndham Lewis, would see the need for an artistic vortex to energize all of the arts, and the three would be at the center of this movement in the near future.

When Pound was invited early that fall to the house of the Indian nationalist poet Sarojini Naidu, he was doubtlessly expecting to spend most of the evening discussing poetry with the charming "Nightingale of India," but Sarojini had been prevailed upon by the already mentioned Mrs. Mary McNeill Fenollosa to arrange the appointment so that she could look over the young American poet for the job as literary executor of her husband's estate. On October 2, Pound told Dorothy about the dinner, saying that he was "getting orient from all quarters" (*EPDS*, 264). Then on October 11, he said that Mrs. Fenollosa had taken him to "two bad plays & to dinner with Heinemann," the publisher. Clearly she had decided very soon that Pound was the man to inherit her husband's unfinished work, and she was not going to be brushed aside. She herself had issued Fenollosa's *Epochs of Chinese and Japanese Art* in two volumes from a rough pencil draft, but she did not want to attack the sixteen or so notebooks that remained, dealing largely with three subjects: Japanese drama, Chinese verse, and the Chinese writing system. Even though Pound was no Oriental scholar, he was a poet, and this was the important thing to her—as it should be to the many critics who simply descry Pound's ignorance at this time of either Chinese or Japanese.

Ernest Francisco Fenollosa (1853–1908) had lived a fascinating life. He was the son of a Spanish musician named Manuel who had come to the United States with a band and had settled in Salem, Massachusetts, where he married a New England girl with the name of Mary Silsbee. Their son entered Harvard College in 1874 and graduated at the head of his class, going on to study philosophy and theology at Cambridge in England. After some work at the Boston Museum of Fine Arts, Fenollosa went in 1878 to Japan, where he taught philosophy at the Imperial University in Tokyo for about eight years. When the Tokyo Fine Arts Academy opened in 1888, he became its first manager. In 1890, he returned to the Boston Museum as the curator of Oriental art, and after another stay in Japan from 1895 to 1900, he spent most of the time before his death in the United States in New York City or in Spring Hill, Alabama, near his wife's native Mobile, although he died in London in 1908.

During his residences in Japan, Fenollosa became vitally interested in Oriental poetry and the Chinese language. Professing Buddhism himself, and even having himself rebaptized with the Chinese name of Tei-Shin, he worked intensively on Chinese poetry from 1896 to 1899, and studied with the Japanese professor Kainan Mori, who spoke no English, from 1899–1900. In order to insure comprehension,

Fenollosa had one of his former students, Nagao Ariga, who was a poet like Fenollosa and Mori, assist him in his work. For a year and a half they glossed a poet whom they called by the Japanese name of Rihaku, but whose true name was the Chinese Li Po; they also studied one Omakitsu, who was Wang Wei. The fact that Fenollosa used Japanese names for these Chinese poets and Japanese sounds for the Chinese characters of their verses was alone a cause for some future confusion, but Fenollosa may have shared a common Japanese prejudice that their language is somehow closer to the "true" Chinese of the ancient past, instead of the monosyllabic, truncated Mandarin dialect that is Modern Chinese. But since Fenollosa was working with Japanese scholars, it was probably simpler to use their language to begin with. The last thing that Fenollosa studied before leaving Japan in 1901 was the Chinese writing system. His *Chinese Written Character as a Medium for Poetry* was captivating to Pound, who tried to publish it in all kinds of journals—unsuccessfully. Finally, he included it at the end of his *Instigations* in 1920, and it has been reprinted several times separately since then. The nature of this treatise is important for a brief discussion here, since the Chinese lyrics and the Japanese Noh plays can be discussed when they appear in book form (articles on these subjects appear as early as May, 1914).

The essay on the written character arouses the ire of most modern Oriental scholars and colors many assessments of Pound's Oriental work because Fenollosa made certain claims about the Chinese writing system that almost every Sinologist denies. Fenollosa held that the Chinese characters are actually representations of ideas (ideograms) which present concepts in a visual form; this notion was extremely important to Pound's study of imagism at the time, since he was striving for a poetry that was visually focused. The Chinese word for "man" shows what looks like a pair of legs, while a "tree" would seem to indicate a stem with branches and roots; the "sun" is an orifice like a mouth, while the "East" can be depicted by presenting the "sun tangled in the tree's branches." The characters with these meanings were shown thus in the later *ABC of Reading* (21):

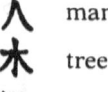 man

tree

sun

 sun tangled in the tree's branches, as at sunrise, meaning now the East.

When one gets to a more difficult concept like "red," the Chinese portray the color by showing pictures of a rose, iron rust, a cherry, and a flamingo (22).

The main argument against this theory is that only a bare 10% of the Chinese vocabulary can be discussed in this way, although that includes most of the basic words. The vast majority of Chinese words consist of about two elements, one of which is purely phonetic, telling the viewer how to pronounce the word and having no relationship to the word's meaning at all. It is true that both Fenollosa and Pound, who were not ignorant of these arguments, obstinately refused to take this into consideration, and so Pound laboriously went through his Morrison Chinese dictionary (which he received as a wedding present that coming spring), trying to make the radicals (which in this dictionary help the viewer to locate the words) an integral part of the ideological concept. Most of this labor was, of course, doomed to failure.

A second great disadvantage that Pound labored under was his ignorance of the *sound* of Chinese. To a poet who later said that *melopoeia* or music-making was an integral part of a poem, he was suddenly faced with the job of translating Chinese concept-figurations with Japanese sound values—or with no values at all. It would not be until he got the Mathews Chinese dictionary years later (which organizes the characters by their sounds rather than by their radicals) that Pound would seriously begin to penetrate the true phonetic structure of the language—with the help of several visitors to St. Elizabeth's. Not knowing the sounds of the originals meant that Pound was truly on his own—but in the long run, when one compares Pound's versions with those of people who supposedly knew the Chinese language, one is not sure that Pound labored at the start under any great disadvantage. During that winter, Pound began first to rework the Noh plays, feeling that it was best to begin with these more polished productions. He worked primarily on *Nishikigi*, which appeared in *Poetry* that May "edited" by Ezra Pound. Although we shall discuss these plays when they appeared as a book, let us say now that, with Mrs. Fenollosa's hand-delivered gifts of October and with parcels arriving from Alabama in November and December, Pound was launched on the Third World of his *Cantos*: the Orient that would accompany the Europe of his family's past and the America of his dreams.

October of 1913 was memorable as a month of malady and marriage. The malady was Pound's recurring jaundice, indicating, as Mother Isabel suspected, that her son was not eating a proper diet.

We know from remarks made by Ford and others that, during these lean years, Pound relied to a great extent for sustenance on the cookies and hors-d'oeuvres of friends, and when he did invest in his own meals, it was usually at a restaurant with rich Italian or French fare—or, from this point on, at a Chinese place in Regent Street. He usually avoided the plain but healthful fare of England, except when eating the surprisingly good cooking of Mrs. Langley. While recovering from this attack, he kept his appointment at Church Walk on October 22 with the noted American photographer Alvin Langdon Coburn, who made some famous portraits of Pound that show a man with a lean, handsome face that culminates in a pointed beard, with a strange glint in the eye. The kindly old landlady Mrs. Langley thought that she detected a trace of "the man from Nazareth" ("begging your pardon, sir") in the face, but Hilda, with her demon-lover fixation, and Mr. Shakespear, with his fears for his daughter, saw an Italianate Mephistopheles there. It was always Pound's fortune, like a true Scorpio, to be billed as either a sinner or a saint.

The marriage after the 18th was that of the Aldingtons, who were finally that in name. As Pound told Ingrid Davies in 1955, he was present at the "hooking" in the Kensington Registry Office—along with the solemn-faced Doolittle parents, who had little to be thankful for except that they had avoided Ezra as their son-in-law. But as things developed, that fate might not have been so bad, since the Aldington marriage was doomed from the start. It was to be a "modern marriage"—that is, one in which each member was free to do as he or she pleased. Given the latitude of Mr. Aldington's desires, that was too broad a range. In order to shake off Ezra's presence, Richard soon arranged for the couple to move around the corner to a cozy cul-de-sac off Kensington Church Street, known as Holland Place Chambers, into building No. 5. Pound and Dorothy would ironically move there too after their own marriage that coming spring.

Since the Aldingtons had already had a long vacation on the continent that previous spring, they did not feel the necessity for taking a honeymoon at this time. At first it seemed as if their marriage was ideal, since, even though Hilda was older than Richard, they were still intensely interested in poetry and Greek culture. But the oncoming war would soon shake their marriage to its foundations, as it did to many others, taking Richard away and driving H.D. to rely first on John Cournos for love and sympathy and then on D. H. Lawrence. Cournos was an American neutral and Lawrence too sickly to fight in the oncoming war. Aldington meanwhile would then fall in love first with Dorothy Yorke and finally very seriously with Brigit Patmore, with whom he was already flirting in 1913. When the Patmore affair finally ended in 1937, Richard courted her daughter-in-law, Netta Patmore, and it was at that time that a formal divorce with Hilda was finally arranged. By 1938, the year of their divorce, H.D. had spent almost twenty years in a long love affair with Winifred Ellerman (alias Bryher, the historical novelist), who was an heir to the millions of Sir John Ellerman, a shipbuilding magnate originally from Germany. In short, the destruction of the marriage could be sensed from the start, and Pound, seeing this, seldom treated the union in a serious way. But although he clearly did not want to marry Hilda himself, he was rather jealous when another man did this.

Next comes an important series of retreats in Pound's life: his three successive winter sessions serving as secretary to Yeats in a country house known as Stone Cottage, located near Coleman's Hatch in Sussex on the edge of Ashdown Forest. Here, about sixteen miles from the sea, the two men rented four of six rooms from Ellen and Alice Welfare, sisters of the owner; Alice cooked and cleaned for them. The first session began in mid-November of 1913 and ended in mid-January of the following year. In informing his mother about his plan to assist the elder statesman of letters, Ezra did not sound enthusiastic. He reminded her that he reveled in city life, and although he would be greatly amused by Uncle William's anecdotes, he would be bored by his talk about psychic research ("the spooks," as Pound often referred to Yeats's ghostly companions); he informed Isabel that he had taken this job largely for the sake of posterity—and, he might well have added, money (*SL*, 25). Pound's letters to Dorothy from November 14 onward indicate that he was not enchanted by Ashdown Forest, where she herself had stayed nearby in October with her own psychic friend, Georgie Hyde-Lees, the future Mrs. Yeats. But Ezra added that Yeats "improves on acquaintance" (*EPDS*, 276), showing that he was only now, after four years, getting close to the man.

Aside from writing Yeats's letters by dictation, Pound read aloud to the older poet from such works as the Hindu *Mahabharata*, the mystical writings of Emanuel Swedenborg, and William Morris's translations of Icelandic sagas. Yeats at this time was deeply involved in assisting Lady Gregory in her researches into the folklore of Ireland and Britain. He later wrote copious notes that were incorporated into her *Visions and Beliefs in the West of Ireland* (1920). Despite Pound's apprehensions about the occult, the two were engrossed in Joseph Ennemoser's *History of Magic* (translated from German in 1854), the *Grimoire* or *Black Book* of Pope Honorius (1629), and an occult novel by the Abbot of Montfaucon de Villars entitled *Le Comte de Gabalis* (1670); Olivia Shakespear later translated the latter, and Pound published it in five issues of the *Egoist* in 1914. At Ezra's request, Homer

Pound sent them his son's copy of a nineteenth-century work on demonism entitled *De Daemonialitate, et Incubis et Succubis*, which had been passed off as the treatise of a seventeenth-century Franciscan friar named Lodovico Maria Sinistrari. These works all fascinated the otherwise pragmatic Pound, and would be more valuable to him many years later when he was trying to write his *Paradiso;* then Yeats's mysticism would be helpful in his attempt to free himself from the economic hell after World War II.

During this winter, Yeats was writing a poem called "The Peacock," which would appear in his 1914 *Responsibilities*. In Canto 83/533–34, Pound recalls the sound of the Irish poet's voice ringing through Stone Cottage in the act of composition, along with the imaginative processes in his own mind as he toiled over a Japanese play:

> The Kakemono grows in flat land out of mist
> > sun rises lop-sided over the mountain
> > > so that I recalled the noise in the chimney
> as it were the wind in the chimney
> > but was in reality Uncle William
> downstairs composing
> that had made a great Peeeeacock
> > in the proide ov his oiye
> > had made a great peeeeeeecock in the ...
> made a great peacock
> > in the proide of his oyyee
>
> proide ov his oy-ee
> as indeed he had, and perdurable

This poem appears on page 119 of Yeats's *Collected Poems*.

We are just beginning to appreciate the importance of these retreats in the development of both poets, and for the development of modernist art. The Noh plays being worked on by Pound offered Yeats a solution to the dilemma that he had faced in the Abbey Theater when he had tried to create a drama that had some ethnic validity. Yeats felt that he had failed and, as he said in his valedictory for Synge, he believed that the Irish theater itself had failed in this respect. The Noh plays indicated to him that he should strive to be more universal, more archetypal, and that is what he proceeded to do in his next plays like *At the Hawk's Well*. In fact, as he moved away from Dublin toward Byzantium, Yeats replaced the ethnic with the archetypal. An important book for both him and Pound at this time was Frank Brinkley's *Japan and China: Their History, Arts, and Literature*.

On Pound's side, the Noh plays tended to involve him in the creation of an aristocratic rather than a popular theater. The subtlety and sensitivity of the dramas seemed to have no bearing on the soon-to-be war-torn and otherwise insensitive culture around him. Instead of blasting this culture, Pound could, with the help of the Noh works, simply run away from it for a time. But this flight was only temporary, for the pragmatic streak in Pound was bound to reassert itself as soon as the war was over and he met Major Douglas. Then in 1918 he would write to John Quinn (*SL*, 137) that the Noh were "unsatisfactory," "too damn soft," too much like the fairy-tale worlds that Yeats had always been drawn to. And so, what was entertaining and expedient in 1914 would not quite serve Pound four years later—although it would continue to be of value to Yeats.

Despite these differences, which were developing even at this point, Pound was determined to remain the older man's friend, and he continued to be at least partially influenced by him, as he showed in his prose poem "Ikon," which appeared in the *Cerebralist*, a journal that became defunct after its first issue in December of 1913. There he insisted that images had spiritual resonances, and were not mechanical reproductions. The two men would, in fact, remain friends, even as they began to go their separate ways: Yeats always on a path toward spiritual fulfillment, Pound increasingly determined to forge an Earthly Paradise before he became absorbed in the demands of a higher world. Their differences, more than their similarities, would be a beneficial thing for the evolution of modern literature.

Even at the edge of the forest, Pound could not break away from political games. He had already accepted Amy Lowell's poem for his anthology (*SL*, no. 26), and he kept hounding Yeats for the name of some bright young Irish writer whom he could add to his fold. In December, the Eagle finally reached back into his memory and came up with the name of a young man whom he had encountered back in 1902, a brash youngster who had informed Yeats that he was too old to help others enter the modern world. This youngster was James Joyce (1882–1941); he had been introduced by Arthur Symons, and he was now eking out a living in self-imposed exile in the Trieste of the dying Austro-Hungarian Empire, teaching English in a commercial high school to supplement his private tutoring. His primary intellectual comrade was one Ettore Schmitz, better known by his literary name of Italo Svevo.

Never a sluggard, Pound dashed off a letter to Joyce on December 15, and another one shortly thereafter. Joyce was astounded and delighted to hear that somebody finally cared about publishing his dormant work. He immediately agreed to let Pound add a poem to his anthology that began: "I hear an army charging upon the land, / And the thunder of horses plunging, foam about their knees: / Arrogant, in black armour, behind them stand, / Disdaining the reins, with fluttering whips, the charioteers."

Pound soon began pushing Joyce's work for *Poetry*, which he had rejoined after a token resignation in favor of Ford, who had resigned back in favor of Pound. He also wrote to his new friend H. L. Mencken at the *Smart Set* about his discovery, and to Henry Davray of the *Mercure de France*, whom he was also close to now. Most importantly, though, he got in touch with Harriet Shaw Weaver, who was gradually assuming editorial as well as business control of the *Egoist* (the new name for the *New Freewoman*), as Dora Marsden retreated in importance on the staff.

Much of the Pound–Joyce correspondence, edited by Forrest Read, is rather disappointing, since the letters are largely business transactions, and the men would not meet until 1920. The Joyce who comes through is often selfish-sounding and money-hungry (although he *was* on the poverty line), while the Pound presented seems to be almost slavishly interested in helping him. When Pound finally did meet the Irishman in Sirmione, he was pleased to find him as witty and brilliant as his writing. Although their relationship after Pound's Paris years was rather removed, they remained good friends, even when they had serious doubts about each other's masterworks in the thirties. Joyce always acknowledged his debt to Pound: "He pulled me out of the gutter," Joyce told Robert McAlmon in Paris. Pound immediately sensed the genius in the man and did everything he could to help him. *Dubliners* would soon see the grace of print, and the *Egoist* would soon serialize *Portrait of the Artist as a Young Man*.

A major event of that winter was the honoring of the old Victorian writer Wilfrid Scawen Blunt (1840–1922). Blunt was really just a minor poet and dramatist who had been more famous as a politician and breeder of Arabian horses, but he had achieved fame among Pound's circle because he had heroically opposed British colonialism and supported Irish home rule; for this courage he was imprisoned by the British government for two months in 1888. A committee of eight paid to have Henri Gaudier-Brzeska carve a stone reliquary in his honor, and inside this were placed poetic homages by the benefactors. On January 18, a group of these appeared at Blunt's house, called Newbuildings Place in Sussex. Six of them appeared in a famous photograph that survived: Victor Plarr, Sturge Moore, Yeats, Pound, Aldington, and Flint. Hilaire Belloc and Frederic Manning were not photographed.

Pound's homage to Blunt was not distinguished, but he did offer the man a beautiful tribute in his *Pisan Cantos*, when, after recalling

Some visitors who honored Wilfrid Scawen Blunt (left to right): Victor Plarr, Sturge Moore, W. B. Yeats, Blunt himself, Ezra Pound, Richard Aldington, and F. S. Flint. (Photography Collection, Harry Ransom Humanities Research Center, University of Texas, Austin)

many of the peccadilloes of his own life, he suddenly changed key and thought of this gesture of kindness:

> Rathe to destroy, niggard in charity,
> Pull down thy vanity,
>   I say pull down.
>
> But to have done instead of not doing
>   this is not vanity
> To have, with decency, knocked
> That a Blunt should open
>   To have gathered from the air a live tradition
> or from a fine old eye the unconquered flame
> This is not vanity.
>   (81/521–22)

The old man received them with genuine aristocratic grace, offering them a roasted peacock for their pleasure.

The general isolation at Stone Cottage has recently been posited as the cause for a negative political attitude in both writers by such critics as Litz and Longenbach (see Works Cited In Text), who see a distinctly anti-democratic stance developing, which in turn would help to color the whole modernist movement. In part, this feeling may have arisen from the works that they were reading, since almost all mystical writers tend to draw a line between the elect, who fathom their mysteries, and the outsiders, who do not.

This distinction was also apparent in troubadour verse: between a hermetic writer like Arnaut Daniel and a "plain" singer like Guiraut de Bornelh. In fact, Pound's constant interest in things medieval reinforced this "courtly" attitude, and the Noh plays doubtlessly contributed to it too. Pound, in fact, linked Provence with Japan in his introduction to the plays in 1916: "The art of allusion, or this love of allusion in art, is at the root of the Noh. These plays, or eclogues, were made only for the few; for the nobles; for those trained to catch the allusion" (*TEP*, 214). One can already see the highly allusive nature of the *Cantos* evolving from these words. Yeats said the same sort of thing in his *Explorations:* he had created "an unpopular theatre and an audience like a secret society" (254). Yeats and Pound were, in fact, a secret society of two at Coleman Hatch; before going there, Pound had joked that he wanted to establish a new brotherhood of Fratres Minores (Brothers Minor) in the arts, so that some notion of patronage could be reinstituted—an idea that he stressed again in "The Renaissance" (*LE*, 224), which he published in 1914.

In fact, during their stay in January, Yeats's old friend George Moore published a part of the third volume of his memoirs in the *English Review*, attacking Yeats for his denunciations of the middle classes, from which the Anglo-Irishman himself hailed. Yeats adopted a patrician manner and refused to defend himself; he simply added two poems to his *Responsibilities*, in the last of which, "Notoriety," he mentioned that his priceless things, his poems, were "but a post the passing dogs defile" *(Collected Poems*, 126). However, the more sensitive Pound was not going to allow this attack to go unanswered. Under the pen name of Bastien von Helmholtz, he wrote an article called "The Bourgeois" that was published in the *Egoist* of February 2 in which he defined the bourgeois not as a social or financial class, but as a state of mind. The bourgeois were the material Philistines of any class who had no use for art, and hence, artists should have no use for them. This attitude toward the middle classes would harden during the coming years, under the duress of war, and it would seriously affect Pound's whole attitude toward his great poem of the future, as well as toward society itself.

Pound's delight in being back in London in late January is apparent in all his letters, especially those written to Dorothy. It is true that he had accomplished a lot at Stone Cottage: he had translated three Noh plays: *Kinuta, Hagoromo,* and *Nishikigi*. The last-named work would appear in the May issue of *Poetry*, along with Pound's glowing review of *Responsibilities*, which he called the work of "the best poet in England." But Ezra had a special reason to be happy on his return, for at long last, he had the permission to marry Dorothy.

11

Toward Amy's *Ism* and Wyndham's Blasts (January–August 1914)

> *In this poetry business there are rings of intrigue.*
> —Amy Lowell
>
> *Their asperities diverted me in my green time.*
> —*Canto 115/794*

Although we are now entering the first year of the Great War, a peruser of Ezra Pound's writings and correspondence would scarcely be aware of this, because nowhere is there any mention of Prussians, Serbians, Turks, Romanovs, or any of the other people who would suddenly be making headlines that summer. Instead, talk that winter and spring centered on the wild life at Madame Strindberg's, or Marinetti's camp orations, or the revolutionary new *ism* that had been baptized by Ezra Pound and fathered by Percy Wyndham Lewis: vorticism.

On his return from the moors, Pound threw himself into the dizzying pace of London life with unshackled energy. He had been distressed back in November about the lack of life in English artistic circles, telling Harriet Monroe that the country was as "dead as mutton," and that unless some standard for world literature was adopted, English literature would become a purely provincial affair (*SL*, 24). Then to Bill Williams, in mid-December, he used the magic word that he had dredged up to christen the new movement that would seek to energize the arts—all of them: "You may get something slogging away by yourself that you would miss in The Vortex" (*SL*, 28). It is clear from the way that he later employed this word in describing circles of French intellectuals whom he had observed in 1912 that Pound was trying to recreate the intellectually alive atmosphere of the French capital in the English.

Now in January, Pound concentrated his efforts on injecting new life into the English scene by doing two things: he tried to continue his promotion of imagism and imagist-related events, and he also tried to hook into the new movement, which was being led by the once cold and diffident Mr. Lewis. Let us consider the imagist campaign first. Pound's attempts to rejuvenate imagism or keep it moving forward depended on his control of a workable organ in which to disseminate new productions. To acquire this, he had to have money behind him, and the person who seemed to possess the funds and the artistic interest was the recently departed Amy. On January 8, he told her by letter that he had resigned from *Poetry* because of its questionable standards, but had since rejoined it for lack of anything better; he also informed her that he was publishing her work in the *Egoist*, trying to warm her to that magazine (*SL*, 29). Then on February 2, he let her know that the *Egoist* might be in its dying throes, and he doubted that an American correspondent (namely her) would be able to save it without some deeper involvement (*SL*, 31). Three weeks later, he made a major pitch to her: "Do you want to edit *The Egoist?*" He let her know that Dora Marsden wanted out of the job, and he suggested that Aldington, who was serving as an assistant editor, might be willing to continue to direct the duller matters (*SL*, 32). But Amy demurred; she was extremely cagey with her millions, and she could sense that Mr. Pound always seemed to have something ulterior on his mind in his moments of kindness.

After a meaningless exchange, on March 18 Pound returned to the driving force of his campaign: "Re *The Egoist*. Of course you won't get it for nothing" (*SL*, 33). He outlined all sorts of possible arrangements, even his moving to Boston. Then, of course, there was the preferable suggestion that Miss Lowell might move to London, "the only sane place for any one to live if they've any pretense to letters"—something of a change from his November comment on the town. When this did not bring a swift response, he delivered what he probably felt was a crushing blow on March 23: somebody (that old angel Harriet Shaw

Weaver) had suddenly thrown £250 in the way of the magazine, and any other deal was off (*SL*, 33).

But Pound continued to try to interest Amy in acquiring a quarterly. Later she told Harriet Monroe that he wanted to buy the *Mercure de France*, which would have required a move to Paris. But once again Amy held her ground. She was not about to rush into anything, and although she baldly fibbed by telling Miss Monroe that she did not have the money to purchase the *Mercure*—a mere $5,000—she had her own plot in mind. Instead of being saddled with a magazine, with all of the work that this entails, Miss Lowell wanted to issue an annual that would serve as a showcase for the Imagistes, whom she was proud to be a part of. What did she want to move to Paris for, sinking thousands of dollars into a scheme that might very well go broke? This "poetry business" was, after all, rather risky. One thing was uppermost in her mind: she could not allow Ezra Pound to call the shots for her annual; she did not trust him; she felt that he was tolerating her entirely for her wealth, and so she determined that the annual would have about five or six contributors, with no one in charge. She then informed Pound that she was planning to return to London in July, but she did not spell out the venture that she had in mind. In mid-July he invited her to join his new group of friends at the "BLAST dinner on the 15th" (*SL*, 37), and he added that he would be pleased to attend her own dinner two days later—both of which were to be held at the popular Dieudonné's Restaurant. These two dinners would mark the formalization of Pound's attachment to vorticism, the end of his attachment to imagism, and the beginning of what he would term Amygism—a Calliopean public relations movement on a worldwide basis that would promote free verse in a way that would be both effective and somewhat vulgar.

Returning now to January, we can chronicle the birth of the new movement that was engaging Pound's renewed energies. At the start of 1913, Ezra had come into the orbit of Percy Wyndham Lewis, the rising star of the London art world. We last left Mr. Lewis back in the spring of 1909, when Pound had encountered him unsuccessfully in the Vienna Café in the company of Laurence Binyon and Sturge Moore. They met one more time that year, and the outcome was no better. The two sullen-faced young rebels merely glowered at each other, and when somebody mentioned the mysterious disappearance of a prostitute, Pound casually pointed to his rival and suggested that *he* might have some information about her.

Wyndham Lewis was often distrustful toward strangers. He worked hard at acquiring the sobriquet "Enemy of the People" and achieved it; indeed, one biographer, Jeffrey Meyers, titled his book simply *The*

Enemy, with an explanatory subtitle. Wyndham's father was a wealthy American with mining and railway interests, but Wyndham acquired Canadian citizenship when he was born on his parents' yacht off the coast of Nova Scotia in 1882—the year of Joyce's birth. Wyndham's father, Charles, was a reckless philanderer who finally ran away with the household maid. Wyndham's mother parted company with him during the 1890s back in her native England, where she and her son had immigrated. Still enjoying some paternal support, Wyndham was able to attend the prestigious Rugby School, and even though he was not idyllically happy there, he was nevertheless able to use this experience as a stepping-stone for entering the elite Slade School of Art. There he became a long-term friend of the rising Augustus John, as well as many other artists. He followed John to Paris for a time, where he lived in the Bohemian milieu that he later described so eloquently in his novel *Tarr,* where he is cast in the title role. Lewis also studied for a time in Munich; he was very conscious of German politics and philosophy, as his later hastily written (and finally retracted) book *Hitler* showed when published in 1931.

Returning to England from the continent in December of 1908, Wyndham had met Pound through his growing associations with painters and writers like Sturge Moore and T. E. Hulme. For a while Lewis was fond of Hulme, but when Hulme began to praise his archrival, Epstein, and to cast lascivious eyes on a young female painter, their relationship went bad. Lewis finally dropped the northman completely, seeing the American Pound as the best spokesman for his many activities. Never very rich because of his father's dissipated career, Lewis supported himself the way Pound did, with hack jobs, often living hand-to-mouth. He sold stories to Ford's *English Review* (as was mentioned in chapter 2) or he peddled an increasing number of art works and home crafts at various workshops and exhibition rooms in London. By 1909, Lewis had drawn *The Celibate,* which the vorticist authority Richard Cork described as a "geometric mask, cold and dehumanised" (I, 12). The same sort of description could be given to many of the characters in Lewis's later brutal satires, such as *The Apes of God,* which picked apart the London art world of the twenties. Lewis was interested in depicting objects in a way that exhibited an "insistent diagonal bias of the composition, its steely control and underlying explosiveness" (I, 12). These features would become the dominant characteristics of vorticist art, and even to some degree characteristics of vorticist prose (especially Lewis's prose in *Blast)* and Pound's satiric writings of the period.

By 1912 Lewis had fallen in with the highly influential critic and entrepreneur Roger Fry, who was organizing his second Postimpres-

Wyndham Lewis as he appeared before World War I in his typical Bohemian garb. (Estate of Mrs. G. A. Wyndham Lewis)

sionist Show in October of that year; his first show in 1910–11 had introduced Van Gogh and Gauguin to a shocked England that was living in a fantasyland of still-lifes, watercolors, and Arthuriana. At this time, English artists like Lewis were still very much under the influence of French cubists, with their abstract forms, or they were falling increasingly under the spell of Italian futurists, with their mechanical designs and robotlike figures. Signor Marinetti, the mustachioed and flamboyant Italian ringleader of the futurists, visited London first in 1910 and then regularly from 1912 onward, making a deep impression there on painters—for good and for bad. Some of Lewis's most famous drawings, such as those for a never published edition of Shakespeare's *Timon of Athens*, betray the hard, jagged edges and brittle elegance of futurism at its best. When Madame Strindberg's cabaret was on the drawing board in the spring of 1912, she quite naturally chose the exciting Mr. Lewis to execute most of her interior murals; it was his first important concession, and he threw himself into the project, creating those walls of shocking color and composition. When Frida did not pay him for his work, Lewis robbed her till of £60, but the crafty Austrian got the last laugh, for she absconded with his art when she fled England at the start of the war (Meyers, 37).

In July of 1913, Lewis joined the Omega Workshops (which *Blast No. 2* called "a curtain and pincushion factory") under the direction of Roger Fry. But he soon became disillusioned with Fry's alleged "cheating" (actually, mismanagement would be more accurate) and left. These moves brought Lewis into touch with "the Wolves, the Whaleys, and the Stracheys" (LBB, 280), as he called the Bloomsbury Group that held a stranglehold on the London art world. They included Virginia and Leonard Woolf, the renamed Arthur Waley, Lytton Strachey, Clive and Vanessa Bell, and Duncan Grant. Lewis attacked them all openly, much to his later chagrin, for they were powerful and could create many hindrances for him. Unfortunately, Ezra Pound inherited these animosities—and paid the same penalty. Pound viewed the "Bloomsburies" as an overprivileged, undertalented lot who pretended to be "trendy," but who did not really want to ruffle the safe world of the establishment that they lived in. Neither Pound nor Lewis could tolerate their bored indifference the way Eliot could. Pound described Wyndham's depiction of Timon of Athens' mind as "the fury of intelligence baffled and shut in by circumjacent stupidity"—and he might just as well have been describing his own or Lewis's mind. Pound would eventually escape this world by fleeing from England—much sooner than Lewis would.

When the poet reestablished ties with the painter, Lewis was attracting a group of young artists whom Pound found very amenable. They included Edward Wadsworth, a wealthy young man who lived nearby on Gloucester Walk (and was not related to Pound's American relatives), David Bomberg (who was a favorite of Hulme's for a time), William Roberts, Frederick Etchells, and, more briefly, Christopher Nevinson, who split away from them irrevocably to join forces with the invading Mr. Marinetti. During 1913, Jacob Epstein, whom everyone (including Pound) saw as the crowning genius on the London art scene, also joined forces with the young rebels, as did Gaudier-Brzeska. Pound knew and praised most of these artists in the avenues open to him, especially after Lewis was back in his entourage in 1914.

On January 22 of this year, Hulme, who was always quick to ride the crest of a gathering movement, gave another of his lectures at the Kensington Town Hall that very few could understand because of his mumbling and his intellectual imprecision. Pound called the talk "almost wholly unintelligible," but he agreed in his *Egoist* review of February 16 that Hulme had stumbled onto something when he had said that the "new tendency toward abstraction" was the main road to be followed by modern art; yet Hulme did not feel that it lay with futurism, given that movement's deification of the flux. (Strange to hear a disciple of Bergson turning on his master's underlying principle!) Hulme predicted that the best of modern art would not show the "simple geometrical forms found in archaic art, but ... the more complicated ones associated in our minds with the idea of machinery" (Cork, I, 141). Still, he did not want to link art with futuristic adorations of the machine and with nihilistic attitudes toward the past. Hulme felt very strongly that art had to return to "something organic," and he could see this movement in Epstein's evocative forms, which were close to natural figurations. Actually, in his own thought Hulme was returning to religion, especially to a doctrine of Original Sin that both Pound and Lewis found offensive; neither could buy this sudden flip-flop of the mind that turned against the most exploratory art and seemed to show a dangerous tendency to revert to a lost past (Cork, I, 140). And so Pound stepped forward with his term "vorticism" to fill the void that had to be filled to carry the new movement forward.

The etymology and source of the word "vorticism" have been widely debated. Timothy Materer has linked it to the Neoplatonist philosophy of Plotinus (about whom Pound had written an important poem in *A Lume Spento*). Pound was also probably influenced by the occurrence of a vorticist concept in the Prophetic Books of William Blake, which he and Yeats were reading together at this time. Their mutual friend Allen Upward had also used the term poetically in *The New Word* (195) back in 1907. In a very different way, Eva Hesse has linked it to the cosmic whirlpool that a Yogi pupil must transcend (*Paideuma*, 9, 329). As it is usually defined, a vortex is a swirling descent of ideas and forces from a spiritual Absolute into a world of time. Lewis himself said: "At the heart of the whirlpool is a great silent place where all energy is concentrated." As such, it is mystical in its origin, but pragmatic in its manifestation. Vorticist art would express the mystical element in its search for the geometric designs underlying all things, and it would express its timeliness in its satiric drawings and prose.

As one can see from the preceding definition, the movement was both idealistic and negative. Although many readers saw only the negative side of a publication like *Blast*, the positive aspects were also there—in the artwork. Lewis's earlier *Smiling Woman Ascending a Stair* (1911–12) was patently satiric, as were most of Pound's poems in *Blast No. 1*. From the start, however, it was hard to see any clear-cut links between vorticist literature and vorticist art. Many people, such as Cork, believe that the literature was a mere handmaiden to the art, which did not survive the oncoming war. When Gaudier-Brzeska was quoted in Pound's memorial to him, the sculptor discussed vorticism largely in terms of masses of energy and their interrelationships. When Lewis tried to define the movement in 1915, he said: "By Vorticism we mean (a) *Activity* as opposed to the tasteful *Passivity* of Picasso; (b) SIGNIFICANCE as opposed to the dull or anecdotal character to which the Naturalist is condemned; (c) ESSENTIAL MOVEMENT AND ACTIVITY (such as energy of a mind) as opposed to the imitative cinematography, the fuss and hysterics of the Futurists" (Cork, I, 280). Meyers says simply that, although Pound tried to make a case for Lewis's early writings, "there was no school of Vorticist writers" (63). This view, however, can be disputed, as we shall see.

March was a particularly hectic month in the life of Ezra Pound. Aside from translating more Japanese plays and taking part in numerous art meetings, he was suddenly invited by "Aunt Eva" Fowler to Oxford to meet the Poet Laureate, Robert Bridges, during the first week of that month. One might have thought that Pound would be far too busy to meet fussy old men like Bridges, but the younger poet's insatiable curiosity got the better of him and he went along. Quite unsuspectingly, as he reported to Dorothy in Rome (*EPDS*, 310), he had a delightful time. Later he told Donald Hall that Bridges was one of four people whose advice had greatly influenced his life. When quizzed, Pound said that "Bridges' was the simplest. Bridges' was a warning against homophones. Hardy's was the degree to which he would concentrate on the subject matter, not on the manner. Ford's in general was the *freshness* of language. And Yeats you say was the fourth? Well, Yeats by 1908 had written simple lyrics in which there were no departures from the natural order of words" (*PR 28*, 29; in chapter 19, see the entry for July 8-9, 1922, for a somewhat different version). Pound saw Bridges again later.

All that spring, battles raged between the art factions, with Hulme very much in the center. Back in December of 1913, a wealthy young artist and patron named Kate Lechmere had given Lewis the princely sum of £100 in order to supply an organ to express the new ideas for his group. The first announcement came in the January 8 issue of the *New Age* in the editor's column, mentioning a journal "to provide a platform for the discussion of Cubism." Pound wrote to Joyce later that Lewis was "starting a new Futurist, Cubist, Imagist Quarterly" that was aimed mainly for painters, but would use Pound "to do the poems" (*PJ*, 26).

By March, Miss Lechmere gave Lewis some more money for some space at 38 Great Ormond Street near Queens Square, where he established a meeting place that was known as the Rebel Art Centre. There young rebellious artists could assemble and exhibit their work, and young poets (as well as some older ones like Ford) could also hold forth. Pound hung up a defiant banner at the Centre that proclaimed END OF THE CHRISTIAN ERA, even though Lewis objected to its being too showy and inflammatory.

In the early part of the spring, Kate Lechmere was introduced to Hulme at a triple lecture held at the Kensington Town Hall on the subject of modern poetry. Hulme spoke first, in his usual inaudible manner (as Lechmere herself reported later), and he was followed by Lewis, who was equally inaudible. The evening was saved by Pound, who cut through the mumbo-jumbo with some bell-like readings of modern poems written by himself and others, recited with a distinctly American accent that many Britons felt was a trifle grating on the ear.

In a short time, Miss Lechmere was quietly abandoning the company of Mr. Lewis and gravitating toward Mr. Hulme. Wyndham, who was never a good loser, immediately flew into one of his patented rages. He stormed into Miss Kibblewhite's Venetian palace intent on drawing blood, but the brawny philosopher simply took the frothing Bohemian by his flowing scarf and cape, dragged him out into Frith Street, and hanged him upside down from a railing on Soho Square, as Lewis himself later confessed in a rather oblique manner that salvaged his pride (LBB, 39). By July, the checks from Miss Lechmere had stopped coming, and the Rebel Art Centre quite unceremoniously closed its doors.

Also in March there was an exhibition of modern artwork at the Goupil Gallery in Camden, where Lewis exhibited his well-known drawing *Enemy of the Stars*, as well as *Plan of War*. Gaudier, who was beginning to drop the "Brzeska" part of his name, participated, along with Jacob Epstein; but Henri could not sell anything, and so poverty continued to dog him. In lieu of other work and out of friendship, Henri now decided to sculpt the famous *Hieratic Head of Ezra Pound*. This monumental work involved the biggest piece of stone that Henri had ever worked with—a gift from the model. It was soon finished and was placed in the front garden outside of South Lodge, until it was moved to Pound's daughter's home at Castle Brunnenburg in the

The *Hieratic Head of Ezra Pound*, sculpted by Henri Gaudier-Brzeska, now in the Nasher Collection in the United States. (Photo Hirschl and Adler Gallery, courtesy Patsy R. and Raymond D. Nasher Collection)

Tyrol; it was sold to Raymond D. Nasher of the United States in 1988. Pound appeared dutifully for the sittings and even helped Henri to heat up his antiquated Italian forge to temper his chisels. He was pleased by the intense power of the head, which resembles a phallus from the rear (quite intentionally), but has the archetypal force of an Easter Island head from the front.

Another famous model for Henri at this time was the vivacious Nina Hamnett (1890–1956), who had studied art in London and Dublin, and who met the Frenchman in 1913 at the Albert Hall exhibition. Having no money for models, Henri asked the emancipated girl if she would pose for him in the nude. She did indeed, and his three torsos of her (one of which was bought by Olivia Shakespear) appeared. Nina's autobiography, appropriately titled *Laughing Torso*, tells of the fun she had with Henri (who also posed for her) and with Ezra, to whom he soon introduced her. Called "The Queen of Bohemia" by her biographer Denise Hooker, Nina was living the pre-1920s life of the unshackled young lady; besides Henri, she numbered among her lovers Amedeo Modigliani, whom she met in Paris this year, and later Roger Fry and numerous other artists, especially during the twenties in France. Pound put her and Henri together in a brilliant passage in Canto 107, along with Confucius, a Neoplatonic philosopher, a lawgiver, and a scientist—all of whom defended the natural impulse against the unnatural thrust of much Christian mysticism during the Middle Ages:

> So that Dante's view is quite natural:
>   this light
>   as a river
> in Kung; in Ocellus, Coke, Agassiz
>   ῥεῖ, the flowing
>   this persistent awareness
> Three Ninas from Gaudier,
>   Their mania is a lusting for farness
>   Blind to the olive leaf,
>   not seeing the oak's veins.
>   Wheat was in bread in the old days.
> . . . .
>   Alan Upward's seal showed Sitalkas.
>   (762)

Meanwhile, much of Pound's prime energy was devoted during this spring to his oncoming marriage. Before that occurred, he abandoned his too-small quarters at 10 Church Walk, which were grabbed by

John Cournos, and moved to an oddly shaped two-room apartment not far away at 5 Holland Place Chambers, where the Aldingtons were already living. The small front room, which was used to receive guests and to hold informal readings, had an angular far wall, while the darker back room was used by Ezra for cooking, since Dorothy firmly declined to stoop to that female occupation until she was forced to during World War II. Hilda describes her shock on seeing that her unfaithful lover, who had finally espoused her strongest rival, had the audacity to move in across the hall from her:

> Wyndham Lewis used to come to our little flat in Kensington to borrow Richard Aldington's razor. This annoyed Richard. Ezra and Dorothy had a slightly larger flat across the narrow hall. I found the door open one day before they were married, and Ezra there. "What—what are you doing?" I asked. He said he was looking for a place where he could fence with Yeats. I was rather taken aback when they actually moved in. It was so near. But we went soon after to Hampstead, to a larger flat that a friend had found us. (*Torment*, 5)

In a letter written all of ten years after the marriage, Hilda still showed the jealousy that she felt when she heard the final news of the event. Writing in 1924 to Viola Baxter Jordan from Utica, now living in New Jersey, she said:

> Yes, Ez is "married" but there seems to be a pretty general concensus [*sic*] of opinion that Mrs. E has not been "awakened" ... She is very English and "cold" and I personally like her although she is unbearably critical and never has been known to make a warm friend with a man or woman. She loathes (she says) children! However that may be a little pose. She is a bit addictive to little mannerisms. I don't think she can be poignantly sensitive or she would never have stuck Ezra. (Guest, 64)

Hilda's feeling of being alienated from her old lover was further intensified by all of this mystifying new vorticist activity. Like Richard and others, she soon guessed that Ezra was perhaps laying them aside. As a result, when Amy Lowell reappeared, Hilda was ripe for exploitation. In speaking of her future, Hilda said in *End to Torment*:

5 Holland Place Chambers. The rooms on the left had angular walls, and so Pound had to design some imaginative furniture, especially a triangular typing table. (Kenneth Alcock)

> I did not see him at the time of my first confinement, 1915. I lost that child. The second was four years later, 1919. He hurtles himself into the decorous St. Faith's Nursing Home, in Ealing, near London.... He seemed to beat with the ebony stick like a baton.... "But," he said, "my only real criticism is that this is not my child." (7–8)

She then chronicles the other times when she saw him later in her life:

> This Canto IV is listed alone as from the Ovid Press, London, 1919. That is the year that Ezra came to St. Faith's Ealing, London, and stormed into my room. . . . Perhaps there was passion and regret "that this is not my child. . . ." I did see Ezra in Paris, once, twice (perhaps three times) in those intermediate years. I did see him and for the last time in London, after Mrs. Shakespear's death—was it about the time of *The Fifth Decad of Cantos*, 1937? (45)

This was the beginning of a long hiatus in their friendship, which was only renewed years later when they were both confined in different ways.

As for the wedding itself, despite the announcement of a reception to be held at Brunswick Gardens on April 18, it was held two days later, on Monday, April 20, shortly after 10 a.m. in the church of the endless bells, St. Mary Abbots (PC 326). There were very few in attendance, since Pound had tried desperately in his correspondence with Mr. Shakespear to opt for a civil ceremony instead. But old Henry Hope wanted a church wedding for his daughter, and he won the argument (*EPDS*, 307–8). It is hard to know why Mr. Shakespear suddenly relented and permitted the marriage, since Pound's financial position had not noticeably improved, but apparently the old lawyer saw that they were at a stalemate: his twenty-seven-year-old daughter was not getting any younger, and if she did not marry Ezra Pound, she was probably not going to marry anyone at all. There was also the pressure from Olivia.

There is no question about the great love felt on Dorothy's side and her vows to be faithful. But on Ezra's side, as we already know, there was every room to doubt that he would suddenly be faithful to any woman alone. He had known Dorothy for five years, and all during that time, he had dated other women; and his fervent affair with Mrs. Scratton was still going on. Furthermore, as he told Ingrid Davies in the 1950s from St. Elizabeth's, he was just entering the great period of his sexual activity in London, when men were being called away to the front in the oncoming days of the war. In short, the marriage was never, even from the start, a standard Edwardian affair. In his letters to Mr. Shakespear arranging the event, Ezra vented some of his spleen against bourgeois notions of Christian matrimony, but old Henry Hope seems to have dismissed this lightly as simply more of a show of a poet's idiosyncrasy. Pound wanted a "modern marriage," like that between Hilda and Richard, in which each partner was free to go as he or she chose. But as Hilda later told Viola, Dorothy was not really "awakened." Even years later Dorothy spoke of the "creature" she had married in a non-pejorative way that simply revealed a kind of mystification in the face of genius and eccentricity.

In any case, on April 20 the couple took their vows. Dorothy was dressed in a smart coat-and-skirt (no trousseau) and Ezra glowered in a crumpled but "respectable" suit. Only half-a-dozen observers were present: Dorothy's relatives, not Ezra's friends (probably not even Yeats). Pound's parents could not attend, but they would visit the newlyweds that summer. The primary witnesses were Mr. Shakespear and Dorothy's uncle, H. T. Tucker, a brother of Olivia. Wedding gifts included some fancy chairs from Violet and Ford; a necklace and some coral from Isabel and Homer; two early Picasso circus drawings (now at the Hamilton Art Museum) from Mr. and Mrs. Shakespear, along with some communally given money that went to buy the multi-volumed Morrison Chinese dictionary that Pound already needed and a lovely piece of Chinese jade; when Dorothy tired of the latter, she sold it to jade-loving Jepson and bought a finely carved horse. Yeats, who had been lecturing in America, gave them some money which Ezra used to commission a clavichord from Arnold Dolmetsch, and this noble instrument ("the size of a suitcase," Pound later told Quinn) became one of the prized items in their apartment. When Yeats refused an award of £40 from *Poetry* and had most of it diverted to Ezra, the poet bought the already mentioned typewriter, which helped him write ever more articles, and some artwork from Gaudier.

Dorothy and Ezra were going to go to Spain in the fall for a honeymoon, but the war canceled that plan. In the interim, they went off to Stone Cottage, where he corrected some proofs for *Blast No. 1*, which would appear in two months, and worked on the Noh plays. Wilfrid Scawen Blunt, clad in Arab robes, received them in his nearby place and toasted their marriage with champagne. Pound's older male friends seemed happy about the mating, but not, of course, his younger female companions.

Meanwhile, the social scene was more than busy. There was constant afternoon tennis at South Lodge, where Ezra was clearly the champion of Kensington. The nervous Violet was continually patroling the sidelines, telling anyone who would bother to listen that Brigit Patmore was trying to take her lover away from her. Brigit had given Ford an iron cross as a present, and Violet complained that this object of their "illicit" love dangled tantalizingly in her face while she and Ford were making love. Although both Ford and Brigit fervently denied that they were doing anything at all, years later Ford would state quite openly in America that he was the true father of Brigit's son, Derek—something that Derek also vehemently denied. Whatever the truth was, Ford through his contacts with "the young" was finding numerous opportunities to meet attractive and unescorted young women, usually with artistic bents, at Madame Strindberg's place with its easy morality or at the now famous Café Royale or the Eiffel Tower. The last-mentioned haunt of the vorticists was a place that Ford, who fancied himself a gourmet extraordinaire, professed to loathe because of its cheap Mitteleuropa fare; but in actuality, he went there often and ate Mr. Stulik's offerings with relish, increasing his already overdeveloped weight and intensifying Pound's and Lewis's cries of "fattie."

This was a critical period in Ford's life. The scandal with Violet had died down, and he was now engaged in writing his masterpiece, *The Good Soldier*, but he still did not feel at home either with imagism or the new "fad." Although Pound did his best to try to bill Ford as the elder statesman of *les jeunes*, the usurping Mr. Lewis did everything he could to make the blond giant uncomfortable. Ford tried to think of himself like the Ernest Jessop in his later novel, *The Marsden Case* (1923): he was "everyone's Dutch uncle in those days; that, I suppose, is why I have gathered no moss" (115). But in *Return to Yesterday* (1931), he more clearly voiced his insecurity: "Those young people had done their best to make a man of me. They had dragged me around to conspiracies, night-clubs, lectures where Marinetti howled and made noises like machine-guns" (419). Finally, a certain D.Z. (who is obviously Lewis) takes him aside and shouts:

> "*Tu sais, tu es foûtu! Foûtu!* Finished! Exploded! Done for! Blasted, in fact. Your generation has gone. What is the sense of you and Conrad and Impressionism? You stand for Impressionism. It is finished. *Foûtu*. Blasted too! ... This is the day of Cubism, Futurism, Vorticism. What people want is me, not you. They want to see me. A vortex. To liven them up. . . . Blast all the rest." (418)

It was difficult for the older man to tolerate such antics. Eventually Ford felt that Pound, Lewis and Company was an autocratic association that was trying to control the arts in a totalitarian way. That is why, when Miss Lowell appeared that summer with her talk about democracy, Ford veered for a time in her direction.

The intellectual war reached its peak when the much-awaited *Blast No. 1* appeared on July 2 (its dateline read June 20). It was issued by John Lane and printed by the obscure house of Leveridge and Company after some bribery, since no conservative printer would touch it. Measuring an oversized 12 x 9½ inches, the magazine was striking for its brazen pink cover ("this puce monster," Lewis called it), with the title descending from left to right in diagonal black letters. Lewis said that it was "not unlike a telephone book" (LBB, 41). Inside, there were all sorts of typefaces screeching at the reader, pronouncing blessings and curses. Blessings went to Madame Strindberg, James Joyce, Kate Lechmere (the sponsor), and Brigit Patmore, whom everyone loved except Violet Hunt. Those blasted were, among others, Bergson with his flux; Tagore, with his now tiresome Indian stances; the pastor of St. Mary Abbots with his infernal bells; the inefficient Post Office, and cod liver oil. Most of the magazine was taken up by Lewis's bold prose, but it also included the opening pages of Ford's *Good Soldier*, titled "The Saddest Story," and a short story by Rebecca West called "Indissoluble Matrimony."

Twelve of Pound's minor poems were present, including one that was almost banned: "Fratres Minores," which begins: "With minds still hovering above their testicles" and ends with talk about twitchings toward Nirvana (*Pers.*, 148). To avoid banning, the printer blacked out the offensive lines, but in such a way that a reader could decipher them. Another of Pound's twelve poems was "Salutation the Third," which tried to capture some of the energy of the vortex that was missing elsewhere, but which sounded like the satire of any time or place:

Let us deride the smugness of "The Times":
GUFFAW!
    So much for the gagged reviewers,
It will pay them when the worms are wriggling in their vitals.
                                (*Pers.*, 145)

As the hypercritical Mr. Lewis would say later in his influential *Time and Western Man* (1928), what impressed most of his artist friends about Pound was "that his fire-eating propagandist utterances were not accompanied by any very experimental efforts in his particular medium" (39). Then, with characteristic egotism, Lewis branded Pound unforgettably as a "revolutionary simpleton," and tried to cull all of the vorticist glory for himself. But in many ways, Lewis was right; Pound's attempts to join the bandwagon were uninspired and scarcely revolutionary.

Art in the magazine was represented by the drawings of Wadsworth, Epstein, Gaudier, Etchells, Hamilton, Lewis, and Roberts. A general manifesto, written by Lewis, was signed by Richard Aldington (who was along for a brief ride), Gaudier, Roberts, and eight others, including Helen Saunders and Jessie Dismorr. Richard Cork (I, 246) believes that the only true supporters of the magazine were Wadsworth, Pound, Lewis, and Gaudier—as well as the wealthy and and artistic Saunders and Dismorr, who were also sexually attracted to Wyndham. This was hardly the nucleus for a united front for the future.

Although Pound and Lewis probably expected to stir up a storm of controversy and incidentally earn a lot of money, they achieved only the first intention. *Blast* was received by Georgian England like a newborn viper. Most of the critics tended to treat it with disdain, calling it the work of sophomoric iconoclasts who were attacking everything sacred from Christianity to the King: "A VORTICIST KING! WHY NOT!" When the war broke out, lines like the following did not seem quite so clever: "there is nothing Chauvinistic or picturesquely patriotic about our contentions." And yet there was a caché value in notoriety. Lewis was invited to meet Prime Minister Asquith, and he was suddenly asked into the drawing rooms of the wealthy and noble, like Lady Maud Cunard and Lady Ottoline Morrell, who were both extremely sympathetic toward artists. During this period, Lady Maud's daughter, Nancy, was beginning to make her debut into high society, and it was through artists like Wyndham Lewis that she saw another side of London life. Ezra Pound would meet her at tea at her mother's place in 1915 and in 1916 when Maud was turning her drawing room into a theater for Yeats's plays. In short, for this brief season, Lewis loomed high as the King of Soho.

Years later in 1962, the vorticist William Roberts painted a charmingly nostalgic picture of the period which he titled *Vorticists at the Restaurant de la Tour Eiffel: Spring 1915*, but the date was inaccurate because *Blast No. 1* appears on the table in the center of the painting. Lewis dominates the middle of the composition, clad in a heavy overcoat, with scarf and sombrero, and gazing leftward with a dangerous glint in the eye. On his right are C. J. Hamilton, Pound, and Roberts himself, with Etchells and Wadsworth on his left. On the viewer's left in the rear, the young ladies Saunders and Dismorr are entering through a door. The owner of the place, Rudolph Stulik of Austria, smiles with Viennese grace and charm as he shows the group his latest freshly baked *torte* on the far right. A bald waiter, whose name was Joe, is bringing in some champagne to celebrate the occasion.

The Tour Eiffel was beloved by vorticists for its fine food and cheap prices (despite Ford's disparagements). It was just next door to Lewis's apartment for a time at 1 Percy Street, and Herr Stulik was known to rent out rooms to strays like Nancy Cunard on the occasions when she could not find quarters elsewhere. Both the Tour Eiffel and the Café Royal were the favorite haunts of the younger members of the art world—and of Ezra Pound.

Although fame (or infamy) was now lavished on Wyndham Lewis, money was not. Still, this did not in any way diminish his bravado. The same William Roberts in an article of 1957 in *The Listener* described him as having "an assurance and provocative swagger in his bearing . . . [He was a] tall form in heavy overcoat and grey sombrero, with scarf flung flamboyantly over one shoulder, striding along, the broad shoulders tilted slightly, like a boxer advancing to meet an opponent. In a sense, acquaintanceship with Wyndham Lewis was like a contest, in which you came out of your corner fighting—and the best man won" (470). The always crabbed John Gould Fletcher remembered him, when Fletcher was turning down an offer to contribute money to the Rebel Art Centre, as "a grim-jawed, black-haired, and beetle-browed individual . . . disposed to be surly and noncommunicative" (136). Yet T. S. Eliot, who was soon to enter the scene and become a close friend of Wyndham, always defended the difficult Lewis as a highly strung, nervous man who was simply oversensitive to slights. Eliot and Pound were both faithful to Lewis during their lives, watching the alienated man sink helplessly into blindness and die in poverty and undeserved lack of recognition on March 7, 1957.

In many ways, Pound and Lewis were perfect "Brothers Minor"—perhaps a little too perfect for either's good. There is no doubt that they created more trouble for themselves than was absolutely necessary. Lewis says in *Blasting and Bombardiering* that Pound had no luck with the English people: "It was not his fault entirely: but on their side they felt that this was a bogus personage and they had no inducement to be 'taken in' by this tiresome and flourishing, pretentious, foreign aspirant to poetic eminence. . . . To accept this vulgar clown *as a poet!*—that was too much to ask" (281). Yet Lewis, who excelled in criticizing others, might have said the very same things about himself as an artist, since he was a foreigner too. On the other hand, in his final biography, *Rude Assignment* (1950), Lewis praised Pound extravagantly for getting Joyce published, editing Eliot, and determining the whole course of modern poetry (131–32), just as he had done earlier on many occasions.

Meyers' *The Enemy* frankly points up the artist's many foibles, but in a sympathetic way. Like Cork, Meyers believes that vorticism was a rather short-lived movement, not extending much beyond 1919, and in literature scarcely ever getting off the ground. Yet this depends on how one defines vorticism. If one sees the movement as part of a greater drift toward modern art, then it is extremely important, for everyone knows that it was the vorticists and not the traditional representationalists who finally won the struggle. Similarly, in terms of literature, if one tries to align Pound with Lewis's drawings or the

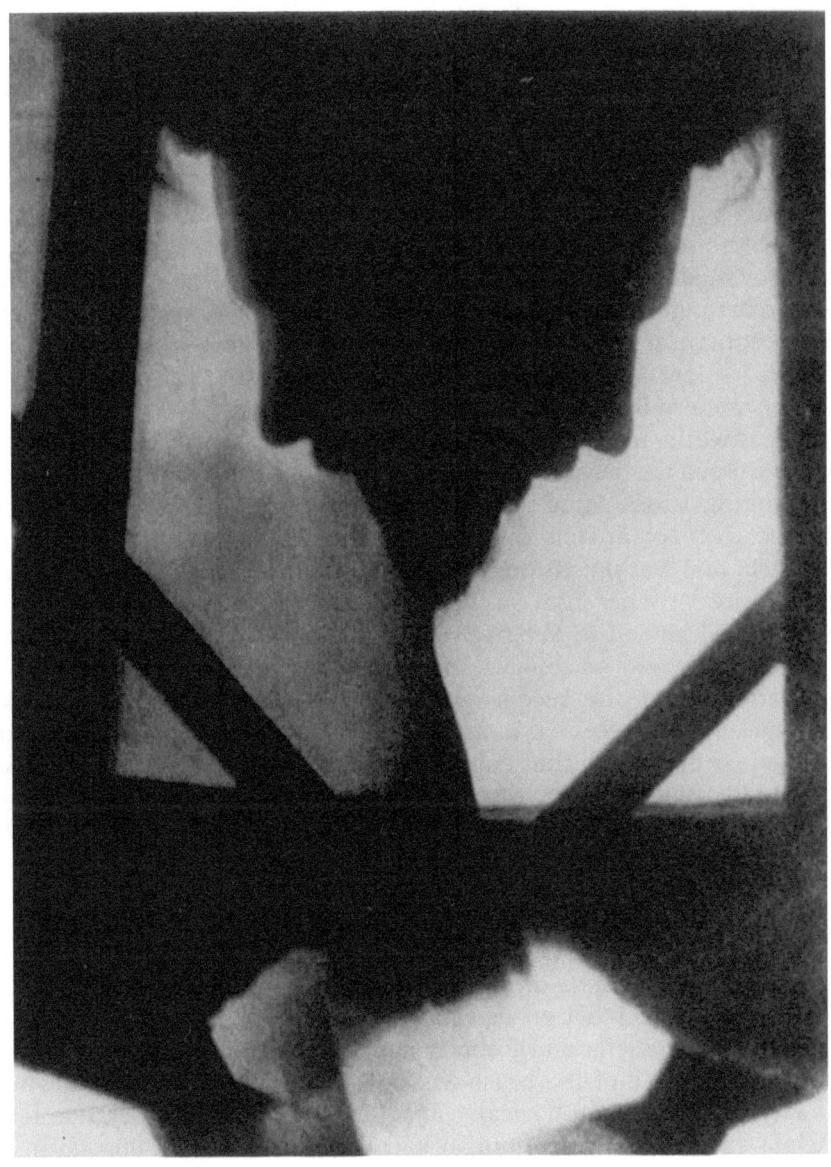

A vortograph with Pound as the subject, done in collaboration with the co-inventor of the process, the American photographer Alvin Langdon Coburn. (International Museum of Photography, George Eastman House, Rochester, New York)

cubists or the futurists, there are not very many features in common, but if one sees that Pound did to literature what the vorticists and others were doing to the visual arts (opening them up, freeing them of pointless strictures), then Pound's affiliation is extremely important. The recent studies of Timothy Materer and Reed Way Dasenbrock have expanded the frame of reference for vorticism in a meaningful way, and this in turn makes Pound's contribution far more than just that of a propagandist. The *Cantos* are the work of a man who has an eye for modern art (Donald Davies' *Poet as Sculptor*); with their radical rearrangements of time and space, Pound's *Cantos* move in an atmosphere of cubism, of montages and collages—not in the staid world of late Victorian painting that accompanies a great deal of other modern literature.

Meanwhile, in July, as *Blast* appeared, so did Amy. She had intrepidly crossed the ocean while the Archduke Franz Ferdinand of Austria was being assassinated with his wife in a remote city, but that did not bother her—or anyone else in her circle. That was the business of Austria and Serbia. Riding away from the ship in her Pierce Arrow limousine with her maroon-liveried chauffeur and footman, she again ensconced herself in her five-room suite atop the Berkeley, with its panoramic view. As soon as she reached town, she was clued in by Fletcher about the recent outrageous conduct of Pound and his friends. Nobody seemed to know quite what they were up to, but it was clear now to all that Pound was bored with imagism and probably ready to give up the throne. This news tickled Amy's heart, since she could see that her mission might resolve itself with a minimum of work on her part.

First of all, Amy reingratiated herself with the Aldingtons, even though Hilda was constantly "indisposed"—still not having recovered from the shock of Ezra's wedding. Then on July 15, Amy appeared at the famous dinner at Dieudonné's on Ryder Street, with only the foggiest notion of what was going on. She did not know artists like Etchells and Roberts and Wadsworth, and she certainly did not approve of the brash Mr. Lewis, who went around blowing his own horn (metaphorically and literally), blessing a chosen few while cursing others. She also had the misfortune to engage in a rather violent tiff with Ford Madox Ford (whom she was trying to woo), but this was soon smoothed over. The one person whom she met there who intrigued her was the tall, lean sculptor with the unpronounceable name. Pound records the fact that his French friend found the voluminous body of the American millionairess equally fascinating:

> Well, Campari is gone since that day
> with Dieudonné and with Voisin
> and Gaudier's eye on the telluric mass of Miss Lowell
> (Canto 77/469)

To Amy, most of this vorticist talk was sheer nonsense, but she cleverly bided her time, waiting for her own party two nights later, when she would be rid of these unwashed artists (neither Jacob Epstein nor Henri was very careful about bathing) and would then be ready to solidify her camp.

Thirteen people assembled on that fateful night of July 17 as Amy arranged her belated celebration of *Des Imagistes*. Since the main table, which was occupied at one end by Amy and at the other by Ezra, could only accommodate eleven diners, two sat off to the side. The other guests included Dorothy, Richard Aldington, John Cournos (who did not fully approve of this aggressive woman who liked to throw her money around [271]), Gaudier, Ford, Flint, Allen Upward, and Miss Lowell's companion, Ada Dwyer Russell (whose close relationship to Amy everyone studiously ignored); there was also John Gould Fletcher, whose memoir provides us with the most reliable chronicle, as well as Violet and Hilda (148ff.).

The dinner itself was an elaborate affair that passed from Norwegian hors-d'oeuvres and lobster bisque to filets of sole and lamb with peas and beans, and ended with various "bombes" and other desserts, along with coffee, tea, and liqueurs. It was enough to satisfy even Amy's appetite—as well as that of "fat Ford" and Ezra (corpulent from his sedentary honeymoon) and John Cournos, a stranger to Fletcher, who kept staring at Cournos' "melancholy, troubled, Russian Jewish face and at the avidity with which he ate his food." After the meal, Amy decided that it was time for speeches, and in a rather schoolmarmish manner, she began calling on people to stand up and say what imagism meant to them. Her first choice was unfortunate—Ford, with whom she had recently quarreled. He made her unhappy by declaring from the start that he wasn't at all sure what the term meant. His own work that had been labeled imagist all derived from the traditional Heine and Browning, and he suspected that the only two real imagists at the table were the Aldingtons—and indeed, at that point, he may have been right.

Although this was an inauspicious beginning for Amy, Ezra was "hugely enjoying himself," according to Fletcher (149). Then Amy asked Allen Upward to speak. Fletcher describes this "obscure barrister" as wearing a pince-nez and a rose in his lapel; he was "a short, stocky figure, with ruddy complexion, iron-gray beard, and hair also turning gray." Upward went along with Ford in declaring his own confusion about the meaning of the abstraction. He said that anything he had ever written that had been labeled "imagist" had stemmed from the Chinese—which delighted the Fenollosa-oriented Pound even more. Upward then told Miss Lowell that if she persevered in trying to be an imagist, she might eventually win an accolade from Ezra, which was the final stamp of approval. This caused laughter among the guests, including Amy, who could read it as a repudiation of Pound's dictatorial methods. But Upward would add more mischief later.

The next speaker, Aldington, bumbled, in his usual awkward manner, into a quarrel with Gaudier. He started off by defining imagism as an outgrowth of Hellenism (which was appropriate for him and his wife), but in so doing he proceeded to annoy the Frenchman, with whom he had argued constantly about the merits of Greek art. Defending himself in broken but brilliant English, Gaudier argued fervently back—but the debate, which was clearly one of a series, soon began to bore everyone else. At this point, Ezra quietly sneaked out a side door and "found" a tub; lugging this back into the room, he summarily dumped it onto the middle of the table, announcing that from this day on, the Imagists were dead, superseded by the Nagistes (Swimmers). This was an elaborate joke aimed at Amy's sole contribution to the anthology, "In a Garden," which ended with the line "Night, and the water, and you in your whiteness, bathing." Acting as if on cue, Upward leaped up and just happened to have a parody of the poem, which he read aloud. Everyone was roaring with laughter—except Amy, who sat there grimly thinking. Later, she regained her spirits, and the evening ended with tolerably good cheer.

Actually, at this point, Pound recognized that imagism was something that he had fathered, promoted, and was now willing to pass on to others. When Amy came to him a few days later with her grand project for the annual-without-an-editor, he saw through her scheme and immediately declined to take part. He also informed her that he regarded the word "imagism" as his own, and he did not appreciate her attempt to usurp it. He suggested that she use a title like *Vers Libre* or *Free Verse* or something to that effect for her own publication. Later she compromised by using *Some Imagist Poets* for the anthologies she would back. The first would include the work of six people besides herself: Flint, Ford, the Aldingtons, Fletcher and—soon to join them—D. H. Lawrence, who was now back in town. In fact, on the night before England declared war, Amy gave another party for her new inner circle atop the Berkeley, and as the curtains billowed in the listless August breeze, she and her guests watched Lawrence bound into the room, bragging that he had just talked with Edward Marsh, the secretary of Churchill at the Admiralty, and that warfare would begin on the morrow. Strangely enough, nobody seemed to be moved. They were all too engrossed in their private war, which they seemed to be winning, since the dictatorial Mr. Pound had been forced to withdraw from the field of combat. Amy was riding high; imagism had become Amygism, and she would promote it to the hilt. The "hippopoetess," as Pound now dubbed her, was triumphant. She had taken the laurels of the Conquest of London away from him.

As for Pound, he had long foreseen that an era was ending. His days of glory were temporarily gone. The grim shadow of desolation that was stalking them all would strike him harder than most, even though (or perhaps because) he would not be involved directly in the fray. Soon most of his friends would be going off to war, but already he felt deserted. The Aldingtons had sided with Amy and soon moved away to Hampstead; he would never feel quite the same with either. When Pound had first met Richard Aldington, he had told the young man that he really felt that he had nothing to teach him, and although Richard took this as a supreme compliment, it could now have a direr meaning. Still, Richard would hover around Ezra, loath to abandon him. Hilda, as we know, would remain loyal but distant, engrossed in her many future affairs with various men and women. Upward would stand by him, and Ford would return to the fold, but Cournos would soon disappear to Hampstead too, where he would be involved in a secret affair with the Dryad and then fade away from Pound's ken. Fletcher had never been a friend; he would alternate back and forth between America and England, deeply engrossed in Amy's campaign to bring imagism to the masses, and he would finally retire (with a Pulitzer Prize) to his native state, where he would pen its epic, *Arkansas*. When Norman Holmes Pearson told Fletcher in the 1930s that Pound had always stood stalwartly by him, Fletcher said that he was indeed sorry for the way that he had been so ungrateful to the man who had helped him get his start.

Flint likewise would write his graceless account of imagism in 1915, in which he would try to denigrate Pound and to praise Hulme to the skies—but he was on his way to obscurity too. Always blaming his Cockney wife for his inability to succeed, Flint showed his own tendency to self-destroy by marrying her sister when she finally died. Violet Hunt (who would soon lose Fordie, first to war and then to other amours) would always stand firmly by Ezra; she was there almost from the start, and would remain a friend to her death in 1942.

Out of that dinner party at Dieudonné's, the best and truest friend was Dorothy. She would say years later that if the war had not suddenly appeared at this moment, Ezra and she would probably have left London for Paris. But the vortex of evil had descended, and the blasts were now suddenly very real.

II

WAR, DISILLUSION, AND DEPARTURE

12

The Delights of Mr. Eliot /
The Horrors of War
(September 1914–June 1915)

The pernicious effects of the war were not immediately apparent to most Britons. The majority of Pound's friends would drift away slowly, and some, such as Wyndham Lewis, were not in positions of danger for at least two more years. The first to go away was Henri Gaudier, as he now called himself, who enlisted in the French Army after several obstacles. Technically, Henri was a deserter because he had not enrolled in the regular French conscription, and he had not kept his passport current. In August he went to the French Embassy and finally persuaded them to issue him a new passport, and then he took off for the continent. But the French authorities on the other side of the Channel rejected his passport, called him a deserter, and threw him into a makeshift jail outside of Calais. Only after a squeeze through a narrow window and a dash across several meadows did he finally work his way back to the Channel and England, where he collapsed in his beloved Sophie's arms. Sophie had feared all along that if Henri went to war, he would be killed. They had both dreamed about his death: his life would end with a bullet entering his skull. But there seemed to be no way of escaping fate. Instead of staying in England, Henri responded to some impassioned letters from authorities in his hometown, urging him to enlist

12 The Delights of Mr. Eliot/The Horrors of War

for the sake of La Patrie; and so he finagled another passport in early September which was accepted as valid, and off he went for a second time—to his death in June.

Suddenly a war that seemed to be tucked away in Bosnia or Hercegovinia or some other unlikely place had moved its way to the English doorstep. The Germans swept in a broad pincer movement through Belgium toward the coast, and elsewhere they advanced southward toward Paris. Then, for some inexplicable reason, they decided not to attack the vulnerable capital, but withdrew northward, where they bedded in and eventually were stalled. Suddenly what looked like a highly mobilized war became a deadly game of trench warfare, and finally a stalemate. All chivalry vanished as battlefields became simply dusty or muddy hellholes where grimy men exchanged mutual insults, played dirty tricks on one another, and lived in a constant state of danger and fear. Henri's letters from the front, which were later printed in Pound's memoir to him, tell the story simply and poignantly.

Meanwhile, life in London also became dangerous as the city was subjected to zeppelin air raids. As soldiers trudged off to the front, the city took on a semi-deserted look, with blackouts, home-defense drills, and inquisitions of aliens. Pound, being American, was not bothered, but anyone with a German name or appearance was suspect, and many often innocent people were subjected to humiliations or assaults:

so in Holland Park they rolled out to beat up Mr Leber
(restaurantier) to Monsieur Dulac's disgust
and a navvy rolls up to me in Church St. (Kensington End) with:
        Yurra Jurrmun!
To which I replied: I am *not*.
"Well yurr szum kind ov a furriner."

(80/503)

As the danger intensified, suddenly around September 22 a new arrival brightened the general depression. An interesting young American appeared for tea in the triangular room on Holland Place with Dorothy and Ezra, who was wearing his usual velveteen jacket and corduroy pants, as the conservatively dressed Eliot would vividly recall. The visitor's name was Thomas Stearns Eliot (1888–1965). He had been born in St. Louis three years after Ezra to a wealthy family of ancient pedigree (as ancient as the Wadsworths and the Westons), had been educated at Harvard (an Ivy League school like Penn), and knew quite a bit about people like Dante Alighieri and even the

French symbolists. Needless to say, there were grounds for friendship, and despite Eliot's inherent shyness, he soon would become one of the stalwart "Men of 1914," as Wyndham Lewis called them, joining Lewis, Pound, and Joyce in the vanguard of the arts.

Eliot had come to London with a Sheldon Traveling Fellowship from Harvard that would enable him to study philosophy at Merton College, Oxford. He had wandered about Europe earlier, and was planning to take a summer-session course in philosophy at the University of Marburg in Germany when war suddenly broke out and it was obviously imperative for him to leave that land that he found much more delightful than he had imagined. Arriving in London around August 22, he felt rather displaced, since he had always liked the French and their culture better than that of his own ancestors. However, soon he would be more English than the English themselves. In fact, Wyndham Lewis would ask the often-quoted question why it was necessary for Eliot to go around behaving as if he were Westminster Abbey in disguise.

It was during this initial period of displacement that Eliot called on Pound, through the introduction of Conrad Aiken, a young poet from Savannah who had known Eliot while they were studying together at Harvard and working for the literary *Advocate*. Aiken, who had been living in London this summer, had already met Pound, who had asked him for the names of bright young poets in America, and the Southerner had offered the name of Eliot. Indeed Aiken had tried to interest Harold Monro in Eliot's "Love Song of J. Alfred Prufrock," but the bookstore owner had been shocked by the poem's "incoherence." Eliot picked up on Aiken's lead and appeared in Kensington around mid-September, while Aiken soon vanished from England and Pound's world because of his adulation of native American verse; in 1952 in his autobiographical *Ushant*, Aiken would refer to Pound pejoratively as "Rabbi Ben Ezra"—though he was not the first to use this name, as readers of Robert Browning are aware.

From the start, Pound told Donald Hall in their *Paris Review* interview, he and Eliot had differences: T.S. was shy and pedantic, whereas Ezra was outspoken and far-ranging. But Pound was not put off by Eliot's Prufrock façade; he detected warmth beneath the waistcoat, just as Lewis perceived the "jokester-trickster" heart beneath the polite and proper exterior: "A sleek, tall, attractive transatlantic apparition—with a sort of Gioconda smile" (LBB, 283).

During the thirties, Pound would tease "Tom," as he always called him, about his religious conversion, using the term "the Reverend Eliot" as a form of address, or even "Possum," implying a certain amount of hypocrisy. But at Eliot's funeral in London in 1965, an aged

"The Reverend Eliot" as Wyndham Lewis rendered him.
(Estate of Mrs. G. A. Wyndham Lewis)

Ezra, accompanied by Olga Rudge, paid his friend the supreme compliment that he would grant to no one else: "His was the true Dantescan voice" (*SP*, 464). At that time he also issued the remark that best catches the spirit of their friendship: "Who is there now for me to share a joke with?" (*SP*, 464). For despite their rivalry and moments of misunderstanding, there was a jovial humor that supported their friendship, and they were usually very loyal to each other. Virginia Woolf, who detested Pound, would wonder at this loyalty, since Eliot (unlike Pound and Lewis) was tactful enough to cultivate her and the other "Bloomsburies" who dominated the London world. Needless to say, when Pound was in grave trouble with his native land after World War II and Eliot was riding high as a respected poet and major figure in publishing with Faber and Faber, the established Eliot tried to do all that he could for his vulnerable friend.

Eliot had known Pound's poems from his Harvard days, as early as 1910 when he was writing "Prufrock," but he had not liked them, and even now he told Aiken that he found Pound's work "well-meaning but touchingly incompetent" (*TSEL*, 59). But after that first encounter, Eliot warmed to Pound the poet as well as to Pound the friend. He could see that Ezra, now famous for his generosity, was sincerely interested in helping novices. After "Tom" left his flat, Ezra dashed off a note to Harriet Monroe, telling her that a new talent had surfaced. Then on September 30, a week after the first encounter when Eliot had given him some work to read, Ezra exclaimed: "I was jolly well right about Eliot. He has sent in the best poem I have yet had or seen from an American. PRAY GOD IT BE NOT A SINGLE AND UNIQUE SUCCESS. . . . He is the only American I know of who has made what I can call adequate preparation for writing. He has actually trained himself *and* modernized himself *on his own*" (*SL*, 40). Despite this enthusiasm, Miss Monroe was difficult. Since T.S. was an American, she expected the "Boom-a-lays" of Vachel Lindsay or the stockyards of Carl Sandburg; when she found that Eliot's poetry was set in fancy drawing rooms with upper-class people speaking, she was disappointed. This response then aroused further cries of exasperation from the promoter (*SL*, 44–45), for Pound was not about to give up. After months of prodding (April 10, 1915: '*Do* get on with that Eliot"), she finally gave in. "Prufrock" appeared in the June issue of *Poetry* that year, and other work by Eliot would appear in Lewis's *Blast No. 2* and Alfred Kreymborg's *Others*.

After the September meeting, Eliot went over to Merton College, Oxford, to read philosophy, but the two poets were in constant communication. Pound kept the novice abreast of his plans in promoting him, often in impassioned letters, while Eliot, who had had some schooling in Buddhism, replied in a calmer, more guarded manner. In this sense, Eliot's presence (unlike Wyndham's) was beneficial to Pound because it helped to tone the choleric poet down. By the time that Eliot returned to London that following summer, he and Pound were firm friends. Eliot then introduced Pound to a young woman named Vivien Haigh-Wood, who became Mrs. Eliot on June 26. At first Ezra and Dorothy found Vivien charming; the Eliots and the Pounds sometimes went dancing at various "palaces" in Hammersmith and elsewhere, but soon it was apparent to all that Vivien was far too neurotic to be the right wife. She would cause "Tom" and his friends a great deal of embarrassment and agony for many years. But for the time being, English literature was in excellent shape as the Men of 1914 joined ranks to fill the vacuum created by the Amygists.

During mid-October of 1914, Pound had another confrontation with Amy. She had the audacity to have her publisher send him a prospectus for her new book, *Sword Blades and Poppy Seed*, which touted her as the "foremost member of the 'Imagists'—a group of poets that includes William Butler Yeats, Ezra Pound, Ford Madox Hueffer" (*SL*, 43–44). Ezra was infuriated. He immediately demanded that she apologize to all concerned. She did indeed send him an apologetic letter, blaming the whole embarrassing affair on her insensitive publisher. Yeats merely laughed the thing off, as did Ford, and so Pound let the matter die. By this time he was so busy promoting Eliot and Joyce that he had no time for her. By November 30, in fact, he was starting to work on Fenollosa's rough notes for the Chinese poetry that would appear that following March as the book *Cathay* (PC 358).

All during that troubled fall, Pound was busy taking care of family and friends. Homer and Isabel had arrived in London in July to belatedly celebrate the marriage. They stayed in Pound's old place on Langham Street by the noisy pub, but Homer had to get back to his job after a month. Isabel, however, stayed on until October 16, moving into the same building with the Pounds and the Aldingtons, who would soon vacate to Hampstead. Then she went back to the States, fearing German submarines during the entire voyage. A month later Ezra got the bad news that old Grandfather T. C. Pound had finally succumbed on November 21 after a series of problems, mostly with his eyes. This caused him great sorrow. When Pound began to write his autobiography five years later, his parents would send him many clippings about Thaddeus that would intrigue and inspire him. Also that fall, Pound tried to establish a College of Arts, which would be a kind of "super-college" for artists of every kind. He envisioned a faculty that would include Lewis, Kitty Heyman, Dolmetsch, the designer Edmund Dulac, Gaudier, Cournos, Wadsworth, the photographer Coburn, and others (*SL*, 42). But like many other idealistic dreams, this one also faltered—thanks to general lethargy and, of course, the war.

It was a cold, bleak winter. From across Kensington Church Street, Dorothy and Ezra could hear the intermittent crackles of antiaircraft guns coming from barracks that had been established there. Food was now being rationed, and civilians were engaged in regular drills, like the artist Wadsworth, who was partially invalided. Hulme was being trained as a gunner, Ford was debating whether to enlist, and May Sinclair was off with the Red Cross in Belgium for a brief stint. The Pounds' company soon was being restricted to aliens, women, and oldsters, but as Ezra told Ingrid Davies later, the lack of available men meant that liberated fellows like himself were suddenly very popular. Stella Bowen, Ford's later lover, recalls in *Drawn From Life* that, soon after this time when she was studying art in London, she met Pound at parties in Chelsea and Kensington, where he was quite popular with young women like her friends Mary Butts and Phyllis Reid—and was always quite alone. Wyndham Lewis and he spent the latter part of that winter working on *Blast No. 2*, not quite realizing that a civilization being blasted from the outside scarcely needs the same from within. Most importantly for the future, to accompany his translating, Pound was now reading Confucius in translation, often in the French of M. G. Pauthier, which would eventually yield the beautiful Canto 13.

As December turned into the new year, Ezra and Dorothy joined Uncle William at the cottage by the forest, but the sounds of guns along the coast destroyed the usual pastoral calm. The two poets continued their readings of William Morris's versions of northern sagas and various mystical writings such as the works of Joseph Ennemoser, the nineteenth-century French occultist Eliphas Lévi (Alphonse Louis Constant), and the *Holy Guide* of the seventeenth-century Neoplatonist John Heydon, "secretary of nature" (Canto 87/ 573). They tackled seven volumes of Wordsworth, despite Pound's apprehensions, and started to follow C. M. Doughty in his *Travels in Arabia Deserta* (1888), as well as through his epic poem *Dawn of Britain* (1906):

> and his hearing nearly all Wordsworth
> for the sake of his conscience but
> preferring Ennemosor [*sic*] on Witches
>
> did we ever get to the end of Doughty:
> The Dawn in Britain?
>   perhaps not
>   (83/534)

Pound was also reading aloud from Robert Browning's *Sordello*, as well as the *Autobiography* of Herbert of Cherbury (1583–1648), who would appear in his final cantos. He completed the proofs of *Cathay* in February and tried to sell John Quinn some of Corporal Gaudier's artwork.

By the first week of March, Ezra and Dorothy were back in the city and happy, despite the threat of air raids. Pound's own attitude toward the war was at first a bit cavalier. He told his parents that a German victory might not be such a bad thing for the world (PC 366), and he was fond of quoting Yeats's friend, the designer Charles Ricketts, saying that it was a pity that *everyone* couldn't be beaten; but he did pen a war poem that was unpublished until James Longenbach's *Stone Cottage* (119ff.).

All during this period, Pound clung to both imagism and vorticism. Back in September, he had published an article in the *Fortnightly Review* called "Vorticism," where he tried to align the two movements, showing vorticism as an outgrowth of imagism. At Coleman's Hatch he wrote to Harriet Monroe some of his most quoted lines about imagism:

> Objectivity and again objectivity, and expression; no hindside-beforeness, no straddled adjectives . . . no Tennysonianness of speech; nothing—nothing that you couldn't, in some circumstance, in the stress of some emotion, actually say. . . . Language is made out of concrete things. General expressions in non-concrete terms are a laziness; they are talk, not art, not creation. (*SL*, 49)

He was still promoting his favorites, and he was showing a temporary interest in Edgar Lee Masters, although he later found Masters too verbose and uncontrolled. He was also planning to issue a new anthology that would rival Amy's offering.

The re-entry of John Quinn into Pound's life early in 1915 was important to more people than these two men. As was said back in chapter 5, Quinn wrote to Pound after reading his article on Jacob Epstein in the January 21 issue of the *New Age*, where Pound was casting aspersions on unenlightened art-buyers who favored the old masters over the moderns. Quinn defended himself in a long letter of February 25, and on March 8 Pound wrote his chastened reply (*SL*, 51f.) in which he also tried to promote the art of Gaudier, whom he was touting in his "Affirmations" series in the *New Age* (February 4). Quinn expressed interest in Pound's own work, and so they began a nine-year correspondence in which Pound sounded often less like a creator than an agent for the art of Lewis and Gaudier, and later the writings of Joyce and Eliot. The lawyer supported all these people in one way or another, even though he had certain misgivings later about Lewis.

Then on April 6, a small book of little more than thirty pages appeared, titled *Cathay*. It would, as many great artists declared, color the whole Occident's view toward the Orient. It consisted of only nineteen poems, all of which are printed in the modern *Personae* (127–42), along with four poems that were added later from *Lustra*. Curiously, the Anglo-Saxon "Seafarer" was also included with the Chinese pieces in 1915. It may seem surprising that Pound was able to get this work out so fast, but the presence of Fenollosa's and Giles's notes and versions helped. Most of Pound's translations in the book have become standard anthology pieces. "The River Merchant's Wife: A Letter" is one of the most beautifully understated love poems in any language, while the war poems ("Song of the Bowmen of Shu" and "Lament of the Frontier Guard") are powerfully moving. Pound sent these military poems to Gaudier at the front, and he shared them with his fellow soldiers, who were surprised to find their condition so realistically described centuries earlier. In short, the violence or tranquility of the *Cathay* poems exist with the horror of Pound's war-torn world around them. All of Pound's closest friends praised the volume, but this was perhaps not as telling as the later imitations by his enemies. Amy would soon link up with one Florence Ayscough (whose scholarly credentials were hardly impressive) to produce their *Fir-Flower Tablets* in 1921. Then too, the "corpselike Waley" (*PL*, 83), formerly Schloss, was now mousing around, trying to cast his eyes on the Fenollosa manuscripts (PC 393). Waley at least had academic training, even if he lacked a "true" sense of poetry; Lowell and Ayscough had neither.

Of course Pound made errors. "The River Song," which was offered as one poem, was actually a conflation of two poems, since Pound had not noticed that some of the lines of a second poem were a title. Also, there were some philological bungles: the word *kiang*, meaning "river," was accepted by Pound as the name of a particular river. But given the authority of Fenollosa and Mori and Ariga, whose names were conspicuously mentioned in the subtitle, Pound's work was remarkably accurate and, compared with the later competition, poetically resplendent.

The two most compelling reviews were by Ford in *Outlook* (June 19, 800–801), who said, "The poems in *Cathay* are things of supreme beauty. What poetry should be, that they are"; and by A. R. Orage in the *New Age* of August 5: "If I were to say that *Cathay* contains the best and only good work Mr. Ezra Pound has yet done, my judgment might be defended." Orage went on to criticize writers of free verse (for like

Robert Frost, he felt that these were merely lazy practitioners of verse), but he praised "The Seafarer," saying that it was worth its weight in gold; and he added that the taste shown in the Chinese works was "impeccable." Pound's most authoritative scholarly defender, Wai-lim Yip, much later pronounced the judgment that should be made of all of Pound's renditions: "Thus his translations were first landmarks of his poetry and only secondarily representations of alien literatures" (158). They were far more transformations than translations.

When the *Egoist* (which he was having little to do with at this time) published its special "Imagist Number" in May, on the heels of Amy's anthology, Pound found himself again in the midst of a battle that he wanted no part of. This issue contained Flint's famous attack, "The History of Imagism," which gave all of the credit for the movement to himself and Hulme, and none to Pound or Ford. Of course this elicited a violent volley from Pound, and then an equally ferocious counterattack by Flint, who accused the American of dictatorial, non-collegial behavior. But Flint would soften his position with time (see chapter 19: Jan. 30, 1921). Meanwhile, Amy and Company were now under attack in an article in the *New Republic* of May 22 by Eliot's old college friend, Aiken, who accused the imagists of operating as a closed club that was writing fragile, fluffy poetry. Pound relished this attack, since his defectors were now being assailed just as he had been before.

All during that spring, influenza was striking the home front, while the German zeppelins were assaulting London with bombs, and the foot soldiers on the muddy fields of Flanders were facing one attack after another. Death seemed to be everywhere. Rupert Brooke was killed that spring from an explosion on the Greek island of Skyros, and even Pound was moved by his death, despite their heated differences (*SL*, 59). Then too, as has already been mentioned, Hilda's first infant died stillborn. Before the year had run its course, Rémy de Gourmont would also pass away. Pound considered him as much a victim of the war as anyone else, as he said in the obituary he wrote for *Poetry* (*SP*, 420).

But the death that moved Ezra Pound the most was the sudden, unforeseen slaying of his good friend Henri Gaudier. It occurred on June 5 as some French soldiers were sweeping through some houses in the little town of Neuville St.-Vaast. A German bullet ripped into Gaudier's skull, and he fell instantly dead, precisely as both he and Sophie had dreamed and feared. Despairingly, Pound sent John Quinn a telegram that said simply: BRZESKA DEAD. On July 12 Quinn responded: "There is only the memory now of a brave gifted man. What I can do I will do." He tried, in fact, to purchase as much of Henri's art as was possible—largely to help the impoverished Sophie.

Pound was devastated by Henri's death. He wrote to Professor Schelling of Penn, whom he had bumped into at the British Museum in 1914: "we have lost the best of the young sculptors and the most promising. The arts will incur no worse loss from the war than this is. One is rather obsessed with it" (*SL*, 61). Pound soon after offered his military services to the British Government (since America was still neutral), but they were not accepted. He told Doctor Kavka in St. Elizabeth's that he tried to enlist on two other occasions and was also turned down. In his profound grief, he set to work writing *Gaudier-Brzeska: A Memoir*, which would be published by John Lane a year later on April 14.

The already neurotic Sophie was shattered that summer. She would soon turn into a "bag lady," roaming the streets of London, muttering, wearing disheveled clothes and worn-out shoes, until she was finally institutionalized for the remainder of her pathetic life. It was now suddenly hard to be cavalier about events; the war had struck home.

13

The Quest for the *Cantos* (July 1915–December 1916)

News Item, May 7, 1915: The Lusitania *is sunk off the Irish coast by German submarines, with a cost of 1,195 lives, some of them neutral Americans.*

It was into this hostile environment that *Blast No. 2* made its ill-timed entry in July. Years later, both Pound and Lewis would rue the inadvisability of their venture at this particular time, estimating that the appearance of this satiric publication during a time of war cost them both many kinds of social and financial gains. Pound's eight offerings to the new issue were largely satires, including "The Social Order" (*Pers.*, 115), "Et Faim Sallir Les Loups Des Boys" (*CEP*, 284), and "Our Respectful Homages to M. Laurent Tailhade" (*CEP*, 283). One slight poem, "Our Contemporaries" (*Pers.*, 118), was meant as a comic comment on Rupert Brooke's attempt to seduce a Tahitian princess, but his recent death near the Dardanelles made this inappropriate. Pound was severely criticized for his lack of taste (*SL*, 66), and he responded with apologies, blaming Lewis in part. The poem "Ancient Music," with its rollicking parody of the Middle English "Sumer is icumen in," later became much quoted:

> Winter is icummen in,
> Lhude sing Goddamm,

> Raineth drop and staineth slop,
> And how the wind doth ramm!
> >   Sing: Goddamm.
> >   (*Pers.*, 116)

His best poem in the collection was later titled "The Game of Chess" (*Pers.*, 120), and is probably the finest vorticist poem that Pound ever wrote, if one describes vorticism as energy. The poem presents the quick, colorful movement of some chess pieces in a way that suggests the dynamic composition of Lewis's *Timon* designs. The most memorable poems in the issue were probably T. S. Eliot's "Preludes" (48–49) and "Rhapsody of a Windy Night." Lewis himself wrote a short piece, "Constantinople Our Star," that stuck in Pound's mind, as every reader of Canto 96/661 will remember.

The rest of that troubled summer saw both Yeats and Pound trying to secure some money for Joyce, who had fled Austrian-ruled Trieste for Venice and then neutral Zurich, where he was stranded penniless. With the help of Edmund Gosse, they persuaded the Royal Literary Fund to grant the Irishman £75, which kept him going while he was writing *Ulysses* (*PJ*, 38ff). The following year, Pound secured for him further grants from the British government—one of £100, with the help of Edward Marsh (*PJ*, 77, 80) and Lady Cunard. Pound managed to break up the home-front boredom by engaging in a brief but heated debate with the editor of the *Boston Transcript*, who had foolishly bragged that New Englander Frost was the first American to go to England and successfully publish a book through established channels. Pound curtly cited his own experience with Elkin Mathews (*SL*, 62), and although he clearly won the argument, this did nothing to improve his already sensitive relationship with Frost.

In August, Ford accepted the commission that was offered him, and on the 15th Violet invited numerous old friends to South Lodge to see him off. Her whisky-and-sandwiches party was as convivial as the circumstances would allow, but after the guests left, she and her lover had a violent row. The next day, Ford hustled off to train some Welsh troops in Cardiff. He would appear in town occasionally, until 1916, when he was sent to France; there, in September, he had a close brush with death, and in December he was subjected to a freakish gas accident that caused both a physical and mental breakdown. Not responding well to treatment, Ford was returned to England in March of 1917 in an incapacitated state. The era of South Lodge frivolity had ended. Still, Ezra and Violet tried to manufacture some joy in the midst of gloom by holding weekly dinner parties at Bellotti's Ristorante Italiano at 12 Old Compton Street. They were often joined there by Eliot, Lewis, Sinclair, and others who were still on the London scene.

The owner of this wartime refuge is mentioned in Canto 80/501, along with anecdotes involving an aristocrat (assumed to be Lady Grey; *CC*, II, 435) and the future King Edward VII, whom Pound calls the Caressor, as opposed to the Confessor:

> and in 40 years no one save old Bellotti
>   "There is no darkness but ignorance"
> had read the words on the pedestal
> The things I cd/ tell you, he sd/ of Lady de X
> and of how he caught the Caressor's about to be
>   Imperial coat tails
> and only twice had rec'd 3 penny bits
>   one from Rothschild and one from DeLara
> and brought in about 2 ounces of saffron
> for a risotto during that first so enormous war
>   Jah, the Bard's pedestal ist am Lesterplatz
> in the city of London

The quotation that Bellotti had read is from Shakespeare's *Twelfth Night* 4.2.45–47, which is engraved on his statue in Leicester (pronounced Lester) Square or Platz; the particularly stingy Rothschild is not identified, while DeLara seems to be the composer Isidore. The fact that Bellotti would be so concerned about bringing in saffron to cook his risotto dishes during the war testifies to his dedication to the art of Italian cuisine, an art that Pound solidly favored.

During that fall of 1915 so many things were happening intellectually to Pound that it is hard to recount them all. He had finished his memorial to Gaudier and had persuaded John Lane of Bodley Head to publish it the following year. By September 12 he had collected his *Catholic Anthology*, using that title to convey the non-parochial content of the collection, but thereby evoking outraged cries from Francis Meynell and other devout worshipers. Issued by Elkin Mathews that November, it included Pound's already published "Contemporania," as well as the work of Eliot (five poems, including "Prufrock"—later said to be the sole reason for the whole venture), Yeats, Goldring, Kreymborg, Masters, Bodenheim, Harold Monro, Harriet Monroe, Sandburg, Upward, Rodker, Williams, and others—quite a catholic lot! But the anthology did not have any of the popular appeal of the one issued by Amy. Copies could still be purchased decades later.

During that fall, Pound was writing two articles on the recently deceased Gourmont, as well as continuing his Noh translations. During the previous spring, he had met a young, unemployed actor from Japan (via France and Germany) named Michio Ito(w) (c. 1892–1961), who was descended from a samurai family. In the spring of 1916, Pound and Yeats would call on Ito to perform the dance of the Hawk in Yeats's play *At the Hawk's Well*, and although Ito really knew rather little about dancing in the Noh, he performed beautifully. When Ezra vacated his place on Church Walk, Ito followed John Cournos in renting it. Years later in Pisa, Pound could still remember the charmingly strange way that Ito talked:

> So Miscio sat in the dark lacking the gasometer penny
>   but then said: "Do you speak German?"
>   to Asquith, in 1914
> "How Ainley face work all the time
>   back of that mask"
> But Mrs Tinkey never believed he wanted her cat
> for mouse-chasing
>   and not for oriental cuisine
>
> "Jap'nese dance all time overcoat" he remarked
> with perfect precision
>   (77/469)

The meeting with Asquith actually occurred at Lady Cunard's house, where the Japanese actor met the Prime Minister without an introduction, and the two found that they could communicate best in German—the language of the enemy at that time. Henry Ainley played the starring role of Cuchulain in Yeats's *At the Hawk's Well*, while Mrs. Tinkey was a neighbor on Church Walk who had heard various stories about what orientals do with cats, especially when meat is scarce. Pound told Quinn on August 11, 1915, that Ito was the most intelligent Japanese he had ever met.

Another Japanese friend of the period was Tami Koume, who painted a large canvas that Pound took along to Paris and then to the Hidden Nest in Venice; during World War II it unfortunately disappeared as he and Olga were forced to yield the Nest to an Italian occupant. In *Discretions*, Mary de Rachewiltz described Koume's work as a large, "grey opaque canvas into which I read nothingness; chaos, the universe or the torso of a giant, crucified" (22). Koume, who was tragically killed at an early age in the Tokyo earthquake of 1924, took the role of a spirit in the Noh play *Hagoromo*. Pound said that his movements on the stage were the most sensitive he had ever seen—showing a much more refined understanding of the work than what any critic revealed.

In late October of 1915 appeared the *Poetical Works of Lionel Johnson*, Dorothy's ill-fated relative, with an introduction by Ezra Pound. After Elkin Mathews's English edition, Macmillan brought the book out in America in December—but without the introduction. The explanation was that Johnson (not Pound) had made disparaging remarks against "important" people like Arthur Symons and Francis Thompson. Pound was quite understandably enraged by the sudden, unannounced excision, and the ensuing friction was costly to him, for when John Quinn tried to persuade Macmillan to bring out the American edition of *Lustra*, the memory of this altercation blocked it, along with another unfortunate event. During 1916 Pound wanted Macmillan to publish a multivolumed anthology of world literature, and seemed to be having success until he said in his promotional material: "It is time we had something to replace that doddard Palgrave." Yet Palgrave's *Golden Treasury* was the staple of the firm, and so in this case Pound's unchecked vitriole was his own undoing, as it would often be in the future.

It was once believed that Pound began his *Cantos* around this time in 1915, but he told Donald Hall in their later interview that he first dreamed of the project at Hamilton College around 1905; even then, he had wanted to write a world epic treating good and evil in history. In chapter 5, we noted that Rummel spoke of an epic work in progress as early as 1910, and Dorothy mentioned a "long poem" in 1911 (*EPDS*, 82). Then on May 23 of 1915 Pound wrote to Isabel: "I am working on a long poem" (PC 391). By September 21, he wrote openly to Milton Bronner, an admiring journalist with the *Kentucky Post* of Covington, about a "chryselephantine" work—what he described two years later to John Quinn as his "new long poem (really LONG, endless, leviathanic)" (*SL*, 104). As for a title, he always spoke of "some" cantos, never *The Cantos*, a title that gradually evolved.

From the start, the major problem was one of order or design. Pound told Hall that he was consciously trying to imitate Dante's comic vision in the *Comedy*, but in a modern way; he could not simply transfer medieval values to the modern world: "I had various schemes, starting in 1904 or 1905. The problem was to get a form—something elastic enough to take the necessary material. . . . Obviously you haven't got a nice little road map such as the middle ages possessed of Heaven. Only a musical form would take the material, and the Confucian universe as I see it is a universe of interacting strains and tensions" (23). Because of these uncertainties, the next few years would indeed be a period of great mental torment. To his inner struggle must be added the terrible strain on everyone stemming from the war. The Belgian town of Ypres was under constant attack that fall, and poisoned gas was used for the first nightmarish time. It would be a gas attack that would deal Ford such pain a year later, triggering his second breakdown.

Before going off with Dorothy to Stone Cottage to serve for the last time as Yeats's secretary, Ezra mentioned his new epic to his father, who had liked a long poem called "Near Périgord" that Pound had recently sent him. The Périgord poem deals with the life and loves of the manly troubadour Bertran de Born of sestina fame. Pound told Homer that if he liked the Périgord poem, he would probably also like Browning's *Sordello*, and indeed the First Ur-Canto (later rejected) opens with the line: "Hang it all, there can be but one *Sordello!*"—which was finally transferred to Canto 2. Pound's attraction to this long poem of Browning (which he and Yeats read together the previous winter) was inexplicable to most people, including Homer. Even the later Browning seemed puzzled by it. Pound confessed in this letter (PC 406) that it had taken him six readings before he could begin to cope with the work, yet he insisted that it was the best long poem in English after Chaucer.

The most convincing explanation for this attraction has been offered by Ronald Bush, whose *Genesis of Ezra Pound's "Cantos"* is the most complete and detailed guide for this difficult period, when Pound was desperately trying to get a hold on his dream. It would take Pound ten more years before the first sixteen cantos were finally published in a definitive form in Paris. Bush explains:

> *Sordello*, then, and the Cantos modeled after it, intend to be a new kind of narrative poetry—a poetry that portrays not just an action but an authentically modern dramatization of the way an action acquires significance within the individual intelligence.... Sordello's speaker is the type of a poet seeking a modern poetic identity, and the "plot" he projects recounts a series of tentative postures assumed by a developing fellow poet. (83)

The Sordello at the center of Browning's poem is not the poet presented in Dante's *Purgatorio:* a thirteenth-century troubadour from Italy who seduced the beautiful Cunizza da Romano from her husband and then fled to Provence to write poems in Old South French and to distinguish himself as a diplomat and warrior. Instead, as Bush indicates, the real center of the poem is Robert Browning, just as Pound is the focus of the *Cantos*. Unlike the "invisible poet" T. S. Eliot, Pound is *in* his poem often as himself, although he also adopts persona after persona, just as Browning did: sometimes serious, sometimes scurrilous, sometimes joking. Both poets use Dante's guiding principle of "popular eloquence" (*volgar eloquio*) as the dominant form of their rhetoric. Yet Browning could not begin to answer all the questions needed for beginning Pound's poem, since Browning had a single story line to follow, and Pound eventually selected world history as his background and central plot, with obvious omissions and selections. The problem of how to order a poem that wanted to tell "the tale of the tribe" (in Kipling's phrase) would occupy Pound for the next decade.

That winter was the last one spent at Stone Cottage with Yeats. The younger man toiled on his long poem while the older one worked on his play, while both thought about Japanese drama, Norse sagas, *Sordello*, and leftovers from Wordsworth and Doughty. With Dorothy often listening, they alternated their reading of Walter Savage Landor's *Imaginary Conversations*, which Pound had previously ignored. Suddenly Landor seemed to be a sensibility worth studying, since he had developed personae who spoke out of the course of history. As a result, Pound praised him in an article published in *The Future* of November, 1917 (*SP*, 384ff.). He also translated twelve of Bernard de Fontenelle's *New Dialogues of the Dead* (1683), Landor's primary French source, which were published in the *Egoist* from May 1, 1916, to June 4, 1917, and then in 1917 as a book.

The peace of the countryside was ruffled that winter by snoopy military detectives who wanted to know what American aliens were doing so close to the seashore installations:

> Summons withdrawn, sir.)
> (bein' aliens in prohibited area)
> (83/534)

Ezra and Dorothy were almost hauled in for a trial, but the potential farce ended with the intercession of Robert Bridges and C. F. G. Masterson, a politician friend of Ford. Then when the Pounds returned to London, there was a problem of getting passports. This infuriated Pound, as he showed years later when he was describing Lombard history in Canto 96/651: "Authar, marvelous reign, no violence and no passports."

The year 1916 began ominously for the Allies. In February, the Germans attacked Verdun, and they seemed to have the upper hand for a time, until the British and the French counterattacked along the Somme River. Tanks were being used for the first time, increasing the horror of mechanizaton in a way that the futurists never anticipated.

Both sides were clearly drained by the endless agony and boredom. Deep snow covered southern England in February, and when Henry James died on February 28th, Pound felt so depressed that he would write Quinn only a very understated notice: "He'd done all he could."

Pound was still in touch with Joyce, but a letter of March 16 (*PJ*, 74) shows an impatience with the perennially needy Irishman. Pound had his own problems with money. His income for one twelve-month span was only around £45. To this one could add Homer's doles and Dorothy's annuity of £150 to £200, which he did not touch for himself, but which certainly helped with general expenses. In order to make more money that winter, Pound had put together a collection of his essays called *This Generation*, which meant to trace the great transformation that had come over poetry in the last decade. In New York, a young publisher named John Marshall, who had worked for the bookseller Laurence Gomme, offered to publish it. In a gracious act, Pound offered to step aside if Marshall would publish Joyce's *Portrait* instead. Marshall was considering both works when disaster struck. His young bride suddenly developed tuberculosis, and they fled to Canada, taking Pound's manuscript with them. That was the end of that book, but John Quinn (who had been suspicious of Marshall) and Alfred Kreymborg both wasted a lot of time and energy trying to track it down. As a result of the mishap, Quinn decided to find Pound a good publisher and did: Alfred Knopf.

Suddenly that spring there appeared a new and interesting personality through the mails, a young poet from Birmingham named Iris Barry (real name Crump). Pound had seen some of her work in Harold Monro's struggling *Poetry and Drama* and had written to her, trying to solicit some poems for *Poetry*. Her prompt reply initiated a brief but interesting correspondence (*SL*, 76ff.) that shows Pound the Master at his best with a new disciple. This pattern would be repeated again and again with Marianne Moore, Ingrid Davies, and many other writers. In the letters to Iris, Pound points out infelicities in the novice's work and recommends books for further reading, usually works that are tangential to his own work. She visited the poet in July, and by September, they were talking about her moving to London, which she did the following year, taking a job with the Ministry of Munitions and later with an Oriental Studies Library. She described the Pound of this period in an article in the American *Bookman* in 1931: "his exuberant hair; pale cat-like face with the greenish cat-eyes, clearing his throat, making strange sounds and cries in his talking, but otherwise quite formal and extremely polite" (165). She also described Dorothy carrying herself like "a young Victorian lady out skating." Ezra told Iris many tales about the battles of imagism, Frida Strindberg's troop of performing monkeys, and the riotous times among the artists in the Café Royal.

All that spring, Pound was immersed in things Oriental. Back in January, Yeats had arranged to have his sister publish some of Pound's translations of Noh plays; these would appear in September 1916 as *Certain Noble Plays of Japan*, issued by the Cuala Press, Churchtown, Dundrum. Japan was very much on both poets' minds. Yeats had dictated his Noh-influenced *At the Hawk's Well* to Ezra that winter at Stone Cottage and dedicated it to him. They arranged to have it presented in Lady Cunard's drawing room as a premiere on the afternoon of April 2, followed by a performance in Lady Islington's home two days later. To the premiere were invited "select royalty" like Edward Marsh (and T. S. Eliot), while about three hundred people with money showed up for the second performance, a charity event for the war. For designs and costumes, they used Edmund Dulac and Charles Ricketts. Pound accompanied Michio Ito to the London Zoo before the premiere, so that the Japanese dancer-actor could imitate the movements of birds as precisely as possible. He was a great hit, but he moved on to New York not long after, and then to Hollywood, finally returning to his native land, where he operated a string of dance halls so successfully that he became a millionaire, according to Michael Reck (96–97).

Two weeks after the performance, *Gaudier-Brzeska: A Memoir* appeared. This moving book suddenly made Pound well known to many art lovers and in some ways compensated for the *Blasts*. Decades later, Nancy Cunard still commented on its impact on her and her upper-class crowd. Her mother, Lady Maud, was now very friendly with Ezra. Aside from helping him support Joyce (*PJ*, 78), she also tried to support Pound by giving him a commission to translate Jules Massenet's *Cinderella* for her lover Thomas Beecham's Opera Company. All during that summer Pound labored over this uninspiring job, and when he finished the following year, he was handsomely paid, although the libretto was never used. At this point, Pound was moving in the upper circles of London, which seemed to forgive him for earlier excesses.

Suddenly the quiet on the home front was shattered by the violent Easter Rebellion in Ireland against British rule. This caused Yeats, who was stunned by the unforeseen event, to write his famous "Easter 1916" poem about the terrible beauty that was being born in the world. In this poem, he mentions Maud Gonne's estranged husband, John MacBride, who was later executed for his part in the affair. Despite the war, Yeats rushed off to Normandy to care for the now hysterical Maud and her extravagantly beautiful daughter Iseult, with whom the old poet was already falling in love. Pound was also deeply moved by the rebellion. The plight of the subjugated Irish was just one more tragic circumstance to consider in a world gone mad, what in *Hugh Selwyn Mauberley* he would refer to as "an old bitch gone in the teeth, / . . . a botched civilization" (*Pers.*, 191).

In May, Pound took Elkin Mathews, who was once again his publisher *faute de mieux*, the copy for his much-delayed collection *Lustra*. Elkin committed the unforgivable crime of sending the manuscript off to the printer without reading it. When the sensitive printer, William Clowes (Canto 82/524), saw the "indecent" things that he was being asked to print, he summarily returned it. The shocked Mathews then informed Pound categorically that he could not publish the poems as presented. Yeats interceded, and he won some concessions for Pound, but he agreed that a few of the poems were lacking in taste. As a result, a compromise was reached whereby 200 copies of the work were published without the "indecent" poems, which were then sold under the counter. The omitted works included "The Temperaments" (*Pers.*, 100), "The Lake Isle" (117), "Pagani's, November 8" (161), and the parodic "Ancient Music." All of these poems are included in the modern *Personae*, where they seem quite un-scandalous, but D. H. Lawrence was stirring up shock waves with his *Rainbow*, and the authorities were extremely sensitive, despite the surrounding havoc of war. No longer do such phrases seem offensive: "64 fornications / and something approaching a rape" (100); "And the whores dropping in for a word or two" (117); or "the eyes of the very beautiful / Normande cocotte" (161). When Mathews issued a second printing, he dropped nine more poems which he thought were "nasty" or "very nasty," and the title of "Coitus" was changed to "Pervigilium." When the book was finally published in September, anyone could buy the unexpurgated edition without any trouble in Mathews's shop. The role that Ezra Pound played in fighting puritanism in publishing has never been properly emphasized; he was every bit as much in the vanguard with Lawrence and Joyce.

Despite the war, the summer was desultory and dull, especially since travel was restricted. Pound tried to enliven things by competing for a $1,000 prize offered by the city of Newark for a poem celebrating its 250th Anniversary. Needless to say, his contribution, "To a City Sending Him Advertisements," was more calculated to shock than to win prizes, but he surprisingly did get a $50 consolation award that was offered almost tongue-in-cheek. Today Newark is prouder of this also-ran than it is of the poet who won.

After taking a brief trip to the shore, Pound was pleased to see that Eliot was circulating widely again. Eliot had taken a job during the winter teaching high school, and he was planning to return to Harvard to defend his thesis; he also intended to carry some art with him for a vorticist show that Quinn was arranging in New York. But at the last minute, the whole trip was postponed. The thesis was accepted anyway in June, and the way was open for gaining the doctorate, but, partially under the influence of Pound, Eliot rejected the academic life completely. Although he taught school for a further spell, by March of 1917 he was working in the foreign department of Lloyd's Bank at 17 Cornhill, and was a permanent fixture on the London scene. Eliot's presence made Pound extremely happy, since he desperately needed people to converse with. Wyndham Lewis was talking all that summer about enlisting, while the poet John Rodker had declared himself a conscientious objector—an act that displeased many people, including Mary Butts, his wife at this time.

During that summer Pound was translating the *Twelve Occupations* of Jean de Bosschère, which was part of a longer work called *Le Bourg*. Pound's translation was published as a small book by Elkin Mathews in September. Years later when Pound wrote his canto about the city of Byzantium and the way that the occupations there were regulated by Emperor Leo the Wise and other rulers, he remembered this work and the kindly Belgian, transplanted by the war, who had authored it (Canto 96/660). Jean was one of the few people who accepted the Ur-Cantos with enthusiasm; in fact, he was almost too extravagant with his praise, as Pound confessed to others.

When the fall arrived, Pound was clearly at sea intellectually. He was torn in too many ways to work on his long poem with any clear direction. And the depressing war did not help. As a result, his letters are often ill-humored and vindictive. He wrote to H. L. Mencken: "Religion is the root of all evil" (PC 438); and for the first time, he began to speak in his letters pejoratively about the Jews. He mentioned a "jew theatre" that stood in opposition to Yeats's concept of an aristocratic theatre dedicated to the highest taste (PC 410); he also mentioned to his father Voltaire's alleged warning that the activities of the Jews had to be restricted—a warning that the world had not heeded (PC 436). Economics and politics were very much on his mind, but in a disorganized way. He was waiting for someone like Major Douglas to come along to show him a way out of the morass.

As a result, when *Lustra* appeared in September, it was more a monument to his past than an expression of his present. Dedicated to someone romantically called "Vail de Lencour" (who was in actuality Brigit Patmore), this was the last of Pound's great collections of serious new lyric material, since *Mauberley* can be thought of as one poem. *Lustra* offered the jewels of imagism, like "In a Station of the Metro," much of *Cathay*, and many freshly written epigrams, such as

"Phyllidula" and "Society." The dedication to Brigit was from Catullus' Poem 1 ("To whom I give my pretty new book"), and the title was Latin too: a *lustrum* is "an offering for the sins of the whole people," according to the epigraph. Although elements of imagism and vorticism are in the book, the epigrams remind the reader of Pound's studies at Penn, when he was patiently translating Catullus and Martial. Pound was back in touch with Old Schelling, and Penn was still very much on his mind. He was badgering Schelling to help him get the doctorate, but of course to no avail.

The new poems in *Lustra* (which appear in the modern *Personae* from page 151 forward) include the recently mentioned "Near Périgord," where Bertran de Born's attempt to create an ideal, imaginary lady is set against a background of war and economic struggle. Clearly Pound was beginning to ask himself political and economic questions:

> How would you live, with neighbours set about you—
> Poictiers and Brive, untaken Rochecouart,
> Spread like the finger-tips of one frail hand;
> And you on the great mountain of a palm—
> Not a neat ledge, not Foix between its streams,
> But one huge back half-covered up with pine,
> Worked for and snatched from the string-purse of Born—
> The four round towers, four brothers—mostly fools:
> What could he do but play the desperate chess,
> And stir old grudges?
>   "Pawn your castles, lords!
> Let the Jews pay."
>
>   (152)

The suggestion here is that chivalric clashes of medieval war were cavalier games (unlike the current war), and that if one lost, the Jews would be more stuck with their loans than would be the mortgager.

But in the end, Pound is more concerned with aesthetics than politics, with the loss of Lady Maent, who is in many ways a construct of the poet's mind:

> There shut up in his castle, Tairiran's,
> She who had nor ears nor tongue save in her hands,
> Gone—ah, gone—untouched, unreachable!
> She who could never live save through one person,
> She who could never speak save to one person,
> And all the rest of her a shifting change,
> A broken bundle of mirrors . . .!
>
>   (157)

In many ways, this poem is a lyric trying to be a narrative. Conversely, the *Cantos*, when they were finally written, would be an epic that often breaks up into a series of lyrics, precisely as Pound viewed Dante's *Comedy*, or a set of small plays, like the Noh plays.

The reception of *Lustra*, despite its importance and brilliance, was mixed. A young American woman who had recently corresponded with Pound (*SL*, 71ff.), Kate Buss, praised him in the *Boston Evening Transcript* of December 6, but confusedly dated the *Cathay* poems before the imagist productions, falling victim to the time lag discrepancy of the work. Pound thought that Miss Buss might be another Iris Barry, but he soon dismissed her as a "discipular imbecile" (PC 420). She was a close friend of Amy Lowell.

The anthologist Louis Untermeyer, who would later collect Pound's work, found this book "a confused jumble and smattering of erudition" in the *Dial* of 1920 (a delayed response); it was "the record of a retreat, a gradual withdrawal from life," and indeed, Pound was haunted himself by this very fear. The poet Babette Deutsch, however, found the work fascinating in *Reedy's Mirror* (Dec. 21, 1917), seeing Pound as a rebel, a romantic, and a "vorticist, to paraphrase his own definition, 'from whom and through whom and into whom ideas are constantly rushing.' " Joseph Conrad was too old-fashioned, he confessed, to like Pound's work, but he told John Quinn on receiving a complimentary copy of the book, that Pound "has many women at his feet; which must be immensely comforting" (RJQ, 340).

The finest tribute to Pound was an anonymous brochure that was appended to the American edition by Knopf much later in January of 1918: *Ezra Pound: His Metric and Poetry*. The author was T. S. Eliot, but the bibliography was the work of Pound. It was clear from this testimony that Eliot was not only a good friend, but also an impeccable critic. His words about Pound's work were among the most intelligent that Pound ever received. Eliot was also one of Pound's last male companions in London. Lewis enlisted in the service finally in March of 1916, after a bout with complications from gonorrhea; he went off to learn the art of "bombardiering" (shelling) later in the year, and in May of 1917 departed for the front. Richard Aldington left in the Christmas of 1916 draft, as Pound informed Quinn on December 31, while poor Ford was recuperating in the hospital from his gassing. This same letter also dropped the first direct mention of the *Cantos* to the lawyer-patron: "Am at work on a long poem. Which last two words have an awful sound when they appear close together." Pound and Quinn were now the best of friends, after their rocky beginning.

As far back as 1915, when Quinn read in a letter of May 22 that Pound had failed in his bid to take over an aged and ailing weekly called the *Academy,* the lawyer had generously agreed to back him in a publishing venture, and he called for an estimate. Pound replied that he believed that he could run a weekly on the cost of printing plus £10 per week: which included 2 for himself and 5 a month for an assistant (Douglas Goldring was a candidate at that time). Quinn thought that it would take an opening investment of $10,000 (assembled from several patrons) to get something moving. Eventually they decided that it was more feasible to run a monthly—preferably one already in existence.

On March 1, 1916, Pound had asked if the *Egoist* was not too "one-horse" to be considered worth subsidizing, and Quinn had promptly offered him a grant of £100 a year for two years "to make something of that paper" (March 15). Yet that negotiation collapsed, Pound informed him on April 8, because Dora Marsden was a fool and she and Weaver would not grant him the kind of power he wanted. Also, his feelings toward that review had steadily deteriorated, especially after Aldington took over as assistant editor (followed by his disorganized wife); this situation would only be remedied in June of 1917 when Eliot assumed control of the helm at Pound's urging. Ezra still valued Harriet Shaw Weaver as a source for book publication for Joyce, Lewis, and himself, but he wanted no part of her operation on a day-to-day basis. Still, the idea of taking literary control of a major publication lay dormant in both men's minds.

For months during 1916, Pound had struggled to get some of the artwork of Lewis, Etchells, Dismorr, Roberts, and others over to New York so that Quinn could open the eyes of Americans to vorticist art. There were enormous difficulties involved in the assembling and packing of these objects, but finally they arrived during that summer, although it was not until after the beginning of the new year that Quinn was able to find a suitable exhibition space. In the end, the show was a great disappointment, and the lawyer wound up buying most of the art himself.

This failure did not dampen the relations between the two men. Pound continued to act as Quinn's agent in Europe, and Quinn continued to support Pound and his friends in a myriad of ways. Not long before he died, Quinn confided that a major reason for his initial interest in Pound was the poet's fascination with the troubadour country of southern France. Now that they were close friends, Quinn guessed that the secret of both of their successes in life had been their supportive families, especially their fathers. Old James Quinn from County Limerick, Ireland, had established a thriving bakery business in Fostoria, Ohio, and had gladly helped his son through the University of Michigan, and then Georgetown and Harvard Law Schools.

Homer Pound's support has been mentioned many times in this book. With John Quinn solidly behind him now, Pound felt more secure. It is clear from reading their correspondence that the older lawyer was in many ways Father Number Two.

14

The Little Review and La Belle Iseult (1917)

On the twelfth day of the new year, Macmillan and Co. at last published *"Noh" or Accomplishment: A Study of the Classical Stage of Japan* by Ernest Fenollosa and Ezra Pound, which is now most readily available in *Translations* (211ff.), with the incorrect date of 1916 taken from the original title page; the work appeared a month later than planned. Expanding the smaller book of September 1916 issued by Lily Yeats, this new work added ten plays, along with Fenollosa's notes, records of his conversation, and appendices. Pound frankly confessed that the vision and the plan of the book were Fenollosa's; he was simply concerned with "arranging beauty into the words." Most readers felt that he did an excellent job in this respect.

However, because of the time lag, Pound's heart was no longer with these delicate, subtle dramas. Two days before publication he wrote to John Quinn, who arranged for the American edition by Knopf in June: "China is fundamental. Japan is not. Japan is a special interest, like Provence" (*SL*, 102). Pound found the ending of *Kagekiyo* "Homeric" and certainly the *Nishikigi*, a tragic story of two separated dead lovers, moving, but the Chinese material now seemed to him more "solid."

Despite this opinion, Pound never forgot these lovely plays. When he was writing the final Fragments of his *Cantos* and was studying

Joseph Rock's work on the Na-khi tribes and language near Tibet, Pound saw correlations between the two Oriental cultures. As a result, one finds the titles of the Japanese plays mentioned occasionally: *Awoi (No Uye)* and *Komachi* (Canto 110/781), and they also occur in the *Pisan Cantos*. Pound was not a playwright, and hence the dramatic form did not interest him per se; also, the plays seemed insubstantial against a background of violence. However, his book was reviewed well, and Pound solidified his reputation as an Oriental translator. The long poem announced again on January 24 to Quinn was now his main preoccupation, despite a host of other projects.

The dream of having a voice in his own magazine seemed to have totally faded, when, almost as magically as Harriet Monroe had risen out of the cornfields, two female editors emerged once again from Chicago—the pert, stylish, feminine Margaret Anderson and her often crew-cut companion, Jane Heap. They had heard of Pound's work from Harriet, and they wrote to him from their newly established New York office, asking him if he would like to become the foreign editor for the magazine that Margaret had founded three years earlier, the *Little Review*. Pound was exhilarated. Although his first letter at some undated point in January (*SL*, 106) was a bit testy, he nevertheless could not conceal his delight. He told Margaret that he wanted a place "where I and T. S. Eliot can appear once a month (or once an 'issue') and where Joyce can appear when he likes, and where Wyndham Lewis can appear if he comes back from the war."

Soon the arrangement was made, and a new era was launched in American publication as the great American expatriates suddenly found a reliable home back in their mother country, apart from *Poetry*'s puritanical editorial board. Margaret was a fearless and honest editor; she one time ran a string of blank pages because she could not find any suitable material to publish; how like Confucius recalling the day when historians left blanks in their writings for the things that they didn't know (Canto 13/60)!

Although the ladies were clearly lesbian lovers, and Pound was not overly fond of homosexuals, he nevertheless made exceptions when called for—even with the didactic Miss Heap, who wears a man's bowtie in the famous Man Ray photograph of her. Jane "talked tough" to Mr. Quinn when that ubiquitous connoisseur of women and art began stopping by their place on West 14th Street, having been drawn there by the stylish Miss Anderson. Pound was worried that the whole deal might be destroyed by these personal bickerings with sexual undertones. In an undated letter of that spring he tried to convince Margaret of the virtues of Mr. Quinn (*SL*, 111), telling her that the lawyer was no tightwad, had a keen eye for beauty (which she now realized), and was not the male chauvinist that he appeared to be. Quinn, unfortunately, did tend at times to be pushy, obstinate, and demanding. He often rewrote or marked up samples of writers' works and sent them back with curt, uncomplimentary comments. He held up the American publication of *Lustra* later that fall by making endless demands on Alfred Knopf about such minor details as spacing, capitalization, and even the appearance of the dog in the Borzoi logo, which Quinn thought was tasteless. Margaret did not receive Pound's lecture too kindly, as she revealed in her ill-written, poorly organized *My Thirty Years' War*—especially his suggestion that her lover was "cheeking" Quinn too much. When the two ladies finally met their foreign editor in Paris in 1923, they were quite disturbed by his nervousness, obstinacy, and didacticism, just as they had been by Quinn's. Margaret's final judgment of Ezra—given the fact that she was well aware of his brilliance and kindness to others—was that he was a bit immature.

Nevertheless, despite the squabbles and misunderstandings, the *Little Review* became one of the most important journals in American literary history, and Ezra Pound was in the forefront of its development. Until it closed shop in 1929, when Margaret was happily settled in France and Jane was back in New York, it published one important poem or story after another—including the serialization of Joyce's *Ulysses*, which got Miss Anderson hauled into court, despite the assistance of Mr. Quinn. With a taste that was far surer than that of the provincial Miss Monroe, the Misses Anderson and Heap helped to shape the course of twentieth-century literature. When the unstoppable Amy Lowell tried to muddy the waters by suggesting that Pound was difficult to deal with, the editors ignored her, and Pound himself silenced her with a quick salvo (*SL*, 122).

As for Pound's own publications during that winter of 1916–17, in an undated letter to his father (PC 447), Ezra wrote that he had completed his first three cantos, and he sent these off to Miss Monroe that spring. She took a bit of time before she let him know that she was not exactly pleased with the new poems; however, she did agree to publish them, despite the fact that they were overly long. Pound told her to string them out over the June, July, and August issues (which she did), and he then cut them down a bit for their subsequent publication in the American *Lustra*. In February she also published twenty of his poems (twelve for the first time in America) in her and Alice C. Henderson's anthology, *The New Poetry*. She was still trying to be a friend.

From the violent Easter Uprising of 1916 to the spring of 1917, Yeats was once again deeply concerned with Irish politics, particularly as they affected that ageless and incurable "revolutionary simpleton" Maud Gonne. Although Maud was now in France, barred from

Ireland after her husband John MacBride was executed for his part in the abortive scheme, she had persuaded Yeats to help her get a pass to enter England by the beginning of 1917. During this time Yeats was again entertaining the hope that she would become his wife, but she refused him in 1917 just as she had so often in the past. Having failed to win her for over a period of twenty-eight years, the old man had gradually fallen under the spell of her beautiful daughter Iseult, who was now in her early twenties.

Iseult Gonne MacBride was born in 1895, the illegitimate child of Maud and the right-wing, French journalist-politician Count Lucien Millevoye. Iseult took after her mother, and was famous for her beauty. Lady Maud Cunard had never seen such a complexion! Because Yeats was in constant touch with the mother, he had known Iseult all during her childhood, much of which was spent in Dublin and Paris, or in their Norman country place called Les Mouettes. Yeats and the black-clad Maud had strolled thoughtfully on the rocky Norman strand after the ill-fated Irish uprising—not mourning the death of the debauched Major MacBride, but the fate of the captive nation.

Iseult had been educated largely in a French convent in Caen, but she was bored by religion and was soon following in the footsteps of her worldly mother. Even in her late teens, she seems to have been having an affair of some sort with the old poet. On August 12 of this year, Yeats wrote to Lady Gregory from Colleville, Normandy, that he and Iseult were back on "our old intimate terms," and that he had proposed to her—even though he was old enough to be her father. This proposal caused great friction between mother and daughter, even though Maud did not want to marry William herself. After weeks of soul-searching, Iseult finally said no too—but only after a long, tearful speech in which she promised to be Yeats's friend for life.

By the middle of September, the two MacBride women were back in London with Yeats, and Pound resumed his casual friendship with them. Maud took an apartment in nearby Chelsea, although she moved to the Woburn Buildings flat later that winter. Iseult began working as an assistant librarian at the School of Oriental Studies and also did some typing for Pound, while Ezra tutored Iseult's younger brother, Seagan (Shawn), who even stayed with him and Dorothy for a time. It is hard to know what Dorothy made of all this, for very soon Ezra and Iseult were engaged in a passionate love affair. We know this, not from correspondence, but from the candid report by Iseult's later husband, the Irish novelist Francis Stuart. In 1920, Iseult married this "tall young republican from Ulster . . . eight years younger than herself, with a shock of golden hair cut in a fringe, eyes like a faun's" (according to Nancy Cardozo, Maud's biographer; 339). In Stuart's revealing *Black List/Section H*, where he is the protagonist "H" and everyone else has a real name, Stuart says very frankly: "Iseult told him that while alone in Yeats's house . . . she had become the mistress of the poet Ezra Pound" (25)—which shocked the young man terribly.

For the entire period from the autumn of 1917 until after the Armistice, when the MacBrides finally were allowed to return to Ireland, Ezra and Iseult engaged in their secret affair. The power of this is shown in some lines from the *Cantos* where the name Yseult (long thought to be the mythic lover of Tristan) was identified by Eva Hesse as the true person she was:

> Yseult is dead, and Walter,
> and Fordie,
> familiares
> (104/741–42)

Iseult Stuart died on April 27, 1953, about when Pound was penning these lines. The "Walter" here is Rummel, whom Iseult knew from her frequent stays in Paris; in fact, Stuart also tells us in the same passage quoted above that Yseult informed him that Rummel was the devoted lover of Isadora Duncan. Even after she moved to Dublin, Iseult returned to London and managed to see Pound until he departed for Paris permanently. Then their affair ended. It seems extraordinary that Pound was able to see so much of her, considering his ongoing affair with Bride Scratton, but, as Joseph Conrad had told John Quinn, Pound had many beautiful ladies at his feet.

During the first half of 1917, Pound was occupied by his usual bewildering array of activities. In February there was an exhibition of "Vortographs"—surrealistic photographs made on an instrument called a vortescope, which Pound had created in October of the preceding year working in cooperation with his photographer friend Alvin Langdon Coburn. The photographs produced by this instrument tried to reveal geometric designs beneath the outward appearance of things. George Bernard Shaw attended the show and received the new invention kindly. Although Coburn tried to carry the project further into cinematography, Pound abandoned it for other interests. All during that spring, Pound kept acting as the executor of Gaudier's estate. He was still trying to arrange for Quinn to buy the dead sculptor's art, but they were again balked by the unruly Sophie, who was well on her way to permanent institutionalization. Sophie speaks bitterly about Pound in her private diary. It was especially irksome to Quinn to be frustrated by this intractably neurotic woman, but he continued to support Pound's artistic friends.

By March, Ezra was in full swing as the *Little Review*'s London agent. For the May issue he sent the two editors a sketch about Indian desuetude called "Jodindranath Mawhwor's Occupation," an editorial accepting his new job, and some "Pierrots" written in imitation of Jules Laforgue, the French poet whom he had discovered with Eliot and whose work he was now devouring. The voice of Laforgue—so intellectually cool and sophisticated, so deliciously detached—was very important for both him and Eliot at this time. It would be heard in Pound's coming translations of Propertius and in Eliot's lyrics. Ezra also sent them a prose satire by Eliot called "Eeldrop and Appleplex," in which Eliot was the former and Pound the apoplectic latter, who was described as having "the gift of an extraordinary address with the lower classes of both sexes."

In this magazine Pound steadily promoted the work of Joyce, Lewis, Yeats, and himself, without meeting the kind of resistance that Harriet Monroe and company constantly threw his way. For May, he also sent Anderson and Heap three "imaginary letters" by Lewis, who was writing him poignantly real letters from Belgium (*PL*, 73ff.). Pound continued the former with his own contributions in the autumn issues of the magazine, and they were eventually published by Caresse Crosby on her Black Sun Press in Paris in 1930 as the slender *Imaginary Letters*. Pound's creations were a series of eight rather comic letters from a stilted Walter Villerant to various young women in the hope of educating them; they are now available in *Pavannes and Divagations* (55ff.).

The October issue of the *Little Review* was suppressed because of Lewis's prose piece "Cantleman's Spring Mate" (a wartime seduction story that now seems very tame). Pound set up the usual howl about puritanism, while the fearless John Quinn sprang to the defense of the two damsels in distress—but to no avail. The law case dragged on through that coming winter, but Pound seems to have been so preoccupied with other matters that when a negative decision was handed down, he did not have the energy (nor did anyone else) to press the matter.

Finally during the summer of 1917, *Poetry* begrudgingly published Pound's "Three Cantos," which are totally different from the first three cantos of the poem as they stand now. These so-called Ur-Cantos were prolix, sprawling, tentative, pretentious, and completely unsure of themselves. Originally, the long poem was supposed to start in this way:

Hang it all, there can be but one *Sordello!*
But say I want to, say I take your whole bag of tricks,
Let in your quirks and tweeks, and say the thing's an art-form,
Your *Sordello*, and that the modern world
Needs such a rag-bag to stuff all its thought in;
Say that I dump my catch, shiny and silvery
As fresh sardines flapping and slipping on the marginal cobbles?
(I stand before the booth, the speech; but the truth
Is inside this discourse—this booth is full of the marrow of wisdom.)
Give up th'intaglio method.

This was a most unpromising beginning. Almost nobody, including Pound, liked it. Eliot *tried* to like it, and Homer Pound tried to like it, just as he had tried to read Browning's *Sordello* at his son's urging—and finally gave up. The dependence on Browning throughout the first three drafts is almost embarrassing. For one thing, who would have guessed that one could pin a major poem on one of the least satisfactory works of a man who is now considered a fine poet, but hardly in the class of Homer or Dante? When these Ur-Cantos were junked, Pound finally decided to begin the poem with Odysseus' descent into the Underworld to talk with the shades of the past, an episode that already appeared in Ur-3:

"And then went down to the ship, set keel to breakers,
Forth on the godly sea;
We set up mast and sail on the swarthy ship,
Sheep bore we aboard her, and our bodies also
Heavy with weeping. . . ."

But even this episode, which is an excellent way to begin a poem that is essentially a series of dialogues with the dead taken from the beginning of Western literature to the present day, lacks the vigor and organization of the true Canto 1. For one thing, the translation above is prolix, lacking the precision of the *Seafarer* imitation and the Anglo-Saxon alliteration that the final version has.

The biggest complaint with the Ur-Cantos was precisely their formless sprawl. The final versions of the early cantos are organized around various centers: Canto 1 around Homer's presentation of Odysseus speaking with the dead; Canto 2 around a scene involving Bacchus from Ovid; Canto 3, around Pound in Venice in 1908, the *Cid*, and a story from Camoëns; Canto 4, troubadour vidas blended with Greek myth, and so on. There is no such basic hint of organization in the Ur-work. Ur-1 leaps from Browning to the troubadours to Catullus to Pound in Venice sitting on the Dogana's steps (the later opening for Canto 3) and several other sites. Along the way such diverse things as Renaissance art and painting, Confucius, Dante, Guido Cavalcanti, and modern painters are mentioned (Puvis de Chavannes, whom Fred Vance of Crawfordsville had studied with; Picasso and Wyndham Lewis). It is clear that Pound was trying to apply vorticist or modern surreal techniques to poetry: "If for a year man write to paint, and not to music—" he says at the end of Ur-1. But the "painting" technique is not successful here because it seems uncontrolled. In the final versions of the cantos, Pound is able to do the same thing because he establishes certain solar centers to hold in orbit his streaking allusions and images. But in 1917, Pound still did not have his centers fixed. For one thing, the whole economic heart of the *Cantos* had not yet been determined. Also, the Confucian base was not established. Confucius is mentioned in Ur-1, but only in passing:

> (Confucius later taught the world good manners,
> Started with himself, built out perfection.)

The road ahead was long and hard, and nobody understood this any more than Ezra Pound.

The careers of most of Pound's friends were still held up by the war. Lewis spent much of the summer of 1917 recuperating from brushes with death at the front, while Ford was still lying low from his freakish gas attack. Eliot, now a banker, had made his debut into English literature with the publication of *Prufrock and Other Observations* by the Egoist Ltd. in June, thanks to Pound, who secretly advanced one-third of Eliot's salary as the new assistant editor of the *Egoist* (*TSEL*, 179). Eliot was now able to publish Pound's essays, such as "Elizabethan Classicists," which ran there that fall and winter (see *Literary Essays*, 277ff.). Eliot had a passion for these dramatists, whom Pound had previously ignored, and this was one of the ways once again in which Pound was influenced by someone whom he himself was helping.

In September Pound's longish poem "L'Homme Moyen Sensuel" appeared in the *Little Review* (*Pers.*, 238ff.), and his series of essays "Provincialism the Enemy" ran through numerous summer issues of the *New Age*. Despite the war, Pound was publishing constantly—in part to support himself—in at least four major periodicals. Finally, in November he got the job of being the regular art critic for Orage's *New Age*, writing under the pen name of B. H. Dias (see his art criticism edited by Harriet Zinnes). In December, he also took on the name of William Atheling, the new music critic for the same journal (his music criticism has been edited by Murray Schafer). These were important jobs because they brought in regular money and they also allowed Pound to become well-known to many new people. Ezra bragged to his parents during the following year that Mr. Atheling was becoming widely respected (PC 497). It was he who three years later would review a performance by a young violinist named Olga Rudge.

In August Joyce had an attack of glaucoma and was very much in need of money for an operation. Pound wrote to Quinn on August 27 telling him to try to sell two autograph manuscripts in his father's safe written by King Ferdinand and Queen Isabella of Spain around the time of Columbus' voyage, in order to assist the perennially impoverished novelist (*PJ*, 126). Pound's generous sacrifice greatly impressed Quinn, who was used to callous ingratitude from most of the artists he helped, such as Epstein; he immediately dashed off a check to Joyce, who had just completed the first three chapters of his monumental *Ulysses*. These chapters were forwarded to Pound in December, and Ezra later called them "an epoch-making report" on the modern mind (*PJ*, 128). Because of English censorship, they were aimed for serialization in the *Little Review*.

Then in October, Yeats sprang his bombshell. Fresh from his dual rejections by the MacBrides, he decided to marry Dorothy Pound's longtime friend Georgiana (Georgie) Hyde-Lees, the stepdaughter of Dorothy's uncle. At first Maud Gonne jeered at this idea because of the disparity in their ages, but later she accepted it—as did Ezra, Dorothy, Olivia, Iseult, and Lady Gregory. "Georgie," as Yeats called her, proved to be excellent company for the older man. She was levelheaded, but also interested in the occult; in fact, very soon she demonstrated a skill for automatic writing at the behest of spirits. In no time, Georgie and Iseult became close friends, and so the family circle widened. Yeats had bought a tower in Ballylee, Ireland, back in 1915, and now that he was married, he would soon retire there.

Toward the end of 1917, Pound was once again devoting himself to the translation of troubadour verse, and he was once again trying to blend it with music. He was using the clavichord that Dolmetsch had made for him, even though, according to Yeats and others, he was tone-deaf. Pound was very anxious to continue his collaboration with Rummel, but Walter was stranded in wartime Paris, which was full of wounded soldiers and refugees. Still, the two kept in touch, and Ezra was already promising to move to France as soon as the war was over.

Meanwhile, through his reviewing, Pound discovered a French female singer named Raymonde Collignon, who, he thought, was ideally equipped to bring the troubadour songs to life. He reviewed her in the January 3, 1918, issue of the *New Age* quite favorably. In December of 1917 he completed his "[Homage à la] Langue d'Oc," which would appear in the next collection of his lyrics, as well as a set of satires called "Moeurs Contemporaines" (in the modern *Personae*, 171 and 178ff.). The troubadour poems include translations from Provençal, such as "Vergier," a lovely dawn song that mentions an adulterous lover and a cuckold, while the second group includes "Mr. Styrax" (a male "virgo"), as well as the moving "I Vecchii," cited in chapter 1. Miss Monroe, as usual, found the poems too frank: she rejected the lot when she received them in January of the next year. But she was already passing out of Pound's world. Anderson and Heap accepted the batch and published them in the May 1918 issue of their magazine; they were also included in *Quia Pauper Amavi* a year later. Lewis, reading them on the front, found them charming, as did his girlfriend Helen Saunders.

The end of 1917 was a particularly trying period in Pound's life. He was wracked by doubts about his own work, since only Eliot of the people he trusted was offering him comfort and positive criticism for his efforts (*SL*, 115). He wrote Margaret Anderson (PC 472) that he desperately wanted to keep writing his long poem and to simultaneously resurrect the dead art of the true lyric, but neither cause was going well. There is no doubt that the war itself was exacting a toll, as it was on Eliot and others. The year 1917 was especially brutal, despite the entry of the United States into the action. T.E. Hulme was killed suddenly on the front that September near Ostend, Belgium, when a shell exploded in his face, blowing him to bits. Despite their differences, Pound mourned his passing in what would eventually become Canto 16, along with the sufferings of others:

> And ole T.E.H. he went to it
> With a lot of books from the library,
> . . . .
> And Wyndham Lewis went to it,
> With a heavy bit of artillery,
> . . . .
>   and a shell lit on his tin hut,
> While he was out in the privvy,
>   and he was all there was left of that outfit.
>   (71–72)

Poor Edward Thomas, the reputation-maker of 1909, was also killed that year. Pound was obviously delighted in December when he heard that the art critic P. G. Konody was able to wrangle Wyndham Lewis's release from the trenches and his installment as a war artist and propagandist for the Canadian War Records Office, through the help of Lord Beaverbrook and Lady Cunard.

It is clearly during these last years of the war that a major change came over Ezra Pound. He now felt that all men, including poets, had to devote themselves to something more than a lifetime quest for beauty. The word "aesthete" became increasingly objectionable to Pound as he began to ask what had caused this terrible and destructive war. His suspicion that the causes were economic rather than idealistic (fed to a great degree later by Orage) led him to take an ever-increasing interest in economics. Why, with the abundance of nature around us, do men have to kill themselves and turn the planet, which could be an earthly paradise, into an inferno? Pound's long poem was an epic; he had gradually come to the conclusion that an epic is "a poem including history," and that one cannot understand history without understanding money (ABCR, 46). But where was one to get that understanding? Surely not from most university professors, who seemed to be in the employ of the establishment. Despite his connection with *New Age* socialism, he had always been leery of that political stance; also the Russian Revolution eventually convinced him that communism was a disaster in its attempt to reduce everyone to the same size.

Toward the end of the oncoming year, a man would suddenly emerge from the London mist and appear at Orage's office saying that he had certain new answers to the problems that were plaguing the world. That man, Major C. H. Douglas, was preaching a gospel called Social Credit, which seemed to offer some hope to a world gone mad. To Ezra Pound, who was desperately searching for an answer, this man and his ideas seemed to point toward a way of regaining a paradise that was otherwise irrevocably lost.

15

Peace and Major Douglas (1918)

The year 1918 will always be remembered as a year of peace and pestilence. The plague was influenza, which struck almost everyone, including Pound. As for the war, Russia collapsed in March, signing the humiliating Treaty of Brest-Litovsk with Germany. Communism was now established as Russia's basic way of life, even though there would be three more bloody years of struggle before it finally triumphed. In April, the Allied Forces concentrated their troops under the French General Foch, while the American General Pershing moved his forces into the heart of the action. In July and August, the Allies met the Central Powers' attack in the outskirts of Paris in the Second Battle of the Marne, driving them back to their original battle positions at the start of the campaign. On all sides except Russia, the United States and Britain and France seemed to be winning. Pound's friend T. E. Lawrence achieved miraculous victories in Arabia, while the British General Allenby captured Jerusalem; Bulgaria fell, followed by Turkey, and even Italy recovered from its previous embarrassing defeat by the Austrians at Caporetto to achieve a decisive victory at Vittorio Veneto, where Hemingway was involved in the action as an ambulance driver for the Red Cross. Shortly after this last defeat, the Austro-Hungarian Empire collapsed on November 4. Then on November 11 the Germans signed the armistice at Compiègne, following riots in the major German cities.

The last year of the war was not a particularly brilliant one in the life of Ezra Pound. He was as busy editing and writing reviews as ever, but much of his work was routine or hack, as he told his father on January 24 (PC 476). He was now contributing to *The Future*, which published his first three cantos in still another reduced form, with pretentious, temporary titles, such as "Images from the Second Canto of a Long Poem." The magazine also ran reviews by Pound of Arthur Waley's Chinese translations and Joyce's *Exiles* in November. (See the Gallup bibliography, Part C, for a complete list of Pound's many reviews and articles of this year.)

Continuing his work with the troubadours, Pound sent off some newly polished translations of Arnaut Daniel to Reverend C. C. Bubb of Cleveland in January. When that volume never arrived (presumably because of German submarines), Pound sent a second copy in November, but that never arrived either. Clearly, the work was hexed. However, Raymonde Collignon did deliver a splendid recital of the Pound-Rummel troubadour songs at the Aeolian Hall on April 27, and it is not surprising that the critic Atheling, who could frequently be scathing, found them enjoyable.

Pound's major work for this year consisted of essays. His interest in French literature was at its height in 1918, thanks in part to Eliot's influence. The February issue of the *Little Review* contained a sixty-page article called "A Study in French Poets," dealing with the now familiar Laforgue, Rimbaud, Spire, Vildrac, Romains, Tailhade, Corbière, and Verhaeren. Pound would praise Laforgue especially—even as late as Canto 116/796:

> And I have learned more from Jules
> 					(Jules Laforgue) since then
> 	deeps in him,

But that was much later; in 1918 he saw Corbière as "the greatest poet of the period" because of the poignancy of his art. Many of these other writers are mentioned in the *Pisan Cantos:*

> "You will find" said old André Spire,
> that every man on that board (Crédit Agricole)
> has a brother-in-law
> 					(Canto 81/518)

Also in February, *Poetry* published his essay "The Hard and Soft in French Poetry," which appears in *Literary Essays* (285ff.).

When John Quinn finally arranged to have Pound's book of essays

Pavannes and Divisions published by Knopf on June 29, one of the key essays was "Rémy de Gourmont." Gourmont had long occupied a high place in Pound's mind as an exemplary European intellectual who was free of British puritanism and provincialism. Gourmont had the kind of far-ranging mind that Ford had, but also a Gallic wit and tolerance that most other Britishers did not possess. Pound called him, in a memorable phrase, "an artist of the nude" (*LE*, 340). Although the influence of Gourmont would wane after Rémy's death, and would continue to wane in the years to come, Pound never totally forgot his impact. Richard Sieburth's *Instigations* points up the various common points of the two writers in terms of literary style, thought, and general sensibility. As for style, Pound had been aware of this early, being in communication with Gourmont over the founding of an international magazine, which the Frenchman was all in favor of. Pound admired the following aphorism from Gourmont's *Litanies de la Rose:* "Femmes, conservatrices des traditions milésiennes" (Women, preservers of Milesian traditions); he referred to this as late as Canto 104/742. Pound liked the "tonal variations" of the sounds in the French (*LE*, 345), and he also liked the insight: That women preserve the basic chthonic feeling—in fact, he applied this adjective to Maud Gonne in a letter to Quinn (*SL*, 140) but defined it negatively: "people who have no sense of 'civilization' or public order."

Even into the final cantos, Pound quotes from Gourmont's *Le latin mystique*, citing such key phrases as the medieval Goddeschalk's statement that "you love in order to make yourself beautiful": "("ut facias"—Goddeschalk—"pulchram")" in Canto 93/626. Pound was especially intrigued by Gourmont's studies in botany and sexuality, and he would soon be translating *The Natural Philosophy of Love* (1922). Gourmont, in short, represented to Pound the intellectual freedom of Paris, and that was much to be desired in those dreary war years. To make things even more depressing, Quinn suffered terribly from an ulcer of the lower intestine this winter and submitted to an exhausting operation. Although he was still young, the indefatigable lawyer and warrior for the arts was actually losing much of his strength; he would die in the near future, years before his time.

The remainder of the essays in *Pavannes and Divisions* included some of Pound's classic statements on imagism, "Religio," the Fontenelle dialogues, and "Troubadours: Their Sorts and Conditions," blended with some recent poems, such as "Pierrots" (*Pers.*, 247) and "L'Homme Moyen Sensuel" (*Pers.*, 238ff.). It was a workmanlike but hardly great book. Still, Pound's recent awareness of French culture had now made him respected in Paris, as he told his father in May (PC 488). Old Albert Mockel, who had founded the Belgian symbolist magazine *La Wallonie*, had praised his work, as well as Tailhade and Romains and the people running the *Mercure*. Pound honored these men in Cantos 78/480 and 80/504.

Pavannes and Divisions, which had been dedicated to John Quinn, was well reviewed in the *Times Literary Supplement* of September 19. Before that, Pound was already at work on his long essay on Gourmont that would apprear later in *Instigations*. In August he supervised a special issue of the *Little Review* in memory of Henry James. But as his central essay "Henry James" shows when it is compared with the longer Gourmont piece that follows it in *Literary Essays* (295 and 339ff.), he now clearly favored the Gallic sensibility over the Anglo-American. In a word, even before the war had ended, he was drawn to Paris.

From August to October, the *Egoist* under Eliot's direction published Pound's essay "Early Translators of Homer" (*LE*, 249ff.). This contained a Latin version by Andreas Divus of part of Book 11 of Homer's *Odyssey*, which was in turn translated by Pound into an English that was alliterative and Anglo-Saxon in style:

> And then went down to the ship, set keel to breakers,
>   Forth on the godly sea . . .
>
>   (*LE*, 262)

Eventually this would become the opening for the *Cantos*, although Pound was not aware of it yet. In fact, all during this year, he had grave doubts about his work. He feared that he was losing his natural poetic voice, relying too much on the work of others; indeed, there was cause for concern, for the long poem was not progressing well. Still, during that most dismal of summers, Pound turned to the past for inspiration: he was translating Propertius. He had told Iris Barry that if nobody else translated the Roman, he would have to do it himself. In November, he sent some versions of Propertius to Harriet Monroe, since he was desperate for money and he wanted to make a last attempt to be friends with her. She would print part of what he sent in March of 1919, while more would run in the *New Age*.

In the September *Little Review*, Edgar Jepson published an explosive attack on "The Western School" (in American letters) in a way that infuriated William Carlos Williams and many others. Jepson praised T. S. Eliot as an exemplary American poet who avoided provincialism. A letter in the Beinecke Library at Yale shows clearly that Pound paid Jepson for this attack with Quinn's money—and repercussions would soon follow. Then unexpectedly in October, Pound had lunch with H. G. Wells, a good friend of Orage whom he had not seen for six years. This seemed to stay in his mind because Wells launched an attack on the well-known statue of the redoubtable Queen Victoria standing by Buckingham Palace as a last symbol of a decadent world empire:

> 'And how this people CAN in this the fifth
> et cetera year of the war, leave that old etcetera up
> there on that monument!' H.G. to E.P. 1918
> (42/209)

An important artist of the future whom Pound met this year through the mails was the American poet Marianne Moore. In a letter of January 9, 1919, she said that she had heard of him as early as 1911, when she and her mother visited Elkin Mathews's bookstore, and Elkin showed them Pound's books and his photograph. Marianne was fascinated by the poet, although she confessed that she was also somewhat afraid of him, because of what she had heard about his famous temper. She wrote him first around April of 1918, and on November 26, at his urging, she sent him two poems and a prose note. Pound was immediately delighted by her eccentric and opaque work, especially her unique handling of meter.

Born in 1887, this lively, sprightly woman, whom Pound did not meet until 1939, had received a B.A. from Bryn Mawr in 1909. At college she had known Hilda Doolittle in passing, and she kept up with Hilda's reputation. In 1915, Marianne worked up the courage to send H.D. some poems, which the Dryad and Richard admired for their "fierce hardness." These were published in the October issue of the *Egoist* that year. Hilda then wrote a laudatory review of Marianne's work in the August 1916 issue, when more poems were published. It took Miss Moore, who lived like a church mouse with her mother, two more years to approach Ezra, who welcomed her contributions to the *Little Review*. He warned her on December 16, 1918, that she would never sell more than five hundred copies of her books (*SL*, 143). He also inquired nosily about her life and looks, obviously hoping that perhaps another Iris Barry had come upon the scene. In a very sensual letter of February 1, 1919, Pound aligned himself with the licentious Zagreus (his adopted natal god), but the sly Miss Moore simply treated "Mr. Pound" with civility and respect. She was content to be an intellectual conquest.

Pound was in London when the war ended. In a letter written home on November 15, he described the general hilarity that gripped the city when peace was finally proclaimed. He saw King George riding around the town in an open car in the November drizzle, looking happy for perhaps the first time in his life (PC 499). The sight of the ingenuously happy king stayed on with Pound for years, recurring as late as Canto 105/749:

> George Fifth under the drizzle,
> as in one November
> a man who had willed no wrong.

Although he was not in especially good health, Ezra rode around the city with Stella Bowen, whom he was seeing a lot of and had introduced to Fordie, who was not in town. In *Drawn From Life* (60), Stella describes "Ezra with his hair on end, smacking the bus-front with his stick and shouting to the other people packed on the tops of other buses." It was a day of unbridled joy. The usually staid Londoners were kissing in the streets; there was ring-dancing in Trafalgar Square, in ways that recalled Merry Old England; crowds milled around Buckingham Palace; and everyone raised hurrahs in belief that they had just ended the War To End All Wars. Even Pound, for a brief moment, believed this, but he perspicaciously told Isabel that he feared the Allies would now begin the "process of extracting payment from the Hun pfennig by pfennig" (PC 499). And indeed, the severe treatment of Germany after the war was in part responsible for the eventual rise of Hitler.

We get an excellent picture of the life of Ezra Pound and Wyndham Lewis at this time from the teasingly brief autobiographic essay contained in Herbert Read's reminiscences in *The Contrary Experience*. This book tells how Read, about to give up the army, was hitting the London scene that fall, trying to start a new magazine, *Art and Letters*, with Frank Rutter of the Art Gallery of Leeds, where Read had attended the University. With some financial backing from Osbert Sitwell, the two succeeded, and Read went on to become Sir Herbert, establishing a career in aesthetics. Although he is perhaps most responsible for creating Hulme's reputation, Read said when *The Contrary Experience* was published in 1963: "by now his five short poems have begun to assume rather too much prominence in the history of this period" (174).

That fall Read met Wyndham Lewis, who, in his art work for the Canadian government, had moved from a château in France that he was sharing with Augustus John back to a spacious, top-floor flat on the Great Titchfield Street so beloved by the youthful Ezra Pound and the "Alfie Venison" Pound of the 1930s. Read says: "He had a girl there 'to pour out the tea'—I did not catch her name, but she is a young poetess who has not yet published" (139). Lewis's biographer Jeffrey

Meyers (89ff.) assumes that this is the Iris Barry whom Ezra Pound had lured down from Birmingham into the wicked life of the capital back in 1916. Indeed Meyers tries to prove (largely from oral reports) that Iris and Wyndham were lovers from 1918 to 1921, when she modeled for his monumental *Praxitella*. Iris supposedly bore him two illegitimate children, both of whom were rather unfeelingly discarded (91). The point would be that if Iris was engaged in an affair with Lewis at this time, then most probably she would have also been engaged in one with Pound from 1916 to 1918. But as far as Pound is concerned, the evidence is purely circumstantial.

The same holds true with Meyers's contention that both Lewis and Pound carried on somewhat briefly with Agnes Bedford, the pianist who was collaborating during this period with Pound on troubadour music and who eventually inherited his apartment when he and Dorothy moved to the continent. Agnes was not a very attractive woman; she had a rather large, hooked nose and plain features. As a result neither artist is believed to have been romantically associated with her for very long. With Nancy Cunard, who Meyers also postulates as a lover of Lewis in the early twenties, there is definite written proof of a liaison with both men. In Pound's case, an affair with Nancy can be documented in 1922, as we shall see.

If Iris Barry had the misfortune to be exploited by Wyndham Lewis and then discarded in favor of Nancy Cunard (as Meyers claims; 92, 94), Iris does not seem to have suffered as much as Lewis's own wife Froanna did. After the war, Miss Barry dropped her munitions work for the government and, like Iseult Gonne, toiled in the School of Oriental Studies for a brief period. She then began to establish a wide reputation as a film critic, writing for the *Daily Mail* in the twenties. In the 1930s, she abandoned Depression-ridden England for New York, finding a post in the Museum of Modern Art which she held for years. When she died in 1969, after having lived with a couple of formal husbands, she was prominent in two glamorous worlds: New York art and Hollywood film. It is therefore hard to view her as a victim, as Meyers tends to portray her.

Herbert Read gives us a reliable background for this fast-moving world that we cannot get elsewhere. Here, for example, are his activities for a typical whirlwind day (October 28, 1918):

> "Met Ezra at 11:30. He is really quite a decent sort: his side whiskers, dainty beard, byronic collar and huge square blue buttons seem rather absurd. But I believe the man is actually *shy*. He is certainly a sincere artist and no fool."

Read then goes to see Orage, who is out of his office.

Then Read goes to a concert: "Ezra was there (and he, by the way, is William Atheling of the *New Age*): also the Sitwells, Nina Hamnett (a painter), Guevara (another), Wolff (another), and we all went to Helen's [Saunders] for tea."

After tea, they went to the Sitwells' "wonderful house in Chelsea full of all things precious and extreme." Lewis was there, acting bitter about the war; in fact, he was starting to deduct four years from his age, which he felt that he had lost because of it. The perceptive Read then offers an excellent judgment of the artists whom Pound and Lewis called the "Shitwells": "The Sitwells are rather too comfortable and perhaps there is a lot of pose in their revolt. But they are my generation. . . ." Ezra told Read that he and his generation should put in a solid ten-year apprenticeship learning the craft of poetry, and then the world would be theirs.

Read goes on to paint a brief but fascinating portrait of the London scene, which was in transition at this time. He dined with the aged but witty Violet Hunt, who was lonely without Ford. He also ate with Lewis at the expensive Carlton House, along with the art critic Konody, who had arranged for Wyndham's sinecure; Eliot was a part of that party. Eliot impressed Read as having "a keen, intelligent face and good eyes. Not at all flamboyant or Bohemian. He has brains. Of all this crowd I begin to distinguish the poseurs and the real talents. Lewis and Eliot are by far the most *important* figures. They have *strength;* Pound is a curious mixture. He makes his undoubted talent less effective by his personal expression of it. He does not allow his brains frank egress" (142). But at another time in this often undated diary, Read says about Ezra: "He is really very nice, though his conceit and affectation would alienate you. But his conceit is largely justified and his sincerity excuses his affectation" (144). This judgment explains some of the difficulties Pound had in dealing with people at this time; he would soon be alienating himself from almost all of his publishing outlets in a way that severely disturbed the more "balanced" Eliot (*TSEL*, 358).

We can also see from this portrait why Pound was not able to ingratiate himself with the wealthy and more traditional eccentrics like the Bloomsbury crowd and the Sitwells. Both he and Lewis insisted on being their own men. There was always something poseurish about the Sitwells that neither Ezra nor Wyndham could stomach. Read's reminiscences show that at the end of the war, Pound was still traveling close to several lovely young artists, like Nina Hamnett, Gaudier's model of the past. Others with whom he socialized were

Iris Barry, Stella Bowen, Helen Saunders, and eventually the notorious Nancy Cunard.

Nancy Cunard (1896–1965) had been introduced to the easy-living art world as early as February of 1914 through her patroness mother, Lady Maud (Emerald) Cunard. She had met Wyndham Lewis about that time while he was designing the dining room in the mansion of Lady Kathleen, Countess of Drogheda. She then met Ezra Pound in 1915 at a tea in her mother's place. In 1918 Nancy was just getting over a disastrous marriage made back in 1916 with a stupid, muscular Australian Guardsman named Sydney Fairbairn. She had been lying low in the country for a time but was now reappearing in London society. Nancy was almost constantly on the move ("If there's a train, I have to be going"). When she was in town, she was usually at the Eiffel Tower Restaurant, where old Mr. Stulik arranged an upstairs room when she wanted one, or at the Café Royal, where she had earlier fallen under the spell of Augustus John. It was just a question of time before she would become close to Ezra Pound.

Anne Chisholm, one of Nancy's biographers, says that Pound sent Richard Aldington the following warning about Miss Cunard in the late twenties, when her behavior was infamous:

> Behold what perils do environ
> The man who meddles with a siren . . .

But Nancy was not the only person about whom poems of this sort were written. When Wyndham was still in France, Ezra sent him a little ditty known as "The Virgin's Prayer" (*PL*, 115). He professed to have heard it as early as 1909, and he swore that it was not of his own invention:

> Ezra Pound
> And Augustus John
> Bless the bed
> That I lie on.

To be in the same league with Augustus John showed that Pound's amatory powers were indeed prodigious.

For a short time when the war ended, there was a feeling of general euphoria. But unfortunately this did not last long. It soon became apparent to everyone that not very much had changed, and in many ways things were worse. Pound's spirits were uplifted when he heard from Quinn that the wealthy lawyer was interested in backing a new journal. He was now thoroughly fed up with the two females running the *Little Review*, who seemed to have an almost masochistic affection for trouble (PC 505). This new proposal sounded intriguing, but Pound was already seriously considering taking off for Paris, where he could work with Walter Rummel in setting troubadour songs and other poems to music (PC 500). London seemed as dead in the new peacetime as it had been before. With the end of war, one expected prosperity, and yet for Pound and countless other artists and "small people," there was the same old scarcity and want. How could this happen?

Toward the end of 1918 (actual date unknown), Major C. H. Douglas came into close acquaintance with Alfred Orage. It was through Orage that Ezra Pound got to know this striking man who suddenly seemed to have answers for the world's problems. Major Clifford Hugh Douglas was born on January 20, 1879, to a family of drapers who had him educated as an engineer. Like many of the other innovative economists of the century, such as Frederick Soddy (a Nobel-Prize-winning chemist) and Arthur Kitson (an engineer and inventor), he had not been "brainwashed" in conventional economic thought; he was therefore, of course, dismissed by most professional economists as untrained in basic rules. Douglas left England to become the chief engineer and manager of the British Westinghouse Company in India, and he also worked for a time as the chief engineer for a railroad in Argentina. During the Great War, he rose to become a major in the Royal Air Force. As part of his job, he was sent to an aircraft factory at Farnborough to examine the production and cost accounting, which were out of hand. As a result of his scrutiny of the books, he soon became fascinated by the "mystery" of economics, and he developed this interest further after the war when he became an official with the London Post Office tube system.

Douglas's study of the various businesses he was attached to led him to observe something that ran directly counter to the traditional view that the prices of goods are always redeemed by their consumption, that the money distributed in the production of goods is sufficient to purchase them. On examining the books, Douglas was certain that this neat proposition was not true. Instead, he evolved the A-plus-B theorem, which he explained as follows in *Credit Power and Democracy* (21f.), written in 1921:

> A factory or other productive organisation has, besides its economic function as a producer of goods, a financial aspect ... as a device for the distribution of purchasing-power to individuals through the media of wages, salaries, and dividends; and on the other hand as a manufactory of prices—

financial values. From this standpoint its payments may be divided into two groups:

Group A—All payments made to individuals (wages, salaries, and dividends).

Group B—All payments made to other organisations (raw materials, bank charges, and other external costs).

Now the rate of flow of purchasing-power to individuals is represented by A, but since all payments go into prices, the rate of flow of prices cannot be less than A + B. . . . but since A will not purchase A+B, a proportion of the product at least equivalent to B must be distributed by a form of purchasing-power which is not comprised in the descriptions grouped under A. . . . this additional purchasing-power is provided by loan-credit (bank overdrafts) or export credit.

If this theorem was true, it undercut the existing rationale for the price system, and it would with time indict the negative role that bankers played. In B, banks were the primary beneficiaries from the imbalance between the money loosed by a firm and the money recouped through prices. Bankers entered the picture because almost everyone from a farmer to a manufacturer relies on their loans to operate from year to year. Since the buyers are also often indebted to banks, their purchasing power is likewise limited, and hence sales are further restricted. As a result, one has a debt-ridden society where there seems to be no egress from the vicious circle of a productivity system that cannot find an adequate market, except through exports to other countries or more indebtedness.

Wars unfortunately offer a temporary respite from the imbalance because much of the work force is diverted into fighting, many products are curtailed, and the governments willingly plunge deeply into debt because they are determined to win. This explains why the general economy in England was better during World War I (though not for a poet) than after, when the country went into a deep slump. Wars also bring the munitions industry into the forefront, and munitions are a marvelous product because individuals do not buy them, thereby diverting their incomes from more basic goods; only states buy munitions, and they turn to banks to transact the sales. It is almost always the banker who wins. According to Douglas, Karl Marx had gone wrong by indicting the capitalist producer and by wanting to take over the sources of production. It was the financial creditor who was at the heart of the problem. Douglas believed that it was not necessary to nationalize production or even to nationalize the banks;

they simply should be barred from creating money off the credit that belongs to the nation at large and allowed to do their ordinary duties of making individual loans for which there is full and proper backing, superintending savings and checking accounts, and transacting other business under appropriate government surveillance.

When Major Douglas first appeared in Orage's nondescript office during the winter of 1918, he was publishing articles with the *English Review*, which was still under the editorship of Ford's replacement, Austin Harrison. Douglas hit Orage at precisely the right time when the great editor was bored with Guild Socialism and looking for new answers to age-old questions. He liked the way that Douglas analyzed the basic problem of price control and especially admired the way in which Douglas's ideas did not call for a drastic revolution like the one occurring in Russia. The system needed reshaping, but not entire recasting. Capitalism could work if only the banks could be brought under control and made to function for the national, not individual, welfare. Since the major was not an expert English stylist, Orage undertook to help him write a treatise that was then serialized in the *New Age* from June to August of 1919. It was called "Economic Democracy," and it appeared as a book with that title in 1920, being followed by *Credit Power and Democracy* in 1921, where the Theorem was fully voiced (after serialization). Pound heard all of these ideas expounded in Orage's office or over coffee at the nearby Kardomah Restaurant, and he was as taken by Douglas's ideas as Orage was. In fact, he devotes a large portion of Canto 38/190 to a poetic paraphrase of the definition just given, and soon afterward starts to mention Douglas's name and to review his work.

What was Douglas's solution for the imbalance between the costs of production and the prices of goods? He formulated a policy known as Social Credit, by which the state, assuming control of the banks' financial credit, would convert this power into subsidies to support industries and to make up the deficiencies in the purchasing power for certain goods that needed help. Yet another step had to be taken. The banks had not only monopolized control of credit, but they had usurped in almost every nation the even more important duty of issuing currency. The "problem of issue" also had to be solved.

This takes us to the central question of how money comes into being. Most people feel that governments themselves create it: the Bank of England acting as a branch of the English government, and so on. But before World War II, the Bank of England was run by private individuals who were not an integral part of the English government any more than the directors of the Federal Reserve System are elected members of the American government. The dollar or pound is a "banker's note" that is not issued directly by these governments, but comes into being when the government needs money.

A private bank enters a credit line to supply it, creating it out of "air, thin air" after the fashion of Ariel. The bank also charges a fee for this service, and so every dollar or pound that enters the marketplace does so with a debtor's note attached to it. This system, which most people do not grasp, came about because of the notion that private individuals, removed from government responsibility, would be less likely to tamper with the money source than would "graft-ridden politicians"; and so the money-magicians of Wall Street are given the key to their own industry, and determine the economic policies of Washington. One of the most enlightened politicians of the twentieth century, Representative Jerry Voorhis in his brilliant *Out of Debt, Out of Danger*, drew an analogy with the Post Office Department. If the Post Office functioned like the U. S. Treasury, they would have to ask for stamps from some private stamp-printing firm any time they wanted them and would have to pay for this service.

How did this system come into being? It can be traced back to 1694 when the Bank of England, acting under the advice of a canny Scotsman named William Paterson, was allowed to take over the royal right of coinage in a war-torn England (still recovering from the Puritan Revolution):

> Said Paterson:
> *Hath benefit of interest on all*
> *the moneys which it, the bank, creates out of nothing.*
> (Canto 46/233)

It was then introduced into the United States by Alexander Hamilton, whom Pound calls "the Prime snot in ALL American history" (Canto 62/350), over the vehement objection of Thomas Jefferson and Hamilton's colleague John Adams, who said:

> Every bank of discount is downright corruption
> taxing the public for private individuals' gain.
>   and if I say this in my will
> the American people wd/ pronounce I died crazy.

This quotation from a letter written by Adams to Jefferson is cited significantly in Canto 71/416, with a solid black line along the lefthand margin. For both Adams and Jefferson believed that private usurpation of the control of divine bounty runs strictly against the spirit and the letter of the American Constitution—as in Article I, Section 8: "The Congress shall have Power: To coin Money, regulate the value thereof, and of foreign Coin." Hamilton's so-called Bank of the United States was eventually destroyed, but then came Nicholas Biddle with a second plan to restore it. Only the courageous actions of men like Martin Van Buren and Andrew Jackson (the only President to restore the national debt to zero) blocked the reformation.

The door for the bankers was opened by concessions granted by President Lincoln to fight the Civil War that was tearing his country in two. Yet although Lincoln gave the bankers firmer ground to stand on, he also did the most extraordinary thing that a president had ever done: he exercised the long-unused right of the government to control its own coinage by issuing bills called greenbacks to fight the war. These were pounced on by his financial enemies and ridiculed as inflation-makers. Yet it was difficult for the opposition to ridicule anyone, since under their steadily growing power there occurred three major bank panics from 1873 to 1894, the Great Depression, and scores of periods of roller-coaster inflation and deflation, unemployment, and financial ruination.

After the Federal Reserve Act of 1913, the bankers were firmly in control. In its wake, there were heavy taxation (the only way the government could raise money), spiraling debt, and scarcity, instead of the taxless, debt-free, abundant society envisioned by Major Douglas. In the following passage, the "bloke" is Pound:

> Seventeen
> Years on this case, nineteen years, ninety years
>   on this case
> An' the fuzzy bloke sez (legs no pants ever wd. fit) 'IF
> that is so, any government worth a damn can
> pay dividends?'
> The major chewed it a bit and sez: 'Y——es, eh . . .
> You mean instead of collectin' taxes?'
> 'Instead of collecting taxes.'
>   (46/231)

How was this taxless society to function? Major Douglas was not a politician, and hence it took some time before the administrative working out of his ideas could be clarified. In 1933, Maurice Colbourne, one of his most lucid explicators, spelled out what would happen if the English nation took over the currency and credit-issuing functions of the so-called Bank of England in *The Meaning of Social Credit* (227f.). He listed the four main points as follows:

1. *We want the nation's money to be under the nation's control.* . . . The New Economics would simply restore the control of money to the Crown; that is, to you and me.
2. *We want our money to be based on our national wealth,* . . . on the nation's Real Credit [not the Financial Credit assessed by banks or other agents].
3. *We want our money to flow in such a volume and at such a time that it is mathematically and automatically sufficient to buy what we produce immediately.* . . . The New Economics would effect this by a National Discount operated by what it calls the "Just Price."
4. *We want to be able to look upon release from unnecessary work, in practice, as a blessing; instead of, as now, a calamity.* . . . The New Economics . . . would distribute a National Dividend to its citizens, all of whom are really shareholders in Great Britain, Limited . . . whose true wealth, in two words, is nothing but her Good Name.

"Just price," one of Pound's favorite terms (*prezzo giusto*), was medieval and Byzantine in origin (see especially Canto 96). The way to create it and to issue the "national dividend" to every citizen is too complex to go into here. Suffice it to say that a mechanism was created, even though it was subject to argument among the various Social Credit factions.

Douglas believed that if a state was truly in control of its currency and credit, it would be in a position to enjoy the enormous profits that now accrue to the rich—the "wise and wealthy" whom Alexander Hamilton envisioned controlling the country, in direct opposition to Jeffersonian democracy. Artists would benefit as well as automobile workers, though not necessarily equally. If people did not produce, the National Appreciation would decrease, and so would the Dividend. Obviously the more Edisons or Westinghouses in a society, the greater would be the bounty to be distributed, and these would reap their own profits because *nothing* would be nationalized (as with socialism and communism). Instead of having a society constantly living under the shadow of debt (Alexander Hamilton: "A public debt is a public blessing"), Douglas and Orage envisioned a terrestrial paradise where, as Jefferson said: "The earth belongs to the living" (Canto 77/468). Although most loan-making would still fall within the province of the banks, the nation could make loans (as indeed it did to the Chrysler Corporation and several major banks that failed in the 1980s). This idea was so unheard of in 1919 and thereafter that Pound cited some precedents from history:

and the fleet at Salamis made with money lent by the state ...
(Canto 74/429; see also 77/468, 79/486)

Alexander paid the debts of his soldiery.
(Cantos 86/564, 95/644; see also 85/549)

But neither the Greek state nor Alexander the Great had to get its money from a Federal Reserve System in order to do this—and then repay it with interest.

Of course to many people Social Credit was a false Utopia. It was bitterly assailed by bankers and financiers, who saw that they might lose their golden goose. They might be reduced to making small loans, where even here they have a tremendous advantage, in that they are allowed to create "out of nothing" nine or ten dollars for every dollar they have on deposit:

> Bank creates it ex nihil. Creates it to meet a need,
> Hic est hyper-usura. Mr. Jefferson met it:
> No man hath natural right to exercise profession
> of lender, save him who hath it to lend.
> (46/234)

Pound employed the medieval word *usura* to describe the excessive profits taken from wrongful moneylending (but never condemning lending at a just rate of interest, which is necessary for capitalistic development). It was a word that he would make famous in Canto 45, which is a dirge against Geryon, the allegorical beast from Dante's *Inferno* that Pound used as a symbol of fraudulence in finance. Usura is defined in Canto 45/230 as "A charge for the use of purchasing power, levied without regard to production; often without regard to the possibilities of production."

Unfortunately for Douglas and Pound, the only government that really tried to give Social Credit a chance to function was the Province of Alberta, Canada, in the 1930s, the depths of the Great Depression, when farmers were bankrupt and misery was widespread. But the provincial government was thoroughly subverted by the bankers and legislators in Ottawa, and as a result nothing meaningful happened.

Embittered by a world that seemed to reject his dream of plenty for all, Major Douglas became a rather isolated figure before his death in 1952. His famous theorem was attacked by those who said that it did not take into account the time in which B became A, while others said that he argued from too narrow a base, a few industries that he happened to know. Still others said that Social Credit would create rampant inflation, like Lincoln's greenbacks, ignoring Douglas's concept of creating a just price.

Finally, Douglas took to blaming all sorts of people as the underminers of his policy: Nazis, Bolsheviks, Freemasons, and finally, the favorite scapegoat of the 1930s, world Jewry, especially the Rothschilds, whom Pound also attacked. In many ways Douglas and Pound followed the same path from idealistic zeal to bitter rancor and denunciation to a kind of self-effacing silence and isolation. Their notions of a divine comedy crumbled into personal tragedy. In his later years, Pound often said that he was no longer a Social Credit man; yet he never gave up on his idea of an Earthly Paradise, down to the last Fragment of the *Cantos*, and he never "forgave" the usurers and manipulators of fraud.

Both Pound's and Douglas's concepts of economics changed drastically over the years. In 1919, both were in some ways still novices, and neither had a firm grasp of the political structure that would be necessary to make their economic dream come true. Orage would abandon economics temporarily in the early twenties to pursue his interests in the occult, and although he was again active in the 1930s, his temporary absence had hurt the cause. Pound stayed close to Douglas's ideas in the twenties, but he supplemented them with some other theories, such as Silvio Gesell's radical Schwundgeld idea, whereby money would literally disappear if it was not spent. The literary and economic critic Gorham Munson in his brilliant *Aladdin's Lamp* covers the field of most of Pound's economic interests, without sharing Pound's rather tragic faith in fascism. Both Munson and Pound were especially taken with Brooks Adams's *Law of Civilization and Decay* (1896), which links economics with the humanities, especially literature and art. Money is to a society as blood is to the body: its basic form of life-giving circulation. Without money, art struggles to come into being, whereas with it, art flourishes, as during the High Middle Ages and Renaissance, before the usurers and "financiers" managed to subvert lazy, greedy kings and usurp their right to control currency and credit. This view is central to the *Cantos*. It would take a few years before Pound was able to put his ideogram or idea-picture for his great poem together, but after he met Major Douglas, the last big missing piece was present for filling in the picture.

The wide-eyed "bloke" in the ill-fitting pants who sat at the feet of the major was about to enter a new era of his life. His despair in the Temple of Mammon would lead him to want to crush it. He was no longer interested in Aesthetics per se; Beauty had to be part of a larger design. Never again would Ezra write graceful lyrics for the sake of writing graceful lyrics; things now had to have meanings. One could not paint the Earthly Paradise without having some notion of how it could come into being. From now on, his still highly inchoative poem would assume an economic slant. If Dante had his theology of another world as the substructure for his epic, Pound would rely on economics (in Greek, literally: "the rule or order of the house"). Ezra Pound wanted his Paradise here and now, and he suddenly felt that he had the substance to impel himself and his vision forward.

16

Propertius and the Roads of France (1919)

> *But to set here the roads of France,*
> *of Cahors, of Chalus,*
> *the inn low by the river's edge,*
> *the poplars; to set here the roads of France*
> —*Canto 76/455*

With the war over, one might have expected people to settle down immediately, but that did not happen. For one thing, the demobilization process was slow. One of the last to be released was Richard Aldington, who was now estranged from Hilda, who had been living in Cornwall. While Richard was off in France, his wife had become friendly with a young female admirer named Winifred Ellerman, the daughter of a well-known shipping millionaire. May Sinclair had given Winifred the Cornwall address, and soon the two women were inseparable as the neurotic heiress offered protection to the abandoned Dryad.

Hilda was especially in need of help because she was pregnant, and Aldington would have nothing to do with this child, who was clearly not his. One of Hilda's biographers, Janice Robinson, believes that the father was D. H. Lawrence, who was a major force in Hilda's life from 1914 to 1918. Hilda had settled for the war in Cornwall to be near

D. H. and his wife Frieda, who were then ejected from the area for suspected pro-German sentiments. Yet another biographer, Barbara Guest, more plausibly suggests a quiet, bespectacled musician and critic named Cecil Gray. Perdita Schaffner, who was born from this mating on March 31, 1919, told Guest (96) that when she met the rather gloomy but highly intellectual Gray for the only time, at Norman Douglas's house on Capri in 1957, she felt instinctively that this man had much of herself in him.

In any case, as we know from passages already quoted from *End to Torment*, Ezra visited Hilda in the hospital in the London suburb of Ealing, where she said that he issued the dramatic statement that he deeply regretted that the father was not he. Thus Hilda. Pound's visit of 1919 would be one of the last times he would see her, except for a brief encounter or two in Paris and at Olivia Shakespear's funeral, since she would soon be deeply involved in her love affair with Bryher, as Miss Ellerman called herself when she wrote historical novels and other works.

Richard, or "Cuthbert" as the two women called him (the name for a coward or turncoat), resolutely refused to contribute any support for the child and soon the Aldingtons were separated, although not legally divorced until June 22, 1938. Yet miraculously Aldington was able to turn what looked like a total loss into a triumph. This "jolly, open-faced English type—26 years old" (as Herbert Read described him suspiciously at the time) boldly asked Winifred to meet her father (a crony of J. Pierpont Morgan). When that occurred, he touched the old man up for a job in journalism, since Mr. Ellerman owned a share of the *London Times* with Lord Northcliffe (one of the denizens of Pound's London Hell Cantos, soon forthcoming). Ellerman came through, and Richard then entered a successful career in journalism, although Pound saw this as a fatal step in his life as a serious writer. Still, Richard did go on to write several novels, some successful, and numerous essays, as on Proust; and in time, with another partner like Brigit Patmore, he even seems to have become a better person, although he always carefully nurtured any injustices dealt to him by Ezra and his first wife.

James Joyce was faring well now that he could leave constricting Zurich and return to Trieste. He had spent much of the previous year in a foolish flirtation with a Marthe Fleischmann (Martha Clifford in *Ulysses*) and in a silly litigation with an English actor (the "Private" Carr of the "Circe" episode in *Ulysses*). On July 6, Harriet Shaw Weaver confirmed that she was the anonymous donor who had given him enough money to live comfortably for the rest of his life. From 1918 on, Joyce had been sending Pound more chapters from *Ulysses* for publication in the *Little Review*. Pound liked most of them, but when he received the "Sirens" episode, he told Joyce to put in some signposts to help the reader (*PJ*, 157)—which irritated Joyce terribly. The work was causing the editors a great deal of trouble from postal authorities. Miss Anderson was forced to make cuts on the "Scylla and Charybdis" episode (April–May issue); this was one of the most innocuous chapters of all, but the Post Office nevertheless suppressed it. When in September of 1920 the "Nausicaa" episode was "pinched by the PO-lice" (*SL*, 150; misdated), they decided to suspend magazine publication and to go directly into book form. When Pound read the "Oxen of the Sun" episode on October 25 of 1919, he told Quinn triumphantly: "Parody of styles, a trick borrowed from Rabelais, but never done better, even in Rab. Our James is a grrreat man. I hope to God there is a foundation of truth in the yarn he wrote me about a windfall" (*SL*, 152). Pound did not have to worry: Miss Weaver delivered as promised, and Joyce was soon lifted from his back and that of the long-suffering Quinn.

Quinn, meanwhile, was also trying to rid himself of the *Little Review*. He was thoroughly bored by the "cheeky" (one of his favorite words) behavior of the two ladies, who lacked any business sense and loved altercations: "making no compromise with the public taste" was their motto. Pound was also tired of the venture. In 1918 he had foreseen the chance of becoming involved with a new journal just as Quinn was backing away from Anderson and Heap (PC 501). On January 27 of 1919, he asked his father if he would serve as a reader, since Ezra always valued Homer's taste (PC 515); but this new journal, which might have been based in Switzerland with Dadaist connections (*SL* 145), never materialized.

Meanwhile the soldiers were coming home from the war. On December 27 of 1918 Pound cooked a turkey for the victorious Colonel Lawrence, who wanted Arabia for the Arabs. Also present were doughty old Captain Baker, who had weathered the combat but would be permanently felled by the flu this coming February, and Fred Manning, still a friend after a decade (PC 510). Old Victor Plarr was once again orating about the famous Galliffet charge of 1870 in the *Times*, just as he had done ten years before to a wide-eyed and innocent Ezra Pound (PC 508).

By January 28, Ezra told Bill Williams (*SL*, 145) that "Fat" Madox Ford (who would finally drop the name Hueffer this spring) was back in town, along with Lewis, who was still recovering from the flu. Ford refused to move back in with Violet, but he did use her address to receive his mail. He took rather spartan quarters near Ezra at 20A

Campden Hill Gardens and looked impoverished, often wearing discarded army clothing. Still somewhat dazed from his freakish gas attack, Ford was determined to abandon the urban literary life and go off with his now beloved Stella Bowen to a pig and chicken farm. Indeed, they managed to find one that was affordable near Pulborough, Surrey. By early summer, Stella had joined him at Red Ford Cottage, where they entertained the likes of Herbert Read, Mary Butts, her former husband John Rodker (now embarking into publishing), Phyllis Reid, and, from time to time, Ezra Pound—with or without Dorothy. The place was cold, dank, damp, and uncomfortable, as Pound jokingly portrayed it in Section X of *Hugh Selwyn Mauberley:*

> Beneath the sagging roof
> The stylist has taken shelter,
> Unpaid, uncelebrated,
> At last from the world's welter . . .
>
> The haven from sophistications and contentions
> Leaks through its thatch;
> He offers succulent cooking;
> The door has a creaking latch.
>
> *(Pers.,* 195)

Indeed, the leaking and the creaking soon proved to be too much, and so they moved over to a place called Coopers near Bedham, where they determinedly raised chickens and pigs for a while. At least once, Violet sneaked down to the country and spied at them through the bushes, just to be sure that all this was really happening. Here Ford wrote his poorly organized memoir *Thus To Revisit,* complaining that it would take him a decade to get the war off his mind. But after a few years of this rather sodden seclusion, he and Stella went off to France to visit Ezra and see the South—and they never came back. The sale of the place, which helped to finance the *Transatlantic Review,* was transacted by intermediaries.

As was said in the previous chapter, Lewis was already in London in 1918 because of his sinecure. When he was formally released from the service, he took quarters at 1A Gloucester Walk in Kensington, also near Ezra. In addition, he had a studio at Adam and Eve Mews, where he did portraits of such people as the Sitwells, Iris Tree (a wild friend of Nancy Cunard), Iris Barry (several drawings), and Ezra Pound, whose 1920 portrait is like that of a powerful iron mask. Pound was indeed one of Lewis's favorite and finest models. Some of Lewis's drawings were included at the end of this year in a series called *Fifteen Drawings*, which were issued by John Rodker on his new Ovid Press.

As early as February, Wyndham had his first one-man show, at the Goupil Gallery, in which war objects and war scenes were featured. It was reviewed most favorably by the now famous B. H. Dias, who concluded that "Mr. Lewis would seem to suggest that art is a cut above war; that art might even outlast it" (*New Age*, Feb. 20). In the next decade, Lewis would support himself largely by doing portraits of such people as Eliot, Joyce, Virginia Woolf, Robert McAlmon, Nancy Cunard, and his wife Froanna. But try as he might in 1919, neither he nor Pound could restore the triumphs of 1914. And so he and Pound turned to women. Unable to win money, they won hearts. Still, this rather reckless lovemaking had to come to an end, and in Pound's case, deliverance was only a few years away.

Although Eliot was untouched by the war, he perhaps came through it more poorly than anyone else. He had tried to join the U.S. Naval Intelligence the previous fall, with Pound's help, but was balked by red tape. In December of 1918, Pound informed Quinn that "Tom" was back at the bank, but his health was in a "very shaky" state. Pound's concern for his friend would continue for the next few years until Eliot finally got free from his job (which he professed to like) and entered publishing. Aldington would help him here with his journalistic connections.

During 1919 both T.S. and Vivien kept declining in health in a way that was depressing to everyone around them. Yet Eliot's work was definitely catching on. Through Quinn, Knopf agreed in April to bring out a collection of Eliot's poems, but not his prose; this was held up by dickering for another year. But the Woolfs on their Hogarth Press did issue a selection of Eliot's work in June of 1919.

Vivien's diary for this year records the Pounds as dinner guests in their small and rather tawdry flat at Crawford Mansions near Baker Street. In April, "Tom" was exhausted, and his doctor told him to discontinue writing for a time; indeed, very soon this was physically impossible. Dorothy and Ezra were extremely concerned about the way that things were going. They heartily invited him (but not Vivien) to accompany them on part of their long walking tour in the troubadour country of southern France that summer. At first Eliot declined; but he grew more receptive to the invitation as his condition worsened, and by August he was off to join them.

Yeats, meanwhile, was happily settled in his new marriage and was asking Ezra to serve as the godfather for his child, if male (PC 514). He was now ensconced in a little cottage next to the imposing Norman tower that he had purchased at Ballylee, which Pound, in a letter to Quinn on June 1, 1920, jokingly called "Ballyphallus or whatever he calls it with the river on the first floor." Soon Yeats was closing down his Woburn Buildings flat, giving it to Douglas Goldring for the last months of its lease. He was feverishly working on his "tower ... restored ... for my wife George," as he says in his little poem "To Be Carved on a Stone at Thoor Ballylee" (YCP, 188).

Yeats was trying to forget the Great War that had taken the life of such friends as Major Robert Gregory (YCP, 130 and 133). He was also trying to keep removed from the lawlessness that was gripping his native land, as the British-supported black-and-tans constantly harassed the loyal Irish forces and ordinary citizens. Yeats would make an extended trip to America in 1920 at Quinn's behest. On returning in 1922, he would settle down in the newly declared Irish Free State and, after some internal troubles in 1923, he would play a prominent role in the nation's history as a senator. In 1924 he received the Nobel Prize for Literature, still years before he wrote many of the greatest poems of his career, such as those dealing with Byzantium. His poem "Nineteen Hundred and Nineteen" is sad and ominous: "Now days are dragon-ridden, the nightmare / Rides upon sleep" (*YCP*, 205), and his famous "Second Coming" (*YCP*, 184) is a brooding prophecy of the militant violence to come. Of Ezra Pound's many friends, Yeats was perhaps the one who was destined for the greatest share of fame, fortune, and—most importantly of all—happiness.

As for Ezra Pound, the two most important events of this year were the publication of his Propertius renditions and his walking tour with Dorothy in the South of France. Early in the year, he gave up his position as foreign correspondent for *Poetry*—after many previous resignations, as he informed Marianne Moore (*SL* no. 159). And although he continued to supervise the serialization of *Ulysses* for the *Little Review*, by April he abandoned the job of acting as their London editor in favor or John Rodker. One of Pound's last acts for the Misses Heap and Anderson was to turn their February–March issue into a memorial for Rémy de Gourmont. In the just-mentioned letter to Marianne Moore, Pound complained that Harriet Monroe had accepted only four of the twelve sections of "Homage to Sextus Propertius." He therefore felt that Harriet was publishing a "very mutilated piece" of his composition, and he was angry. Harriet in turn was angered when she learned about this accusation, which was certainly overstated on Pound's part.

As soon as Harriet published the four sections (with the current VI replacing the more lascivious IV), they were assailed in her April issue in a letter to the editor from W. G. Hale (1848–1928), a professor of Latin at the University of Chicago. His letter, one of the most insensitive reviews of all time, is printed *in toto* in Eric Homberger's *Ezra Pound: The Critical Heritage* (155-57). Hale's pedantry shows why the study of classics was declining so rapidly at the time. Without any awareness of the fact that Pound was obviously not trying to be literal, Hale accused him in the most narrow way possible for his many casual expressions ("have my dog's day"), additions, and, of course, errors.

One of the most famous of these howlers, which Richard Aldington never tired of quoting, was Pound's apparent mistaking of the verb *canes* (you will sing) for the noun *canes* (dogs). Yet, as Pound's most lucid defender, J. P. Sullivan, has shown in his highly regarded *Ezra Pound and Sextus Propertius*, the line makes perfectly good sense and is faithful in Pound's version:

Hale: You will sing of the drunken evidence of a nocturnal episode.

Pound: Night dogs, the marks of a drunken scurry

(*Pers.*, 211)

Hale merely fell into the trap that has caught others: as Ezra said to his father Homer, "my poem never for a moment pretends to translate" (PC 521). Pound said to Orage, who was about to serialize the entire sequence in his June 19 issue of the *New Age:* "My job was to bring a dead man to life...." (PC 523). We shall return to this argument after discussing Pound's trip to the Midi, since that vacation mercifully interrupted the furor.

It was not easy to get away. There were stiff post-war restrictions on travel that required information about one's business, birth, health, and so on before they could get a passport and be on the road. Finally on April 22 they left England by ship from Southampton. If Pound was anxious to go, probably Dorothy was even more so, since she had to be aware of at least some of his many amours with other women. It has been suggested that she was rather naive about these matters at this time, but that is difficult to believe. It has also been suggested that her natural frigidity made her welcome Ezra's attentions to other women, but that is difficult to accept too. Certainly at other times she showed that she was not the least bit happy about sharing her husband with anyone else.

Their first stop was Paris, where they stayed near the Mapel sisters, whom he knew from the Spain of 1906; they then proceeded to Toulouse, the home of the troubadour Peire Vidal, who figures prominently in Canto 4, which was soon to be published. They planned on using this metropolis of the South as their central base of operation. A postcard to Olivia on April 24, showing the impressive Basilica of St. Sernin, says that they have finally arrived. They were being assisted by Pierre Aristide Dulac, the father of Edmund, who had helped to stage Yeats's plays and who had designed the orange-red stamp with the "EP" intaglio that appeared in the first edition of *Lustra* in 1916. The father followed his son's request and found them a nice room at 13 Rue St. Ursule. He also played the perfect host, treating them to meal after meal of the delicious cuisine of the South, including the cassoulets and terrines of rabbit and beef. The food was so good that:

>   ... Tosch the great ex-greyhound
>   used to get wildly excited
>   at being given large beefsteaks
>   in Tolosa
>   and leapt one day finally
>   right into the centre of the large dining table
>   and lay there as a centre piece
>   near the cupboard piled half full
>   with novels of "Willy" etc
>   in the old one franc editions
>   and you cd/ hear papa Dulac's voice
>   clear in the choir that wd/ ring ping on the high altar
>   in the Bach chorals
>   true as a pistol shot
>   (Canto 80/503–4)

The "Willy" that Father Dulac was reading was the novelist Henri Gauthier-Villars (1859–1931), whom Pound knew in Paris and tried to enlist as a writer for the *Dial*, although he never succeeded.

One of the buildings that Pound most admired in Toulouse was the Basilica of the Daurade (the Golden) on the banks of the Garonne, which was noted for its colorful dome and golden mosaics. Latter-day troubadours (after the Inquisition) used to receive prizes here, and earlier in the late 1200s Guido Cavalcanti saw it on a pilgrimage to Spain, since he mentions it and a girl from Toulouse in his Ballata 7 (*Trans.*, 112–13). Pound included the Church in early versions of Canto 4, but it was later cut, only to be cited in Canto 52/258, where the Golden Roof puts it in a category with the beautiful temples of Ravenna and Istanbul.

It is difficult to account for the first six weeks of the Pounds' stay, but there are numerous postcards to follow their later movements. Several of these were published in *Ezra Pound: The London Years*

(1978), edited by Philip Grover after the First International Conference in honor of Pound, held at the University of Sheffield. A letter to Wyncote sent on May 30 explains that they have been resting for a month (PC 523), taking small tours in the immediate vicinity. Actually Pound was also checking the proofs for his next collection of poems, *Quia Pauper Amavi*, and was following installments of Joyce's opus. He had been commissioned by Orage to write a series of loose pieces on travel or other meditations for the *New Age*, and these, titled "Pastiche: The Regional," helped to pay for the trip. The first appeared on June 12, saying that Pound had visited Nîmes with its Roman amphitheater and the beautiful marble Maison Carrée, which he admired for its Greek symmetry (see Cantos 31/154 and 100/714); he had also seen Arles, with its lovely cloister of St. Trophime (Canto 45/230 and 51/250). Other pieces, which ran on into November, spoke about anything from the deadness of the nightlife in Toulouse to the glory of French romances.

In the first week of June, according to a plan enunciated to Homer Pound on May 30 (PC 523), they intended to head eastward by train to Nîmes, Beaucaire (96/659), Tarascon (76/455), Avignon, St. Rémy, Les Baux (a largely deserted site where some patrons of Sordello had resided), Arles, and Carcassonne, which disappointed Ezra because of its excessive restorations (PC 525).

Returning to Toulouse, they then headed southwest. On June 6 Dorothy sent her mother a card from Montréjeau, saying that the proofs of *Quia* had been forwarded, and they were feasting on the Italianlike cuisine, which had a lot of cinnamon and saffron in it. Ezra told Olivia on a later card that showed the Valley of the Garonne that "Coz" (Dorothy) was "industriously painting" landscapes, and indeed many of her watercolors, especially of the mountains, survive. The couple liked this town, as well as its neighbor up the hill:

> As from the terrace, Saint Bertrand
>   to southward from Montrejeau
>   (95/645)

They often walked the road leading up to St. Bertrand de Comminges.

This was alleged to have been Albigensian country, the home of dualist heretics who were brutally killed by the North French in conjunction with the Papacy in the infamous Albigensian Crusade. Here, high in the crystal air of the Pyrenees, they climbed to the site of the old solar temple of Montségur (Mount Secure), which was sacred not only to the Albigensians but also probably to the Gallic druids and other tribes long lost to history. Hundreds of people had been burned at the stake here in 1244 when they refused to recant their allegedly heretical beliefs. Pound wanted to link these rebels to the Greek cults of Eleusis, the worshipers of earthly fertility, as well as the forces of the Sun, Helios:

> Mont Ségur, sacred to Helios,
> and for what had been, San Bertrand de Comminges.
> (87/574)

In fact, he saw the whole of the troubadour tradition opposed to the rigid policies of the Church, which often worked against the beauty of Art, Nature, and Earthly Love. He linked the troubadours and their masterful compositions to the great architects who built cathedrals with symmetric proportions and with the liberal Irish philosopher John Scotus Erigena of the ninth century, who refused to acknowledge Heaven and Hell in his life-affirming *On the Division of Nature:*

> That is Sagetrieb,   [the instinct to express; Pound's word]
>   that is tradition.
> Builders had kept the proportion,
>   did Jacques de Molay
>   know these proportions?
> and was Erigena ours?
> (90/605)

June 11. A card shows the Market of the Carmelites, Toulouse. Ezra tells Olivia that the Dryad is free to move into their apartment with her baby if she chooses. He is pushing a portfolio of Gaudier's drawings to be run off by Rodker on his Ovid Press.

June 15 or thereabouts. Mauléon. Hometown of the troubadour Savairic, who received Gaubertz de Poicebot (Professor Shepard's man) into the knighthood after he abandoned his monastery. The card shows the Square of the Bridge and the Tower, but the castle was largely Renaissance, and hence disappointing.

June 22-28. Foix. They enter this dramatic mountain town on the 22d, just as it is prepared to celebrate the formal signing of the peace. Flags are waving everywhere, people shouting, bands.

July 12. Back at Montréjeau and San Bertrand de Comminges, with its many Roman ruins:

> ... the stair there still broken
> the flat stones of the road, Mt. Segur.
> From Val Cabrere, were two miles of roofs to San Bertrand

> so that a cat need not set foot in the road
> where now is an inn, and bare rafters,
> where they scratch six feet deep to reach pavement
> where now is wheat field, and a milestone
> an altar to Terminus, with arms crossed
> back of the stone
> Where sun cuts light against evening;
> where light shaves grass into emerald
> Savairic; hither Gaubertz;
> Said they wd. not be under Paris
(Canto 48/243)

July 13. Montségur again. Ezra writes Homer that he has seen an unforgettable festival in which people competed by trying to climb a greased pole, at the top of which were attached a live chicken and a goose (PC 526). He was sure that this was some holdover from ancient pagan rites that had been subsumed by the Christians in a way that he approved of. Earlier, he and Dorothy had seen a vermiform or wormlike procession threading its way through a crowd in a Catholic rite outside the Church of St. Nicholas in Toulouse (PC 511). This would find its way into the final version of Canto 4:

> The Garonne is thick like paint,
> Procession,—"Et sa'ave, sa'ave, sa'ave Regina!"—
> Moves like a worm, in the crowd.
> (16)

July 16. Still in the Foix-Montségur region.

July 24. They have now moved north to Brive of the laughing waters, having traveled through the infamous usury city of Cahors past Rocamadour to this lovely valley town on the banks of the swift-running Corrèze. They pause here, using Brive as a base to explore the area beloved by Bertran de Born and Bernart de Ventadorn, two of the most famous troubadours.

July 25. Excidueil. The town of Guiraut de Bornelh; but since Dante disapproved of his work, Pound paid little attention to him. Yet this hamlet on the still-flowing River Loue contains the ruins of a once-imposing castle that had belonged to Talleyrand, the friendly enemy of Bertran de Born, and was a good place to reside in. They stayed in the little Hotel Poujol run by Madame Poujol (74/428). It was extremely hot that summer, and so they had to flypaper their bedroom and kitchen.

July 28. They took a long side trip northeast to Clermont, where the

First Crusade was announced. Along the way, they passed through Ussel, the home of at least three troubadours. On a side road that was difficult to locate, they found the high, windswept ruins of the parapets of Ventadorn/Ventadour, where Bernart may have composed his famous Lark Song:

> When I see the lark moving
> His wings with joy toward the light,
> Then forget and let himself fall
> From the sweetness that enters his heart . . .
>
> *Can vei la lauzeta mover*
> *De joi sas alas contra·l rai*
> *Que s'oblid'e se laissa cader*
> *Dal doussor que al cor li vai . . .*

Pound remembered both Bernart and his castle early in Canto 26/132:

> Where was the wall of Eblis
> At Ventadour, there now are the bees,
> And in that court, wild grass for their pleasure
> That they carry back to the crevice
> Where loose stone hangs upon stone.
> (27/132)

And late in Canto 74/436:

> Past Malmaison in field by the river the tables
> Sirdar, Armenonville
> Or at Ventadour the keys of the chateau;
> rain, Ussel,

August 1. Hautefort, or better (because Provençal), Altafort. The famous castle of Bertran de Born, whose voice Pound had borrowed in his vigorous sestina. The castle has been reconstructed through the years, but it still glowers menacingly over the valley on its stout, impregnable base.

August 2. Montignac, the village where Bertran's girlfriend Maent lived. The Pounds slept close to the place where King Henry II of England had besieged Bertran in his castle.

August 5. Rocamadour (either St. Amadour's Rock or, as Pound was more likely to construe it, the Holy Lover's Rock). A card to Olivia from Dorothy says that they approached this eyrielike town through scrub trees, where they stirred up thousands of butterflies (years later Pound would also remember stirring up a field of larks at Allègre). Rocamadour is a religious town; it was filled with tourists who had come to see the Black Virgin and to hear the peals of the Miracle Bell. Penitents and modern lepers crawled up the many steps leading to the central shrine, while that night the little central cafe had some rollicking Russian soldiers swigging vodka in celebration of the end of the war. The next day the Pounds took the train to:

August 6. Brive again. At this point, until Eliot arrived nine days later, the couple took numerous side trips, collecting postcards that they kept as mementos:

They visited Rocafixada, where they had to huddle against a wall during a driving thunderstorm.

They saw Ribérac, the hometown of Arnaut Daniel, which has only melancholy ruins, and nearby Marueil, where the Lesser Arnaut of Marueil lived.

They saw Angoulême, which squats proudly on its hill, and Barbezieux, where Richart or Rigaut wrote amusing poems heavy with animal imagery: "Exactly like the elephant. . . ."

They saw Blaye, where Jaufre Rudel pined for his far-off love . . . *de lonh* . . . (65/371).

They saw Poitiers, the cradle of troubadour poetry, since the first surviving troubadour, Duke William IX of Aquitaine (or Guillaume of Poitiers, as Pound calls him) came from there, along with his lovely granddaughter, Eleanor of Aquitaine . . . destroyer of ships like Helen, her namesake, destroyer of men . . . but also the patron of Bernart. . . .

In this city, Pound was fascinated by the room in William's palace where you cannot cast a shadow (now the Hôtel de Ville) and the beautiful Church of Notre Dame la Grande, whose turrets resemble acorns or perhaps the scales of fish; and there was also the magnificent Church of St. Hilaire, whose soaring vaults combined mystic rapture with rationality:

> Not by usura Saint Hilaire
>
> (45/230)
>
> Nor St Hilaire its proportion
>
> (51/250)
>
> Like a fish-scale roof,
>   Like the church roof in Poictiers
>   If it were gold.
>
> (4/14)

1919

> And from the San Ku
> . . . .
>   to the room in Poitiers where one can stand
>   casting no shadow,
>   (90/605)

He never forgot this town.

They also saw Talleyrand's castle in Chalais (101/723), as well as neighboring Aubeterre (101/723), where the charming translator and occultist Mademoiselle de Pratz of Paris came from originally:

> and at Ventadour and at Aubeterre
> or where they set tables down by small rivers,
> and the stream's edge is lost in grass
>   (80/509)

Other treasured postcards show that they did not miss Périgueux, a town connected with Talleyrand, who warred and exchanged poems with nearby Bertran; his family continued down to the time of Napoleon (salubriously, Pound ultimately felt, although at first he disliked this family because of what John Adams said about them). With its impressive walls and towers, Pound saw here a miniature New York: "But that New York I have found at Périgueux" (80/508). Dorothy notes on one card that Talleyrand was pronounced Dalleyrand and Périgord Berrigord (105/749).

Finally on August 15 Eliot arrived, looking pale and thin and nervous. Ezra and Dorothy proceeded immediately to get him out into the sun and into mineral baths (there was an excellent one at Brive), into a world of healing nature. While Dorothy stayed behind at the Hotel Poujol at Excideuil, Ezra and Tom embarked on several trips: to Thiviers (Aug. 17) and Brantôme (Aug. 18), where poor Eliot, who was not accustomed to such exertions in walking, suddenly sprouted seven blisters. He and Ezra therefore switched over to the train.

August 21. Around this time before leaving Excideuil, Eliot and Pound examined the ruins of the local castle, where Pound showed his friend an interesting wave pattern sculpted into the walls (see Kenner's *Pound Era*, 337). Ezra was convinced that this engraving was a link between these people with the Mediterranean cultures of Greece and Rome:

> and the wave pattern runs in the stone
> on the high parapet (Excideuil)
> Mt Segur and the city of Dioce
>   (80/510)

During this examination, Eliot turned suddenly and said something that sounded strange and ominous to his companion—something that Pound did not forget, although he substituted the name "Arnaut" because he did not want to embarrass his friend:

> So Arnaut turned there
> Above him the wave pattern cut in the stone
> Spire-top alevel the well-curb
> And the tower with cut stone above that, saying:
> "I am afraid of the life after death."
>
> (29/145)

Eliot soon loved the South of France as much as Dorothy and Ezra—and numerous others whom Ezra proselytized over the years, like Olga Rudge and Nancy Cunard and Stella Bowen. At one point, Eliot went off on his own to inspect the primitive cave paintings at Les Eyziès and Font de Gaume.

All too soon it was over and time to go home. By August 26, the Pounds were north in Orléans, and by September 3, they were back in a large room at the Hotel Elysée, 3 Rue de Beaune, with a view of the Seine. They had dinner with Ida Mapel, whose "inseparable" sister Adah was now back in West Virginia. Pound saw and talked to Fritz Vanderpyl, a Flemish art critic and poet who wrote in French, old Albert Mockel, and many, many painters. France was once again calling.

By September 11, three days before Dorothy's birthday, they were back in London, thanking both Alfred Orage for his underwriting and Edmund Dulac for his father's hospitality.

It was a glorious tour—one that none of the three travelers would soon forget. Dorothy had her paintings, Pound his future lines of poetry, and Eliot a new lease on life. But Eliot was soon back in the debilitating grind of bank routine (he was working on German debts to England) and in the increasingly difficult clutches of his neurotic wife.

In the interim, the publication of the Propertius renditions in the *New Age*—as well as their inclusion in *Quia Pauper Amavi*—continued to stir up adverse criticism. Although Orage himself defended Pound (Homberger, 158), he published an anonymous review in the *New Age* of November 27 that was more controlled than Professor Hale's, but equally devastating. Paul Selver identified the reviewer as Adrian Collins, who had studied classics at Oxford. Collins was perceptive in that he stated flatly: "It is obviously not meant as a translation," but he then went on to point out a myriad of errors. Pound replied to this review on December 4, and he then invited Collins to dinner; ultimately the two got along together very well, but the attacks and the counterattacks went on.

The lyrics of *Quia Pauper Amavi* were largely forgotten. Indeed, the book had almost nothing new in it. The title, incidentally, was taken from Ovid's contention that love and poverty go well together: "Because I loved as a pauper" (*Art of Love* 2.165), as Pound explained to Homer (PC 511).

Probably the last thing to be said about the Propertius transformations is that they present that first-century B.C. author in a more vigorous way than anyone else has presented him. Pound himself acknowledged to his father that he might have "overemphasized the correspondence between Augustan Rome and the present" (PC 520; apparently he thought of the modern Augustus as President Wilson, whose policies he detested). Even though Propertius did not want to write imperial propaganda any more than Pound did, he nevertheless seems to have had a much stronger feeling for Rome than Pound had for the United States or England. There is also the question of whether Propertius was as witty as Pound made him out to be. Yet the unstated factor that may have irked reviewers more than anything else was Pound's free handling of the suggestive quality of the verse. Propertius is erotic, and Pound's renditions of him are frankly sensual. In 1919 this license was not acceptable, and that is why Elkin Mathews would not issue *Quia* (the Egoist Ltd. did), although he did agree to bring out a large collection of Pound's lyrics the following year.

Pound meanwhile continued to publish constantly in the *New Age*, and his publications were becoming increasingly more political and economic. In one of his last "Pastiche" pieces on November 6, he made the bold statement that artists followed the Greeks and the Romans, while others followed the Jews. This was the first even vaguely anti-Semitic remark of his to appear in print, and the reaction was immediate. As a result, in the next issue of the 13th, he was quick to apologize: "Inasmuch as the Jew has conducted no holy war for nearly two millenia [*sic*], he is preferable to the Christian and the Mahomedan." In an earlier piece on October 30, Pound showed the first sign of being influenced by the ideas of Major Douglas. He said that it was important for manufacturing systems to overproduce so that their goods would be available for everyone. Aristocratic governments could back a productive system that was selective and meant to be luxurious, but it was the *duty* of democracies to make goods available to all of the people. When this series ran its course, Orage immediately commissioned Pound to write "The Revolt of Intelligence," which ran on until March 18 of the next year.

The fall of 1919 was brightened by the appearance of Canto 4 as a small, four-leaf brochure from John Rodker's Ovid Press. Printed on expensive Japanese vellum, it was distributed free when its forty copies appeared on October 4. This version of the canto was still quite different from the one circulated today, especially in its ending, but progress on the long poem was clearly being made. On December 13, Pound notified his father that he had now finished Cantos 5, 6, and 7, and that each one was more difficult than the one that came before it (sad news). He also lamented to John Quinn that his long poem was becoming much more abstract and obscure, and could never hope to have a large, popular audience (prophetic words).

A marvelous opportunity for the future seemed to present itself that same October when a publication called the *Outlook* asked Pound if he would like to serve as their drama critic. The pay was excellent, and Ezra was ecstatic. But Paradise, as Pound soon learned, was indeed *spezzato:* he was fired in the "most caddish possible manner" after "two opulent weeks," he told Quinn on October 25.

It is clear that 1919 had been a year of very mixed blessings. The Propertius had been stormily received, yet was by no means a total loss. He was now drafting his Hell Cantos, using London as his modern Inferno, and so the long poem continued to move along. But in retrospect, the year had been saved by that walking trip in the South. It had restored the health of both Eliot and Pound, although Eliot was due to go under again shortly. Even when Pound was writing the very last of his *Cantos*, he remembered that sunny, brilliant world of southern France with its lovely poems like the Lark Song of Bernart de Ventadorn. He thought of those roller-coaster roads from Brive to Tulle and Moissac and Cahors, along with the rise and fall of Bernart's bird on its ill-fated flight toward the sun. He also mentioned the bankruptcy *(faillite)* of a famous publisher friend of Gourmont, Cocteau, and Cunard, whose firms failed because he spent too much money on making his books look beautiful:

> La faillite de François Bernouard, Paris
> or a field of larks at Allègre,
>   "es laissa cader"   [and lets herself fall]
> so high toward the sun and then falling
>   "de joi sas alas"   [with joy her wings]
> to set here the roads of France.

(117/803)

17

Mauberley (and Pound) Say Goodbye (1920)

I know that I am perched on the rotten shell of a crumbling empire but it isn't my empire, and I'm not legally responsible, and anyway the Germans will probably run it as well as you do. If they don't run it rather better I shall go to Paris, for I am not particularly fond of Germans.
—"Through Alien Eyes, I"

*so that leaving America I brought with me $80
and England a letter of Thomas Hardy's*
—Canto 80/500

Ezra Pound's last year in London was filled with the same kinds of triumphs and frustrations that had marked his earlier years there. The triumphs, as usual, were literary. On April 25, Boni and Liveright of New York brought out his collection of earlier essays called *Instigations*, dedicated to Homer Pound. Then in June, Elkin Mathews made good on his word and published *Umbra*, "The Early Poems of Ezra Pound: All that he now wishes to keep in circulation from *Personae, Exultations, Ripostes*, etc." Also in June, John Rodker published *Hugh Selwyn Mauberley* on his Ovid Press.

Instigations consisted largely of previously written or newly patched pieces concerning modern French poets, Gourmont, James, Eliot, Joyce, Lewis, and earlier translators of Greek—as well as an essay on Arnaut Daniel with some newly revised translations (reprinted in *Literary Essays*, 109ff., which also contains some of the other work). *Instigations* also contained as chapter IX the first complete book publication of Fenollosa's *Chinese Written Character*, and was as important to Pound for this fact as for containing his own work. The book was fairly well received, earning him over $100 that fall.

Umbra was likewise retrospective in content, but it did add "The Alchemist," which had been written in 1912 but had never been published before. It also contained some updated translations of the poems of Daniel and Cavalcanti, as well as still another collection of the works of T. E. Hulme. In many ways, *Umbra* is a fitting last reprise for Pound's twelve-year stay in London.

The primary reason for Pound's leaving London was perhaps more mental than material, since Paris did not promise him any financial windfall and did not deliver one. The war was over, and yet British society still seemed hampered by past mistakes, whereas Paris was swarming with immigrants seeking that famous freedom that France had offered since its revolution. One could be a poor artist in Paris and still be happy, as both Puccini and Modigliani had portrayed. Early in 1920, Pound was richer than he had ever been—and this had nothing to do with Dorothy, as some biographers claim. His job as a drama critic with John Middleton Murry's *Athenaeum* (gained through Eliot) was wondrously lucrative, even sybaritic, he claimed to several people. But when, under the initials T.J.V., he severely criticized Mary Grey in Gogol's *Government Inspector* on April 23, the magazine apologized for these remarks on May 7, and his job would soon be given to someone else.

In March, the ever-faithful John Quinn persuaded Scofield Thayer and Gilbert Seldes to hire Pound as the foreign correspondent for their *Dial*, a magazine that had been resuscitated with the help of the wealthy J. Sibley Watson, Jr. T. S. Eliot knew the equally rich Thayer from their days together at Milton School and Harvard, but he was a bit skeptical about their publication, which he considered a dismal imitation of the *Atlantic Monthly* (*TSEL*, 359). On March 24, Pound wrote Thayer a long, pompous letter accepting the job but testily querying the magazine's responsiveness toward such writers as Joyce and Fenollosa. He also offered them Cantos 4, 5, 6, and 7 (in their then-current form), promising at least two cantos per year in the future. The *Dial* did, in fact, publish Canto 4 in its June issue, as that

A famous sketch of Pound made in 1920 by Wyndham Lewis. (Estate of Mrs. G. A. Wyndham Lewis)

palimpsest continued its journey toward its final state, a course traced by Christine Froula in *To Write Paradise*. On April 23, Quinn, upset by Ezra's tactless letter, warned him to use diplomacy in dealing with the wealthy editors, who were young and not eager to be manipulated by their elders.

On April 20, Pound told T. E. Lawrence, who was considering publishing as a postwar occupation: "*The Dial* is an aged and staid publication which I hope, rather rashly, to ginger up to something approaching the frenetic wildness of *The Athenaeum*" (*SL*, 152). Meanwhile T. S. Eliot was writing Quinn foreboding letters about the way that Ezra was cutting himself off from his last English contacts, while Pound conversely was urging Quinn to help him to try to get Eliot pried free from his bank. Quinn, as usual, supported both men to the full.

Orage also continued to prove loyal to Pound, subsidizing "The Revolt of Intelligence," which ran from November of the previous year to this March. This was not a brilliant set of essays; in a rather loose and hackneyed journalistic manner, it discussed a variety of political and cultural topics ranging from Ireland (January 8) to the Rockefellers and usury (March 11). When Pound announced that he and Dorothy were heading south for a long vacation, Orage commissioned the poet to write a biographic series about his early years in America, to be titled "Indiscretions."

The Pounds left London for Italy in the last week of April, traveling through Paris and Milan to Venice. Ezra originally had planned to continue by train to Trieste to hold his much-awaited encounter with James Joyce, but he decided to stop instead in his favorite refuge. Pound wrote Joyce that they intended to spend the whole month of May in Venice, and would then move on to Trieste, where the Irishman was bored to death by the lack of conversation after his return from Zurich; he was also still smarting somewhat over Ezra's harsh words about his "Sirens" chapter, he confessed to Harriet Shaw Weaver.

By April 29 (PC 549), Pound and his wife were splurging in the rather elegant Hotel Pilsen-Manin, a Venetian hostelry that honored German beer and Italian patriotism in its name. There Pound was beginning his twelve-part autobiographic series, which is still one of the primary sources for his early years, even though it is written in an intentionally cryptic manner in a prose that is sometimes more intricate than the subject matter demands. *Indiscretions* forced Pound, now at a critical crossroad in his life, to confront his past. In his letters home, he asked many questions and was already receiving valuable clippings about T. C. Pound that would influence his later thought. Pound, in fact, was even seriously considering a return to America. He queried Quinn about the possibility of work in teaching or publishing in New York, but the lawyer (who was now in a cranky state of health preceding his terminal illness, cirrhosis) wrote him a long, bitter, ill-humored letter on October 21, warning him away from "New York with its million Jews. You would be thoroughly disheartened by the hostile atmosphere of this vulgar and sinister city" (RJQ, 437). To the Jews, Quinn added thousands of "dagos," Slovaks, Croats, and "pissing" Germans—everyone except the Irish.

The vain dream of entering the teaching profession again entailed the acquisition of the elusive Ph.D., and so Ezra prodded his father into going to the Penn campus and talking to Professors Schelling and Rennert about the awarding of the degree—on the basis of publications after leaving school. Obviously this was out of the question, since Pound had not completed his coursework, but Homer enacted his role, and Schelling did discuss the matter with his peers, even though nothing came of it. In February, Ezra calumniated Rennert as backboneless (PC 544) and as late as August was still trying to enlist the help of Wharton Barker, Esq., of Philadelphia in quest of this pointless dream (PC 563). He would not admit that, after the experience of 1908, he and Academe were incompatible. In fact, during this year he even entertained the notion of returning to school to study medicine, but the cost of tuition ruled against this.

Suddenly Dorothy fell sick in Venice, apparently from the "bad air" off the canals, as Pound informed Joyce on May 8 (*PJ*, 164). As a result, they were "ignominiously retreating" to Pound's favorite hotel, the Eden in Sirmione, as soon as possible. A few days later, Ezra was once again looking out over Lake Garda, whose blue was deeper than any except that in the famous Grotto of Capri (*PJ*, 167). Then began a marvelous comedy of errors in which the travel-fearing Irishman, who was deathly afraid of thunder, tried to meet with the indecisive American. (Perhaps both men secretly dreaded the long-postponed meeting.) In any case, Pound kept giving Joyce difficult instructions about traveling to Desenzano, the main rail link from Sirmione to the outer world. Affairs were complicated by a very poor schedule that called for overnight sleeping and included that bane of Italian travel—a sudden rail strike.

Forrest Read's edition of the Pound-Joyce correspondence details the moves and countermoves of this elaborate comedy. Joyce did leave Trieste on one occasion, but was forced back by a walkout. Pound kept making pensione reservations that he was forced to cancel. He was trying to persuade the Irishman to leave Trieste for good—to bring his entire family to Sirmione, where they could then proceed to the magic city of Paris, where all true artists belonged. Joyce himself was thoroughly amenable to the relocation, but it was hard to collect himself, his family, and his belongings. When the strike seemed to be over, Joyce took the plunge, despite the threat of thunderstorms. A letter that Pound was writing to him on June 7–8 breaks off suddenly: one imagines that Ezra has received word that Joyce and his son Giorgio are waiting for him at Desenzano. Pound rushed there and led the father and the son (who was acting as a "lightning conductor," as Joyce told Harriet Weaver [*PJ*, 175]) to the peninsula, where Dorothy greeted the two "very Irish" visitors as warmly as she knew how. The guests stayed for only two days in the quarters arranged by Pound, but this meeting had a profound effect on Joyce's life, since he did indeed permit Pound to persuade him that Paris was the only possible center for the future.

There are no dramatic photographs surviving of this momentous encounter of the two great epic-writers of the twentieth century—the one an outright poet and the other a master of poetic prose. One likes to picture the long, lean, angular Irishman and the lithe, red-haired American playing tennis together or just sitting in the ruins of Catullus' villa discussing the fate of modern literature. At this point, the two writers were still very much in agreement about most matters, but soon their paths would diverge. Joyce would finish *Ulysses* shortly, and Pound would help him get it published in Paris, while Joyce would then embark on that massive sea of words known as *Finnegans Wake*, a work that Pound deplored because it did not probe reality in a way that his *Cantos* would. In Pisa, Pound remembered their encounter this way:

> In fact a small rain storm . . .
>   as it were a mouse, out of cloud's mountain
> recalling the arrival of Joyce et fils
>   at the haunt of Catullus
> with Jim's veneration of thunder and the
>   Gardasee in magnificence
> But Miss Norton's memory for the conversation
>   (or "go on") of idiots
> was such as even the eminent Irish writer
>   has, if equalled at moments (? sintheticly)
>   certainly never surpassed
>
>   (Canto 76/456)

The woman who could also re-create an unmediated flow of language was Sarah Norton, the daughter of Charles Eliot Norton of Harvard and friend of Julia Wells, whom Pound knew well in Venice in 1908.

After the visit, Pound described his friend this way in a much-quoted letter to Quinn:

> Joyce—pleasing; after the first shell of cantankerous Irishman, I got the impression that the real man is the author of *Chamber Music*, the sensitive. The rest is the genius; the registration of realities on the temperament, the delicate temperament of the early poems. A concentration and absorption passing Yeats'—Yeats has never taken on anything requiring the condensation of *Ulysses*... He is, of course, as stubborn as a mule or an Irishman, but I failed to find him at all *unreasonable*. Thank God, he has been stubborn enough to know his job and stick to it. (*SL*, 153)

Joyce considered his tireless promoter "a miracle of ebulliency, gusto, and help," "a large bundle of unpredictable electricity" (*PJ*, 178). But Joyce always suspected that underneath Pound's surface respect there lurked the feeling that he was a rather dull bourgeois—and, in fact, that was sometimes the way that Pound would think of "Joyce the man" in the future. Still, the two writers got along very well together. In the ride from Desenzano to Sirmione, Pound bluntly asked Joyce if his new secret patron was Quinn. Joyce could be heard for a distance as he sputtered, "Who?!" since he and Quinn had had several run-ins over money. Quinn, in fact, was now purchasing the manuscript of *Ulysses* in sections. When Joyce revealed that his "angel" was Harriet Shaw Weaver, it was Pound's turn to sputter. Ezra was very happy to hear that his once impecunious friend now had the handsome sum of £250 a year guaranteed for life.

Still, Pound's altruism was not to be brushed aside. Wyndham Lewis tells an anecdote about how this generosity could misfire in his *Blasting and Bombardiering* (270ff.). Later this summer, when Joyce was safely settled in Paris, T. S. Eliot and Lewis decided to meet him while they were en route to the Bay of Quiberon for a vacation. When they left London, Pound gave Eliot a brown parcel to deliver to Joyce when Joyce stopped by to visit them at their hotel. Lewis then describes the appearance of the tall man with the "large powerful spectacles, and a small gingerbread beard," accompanied by his son, Giorgio, "a scowling schoolboy" to whom Joyce spoke almost entirely in Italian. When Joyce opened the package, he found, to everyone's astonishment and dismay, a battered pair of worn-out brown shoes. The son, who was more Italian than Irish, angrily gathered the present up and departed, leaving the three to go on to dinner together and to brush over the event as swiftly as possible. From that point on, Joyce treated the pair with great hospitality, as if to prove that his days of penury had ended.

Earlier that spring, Pound had also tried to persuade Eliot to join him and Dorothy in Italy, but Eliot wrote back that he and Vivien were apartment-hunting and could not come. By mid-June, Ezra and Dorothy were ready to leave Lake Garda, but the specter of a railway strike struck again, and they got no further than Milan. Using various improvised forms of transportation (finally a tram, Pound told both Quinn and Agnes Bedford), they at last crossed the frontier, and were in Paris by June 19 (*SL*, 153). This horrendous journey made any move to Italy seem totally untenable. Also, as Pound had preached to Joyce, there was too little of an Italian intelligentsia: The Joyce translator, Carlo Linati of Milan, and a handful of others. Paris, however, was bleak and rainy, and did not seem to be an immediate goal at that time either. The comfortable job with the *Athenaeum* was still beckoning, reinforced by a friendly letter from Editor Murry.

It was in late June that Ezra Pound passed for the first time through the portals of Sylvia Beach's already well-known bookstore, Shakespeare and Company, which was then located at 8 Rue Dupuytren, a stone's throw from its later site on the Rue de l'Odéon. She was struck by his elongated, feline appearance, his nasal drawl, and his natural friendliness, since he offered to do some carpentry work if she needed it. Their only source of contention at this time was probably Woodrow Wilson, whom Pound detested and Sylvia admired, since the president during his Princeton days had been a good friend of her father, who preached in the college town.

Joyce and his entourage arrived in Paris on July 9, his way cleared by his unofficial promotional agent, Pound. Ezra soon persuaded the future mother-in-law of John Rodker, Madame Ludmila Bloch-Savitsky, to give Joyce free quarters in her apartment in Passy until he could become settled. Thanks also to Pound's extravagant praise, Madame Savitsky later agreed to translate *Portrait* into French. This task took much longer than they originally anticipated, and her *Dedalus*, as she called it, did not appear until March of 1924.

At Pound's prodding, Madame Savitsky finally persuaded the influential Zionist poet André Spire to entertain the Joyces (sans children) at a Sunday tea and early dinner in his bucolic apartment at 34 Rue du Bois de Boulogne. Spire also invited the Pounds, Mrs. Savitsky's husband (the poet André Fontanas), the Jewish intellectual Julien Benda (whom Pound would come to admire greatly for his recent controversial book *Belphégor*), and Adrienne Monnier. Miss Monnier insisted on bringing along her devoted friend and lover, Miss Beach, who was "dying" to meet the Great Joyce. While Benda attacked spineless intellectuals like Valéry, Gide, and Claudel—all friends and idols of Miss Monnier, who defended them vigorously—Sylvia was able to corner the shy and retiring Irishman, who refused to drink any wine before 8 p.m., despite Pound's many temptations. When Joyce sidled off into the library to elude the rapid-fire French argument, Sylvia pursued him and asked breathlessly: "Is this the great James Joyce?" He smiled and extended a flaccid hand. The next day he appeared at her store wearing a blue serge suit, a black felt hat, dirty tennis sneakers, and thick glasses to cover his myopic eyes. He told her he wanted some tutoring jobs, and she promised to help; indeed from this point on, her help was never-ending for "Crooked Jesus," since it was she who would finally publish *Ulysses* in book form.

Pound himself loaned Joyce some pin money to ease his relocation, and Quinn came through with a large payment for the manuscript of the novel. Joyce also touched up Fritz Vanderpyl for a loan at their first meeting, and the jovial Belgian author-critic gave it to him without any questioning.

Before the Pounds returned to London, Ezra unearthed some unpublished meditations of Gourmont, which he translated as "Dust For Sparrows ('Things Thought, Felt, Seen, Heard, and Dreamed')." These appeared in the *Dial* in nine installments beginning with the issue of that September; they appear now in Pound's *Translations* (363ff.).

Back at Holland Place Chambers, Pound bragged on brand-new stationery that the *Dial* would publish the work of such writers as Julien Benda, Marcel Proust, Paul Valéry, and Louis Aragon. He especially admired Benda's defense of the intellect against feeling in his *Belphégor*, and he always considered Benda's *Treason of the Intellectuals* (*Trahison des clercs*, 1927) important because it defends free and unchecked speech among politicians and intellectuals. Pound mentions the Jewish Benda positively in a passage where he attacks the "kikery" of two Christians, Jacques Maritain, the ardent neo-Thomist, and Robert Hutchins, the "reforming" (diluting?) President of the University of Chicago:

> *Democracies electing their sewage*
> *till there is no clear thought about holiness*
> *a dung flow from 1913*
> *and, in this, their kikery functioned, Marx, Freud*
>   *and the american beaneries*
> *Filth under filth,*
>   *Maritain, Hutchins,*
> *or as Benda remarked: "La trahison"*
>   (Canto 91/613–14)

Pound threw the word "kikery" around far too freely in his later years, and although some of those close to him claimed that he meant to be general with this ethnic slur, a poet who fathered imagism should have been far more careful with his diction. After World War II, words of this type were strictly *verboten,* as Pound himself should have known.

As that last fall in London began, two catastrophes occurred. In early September, Pound received a copy of William Carlos Williams's book of improvisations, *Kora in Hell* (a title that Pound in part inspired through his constant talk about the goddess Proserpina). In the Introduction, Pound's old friend suddenly attacked him by name: "Ezra Pound is the best enemy United States verse has" (28). Williams was still sulking about Jepson's attack on most American writers except Eliot. Naturally Pound was both shocked and hurt by this unexpected onslaught. On September 11 and 12, he dashed off three spirited letters (*SL,* 156–61) in his own defense, mixed with some attacks on Williams. Using many expletives that the editor D. D. Paige deleted from his *Selected Letters,* Pound tried to stress how he had battled for *all* poetry against Harriet Monroe and Amy Lowell. He gasped: "I really can't do the whole show" (*SL,* 159). Finally, he praised Williams's improvisations, saying that they were no more incoherent than Rimbaud's *Season in Hell,* ending on a note that approached amity. Fortunately, his friendship with Williams went on.

He also learned of a worse disaster: He had been given "the chuck," he told Quinn, by Murry from his comfortable job. Pound was furious. This job had been his major reason for returning to London, and now it was gone. Of course, he was still reviewing music events for the *New Age* as William Atheling and he was gaining royalties here and there, but the *Athenaeum* job had spelled the difference between subsistence and comfort. That same month the *Dial* began Pound's three-part series called "The Island of Paris: A Letter," in which he praised the French capital as the liveliest city in Europe and expressed his desire to live there in the future. That future was now at hand.

A few happy events did, however, occur. Around the end of September, as he told his parents (PC 566), Dorothy and he traveled down to Lacock Abbey for four days to visit a place that had been owned by a cousin of Dorothy's named Charles Talbot. On his death, Charles had willed it to a Scottish niece named Maud Gilchrist-Clark, who then adopted the Talbot name. In order to maintain the estate, Maud was forced to sell many valuable paintings and possessions, including the Magna Charta. During this stay, Dorothy and Ezra clambered over a roof into a remote turret in order to gaze upon this prized possession before it went to pay the death duties. It eventually wound up in the

British Museum, although later it was brought by Maud to Washington for display when Ezra was in St. Elizabeth's. Henry Hope Shakespear also owned a gold copy of the Talbot family seal, with a canine emblem that formed the handle and was the main subject of the imprint. The seal was eventually passed on to Omar Pound (*Paideuma*, 2, 492). This essentially happy visit, with its unhappy overtones of an empire fading, was recalled by the poet in Pisa in Canto 80/515:

> Chesterton's England of has-been and why-not,
> or is it all rust, ruin, death duties and mortgages
> and the great carriage yard empty
>   and more pictures gone to pay taxes
>   When a dog is tall but
>   not so tall as all that
>   that dog is a Talbot
>   (a bit long in the pasterns?)

Another happy event was the publication of *Five Troubadour Songs* by Boosey and Company "With the original Provençal words and English words adapted from Chaucer [by Ezra Pound], Arranged by Agnes Bedford [for voice and piano]." The Chaucer poems set to music included the lovely "Your eyen two wol sleye me sodenly" (as the words appear in Canto 81/520), while the troubadour songs were by minor poets such as Pons de Capdoil and Faidit. Agnes was now a very close friend of the Pounds, often stopping by to play on the clavichord. It was she who claimed the Holland Place quarters on their departure, faithfully forwarding mail.

The "Proem" to the troubadour book was signed by both Ezra Pound and William Atheling, who had outlived the departed B. H. Dias, who was replaced by one R. A. Stephens in the November *New Age*. It was Atheling who wrote a review of the woman who would dramatically change the life of Ezra Pound: the violinist Olga Rudge. In the November 25 isssue of the *New Age*, Atheling said of a performance that had taken place a bit earlier:

> Olga Rudge charmed one by the delicate firmness of her fiddling when paired with Hela Ziemska, a very alert and promising young pianist, following more or less the Letchititsky tradition. Miss Rudge, however, committed a serious error in changing partners, and was unable to overcome the wooden burden of Mlle. Renata Borgatti's piano whack.

Pound did not meet Miss Rudge at this time; that meeting would take place soon at Natalie Barney's salon in Paris. The memory of this review distressed Pound when he first met Olga, but she was blissfully unaware that it had ever been published in that out-of-the-way socialist journal.

Olga Rudge was living at this time at her mother's place in the fashionable Rue de Ranelagh part of Paris just off the Bois de Boulogne. She had been born on April 13, 1895, in Youngstown, Ohio ("a flower from a desert," said Ford Madox Ford on first meeting her), where she was baptized Olga Ludovica (Louise) Rudge, but she was taken from that steel town while still a child. Her mother was the gifted contralto Julia O'Connell, who came from Canadian fishing people but who had studied voice in Paris and London and sung before royalty. Julia's people had moved from Canada to Brooklyn, and she sang often at the Madison Square Presbyterian Church that little Ray Pound attended with Uncle Ezry and Aunt Frank. Julia then met J. Edgar Rudge of Youngstown, who became prominent in local insurance circles. Edgar's father, George Stock Rudge, had been an Irish sheepfarmer, but as Australians monopolized this business, he moved to Ohio and eventually entered real estate. His son John Edgar was born in the Youngstown suburb of Boardman on September 3, 1860.

Julia was never content in the steel city. She longed for the continent and a more sophisticated life away from Protestant-dominated Youngstown. Soon she packed her bags and took Olga to the Upper West Side of New York, London's St. Johns Woods, and finally Paris, leaving Edgar behind. Olga's only formal schooling occurred in a convent in Dorset and ceased at age ten. But once she and her mother and brothers were in France, she began to study the violin, especially under the renowned Carambet. After Julia died and was buried in France in this year of 1920, Edgar took a second wife, but he always stayed close to Olga, even buying her the little Hidden Nest on Calle Querini-Dorsoduro in Venice shortly before the stock-market crash of '29, when he was forced out of retirement and back to work. He died and was buried in Youngstown in 1935. His grave was visited by the curious Olga in 1969, who was as puzzled by Youngstown as Ezra always was by Hailey, Idaho. On seeing it when the mills were already in decline, she found it a lovely valley city, but she was distressed to learn that the family manse on Bryson Street was now just a parking lot (later an athletic field).

When Ezra first encountered Olga, she was already on her own private course to fame as a musician and as an expert on the works of

Olga Rudge in the early 1920s.
(Mary de Rachewiltz)

Vivaldi. Her social standing at this time was radically different from his, because she moved in a world of Paris aristocrats and millionaires on the Rive Droite, while he would shortly be moving in a world of impoverished artists and students on the Rive Gauche, the Latin Quarter. Yet despite the social disparity, they had many things in common. Olga's high intelligence, liveliness (even into her nineties), and musical brilliance would soon capture Ezra's heart, expelling the meaningless women from his life, as Olga became the La Cara that he both desired and needed, although he never abandoned Dorothy.

During that final autumn in London, reviews, often negative, kept coming in for *Hugh Selwyn Mauberley*, which many readers consider the highpoint of Pound's lyric production, and which is indisputably the end as far as his serious lyrics go. Critics are usually careful to point out that Pound and Mauberley are not the same person, and yet there are obviously some similarities between them and their common world. Both poets are issuing farewells, although Pound is moving on to other things (Paris, the *Cantos*) while Mauberley is going to drift as an idle hedonist, cut off from any tradition. An epigraph that was added in 1926 but is still present in the modern *Personae* reads: "The sequence is so distinctly a farewell to London that the reader who chooses to regard this as an exclusively American edition may as well omit it and turn at once to page 205" (185). The most quoted lines, from Part I, Section V, speak of English society as "an old bitch gone in the teeth . . . a botched civilization," while Section IV verbalizes the poet's new economic interests when it describes soldiers coming

> home to many deceits,
> home to old lies and new infamy;
> usury age-old and age-thick
> and liars in public places.

The *Cantos* might well begin where these lines end.

As John Espey made clear in his pioneering *Ezra Pound's "Mauberley,"* the poem as first published by Rodker showed a clear delineation into three sections:

Part I: "Ode pour l'élection de son sépulchre" through Section XII
Envoi (1919)
Part II: Mauberley: Sections I through V, *Medallion*

The text of Rodker's Ovid Press edition put the initials "E.P." before the opening ode, thereby clarifying the arrangement. The first five poems of the sequence belong to Pound or concern Pound. The next seven sections present the London world common to both Pound and Mauberley, ending with the disappearance of Pound in his *Envoi*.

In Part II, we have Mauberley by himself, trying to face the same world and disappearing with *Medallion* as his last gasp and single production. This rather hollow poem contrasts sharply with the lovely *Envoi* that ends Pound's section, where a world of the beautiful past is revivified in the present:

> Go, dumb-born book,
> Tell her that sang me once that song of Lawes:
> Hadst thou but song
> As thou hast subjects known,
> Then were there cause in thee that should condone
> Even my faults that heavy upon me lie,
> And build her glories their longevity.

Here a live tradition is gathered from an old one—despite hostile critics who considered Pound out of step with his time, wrong from the start in going to the past in order to gather the inspiration for new beauty. The *Envoi* shows that Pound is free, whereas Mauberley is trapped in his wooden or porcelain world where mouths bite the empty air; in his final state, he drifts aimlessly as a hedonist in his "Exclusion from the world of letters" (*Pers.*, 202).

The seven central sections between Pound and Mauberley as personae present the worlds of their past and present. "Yeux Glauques" deals with the inspired but ineffectual world of the nineteenth-century Pre-Raphaelites, while the sections presenting Monsieur Verog (Victor Plarr), Brennbaum (presumably Sir Max Beerbohm), Mr. Nixon (Arnold Bennett), and the nameless stylist (Ford Madox Ford) show a literary world that is going nowhere.

Hugh Kenner said in his groundbreaking *Poetry of Ezra Pound* (1952) that "At the time when *Mauberley* was written, Eliot was getting rid of Laforgue and in collaboration with Pound assimilating Corbière and Gautier" (169). In short, Pound was casting off mere aesthetic irony for deeper modes of statement. He was preparing the way for the "serious" voices that are heard in the *Cantos*, not the bored voice of the frustrated dilettante who can be heard in many of Pound's and Eliot's earlier poems. Pound himself said in a letter to Professor Schelling two years later: "The metre in *Mauberley* is Gautier and Bion's 'Adonis' " (*SL*, 181). Espey's study explores the intricate metrical system that owes something to the ancient Greek, as well as the diction, which is indebted to Gautier's spicy use of words: glauque, cart[o]on, mousseline, still-born.

Once *Mauberley* had been written, there was little more to do than issue the final verbal farewell. But still Dorothy and Ezra hesitated. It is not an easy thing to give up one's native or even adopted land, and twelve years had been a long, long time. Then on December 27, Ezra wrote to his father that he and Dorothy were heading for either Orange or Avignon. He had recently had dinner with Ford, and had seen Rodker, but the continent was calling. Paris was the obvious final destination, but that city was not mentioned, and, in fact, the Pounds spent most of the first months of 1921 in the south of France, where the weather was warmer.

The abruptness of their departure left Eliot stunned: "This is a blow. . . . What happens to the *Dial?*" (*TSEL*, 426–27). When Pound turned his apartment over to Agnes Bedford, most of his possessions were still in it. In fact, as he says in the words cited at the beginning of this chapter, when he left England, Pound was carrying little of value except a letter from Thomas Hardy in which, according to the *Companion to the Cantos*, the older poet (born 1840/died 1928) objected to the title *Homage to Sextus Propertius;* Hardy preferred something like *Propertius Soliloquizes.*

As Philippe Mikriammos has said, Pound did not arrive in Paris until a few days before January 10, 1921, when the Paris edition of the *New York Herald* welcomed him with a long interview that said:

> Mr. Ezra Pound has just arrived in Paris from London. He says that after a visit of several months to the Riviera he will return here to remain indefinitely. His reason is that he finds "the decay of the British Empire too depressing a spectacle to witness at close range...."

The remainder of the article has Pound praising the unacknowledged genius of Major Douglas and concludes by saying that Mr. Pound "will keep clear of England and devote himself to his study of 12th-century music... He is also writing a long poem, although he says that he realises that one should not write long poems in the 20th-century. He is accompanied by Mrs. Pound and they intend to return here in April."

Another farewell of sorts was published in the *New Age* of January 13, 1921, under the title "Axiomata" (reprinted in *Selected Prose*, 49ff.). Attacking entrenched religion, Pound implies that he is forced to leave England because of its constrictions on his free thought and will. France seemed to offer a greater opportunity for self-expression. Kindly Alfred Orage, who had supported Pound faithfully over the years, was not about to let his departure go unnoticed. After Pound's piece, he wrote a lengthy valedictory, saying in part:

> Mr. Pound has shaken the dust of London from his feet with not too emphatic a gesture of disgust, but, at least, without gratitude to this country. I can perfectly well understand, even if I find it difficult to approve. Mr. Pound has been an exhilarating influence for culture in England: he has left his mark upon more than one of the arts... and quite a number of men and movements owe their initiation to his self-sacrificing stimulus... With all this, however, Mr. Pound... has made more enemies than friends, and far more powerful enemies than friends. Much of the Press has been deliberately closed by cabal to him; his books have for some time been ignored or written down; and he himself has been compelled to live on much less than would support a navvy.

Orage scoffed at the notion that modern Paris could offer salvation to anyone. Neither Paris nor Pound, he said, believed in religion or psychoanalysis and hence, in his eyes, both were in trouble.

Orage's article was a touching final tribute from a true friend, a man who was genuinely interested in the well-being of others. Yet Orage himself would soon be passing through a terrible crisis that would result in his fleeing England for the France of his Huguenot ancestors. Shortly after writing this article, one of Orage's best friends ran off with his wife, leaving him desolate. Then too, his attempts to promote Social Credit, especially a plan to take over the mining industry, failed, and he lost faith in social causes. He immersed himself in the ideas of the occultist P. D. Ouspensky and the Russian mystic George Gurdjieff, since the unknown had always fascinated him.

By 1922, Orage had given up the editorship of his journal and was living in Gurdjieff's institute, known as Le Prieuré, in Fontainebleau, not far from Ezra. Six years later, Orage moved to the United States, trying to raise money for mystical causes. He returned to England in 1930, and two years later founded the *New English Weekly*, in a new attempt to promote Social Credit during the depths of the Great Depression. But two years after that, Orage died, much to Pound's grief, since Ezra was deeply interested in economics and Douglas during those troubled thirties. Orage was one of the best friends that Ezra Pound ever had—like Elkin Mathews, who died in 1921, just after Pound's departure. It was Elkin who had gotten him going, and it is rather fitting that Elkin should also have left the scene when Pound did. The end of an age.

Did Pound carry only animosity with him on his departure? Yes and no. However despairing he was about the British social picture and the British temperament, Pound always nurtured a certain love for this land, which was, after all, his mother country. He said in the *New Age* of January 8, 1920: "I am racially fifteen parts English and the remaining sixteenth part Celtic" (though if the name Loomis is Welsh, as it usually is, he was far more Celtic than he allowed). England had taken him in when no place else seemed willing. Ford Madox Ford never tired of reminding him that no other city besides London—not Berlin nor Rome nor Paris nor Vienna nor Athens—could have offered him the opportunity to express himself that London did in 1908. Back in those days, his Italian was minimal and even in 1920 Italy was not in a position to be receiving anyone except perhaps a millionaire. Pound was not oblivious toward the debt that he owed his adopted land. That is why one of the most moving passages in the *Pisan Cantos* concerns his memory of the London landscape seen in time of trouble, when the soothing English green could soften the merciless glare of the broiling Pisan sun:

>   and the Serpentine will look just the same
>   and the gulls be as neat on the pond
>   and the sunken garden unchanged
>   and God knows what else is left of our London
>   my London, your London
>   and if her green elegance
>   remains on this side of my rain ditch
>   puss lizard will lunch on some other T-bone
>   (80/516)

III

THE PARIS INTERLUDE (1921–1925)

Introduction to Part III

Because this period in Pound's life is so filled with many different people and events, it seems wisest to discuss the people in some major constellations, and then to narrate the general events in chronological order. The diary organization helps to stress the crosscurrents of Pound's life, which was much like a collage. The general busy-ness of these years may suggest why Pound eventually felt that he had to leave Paris, despite its excitement and charm.

18

The Constellations of Paris

There are many reasons why Paris was such a magnet for foreigners, especially artists, in the twenties. First of all, there was the perpetual loveliness of the city, as well as the excellence of the cuisine and the wines. Then too, Paris had offered personal freedom from the time of the French Revolution, and it had consistently shown not only a tolerance but even a respect for artists. Still another important reason was economic: Paris was a great bargain for most foreigners, especially Americans. During much of this decade, a dollar was worth 25 to 30 French francs, and one could acquire a great deal with that rate. Shortly after his arrival, Ezra told John Quinn that his meager living money was now going much farther than it ever had in London. Then too, there was the general perception, crystallized by Gertrude Stein, that Paris was where the action was. She and her brother Leo had perceived at the turn of the century that artists like Picasso and others would be drawn to the City of Light. Now in the twenties countless others felt the same way. It is estimated that in the middle of the decade about 20,000 to 30,000 Americans were living in the environs. Only the Great Depression would reverse the influx.

When Pound finally settled in the city after a long vacation in the South, his world included millionaires, writers, musicians, and artists. Each of these worlds was in many ways a self-contained constellation, but their outer limits touched. Although Pound's world was primarily literary and poor, his newly revived interest in music brought him back to Walter Morse Rummel and his wealthy friends. He was also active in the art world, even though he rather crankily informed Quinn on May 26 of that first year that he no longer wanted to go on "valeting" for the difficult Mr. Lewis, and that music was now in the fore. Then too, there was a purely social world that stretched from Montparnasse, where Pound eventually established an apartment, to the elegant house of Natalie Barney, an acquaintance of eight years, near the Seine. On June 19, 1920, Pound described to Quinn the high quality of talk in her salon, noting that he had seen a portrait of the deceased Rémy de Gourmont in her Temple of Friendship. Unlike the American songmaker Cole Porter (whom Pound loathed and doubtlessly envied), Ezra never moved in the world of the very rich for very long, although he certainly encountered them through people like Natalie Barney and her crowd.

The World of Natalie Barney

Natalie Barney's life in many ways resembled that of Olga Rudge. They were both born in Ohio to families with money who soon found their ways back to Europe, where the two young women pursued their educations and artistic careers—Olga as a violinist and Natalie as a writer. It was at one of Natalie's famous Friday evening salons in the St. Germain Quarter that Olga Rudge first met Ezra Pound during the winter of 1922–23.

Natalie was born in Dayton on October 31, 1876, to two wealthy parents. Her father, Albert Clifford Barney, had inherited the vast fortune of his father, who had amassed it by building railway cars at a time when rail expansion in America was booming. Her mother, Alice, was descended in part from the Pikes, a German family (originally called Hecht), who had amassed a fortune from whisky and were noted for their support of music in Ohio. The mother was an accomplished painter who did portraits of Whistler and George Bernard Shaw that have survived in the Smithsonian Institute. Bored with life in Cincinnati and then Washington, Alice took Natalie with her when she returned to Paris to continue her art. Her less artistic husband tended to remain in London, a town that Natalie always looked down on: "In London, nothing is designed for women—not even the men." The mother lived on by herself in Paris until 1924, when she abandoned it for Hollywood, where she died in 1931.

Very early Natalie showed signs of being homosexual, and the fact that the Napoleonic Code was tolerant of homosexuality was still another reason why she and so many like her found Paris congenial. Natalie loved to indulge in sports like tennis—Pound's own favorite pastime, and the two often competed on such courts as those on the long, eel-like Ile des Puteaux in the Seine. She also enjoyed horseback riding. She went out almost every morning in her youth to the Bois de Boulogne, clad in a showy riding habit that the French called an *amazone*. She acquired the nickname of "The Amazon" by appearing one Sunday in 1910 at the chambers of Rémy de Gourmont near the Café de Flore, wearing her garb, and he was so startled by her appearance that he gave her the nickname. Later he wrote his famous "Letters to the Amazon" that were published in his *Mercure* for two years until 1913, and were issued as a book in 1914.

Earlier, Natalie had begun to build a legend for herself when she was associated with a lesbian book entitled *Idylle saphique* (*Sapphic Idyll*, 1901), which was written by the lovely woman-about-town Liane de Pougy. Mr. Barney was furious when he learned that his daughter was associating with such loose and perverse women, and so he tried to marry Natalie off to a man and to dissociate her from "wicked" Paris. But when he died in 1902, he kindly left her $2,500,000, which more than supported her Parisian residence for the rest of her life. For the next decade, Natalie wrote many other works dealing explicitly or subtly with lesbianism. She had numerous affairs with women, such as the novelist Renée Vivien (born Paula Tarn) and Lucie Delarue-Mardrus, the wife of a famous Orientalist and French translator of the *Arabian Nights*.

By 1909, Natalie had taken residence in a two-story *pavillon* or detached house in the rear courtyard at 20 Rue Jacob near the Boulevard St. Germain; this was her home for the next sixty-three years. Very soon she decided to have open house on Friday evenings for selected guests and regular habitués. Her most famous male guests were the art scholar Bernard Berenson, the classicist Salomon Reinach (mentioned in *Hugh Selwyn Mauberley*; it was he who called her "the wild girl from Cincinnati," another one of her nicknames), and even the hermitlike Gourmont, who was lured from his nearby quarters where he usually tried to conceal his lupus-disfigured face. Natalie presided over these salons wearing white tea gowns that accented her blonde hair and blue eyes; when she went outside, she usually wore gray tailored suits.

The downstairs part of her house, where she received guests, was furnished in a style that hovered (so many said) between a chapel and a bordello. A domed, stained-glass ceiling arched over Turkish hassocks and opulent couches, while along the walls were tables laden with delicious tarts, elegant sandwiches, tea, champagne, and vases filled with white lilies. The lilies were reminders of the ill-fated Renée Vivien, who died in 1909 from an almost self-induced melancholia brought on by her unrequited passion for another woman. Natalie continued to honor her memory.

During the twenties, Natalie's primary lovers were the stylish Elisabeth de Gramont, Duchess of Clermont-Tonnerre, and the talented American painter Romaine Brooks. Aside from Pound and his friends, Natalie received Pierre Louÿs, the forger of the lesbian *Songs of Bilitis* (1894), André Gide, Paul Valéry, Jean Cocteau, Isadora Duncan, and Gabriele d'Annunzio. There were also many politicians and some aristocrats like Prince Edward de Polignac (or Polonhac; see Canto 4), and his wife Winnaretta, one of the heirs to the Singer Sewing Machine fortune. Another was Marguerite Caetani, the Princess of Bassiano (who had been born Margaret Chapen in New London, Connecticut, but married an Italian prince named Roffredo); from 1949 on, she subsidized *Botteghe Oscure* from Rome, but lived at this time in the Villa Romaine near Versailles.

Pound's friendship with Natalie endured through World War II, when she fled to Italy to live with Romaine Brooks in the hills outside of Florence near Berenson. Both she and Romaine were extremely partial to fascism. According to Olga Rudge, Natalie gave Ezra a valuable radio during the war, along with the suggestion that he should tune in the broadcasts of Lord Haw-Haw from Germany—little realizing the possible consequences of this act.

During the twenties, Miss Barney (as she was usually called) vigorously helped Ezra in his musical campaigns involving his work and that of her own friend Olga and an American arrival named George Antheil, whom she called "a tiny man with a tiny wife." Antheil's *First String Quartet* was performed in her salon on New Year's Day of 1926. She also supported Pound in his efforts to subsidize T. S. Eliot and Paul Valéry, even though neither was anxious to accept their generosity. Natalie admired Pound's critical judgment so greatly that she submitted some of her own poems for him to judge during his walking trip of 1919. He rather brutally told her that she was "out of touch ... with the best contemporary work." Yet when she published her *Pensées* in 1920, Pound said in his review in the *Dial* of October 1921 that she "has published with complete mental laziness a book of unfinished sentences and broken paragraphs, which is, on the whole, readable and is interesting as documentary evidence of a specimen liberation." Her statement that most clung to him was "Having got out of life, oh having got out of it perhaps more than it contained." He worked this into Canto 84/539, coupling it with a mention of his exuberant Aunt Frank, who rode a mule in Tangiers when women seldom did anything so daring:

> like Natalie
> "perhaps more than was in it"

Natalie was a fierce individualist like Gertrude Stein, whom she was slow to know, until Gertrude moved close to her at 5 Rue Christine in the thirties. As is well known, Miss Stein did not care at all for Mr. Pound. Ernest Hemingway describes in *A Moveable Feast* (28) how Gertrude invited Ezra to her place at 27 Rue de Fleurus, where he broke one of her expensive, fragile chairs, which Hemingway felt was rigged to cause embarrassment. This event occurred in the summer of '21, with Scofield Thayer as a witness. Stein says in her *Autobiography of Alice B. Toklas* that she did not find Pound amusing: "he was a village explainer, excellent if you were a village, but if you were not, not" (246). Pound responded in a variety of equally hateful ways, seldom calling her anything better than "Dirty Gertie" or "Miss Steink."

Unlike Gertrude, Natalie found Pound charming, and he in turn admired her courage. She used to walk home late at night alone through the ribald Latin Quarter to her house. Sometimes she was accosted by would-be robbers, but she always stood her ground. Pound celebrated this courage in Canto 80/505:

> and Natalie said to the apache:
> vous êtes très mal élevé   [You've been badly reared]
> and his companion said: Tiens, elle te le dit [Well, she told you!]
> so they left her her hand bag

A few lines later he recounts an event that apparently occurred in the 1890s shortly after her arrival in Paris:

> And three small boys on three bicycles
> smacked her young fanny in passing
> before she recovered from the surprise of the first swat
> ce sont les mœurs de Lutèce   [These the customs of Paris]

Pound also recalled walking to Natalie's house with its Temple à l'Amitié, a Doric-faced gazebo in the courtyard, with the writer Jean Cocteau. He recalled what Cocteau's old housekeeper said of the neo-Thomistic philosopher Jacques Maritain (who was trying to save Cocteau's soul after the writer had lost his gay lover, Raymond Radiguet), "He seems to me to be a curate in disguise":

> The old trees near the Rue Jacob
>   were propped up to keep them from falling
> à l'Amitié   [for Friendship]
> and M. Jean wanted to save that building
> what do you call it,
> can it have been the old École Militaire?
>   "Il me paraît," said his housekeeper
>   "un curé déguisé"
> (that was Maritain)
>
>   (Canto 80/505)

The building that Cocteau wanted to save was the Hôtel Biron in the Rue de Varenne, where he had a pied-à-terre for a time. As for Maritain's "saving" Cocteau, that endured for about three years in the late twenties, and then faded away.

Natalie Barney was also very friendly to most of Pound's literary friends. She liked Ford Madox Ford's sophisticated manner, and he published two of her poems in his *Transatlantic Review* (II,4) "Arranged by Ezra Pound." She also was friendly toward Hemingway and to Richard Aldington, who translated *Letters to the Amazon* into English. But her favorite was clearly Ezra. She allowed him to practice on her own piano from 1921 to 1926 when he was working on his music, and she also allowed Antheil to bang on his percussion instruments in her house when nobody else would let him do this (he was even forbidden for a time from having a piano in his own small apartment by Sylvia Beach, his landlady). In short, by the time she died in her nineties in 1972 in a world that was much colder and more violent than that of the twenties, Miss Barney had indeed gotten almost more out of life than was in it.

The World of Music

Pound's introduction to the Parisian world of music had taken place back in 1908 when he had stayed with Walter Morse Rummel en route from Venice to London (chapter 1). He knew of Rummel at least from 1906 when the pianist had arranged some music for Kitty Heyman, who played the piano in Utica when Pound was a student at nearby Hamilton College. As stated in chapter 5, Rummel stayed with Pound and his family in Swarthmore in 1910, and for the next few years Pound visited the pianist often before World War I. One of their major collaborations was the *Hesternae Rosae* of 1913, which various German newspapers cited as one of Rummel's greatest achievements at the time of his death in 1953 in Bordeaux. Pound told Quinn and others that Rummel diffused too much of his creativity in performing other people's works.

The son of Franz Rummel, himself a well-known German pianist and scion of a prolific family that had excelled in music for generations, Walter came by the piano easily. His father visited the United States in 1878, where he met and then married Cornelia (Leila) Morse, daughter of the famous telegrapher and code-man. Franz and Leila tended to regard Washington as their American home, but they soon established bases in England and Germany when she came into her inheritance. Besides Walter, they had two other sons: William, an accomplished violinist, and Frank, a cellist and painter who also lived in Paris and was known to Pound.

Born in Berlin on July 19, 1887, Walter had studied piano and composition in that city, but he soon established Paris as his permanent residence, especially on coming into some of his mother's money. Early in his career, he gave recitals in the major capitals of Europe and he visited America often, thereby making himself known to the rising Miss Heyman (both as fellow pianist and as composer-collaborator) and to the Philadelphia music circles in which Ezra and his family, especially his mother, were moving. H.D. knew both Kitty Heyman and Rummel through Isabel—Kitty around 1906 and Walter in 1910, when she met him at the rented house in Swarthmore.

Rummel was a worldly man. He could either be very generous, as he was to the impoverished Pound, or rather aloof, as he was to the troubled Margaret Cravens before she committed suicide back in 1912. Rummel was a student, friend, and promoter of the work of Claude Debussy, whom Pound did not admire. Rummel also liked other composers inimical to Pound, such as Wagner, Liszt, and Sibelius. In Canto 80/493, Ezra describes his friend lost in a Sibelius composition, apparently without any gas:

> and dear Walter was sitting amid the spoils of Finlandia
> a good deal of polar white
>   but the gas cut off.
> Debussy preferred his playing
>   that also was an era (Mr. W. Rummel)
> an era of croissants
>   then an era of *pains au lait*

Since Rummel had the money to pay his bills, Pound must either be referring to the time in 1911 when the two took a house in London and abandoned it, or else he is portraying him as so lost in the act of contemplation that he has overlooked a material thing like a gas bill.

From 1908 onward, Rummel was a close friend of a lovely French pianist named Thérèse Chaigneau, who, with her two sisters under the name of the Chaigneau Trio, sponsored many musical events. It is believed that his marriage to her in 1912 triggered Margaret Cravens' suicide—although Rummel blamed Pound for this act, saying that Margaret had actually been in love with him. With Thérèse, he had two handsome sons, Étienne and Théo, but their marriage ended with a divorce. Later Rummel married an Englishwoman named Sarah Harrington, but that also ended in separation. By the time he died, Walter was quite alone, according to German newspapers.

In his heyday, Rummel was a dashing figure in the music world of Paris. In 1918, when the city was being bombed by German Big Berthas, a secretary named Christine Dalliès introduced him to her employer, the dancer Isadora Duncan. The two carried on a much publicized romance, largely at Cap Ferrat on the Riviera. Isadora was infatuated by the sensitive musician, whom she called "The Archangel." He really looked more like a Lohengrin, but Isadora had already expended that epithet on her millionaire lover Paris Singer. Walter and Isadora swept through the French provinces on patriotic tours (to the tune of the *Marseillaise*), even swinging over to North Africa, which Isadora for a time envisioned as the land of the future, especially for dance. After the war was over, they went off to Greece, accompanied by six lovely German girls whom Isadora adopted, the so-called "Isadorables." The girls formed a Greek chorus while the chiton-clad Isadora danced in the shadows of the Acropolis and Walter played dreamy compositions on a piano that was especially hauled in for the occasion. Usually he played the German Romantics, but he also performed the compositions of Kitty Heyman or Pound's poems set to music by Kitty or himself.

When the troupe returned to the Riviera, disaster struck as Walter fell suddenly and irrevocably in love with one of the youngsters, who was known as Anna. Isadora got wind of this and went into a Medea-like rage, banishing Walter forever from her sight. We have a letter written by Walter on February 21, 1921, from the Hotel de Paris in Monte Carlo, tearfully begging Isadora to take him back: "I wanted to stay with you and work." Rummel commends Anna to Isadora's care and prays that the dancer's inner temple will rebuild itself with Christ replacing Dionysus (mercy triumphing over Eros). But Isadora believed that the Age of Christ had passed, and the world was entering the Age of Bacchus (usually known as Aquarius), and she in no way relented. He never appeared at her funeral after she was tragically and almost grotesquely strangled to death in 1927 when her scarf got caught in the back wheel of a Bugatti racing auto being driven by an Italian playboy.

There is no doubt that the "Archangel" was a highly intelligent, sensitive man. In the Isadora Duncan Collection at the Lincoln Center Library in New York there is a strange notebook for the years 1904 to 1912 that records many of the "Dreams and Visions" of the composer-pianist. These were written from Holland in 1904 to Norway in 1909 and America on the visit of 1910. One entry dated July 1, 1911, seems to foretell the various romantic misadventures of Rummel's life: "They have come, the dark-ones, and / They have taken away my bride from me." Rummel made a complicated drawing that looks as if it might have been lifted from a Neoplatonic text of John Scotus Erigena: it shows clouds symbolizing eternity lying above a world of creation that moves down through several stages of emanation from a divine world of gold to a circle of being that is bounded on the north by blackness and winter, on the east by yellowness and spring, on the south by summer and greenery, and on the west by blueness and autumn. This is precisely the sort of imagination that appealed strongly to Pound, as well as to Yeats. When Rummel died in 1953, the same year as Iseult Stuart, Pound noted the event sorrowfully in Canto 104/741.

Pound's most publicized friend on the Paris music scene was an American interloper, George Antheil (1900–59). Unlike the aristocratic Rummel, Antheil had been born of lower-middle-class Polish-Prussian stock in Trenton, New Jersey, where his father ran a shoe store. Early in life, George had shown a marked talent for the piano, and so under the patronage of Mary L. Bok, who also knew Pound vaguely during his childhood, he was allowed to study under Ernest Bloch and to enter the Curtis Institute of Music in Philadelphia. When he was only twenty-two years old, George bolted off to Europe on an amatory quest, but he carefully found an agent to arrange some concerts for him in London and Berlin. In the latter city, he made the acquaintance of the visiting Igor Stravinsky, but their friendship did not go far because of Antheil's aggressiveness. Meanwhile George's *First Symphony*, which had been scheduled to be premiered in Philadelphia, was successfully offered in Berlin in 1922. In the German capital, the very short and young-looking George met a very short and young-looking Hungarian girl named Boski Markus, and the two formed a liaison that ended with marriage three years later.

Moving to Paris in June of 1923, the couple soon found a small room above Sylvia Beach's bookstore on the Rue de l'Odéon. Pound came by the store almost daily, but Antheil actually met him through the editor Margaret Anderson, who had fled with Jane Heap in 1923 to France to escape puritanical harassment. Margaret had been associated with an artists' colony at Bernardsville, New Jersey, where George had been involved too. Shortly after George's arrival, Margaret invited him to a tea in honor of the beautiful actress Georgette LeBlanc, who would soon become her next long-term lover. At this party Antheil met the arbiter of taste in Paris, Erik Satie, who worked as a postal clerk by day and a critic by night. Also there was a "Mephistophelian red-bearded gent who turned out to be Ezra Pound" (117). Pound said that they should get together soon, and the very next morning he turned up at Antheil's humble apartment "in a green coat with blue square buttons" ready to talk music. (Pound's square buttons seem to have upset almost everybody; Olga Rudge claimed later that he wore them out of poverty, not pretension.)

The preceding narration has been largely taken from Antheil's stagily titled autobiography *Bad Boy of Music*, which was written two decades later, when the composer was living in Los Angeles, having "sold out" to the movies. As a result, Antheil's attitude toward Pound is very different from the one that he had back in the twenties. Earlier, Pound wanted Antheil's advice on his opera, while Antheil wanted Pound's help in crashing the music world. For a brief time, things seemed to go smoothly between them. Ten years later in *Guide to Kulchur*, Pound said:

> Musical moralists have damned in my presence that very tough baby George Antheil. He has gone to hell and to Hollywood a "sub-Medean talent," he has made himself a motley and then some. He was imperfectly schooled, in music, in letters, in all things, but he nevertheless did once demand bits of SOLIDITY, he demanded short hard bits of rhythm hammered down, worn down so that they were indestructible and unbendable ... This is in accord with, though not contained in Jean's *Rappel à l'Ordre*. Cocteau there demanded a music to be like tables and chairs. (94–95)

A year after their meeting, Pound published his short monograph *Antheil and the Treatise on Harmony* through William Bird's Three Mountains Press. When this book appeared, Antheil pretended to be bewildered by it. In his memoir, he seemed surprised that Pound had claimed that "I said that melody did not exist, that rhythm was the next most important thing to develop in music, and that harmony after all was a matter of what preceded and what followed" (117).

Despite Antheil's professions of innocence, he was writing precisely that kind of avant-garde music that shocked the bourgeoisie. On October 4 of 1923, he presented his "Mechanisms," "Sonata Sauvage," and "Airplane Sonata" for the first time, as a prelude to the popular Swedish Ballet. There was a riot at the opening, in which the photographer Man Ray supposedly punched someone, but Arbiter Satie applauded the newcomer's work vigorously, along with Joyce and Pound. Antheil's reputation as an *enfant terrible* was made.

George went on to compose his famous *Ballet mécanique*, which was performed on June 19, 1925, at the Theâtre des Champs-Elysées with the usual sensational audience reaction. The piece called for bass drums, xylophones, rattles, whistles, bells, and an airplane propeller that almost blew away the first five rows of the orchestra seats. In the midst of the screams and catcalls, Pound is reported to have leapt up and shouted to the audience: "Idiots! Imbeciles! Ignoramuses!" This, at least, is the report of the English journalist Sisley Huddleston in his interesting *Paris Salons, Cafés, Studios* (101). There Huddleston also claims that Pound said: "It is possible to imagine music being taken out of the chamber and entering social and industrial life so completely and so splendidly that the whole clamour of a great factory will be rhythmically regulated ... The factory manager will be a musical conductor on an immense scale, and each artisan will be an instrumentalist" (99).

Later Antheil acted as if he had written this last-mentioned piece solely at the behest of Ezra Pound, who "was never to have even the slightest idea of what I was really after in music" (119), and whose support "did me no good whatsoever" (120). This is the kind of ingratitude that Hemingway deplored from many of Pound's so-called friends. After 1925, Antheil abandoned mechanical music and produced his *Second Symphony*, which Pound walked out on, since it seemed to be nothing but a pallid neoclassical revival in imitation of Stravinsky. During the thirties, Pound wrote occasionally to Antheil, telling him to abandon Gershwin's "softness" and Milhaud's "croonings," and to write some good rhythmic music for his two favorite cinematic dancers, Ginger Rogers and Fred Astaire. Antheil instead wrote numerous scores for grade-B movies, such as *The Scoundrel*.

Before Antheil's defection from art, he, Ezra, and Olga formed a strong and active trio, with Pound serving as an advisor and agent. During the summer of '23, Ezra called for ("demanded," said George) several violin pieces for Miss Rudge, whom Antheil described as a "dark, pretty, Irish-looking girl, about twenty-five years old and ... a consummate violinist" (121). He wrote his *First Violin Sonata* for her, and she performed it on December 11 with some works by Pound at the Salle du Conservatoire. He and she also appeared together in Budapest in January of 1927 in a concert that was not very successful, especially since Olga had to cancel an important engagement in Rome in order to play there. She then had to rush back to her flat at 2 Rue Chamfort in order to prevent her landlord from evicting her sublessee. By this time a parting of the ways was in order.

This was, in short, one of Pound's less successful friendships. Ezra introduced the "bad boy" to all of his friends, whom Antheil described condescendingly as follows: Eliot, who was always dressed like a banker (which he definitely was for a time); Joyce, who wore unfashionable "white ducks"; Lewis, who swaggered around in a "jet black suit with hat and cape"; Hemingway, who dressed and acted like a lumberjack; and Pound, who was studiedly Bohemian, wearing "bizarre tweeds with square buttons." The only friend whom Antheil seemed to like was Joyce, because of his "immaculate manners" (155). It is true that Ezra was often unmannerly to his young charge; in his letters, he sometimes sounds brassy, pushy, vindictive. But Antheil was well-known for being difficult. He is mentioned in the *Cantos*, along with Hemingway, in two phrases: "ebullient" and "infantile synthesis" (Canto 74/427). Antheil died in 1959, just after Pound was released from St. Elizabeth's but the musician had long since abandoned communication with his former master and promoter, since, in George's eyes, Ezra had fallen into deep and irrevocable disgrace.

There were other musicians in Paris, especially "The Six" gathered around Jean Cocteau, but Rummel and Antheil—those extremes—were the most important to Ezra Pound.

The World of French Art and Letters

"a Paradise of painters ... lying like the background of Rodenbach's portrait, invites one to anything but a critical attitude."
—*"Island of Paris: A Letter"* (Oct. 1920)

Even though Pound boldly proclaimed to John Quinn on May 26, 1921, that he was now more interested in literature and music than in art, it was hard to escape the latter in Paris. Artists were everywhere—from the older haunts in Montmartre on the Right Bank to the new "in" place, Montparnasse on the Left, as well as in the old Latin Quarter along the Boulevard St. Michel. Picasso had been in Paris from the turn of the century, and Pound had viewed the work of Cézanne and Matisse a decade earlier. Pound's insatiable curiosity and gregariousness simply would not let him cut this area off. Besides, in 1921, he decided to become involved with the *Little Review* again, being listed as part of the "administration" in the Autumn issue, which contained his essay on Brancusi and a long piece by Picabia. When the Misses Anderson and Heap finally fled the puritan persecutions in America in 1923, they turned the magazine into a forum for art as well as literature. Francis Picabia was named their Foreign Editor, even though he never did much for the magazine, leaving it rather soon in 1923. The Autumn–Winter issue of 1923–24 featured French writers and artists, while the Spring of 1924 focused on the Dadaists, and the Spring of 1926 on the surrealists and various Americans. But by the Autumn issue of 1924, Pound had once more abandoned the enterprise, and was concentrating on his own interests.

As far as Pound was usually concerned, Pablo Picasso was the star of the Paris art world. He met the man finally at a New Year's Eve party in 1922 (PC 598). The Spanish-born painter is cited importantly in Canto 2 in poetic lines that in some ways imitate the artist's daring techniques in art. As for others, Pound told Quinn on May 26, 1921, that he considered Constantin Brancusi the best sculptor and Francis Picabia the best artistic "thinker." In letters to his parents, he cited Picabia and Jean Cocteau as "intelligent" (PC 582); and on April 24, 1921, he issued the following judgment, which was constant during his Paris stay: "Brancusi a fine sculptor, Cocteau living spit of Bill Wms. from certain angles. Picabia very much alive" (PC 584).

In the essay "D'Artagnan Twenty Years After," which first appeared in the *Criterion* of July 1937 and is now in *Selected Prose* (452ff.), Pound discussed Cocteau as the liveliest mind in France, with Wyndham Lewis his equivalent in England. Pound claimed that after World War II, there was no presiding genius in either country for the young to follow, but there was a kind of leadership or "very vital critical action" that consisted of "Wyndham Lewis, Picabia, Cocteau. Disjunct, not the conscious process of a conspiracy but lively minds meeting a common need *of the period*" (*SP*, 458). To these, he added the abstract artist Fernand Léger, who collaborated with Antheil on a film based on the *Ballet mécanique* (*SP*, 457), and new writers like Paul Morand and Guy Charles Cros. There were always, of course, older writers like André Spire, the arch-Zionist and exponent of free verse, and the more elusive Paul Valéry, who was writing poetry again after a long layoff, but whom Pound found in the long run rather overrated (*SP*, 433).

Nobody was more important for Pound at this time than Francis

Picabia: "the only man I have ever met who has a genius for handling abstract concepts" (*SP*, 458). Francis Martinez Picabia was born in Paris on January 22, 1879, to a Spanish-Cuban industrialist-politician father and a French mother who had wealthy bourgeois connections. His comfortable circumstances led him to be highly independent, so that, unlike his starving confreres, he lived at this time either in the elegant part of the Right Bank off the Bois de Boulogne (the milieu of Rummel and Olga Rudge) or in the fashionable suburbs; he only visited "the Quarter," as Montparnasse was now dubbed. An expansive Mediterranean by nature, Picabia loved fine food, beautiful women like his lover Germaine Everling at this time, and expensive cars, of which he at one time owned more than a hundred. Pound believed then and later that it was in his studio that post-war modernism found its center.

Picabia was a conventional impressionist in his youth, but he visited the eye-opening Armory Show of 1913 in New York, which was sponsored in part by Quinn, and was soon joining the new cubist and avant-garde bandwagon, as his drawings *Udnie* and *Catch As Catch Can* show. When war broke out in 1914, he was sent on an official mission to Cuba (some said to purchase molasses), but he got off the ship in New York and stayed there, often in the company of his friend Marcel Duchamp, a reject from the French army. Duchamp had shocked America a year earlier with his famous *Nude Descending the Staircase*. Together, they formed a liaison with the photographer Alfred Stieglitz and a rising cubist painter who would soon turn photographer, Man Ray, who had been born Emmanuel Rudnitzky in 1890 in Philadelphia. The group founded the journal *291*, which was named for the number on Fifth Avenue where Stieglitz' gallery was located upstairs. In many ways, their publication prefigured the Dadaism to come.

In 1916 the high-living Picabia decided for health reasons to abandon the debauchery of New York, and so he and his first wife (a different Germaine) moved to Barcelona, where in January of 1917 he founded a new publication called *391*. His literary collaborator was Guillaume Apollinaire, the French poet who was then considered the embodiment of the "new spirit" that was sweeping art and letters, despite the war. This magazine attracted the attention of a Rumanian who was stranded in Zurich by the name of Tristan Tzara, who immediately invited Picabia, then considering a consultation with Swiss doctors, to come to the neutral land and join his group. In 1918 Picabia descended on Zurich, not interested at all in James Joyce but in the mixed circle that gathered in the Café Voltaire. This group, which included Germans like Hugo Ball and Richard Huelsenbeck, as well as the Alsatian Hans (Jean) Arp, was espousing a nihilistic philosophy that had been dubbed Dadaism from the babylike and meaningless word *dada*.

Back in New York, Picabia's circle had spoken about taking something useful and making it useless. Now in his *Manifesto of 1918*, Tzara said: "sweep, sweep clean." One can see why Pound would be able to associate this movement with his and Wyndham Lewis's earlier efforts in *Blast*. After the war, some of the Dadaists drifted north, but Tzara followed Picabia back to Paris. There they were joined by Duchamp and Ray. Tzara was the chief spokesman for Dadaism (which professed not to want one), and Picabia the disseminator of its work. Soon they were joined by a demobilized medical student named André Breton, who was at first fascinated by the extravagant Tzara, but very soon began to differ and then fight with him. Indeed, by 1920–21, when Pound arrived on the scene, the movement was so split internally that Breton was already envisioning leading a splinter group into areas that would be called surrealism. For one thing, nihilism had become a bore.

Breton was deeply involved in psychoanalysis and Freudian researches, and he had always nurtured a profound interest in mysticism and the occult. As Anna Balakian has said in her study of Breton, his new movement would attempt to capture the "surreal" from analyses of dreams, hypnotism, and automatic writing. Breton issued his *First Manifesto* in 1924, and this was followed by his *Second* in 1930, when the movement was clearly swinging to the extreme left, especially communism. Revolving around the journal *Littérature*, Breton and his group tried to hold together as long as possible; fellow members included the painter Giorgio di Chirico and writers like Paul Eluard, Philippe Soupault, and Louis Aragon. But eventually "Pope" Breton could not keep the circle intact, and it dissolved. Pound was never active with the group, nor was Picabia, nor Jean Cocteau, whom Breton disliked intensely.

By contrast, Pound admired Dadaism and even contributed to a few of its journals, always drawn to it by Picabia, whom he called "the dynamic under Dada" (*SP*, 459). He felt that it was Picabia who had "cut the barnacles off Picasso, Cocteau, Marinetti, pitilessly but with consummate good humour." Pound mentions the painter in the *Cantos* largely for one remark: that all of Europe had been exhausted by the conquest of Alsace-Lorraine (87/570; 97/678; 103/733), which was made in the Autumn *Little Review* of 1921 (12). In a *Criterion* article, Pound dwelled on the great humor of the artist, who said to the futurist Marinetti after the war: "I dreamt that it was my great-grandfather who discovered America, but not being an Italian he said nothing about it to anyone" (*SP,* 459). Although many people feel that Picabia's career never matched Picasso's, Pound defended the man to the end. Picabia died in 1953 (the same year as Rummel and Iseult MacBride Stuart), when Pound was still five years away from liberation.

One artist who avoided undue ties to movements was the brilliant Rumanian sculptor Constantin Brancusi (1876–1957). Pound recalled Brancusi's celebrated sculpted bird as late as Canto 117/801, where he imagined it nestling into a tree. He always admired the sculptor's devotion to art:

> "One of those days," said Brancusi,
>   "when I would not have given
> "15 minutes of my time
>   for anything under heaven.
>   (80/559)

The sculptor also used to say often (in French): "I can start anything on a certain day, but—to finish it!" (Cantos 86/560, 97/677).

In *Guide to Kulchur* (84), Pound spoke of the great tranquility that he always felt in Brancusi's barnlike studio, which was cluttered with emerging works and uncut blocks of stone. He frankly called the Rumanian a saint (105), as compared to the "intellect" of Picabia or the "genius" of Cocteau. Dante, of course, would put the saint higher than these other two. The best description of the sculptor comes from Robert McAlmon's *Being Geniuses Together,* where Brancusi is described as a "Rumanian peasant with a patriarchal beard and mild kind eyes" who "loved Americans and things American, and pranced about as the spirit of the jazz age, although at times wearing his wooden sabots" (112). Brancusi's cooking was legendary. McAlmon sampled it with Pound at the studio in the Impasse Ronsin off the Rue de Vaugirard near the Luxembourg Gardens: "The dining table was a huge round slab, and the stove had been made by Brancusi himself of stones piled one on the other. The meals started with a kirsch, Rumanian hors d'oeuvres, and then steak or roast chicken, salad and fruit, and of course, quantities of wine." To Pound, who often dined on omelettes, these repasts were indeed quite welcome. The color of Brancusi's soups was often as vivid as those of the Russian mystic Gurdjieff, Orage's master, who was nearby at Fontainebleau.

But Pound's fondest Parisian friend was unquestionably Jean Cocteau (1889–1963), who was a part of many of the worlds of Paris, yet, like Pound, an outsider when it came to surrealism. Cocteau was a typical poet of the salons and the boulevards who knew as many people in Paris as Pound had known in London. Born in the suburbs, he nevertheless grew up with his mother in the area around the Gare St. Lazare on the Right Bank after his father's sudden death (rumored to have been a suicide). Usually, he maintained a secret pied-à-terre on the Left Bank for his gay amours. Very early in life, Jean set out to conquer the literary world, and he was successful with most people, except for Robert de Montesquiou (one of the models for Proust's decadent Baron de Charlus), Proust himself (who was too retiring to keep up with the tireless Jean), and André Gide, a *macho* homosexual who had no affection for those of the "obvious" school—for Jean made no secret about his sexual preference.

Still, Cocteau also had many powerful friends: Igor Stravinsky (for whom he wrote the oratorio for *Oedipus Rex*), the ballet impresario Serge Diaghilev, Pablo Picasso, Guillaume Apollinaire, and numerous aristocrats who enjoyed having their salons enlivened by his effervescent wit. Many people are surprised that Pound enjoyed this obvious homosexual, since the legend of the super-male boxer that accrued around Hemingway and rubbed off on Pound has given the poet a somewhat homophobic reputation. But that is not fair. Pound could tolerate anyone who had a probing mind.

In "Jean Cocteau Sociologist" (which appeared in 1935 and is reprinted in *Selected Prose*, 433ff.), Pound praised the Frenchman extravagantly. He speaks of Cocteau's sensibility, which was captured by the perhaps too-sensitive portrait of Marie Laurencin, which is also cited in Canto 80/512. This portrait first appeared in François Bernouard's deluxe "Belle Edition" of a journal called *Le Coq*, along with some of Jean's poems, in 1920. Bernouard's publication then went into bankruptcy, as did some of his later enterprises (117/802). Pound admired both this sensitivity and Cocteau's firm, hard style. He recalled often how the playwright Luigi Pirandello wondered if Jean would succumb to Freudianism while working on his Oedipus plays, but the Italian then corrected himself: "NO, on the whole no, he won't fall into Freudian mess. Il est trop bon poète" ("too good a poet," *SP*, 434; see also Canto 77/469).

The language of Cocteau's *Antigone* sounded tough and tensile to Pound, and the numerical litany of the Sphinx in *The Infernal Machine* seemed hauntingly right. There was a line in the latter play that spoke of the city of Thebes being run by "gros légumes" (we would say "fat cats"). Pound liked the reference to economics in a play that was otherwise "aesthetic" and cited it in Canto 87/572. After a life of some trial, Cocteau was finally elected to the French Academy in 1955, but in Canto 77/472 Pound remembered a remark that Jean once made about such hallowed enclaves:

18 The Constellations of Paris

"Thought" said M. Cocteau "that I was among men of letters
and then perceived a group of mechanics and garage assistants"

Pound first "discovered" Cocteau for himself when he reviewed Jean's *Collected Poems 1917–1920* in the *Dial* of January 1921. He praised these poems for capturing the spirit of the city of Paris. His admiration for Cocteau increased over the next decades as Jean produced his plays and films like *Les Enfants Terribles*, which Pound felt were universal rather than merely French. The only time in Cocteau's life that was difficult for Ezra occurred in December of 1923 on the death of Jean's lover, the wonderchild novelist Raymond Radiguet. In desperation, Cocteau turned to opium (which Pound could abide) and also to the neo-Thomistic scholasticism of Jacques Maritain (which Pound could not), as was shown in Canto 77/472.

In *Paris Was Our Mistress* (139ff.), Samuel Putnam tells how loyal Pound was to Cocteau in his time of need, recounting how Jean embraced Ezra with passionate feeling in his "opium den" on the Rue d'Anjou, with its many exotic furnishings. Pound recalled this cluttered apartment in Canto 76/453, which reminded him of the one once inhabited by the poet Théophile Gautier that had been passed on to his daughter Judith, who lived among monkeys and assorted Chinese and Hindu *brocages:*

> Teofile's bricabrac Cocteau's bricabrac
> seadrift snowin' 'em under
> every man to his junk-shop

He also speculates that Cocteau may have paid bills for La Falange in Canto 80/505. This is usually interpreted as either the pro-Fascist party of Spain during the 1930s or a small literary magazine. However, a peculiar book entitled *Holy Blood, Holy Grail* by Michael Baigent and others claims that Cocteau was the Grand Master of a secret sect known as the Prieuré de Sion (130ff.), which was a descendant of the famous Order of the Knights Templar of the Middle Ages. Although this book has not been universally accepted, its thesis would put Cocteau in the middle of an ideogram that Pound was very much interested in, including the Templars, the Albigensians of Montségur, and other "undercurrents" blacked out by most historians.

It is not so easy to document Cocteau's praise of Pound. His most scholarly biographer, Francis Steegmuller, mentions Cocteau's inability to appreciate Pound's music, which he found willfully medieval (277), and his unhappiness over an article of Pound that appeared in the August 1922 issue of *Vanity Fair;* there Pound described the exciting new nightclub, the Boeuf Sur Le Toit (named for a "concert-spectacle" of 1920 by Cocteau and Darius Milhaud), implying that Jean was in some sense a proprietor. Cocteau did not like this at all, even though he was the secret force behind the operation of Louis Moysès and was there almost every night under Picabia's "big eye painting," *L'oeil cacodylate*. Pound went there often too—almost never with Dorothy. Sometimes he was with Kitty Cannell, who had dropped her husband Skipwith and had returned to Paris, where she met the often offensive Harold Loeb and fell in love with him; she would later write fashion pieces for the *New York Times* during the Depression and after that ballet criticism for the *Christian Science Monitor*. Another habituée of the Boeuf was Nina "Laughing Torso" Hamnett, who was modeling for artists when she was not creating art herself and in general having a marvelous time; unfortunately for Nina, her life would change drastically in her old age, and she would become known as the sad, broken-down "Queen of Bohemia" (see Denise Hooker in Works Cited in Text.) The Boeuf would never have been quite itself without the presence of Nancy Cunard in her flashing attires of every design, accompanied by men of all shapes, colors, and sizes. Another regular was Mary Butts, who had dropped John Rodker and was now with a rather debauched Scottish gentleman named Cecil Maitland. And of course, there were scores of others.

In assessing Pound's relation to the French literary and artistic worlds, one has to agree that he did not make the same splash here that he had made in London from 1908 onward. One reason was the language barrier; although Pound could speak acceptable French (his detractors said that it was of the intermediate Berlitz variety), he is known to have complained jokingly that the natives spoke English poorly. Certainly the snobbishness in many Parisian salons worked against him, as it did against even someone as talented and rich as Natalie Barney. Still, Pound was very much aware of what was going on—unlike Robert McAlmon, who, when asked by William Carlos Williams to list the leading French writers of the period, could not come up with a single name. Yet much as Pound liked many of the French artists, he was largely drawn to those who spoke his own language.

The World of English Letters

Everyone agrees that the English literary center at this time in Paris was the bookstore owned by Sylvia Beach at 12 Rue de l'Odéon,

Nine "founders" of the Jockey Club Bar, which opened in 1923. Standing from left are Man Ray, Hilaire Hiler (the American decorator and proprietor), Walter Miller (a retired jockey and part owner), Pound, Lew Copeland (ex-cowboy singer), Vernon Campbell, and Curtis Moffett. Sitting are Tristan Tzara with monocle and Jean Cocteau with cane. The atmosphere was that of a Western saloon, and the star was the famous model Kiki of Montparnasse. (Photography Collection, Harry Ransom Humanities Research Center, University of Texas, Austin)

called Shakespeare and Company. It was directly across the street from Number 7, La Maison des Amis des Livres (The House of Booklovers), which was run by the kindly, peasantlike Adrienne Monnier, Sylvia's longtime friend and lover. Sylvia had been born to a preacher's family in Baltimore in 1887 (died 1962). Her father took the family to Paris after the turn of the century, where he preached for a time, before returning to Princeton, where he was a friend of Woodrow Wilson. Sylvia and her sister fell in love with the French city, and she managed to return there even during the war. She met Adrienne in 1917 after stopping by her store to purchase a copy of Paul Fort's *Vers et Prose*. The two women became immediate friends, and two years later Adrienne encouraged Sylvia to ask her mother for enough money to open her own store. This she did, founding her first place around the corner on November 19, 1919. But in 1921, she took over an abandoned laundry across from the Maison, which became her most famous store. There were two small rooms upstairs, which she rented out to such people as George Antheil.

The interior of the shop has been preserved in numerous photographs that reveal a spacious two-room place with scores of portraits and pictures on the walls. Shakespeare, of course, held a dominating position. Sylvia began her business as a lending library, but she soon started to sell books too, especially *Ulysses*, after she published it on February 2, 1922. Her shop was deliberately modeled after Elkin Mathews's establishment in London. People could stop by at any time during the day to browse or chat around a large table that served as the proprietor's desk. It was a homey place, and very soon acquired a reputation for being a center for tourists and expatriates.

Pound often gravitated to Sylvia's store in the afternoon. In June of 1920 at the first shop, Pound informed Miss Beach that he was a handyman as well as an artist, and would be happy to assist her if she needed any repairing. She gave him a cigarette box and a chair to mend. Dorothy also endeared herself to Sylvia by drawing a map for American tourists to locate the difficult side street. Aside from possible arguments about President Wilson, Pound and Sylvia seem to have gotten along rather well, especially after she met James Joyce. As was said back in chapter 17, Pound took the Joyces to André Spire's apartment on July 11, 1920, where the two first met. Yet in a letter written to John Quinn on February 21, 1922, Pound said that Sylvia was "bone ignorant and lacking in tact"; he added that she insulted him every other time he entered her shop, but always in "*perfect*... unconsciousness." Certainly her autobiography, *Shakespeare and Company*, is often naive and ingenuous. Quinn himself was offended by Sylvia's trying to touch him up for some support for

Joyce when the lawyer believed that Harriet Shaw Weaver was more than taking care of him. Quinn called the bookseller "Miss Bitch," and Pound humorously replied that that was the way the natives pronounced her name.

One person who admired Miss Beach greatly—whom she called her "best customer"—was Ernest Hemingway, who first stopped by her place with its warm stove on a cold December 28 of 1921. Recently arrived, he was living with his wife Hadley at this time in the Hotel Jacob, which had been recommended by Sherwood Anderson, but they would soon take a dreary flat on the Rue Cardinal Lemoine by the Seine. Anderson, who was well known for *Winesburg, Ohio*, had made a triumphal visit to Paris from 1920 to 1921; here he had met Pound, Joyce, Stein, and Beach, and he had given Ernest letters of introduction to all of these. The inherently rather shy and independent Hemingway used some of these letters, but he actually bumped into Pound accidentally in Sylvia's shop shortly after the publication of *Ulysses* in February of 1922. Ezra immediately invited him and his wife for tea, and Ernest later vividly recalled sipping Dorothy's concoction in a "gloomy," art-filled apartment, while the host raved on and on about things literary. Hemingway did not appreciate Pound's appearance or his pomposity. He told Lewis Galantière, Anderson's French translator, that he later rushed home and dashed off a scathing satiric poem about this post-Byronic impostor. Galantière wisely counseled him to destroy the poem, and this Hemingway did—to his later satisfaction. Then he gave Pound some of his work to read, and when the poet was enthusiastic, their friendship was on its way.

Until he shot himself to death in 1961 in Ketchum, Idaho—just a few miles north of Hailey, where Pound had been born—Hemingway spoke glowingly of Ezra, as he often did not do about other people. His sketch of Pound in *A Moveable Feast* (1964) begins: "Ezra Pound was always a good friend and he was always doing things for people" (107). He then goes on to mention how he tried to teach Pound to box, and he says, among many complimentary things: "Ezra was the most generous writer I have ever known and the most disinterested" (110). Pound told John Peale Bishop when he met him in 1922 that "The son of a bitch's *instincts* are right." There could be no higher praise on either side.

Born on July 21, 1899, in Oak Park, Illinois, to Dr. and Mrs. Clarence Hemingway, Ernest very soon developed his skills as a precise writer of journalistic prose. After graduating from the local high school, he won a job as a reporter on the *Kansas City Star*, but when the war began, he enlisted as an ambulance driver for the Red Cross. He was wounded by Austrian forces in a campaign north of Venice in 1918 (that was never as courageous as he liked to make it out to be), and was shipped home to the States as something of a war hero. At least he received a medal for his bravery, although he was never a member of the *Arditi* forces, as he tried to make Pound believe. After a stint with the *Toronto Star*, he returned to his native Chicago and met a sheltered woman, Hadley, who became the first of his four wives. Feeling restless in America and sensing that the creative center was in Europe, he then took off for Paris with his wife's trust money and a free-lance job with the *Star* as his means of support. They arrived in Paris three days before Christmas of 1921.

The friendship between Pound and Hemingway is frequently depicted as that between two male chauvinists. Shortly after they met, Ernest told Galantière: "He's teaching me to write, and I'm teaching him to box." Both Wyndham Lewis and Ford Madox Ford reported watching these exhibitions, which Hemingway clearly controlled; in fact, the teacher claimed that he scarcely worked up a sweat. After Pound left Paris, Hemingway continued to fight, even publicly. He took on a much larger French boxer named Prevot and battled him for several rounds, even though he had a broken hand. Pound could share some, but not all, of his friend's love of heroics; they played tennis together and swam and hiked, but Ezra never went to Spain with Ernest to watch the bullfights. They walked a great deal in Italy in 1923, but Hemingway did not share Pound's love of "Kulchur." He drew the line with most cathedrals, and he certainly did not appreciate Pound's bassoon-playing when Ezra took that instrument up to help himself write his opera.

Pound, as usual, was tireless in his efforts to assist and to promote his new friend. When the *Little Review* ran its "Exiles Issue" in the Spring of 1923, Pound made Margaret Anderson agree to publish the first six sketches of *in our time*, which William Bird would issue later as a book. It was Hemingway who introduced Bird to Pound after meeting him at an economic convention in Genoa in April of 1922. There Hemingway also met (and later introduced) the famous old muckraker Lincoln Steffens, who exerted a strong influence on Pound's political thought, especially as related to Russia. Two years later when Ford Madox Ford was establishing his *Transatlantic Review*, Pound pushed Hemingway hard as an unpaid assistant editor. This was not a successful liaison, as anyone knows who has read Hemingway's bitter portrayal of Ford in his *Moveable Feast* (8ff.). When the magazine quickly needed extra money because of Ford's poor management, the older man had to rush off to America, leaving his review in the hands of Hemingway, who had already persuaded Ford to publish too much of Stein's *Making of Americans* and who overly favored American writers. The August issue displeased Ford enormously because of its bias toward Americans.

Then after Joseph Conrad's death, when Ford decided to run an honorary supplement in September, Hemingway crudely said that he would be happy to grind up the body of T. S. Eliot and sprinkle it over Conrad's grave if he thought that he could revive the corpse. Ford felt obliged to apologize for these words in November. In short, the two were not amenable. Ford was too much an imitation country gentleman for Hemingway and Hemingway a rude Midwesterner for Ford. On March 17, 1924, Hemingway paid Pound the supreme compliment by saying: "You are the only guy that knows a god damn thing about writing" (HSL, 113). He offered no such tribute to Ford, the way Pound habitually did.

Hemingway and Pound could always joke together. Their correspondence is marked with an easy hilarity and enjoyment of life. Hemingway always showed deference to Pound, even though Pound did not extract it. For example, in an unpublished letter in the Beinecke Library written around December of 1925 (since exact dates were never Ernest's strong point) and in another in 1927 (?), Hemingway stated candidly that he stood in awe of Pound's curiosity toward all new things. He bemoaned his own feeble education, particularly in the classics, and even in grammar. When Pound was in grave trouble after the war, "Hem" stood solidly behind him, even though he was having his own problems of an inner nature. When Hemingway received the Nobel Prize in 1954, he very graciously said to many that he was ashamed to accept this award that had never even been considered for Pound.

The two writers also had several enemies to bring them together—and Gertrude Stein was doubtlessly Number One. Hemingway was relatively kind to her in his *Moveable Feast* (9ff.), but elsewhere he was brutal. He especially zeroed in on her lesbianism. Still, Gertrude struck the first blow in 1933 in her *Autobiography of Alice B. Toklas* (216ff.), when she said that he was "ninety percent Rotarian." He revealed his anti-Semitism in a letter of November 8, 1925, to Ezra when he dubbed her one of the "safe playing kikes." Hemingway also disliked Wyndham (The Enema) Lewis ("the nastiest man I've ever seen"; *A Moveable Feast*, 109), Picabia, the "perpetual drunk" F. Scott Fitzgerald, and—one of his closest friends at one time—Robert McAlmon. After McAlmon helped him to get published, Hemingway called him in a 1926 letter to Pound a "fairy" (one of his favorite words), "stage husband," "ass-kisser," and similar epithets. He even socked McAlmon in 1934 in one of Jimmy Charters' bars. Only James Joyce other than Pound seemed to elude the venom. In his letters, Ernest is always solicitous about Ezra's and Dorothy's health, and he constantly asks after the fate of Omar Pound. He does not mention Olga Rudge, who said that Hemingway was one of the most unpleasant men in Paris in the 1920s. He treated her coldly when she begged for his help in freeing Pound in 1951.

An important person in assisting both Pound and Hemingway to get published was William Bird, a journalist and businessman who strayed into the literary set through his newspaper dealings with Hemingway. Bird got the idea for his Three Mountains Press in 1922 when Hemingway informed him that Pound might let him publish a few of his cantos on his private printing press, Bird's favorite hobby. "Oiseau," as Pound liked to refer to him in letters, immediately concurred, and soon he established his firm at 29 Quai d'Anjou on the Ile St. Louis in the Seine. In his *Autobiography* (189), William Carlos Williams described Bird when he first met him in 1924 as a "tall, sharp-bearded American businessman who looked as though he had been mellowed in Chambertin, gentle, kindly and informal." Bird and his singer wife Sally were extremely popular with most people, especially the writers they published.

Born in Buffalo in 1888, Bird graduated from Trinity College in 1912 and then proceeded to organize his own wire service, the Consolidated Press, which had its French office at 19 Rue d'Antin. After meeting Hemingway in Genoa in 1922, Bird named Pound his chief editor in charge of selecting six books for publication. The first book to appear in 1923 was Pound's own *Indiscretions*, assembled from the memoirs that had been published in the *New Age*, and the last was Hemingway's *in our time* in 1924 (not to be confused with the Boni and Liveright *In Our Time* of 1925). In between came Bride Scratton's *England* (under the pen name of B. M. G.-Adams), the Australian sheepfarmer and woolbroker B. C. Windeler's *Elimus* (Pound had met this man in London during the war), Williams's *Great American Novel*, and Ford's *Women & Men*. In 1924, Bird joined forces with Robert McAlmon's publishing venture, known as Contact Editions. In that same year, Ford Madox Ford began publishing his new journal, the *Transatlantic Review*, and Bird generously allowed Ford to run his operation out of the raised loft in the rear of his building on the Island. But Bird's most important publication, as far as Ezra Pound was concerned, was his *Draft of XVI Cantos*, published in 1925. In that year, Bird began to lose interest in his publishing business, and in 1928 he sold his press to Nancy Cunard. Then he went off to work in journalism again in New York, Tangiers, and finally Paris, where he died in 1963.

Bird's publishing associate for a time was Robert McAlmon, a man of many talents. He was the son of a preacher, born in Clifton, Kansas, on March 9, 1896, and he died in Desert Hot Springs, California, on February 2, 1956. After desultory studies in the Universities of Minnesota and Southern California, McAlmon bounced around in a variety of jobs until he wound up in Greenwich Village, where he supported himself for a time as a male art model. McAlmon was considered by many people other than Hemingway to be charming, affable, and strikingly handsome. He was overtly bisexual, if not homosexual. In the Village he met Marianne Moore and also William Carlos Williams, with whom he worked on Williams's magazine *Contact* from 1920 to 1921. Previously McAlmon had published some poems in *Poetry* and had some dealings with the tubercular Emanuel Carnevali, the associate editor, who would eventually die of his disease back in his native Italy.

Through Williams, McAlmon met Hilda Aldington when she arrived in New York after the war with her child and her new companion, the heiress Bryher. Hilda's female lover was in trouble with her wealthy father, Sir John Ellerman, because she was not interested in men and would obviously never be married, thus denying him an heir. Since Bryher needed a man and McAlmon needed money, their marriage made sense, and so it transpired in 1921. Back in London, they convinced old Sir John that McAlmon was indeed a suitable mate, and he generously released floods of money in all directions. The trio then took off for Paris, where McAlmon tended to stay, while the women lived in a variety of places, especially London and Switzerland.

In Paris, McAlmon was advised by both Williams and H.D. to look up their old friend from childhood, Ezra Pound. McAlmon obligingly dashed Ezra a note, which was promptly answered with an invitation. In *Being Geniuses Together*, McAlmon describes how painfully unsuccessful that first encounter was, like many of Pound's first meetings. Pound struck him as being a pompous, long-legged Bohemian with a "Vandyck-ish beard and an 1890-ish artist's getup" (29). McAlmon sensed that there was a heart under this pretentious exterior, but he was very angry when someone told him that Pound said after the visit: "Well, well, another young one wanting me to make a poet out of him with nothing to work on" (29). McAlmon's visit had been purely social, and so in the immediate future he ignored Pound when he saw him in the company of other friends, like Joyce, with whom both McAlmon and Hemingway had epic drinking bouts, Wyndham Lewis, John Rodker, or others. McAlmon describes how, when the quiet Quaker Harriet Shaw Weaver came over to Paris to see her protégé Joyce, Pound came up to the table where she was having a single glass of wine with the Birds, Djuna Barnes, H.D. and Bryher, and tactlessly blurted:

"Why, Harriet, this is the first time I've ever seen you drunk!" (89). The evening was saved only by Miss Weaver's early retirement to bed.

Yet despite a bad start, McAlmon and Pound finally became friends. They had a mutual enemy in Gertrude Stein, whose style McAlmon mercilessly imitated on several occasions, with its ponderous repetitions approaching the infantile at times. Still, he and Bird did publish her *Making of Americans* in a joint effort. McAlmon also disliked Eliot, who was "mouldy and sogs and is everlastingly the adolescent who will perversely be an old man blubbering," whereas "Ezra is hard, and his images flash at you and awaken clear and stimulating response" (30). Still, McAlmon was never as close to Pound as he was to Joyce, with whom he ate constantly at Joyce's favorite restaurant, the Trianon, and drank with in such bars as the Gipsy, the Dingo, and Bricktop's. McAlmon did try to visit Pound at Rapallo in January of 1923, but Ezra and Dorothy had already departed. Later he and Hemingway and Bird went off to Spain to see the toreadors. When Sir John gave him a handsome settlement to dissolve the nonexistent marriage in 1926, McAlmon strayed away from everyone, winding up selling cars for a time with his brother in El Paso, and finally dying lonely and forgotten in the California desert, with little to show but his memoirs and the publication of others.

Another American writer to appear during Pound's Paris stay was Edward Estlin Cummings, who was born in Cambridge, Massachusetts, on October 14, 1894, and died in New Hampshire in 1962. While working for his B.A. from Harvard, where his father taught sociology before becoming a preacher, Cummings established contacts with the men who would redo the *Dial:* Gilbert Seldes, Scofield Thayer, and J. Sibley Watson, Jr. Before his graduation with a B.A. in 1915, Cummings discovered Pound's poem "The Return," and its tight yet free expression made a profound impression on him, according to his biographer Richard S. Kennedy (105–7). During the war Cummings served like many other young Americans in the ambulance corps in France, where he was arrested by the French and charged with pro-German sentiments, thanks in part to his closeness to a reckless friend named Slater Brown. This comedy of errors, which was soon straightened out, led to the writing of his *Enormous Room* (1922). After the war, Cummings wrote many poems, seven of which were published in the *Dial* in 1920. These attracted attention because of their innovative lack of capitalization, peculiar punctuation, and daring rhetoric. Cummings at this time conceived a love for the attractive wife of Scofield Thayer, Elaine, and when he decided to return to France in peacetime, he went with his friend John Dos Passos and the liberated Elaine, whose marriage with Thayer was destined for divorce. Thayer, whom everyone considered brilliant, was already showing signs of being paranoid and schizophrenic; he would end his days as a recluse attended by a single servant.

Arriving in Paris in May of 1921, Cummings was introduced to Pound by Thayer during the early part of that summer. Estlin described Ezra as "feline" and "pantherlike" to friends, and to his parents he described him as a "gymnastic personality." Since these terms could be equally applied to Cummings, the two men got along well together. Cummings exploited the poetic liberties that Pound had created, and he was always free in acknowledging his debt. That summer they saw quite a bit of each other, as Elaine and Scofield obtained their divorce in July, and Thayer then scurried off to Vienna to be analyzed by Dr. Freud (which did as little good for him as it did for H.D. a decade later). Estlin and Elaine had a child named Nancy, who was born out of wedlock, but finally in 1924 he married Elaine—only to divorce her a year later. The relations between many of Pound's friends were extremely complicated.

In any case, Cummings remained in Paris off and on from 1921 to the fall of 1923, when he decided to follow Elaine back to New York. There in 1925 he established his long-term residence on the third floor of 4 Patchin Place, that charming mews off Sixth Avenue where he lived for many more years, and where, ironically, Hilda Doolittle had stayed on her visit to see Ezra back in 1910. Before going to Paris, Cummings had met the founders of *Broom*, Harold Loeb and Alfred Kreymborg, and they had also published his work. Pound, of course, knew Kreymborg years before when he was publishing *Glebe* and *Others*. These two soon followed Cummings to Paris, with stops in Rome and Berlin for their journal along the way. In his *Life Among the Surrealists*, Matthew Josephson, who was also connected with *Broom*, chronicles the journey of that magazine and its editors.

Pound mentions Cummings fairly often in the *Cantos*, and always positively. In Canto 74/432, he groups him with Basil Bunting (the eccentric English poet who briefly assisted Ford with his review before Hemingway) and with Joe Gould (a Greenwich Village Bohemian poet who had gone to Harvard and was a friend of Cummings'), seeing all three as defenders of classical precision "against thickness and fatness." In Canto 80/507, Pound deplores the fact that an old-fashioned poet like Sir Henry Newbolt of his London days could use a locution like "the door behind" and get away with it, but Cummings' more meaningful innovations were viewed with scorn and distrust by the general public. Pound mentions the Patchin Place address in 80/508, when he quotes Cummings saying that he knew that a certain person was his friend because he never tried to sell him any life insurance. Finally in Canto 89/603, Estlin is remembered for calling Pound a "damn sadist"—because he tried to make people think. All of these allusions show admiration and affection. Cummings had the virility of Hemingway without the adolescent boorishness. And like Hemingway, Cummings stood by his friend in his time of need.

The Social World

The first thing to be said about the Paris interlude is that it was just that—a short space of time between London and Italy. In actuality, Pound spent only about thirty out of forty-eight months during the four-year time span in the city. On arriving in January of 1921, he and Dorothy stayed briefly and then were off to St. Raphael on the Riviera. On their return, they stayed at their favorite stopping-place, the Hotel Pas-de-Calais at 59 Rue Saints-Pères off the Boulevard St. Germain, removed from Montparnasse. Some people considered this hotel dark and dingy, but the modern continuation is rather elegant. In a letter, Scofield Thayer said that when one called there and asked for Pound, a young woman at the desk would say immediately that he was "in his bath"; but if a visitor persisted, she would go upstairs, and shortly afterward, Pound would descend, smiling and ready to receive his guests.

Several months after their return from the South, the Pounds found a studio apartment in the rear house or *pavillon* of 70 *bis* Rue Notre Dame des Champs, a famous artists' street where Whistler had stayed for a time in his youth—and Fred Vance of Crawfordsville had actually roomed next door at 72. Pound's studio was a duplex on the ground floor off the rear courtyard, with a bedroom reached by an inner staircase. It was protected by two banks of houses and an outer courtyard from the noises of the street, which plagued Hemingway when he moved nearby in 1924. One passed through a long corridor that led finally to the rear courtyard with its trees, plants, and crumbling statue of Diana. As Olga Rudge said, it was too convenient for any straggler to wander in off the street and knock at the door. Seldom were people turned away. Indeed, a common motif in Pound's letters is the mention of "droves" or "floods" of people. This undue accessibility was one of the many reasons that led to Pound's eventual abandonment of the city.

Upstairs in the same building lived an eccentric opium addict from Detroit named Ralph Cheever Dunning (1878–1930), who published some of his poems in *Poetry* and the *Transatlantic Review*. Pound was for a time an admirer of Dunning's work and tried to help him in any way that he could. When Ezra left for Italy, he even gave Hemingway some drugs to sustain the man's habit (so Hemingway said), but when the drugs ran out, Dunning went wild and had to be taken away by the police. Eventually he died of tuberculosis aggravated to a great degree by chronic malnutrition. No one could ever remember seeing him eat.

Pound's apartment was not overly large, and it was filled with works of art like the Japanese Koume's painting, Gaudier-Brzeska's sculpture, Dolmetsch's clavichord, and countless books and manuscripts, along with fencing foils, tennis rackets, and boxing gloves. One of the distinctive pieces of furniture that Ezra had brought over from Holland Place Chambers was the triangular typing table that had fit neatly into the strangely shaped main room of his old flat. This was the table on which the *Cantos* were pounded out. The studio came equipped with a warm stove that gratified many guests who were lacking one, as well as enough kitchen appliances to enable Ezra to cook, because Dorothy still refused to soil her hands with such duties. Since chairs were needed, Pound took to carpentering, creating some sturdy if rather inelegant wood-and-canvas specimens that are visible in various photographs. Pound wrote to John Quinn on December 19 of his first year that his new place was "magnificently large, larger than I need, but MUCH cheaper than hotel ... I ... have built all the furniture except the bed and the stove." The rent for the place was 300 francs a month, which was cheaper than London (about $12 or $15). He told Quinn that he was cooking in a great deal to avoid the high cost of French restaurants, but in fact he often ate out.

Pound tended to entertain people during the day for tea. He did not throw the kinds of wild parties that Ford did, although he attended these. Since Dorothy usually stayed home at night when Ezra was out on the town, the place was not noted as a nocturnal center; it was an intellectual salon, like Stein's richer residence not far away. When Ezra was deep into his music, he allowed George Antheil and Olga Rudge to practice in his place, which caused complaints from a Swede upstairs, but the Paris police were always prejudiced toward artists, and so the music went on unimpeded.

Pound's street was to the east of the heart of the Montparnasse of the twenties, near the Vavin stop of the Metro. There the Boulevard Raspail, running south from the Seine, transects the Boulevard Montparnasse, which runs from the dirty old Gare Montparnasse on the west past the famous cemetery full of artists' graves over to the Boulevard St. Michel, where it meets the Avenue de l'Observatoire leading south to the Observatory. At the Raspail-Montparnasse intersection were the four major terraced café-restaurants of the period: the Dôme, Coupole, Select, and Rotonde. On the little Rue Delambre behind the Coupole was the famous Dingo (in English, "Whacko") Bar, immortalized by Hemingway's *Sun Also Rises*. Its bartender at this time was Jimmy the Barman (James Charters), the author of *This Must Be The Place*. Pound was anything but a barhound, limiting his drinking to a demi-carafe of wine a day or so; Charters remembered him as a "white-winer" (96), one of those elegant drinkers who could control himself. In his memoir (96–97), Charters told the story of how Pound saved the life of Robert McAlmon one night at the Cloche Restaurant near the Odéon. According to Charters, a crazed Italian sprang at McAlmon with a knife while the others sat shocked and unable to help. Pound rose heroically to the occasion and subdued the man. This story was muddied by others, notably Matthew Josephson (222), who said that Pound got into the middle of a vendetta between the surrealist Robert Desnos and Jean Cocteau, and was barely saved by friends. Olga Rudge, who was there at the time, vouches for the Charters version.

One of Pound's favorite restaurants was the lovely Closerie des Lilas (Closed Court of the Lilacs), which was located at the Boul' Mich', where Pound's street came to an end, directly across from the Ottoman-façaded Bal Bullier, a cavernous dancehall where the students from the Sorbonne assembled at night. Hemingway described the restaurant beautifully in *A Moveable Feast:*

> The Closerie des Lilas was the nearest good café when we lived in the flat over the sawmill at 113 rue Notre-Dame-des-Champs, and it was one of the best cafés in Paris. It was warm inside in the winter and in the spring and fall it was very fine outside with the tables under the shade of the trees on the side where the statue of Marshal Ney was, and the square, regular tables under the big awnings along the boulevard. (81)

Ney, who remained loyal to Napoleon even after exile, waved his sword at the pseudo-Oriental hall across the street because he was executed there for trying to help Bonaparte return to power. These places are both mentioned in Canto 74/433 and 76/453.

Next door to the Bullier was a two-story restaurant that Sisley Huddleston of the *London Times*, a good friend of Orage's, recalled with affection in his atmospheric description of Paris gathering places, already mentioned:

> He [Pound] is a good talker too. What a vivacious evening we
> spent, for example, in an upper room *chez* Emile! Emile is a
> picturesque Alsatian restaurant-keeper, perpetually dressed in
> white twill cloths, and a high cook's bonnet. That evening—
> though it is but one of many—we—that is to say, Ford Madox
> Ford, Pierre Loving, Pound, and myself—gaily played with
> ideas for hours, in the upper room on the Boulevard Saint
> Michel, next to the mock Oriental building of the Bal Bullier.
> Pound was the merriest spirit of the party. (97)

Other places that Pound liked were the more fashionable (and expensive) Sirdar on the Champs Elysées, Voisin at two locations, and two restaurants that were located in the greenery of the Bois de Boulogne: Pré-Catelan and Armenonville. Some of these are gone, as Pound laments in Cantos 74 and 76. "War is the destruction of restaurants." Pound also visited Joyce's favorite eating place, the Trianon in the Boulevard Raspail, and Ford's, the Nègre de Toulouse on the Boulevard Montparnasse, just around the corner from Pound's studio.

Since the poet did not have a surplus of money, he did not idle his hours away, sipping drinks in the famous cafés as the sun filtered down through the plane-trees and chestnuts. He wrote during the morning and did something athletic during the afternoon, often ate in, and then frequently went out at night to socialize—at the houses or studios of friends. One of Pound's favorite pastimes was dancing, as we know from Stella Bowen's report of his London days. When Stella and Fordie descended on Paris finally in the autumn of 1923, they gave parties at their places on the Boulevard Arago near the Santé Prison. When these became a bit raucous, Ford hired out a workingman's dance hall on Friday evenings; this was located at the Rue Cardinal Lemoine, where Hemingway had his first flat. Ford's parties were the highlights of the week's activities. Sisley Huddleston said that Pound was always the star dancer as the phonograph ground out the hits of the twenties. The reporter could not forget the vision he got of Pound "ignoring all the rules of tango and of fox-trot, kicking up fantastic heels in a highly personal Charleston" (144).

An even more dramatic portrait of Ezra in action has been given us by Caresse Crosby, wife of the ill-fated Harry, who published Pound in 1930 on their Black Sun Press. In the early spring of that year, Pound came up from Italy and had dinner with her. When he suggested that they go out on the town, she took him to "the Boule Blanche where a remarkably beautiful and brilliant band of Martinique players were beating out hot music":

As the music grew in fury Ezra avidly watched the dancers. "These people don't know a thing about rhythm" he cried scornfully, and he shut his eyes, thrust forward his red-bearded chin and began a sort of tattoo with his feet—suddenly unable to sit still a minute longer he leapt to the floor and seized the tiny Martinique vendor of cigarettes in his arms, packets flying, then head back, eyes closed, chin out, he began a sort of voodoo prance, his tiny partner held glued against his piston-pumping knees.

The music grew hotter. Ezra grew hotter. One by one the uninspired dancers melted from the floor and formed a ring to watch that Anglo-savage ecstasy—on and on went the two, until with a final screech of [cymbals] the music crashed to an end. Ezra opened his eyes, flicked the cigarette girl aside like an extinguished match and collapsed into the chair beside me. The room exhaled a long orgasmic sigh—I too. (255)

It is obvious from many sources that Pound's extramarital affairs did not diminish during his Paris years. One of his greatest flames was Nancy Cunard, who had moved away from Augustus John and her other London interests, and was now running loose in the liberal world of Paris. For a time she rented a charming apartment on the Ile St. Louis, not far from William Bird's operation, which she would one day take over. She went almost nightly to the Boeuf once it opened, where she consorted with Jean Cocteau and his friends, and to the Cyrano with budding surrealists like Louis Aragon. She was also a habituée of the Jockey Bar, which Pound helped to open, the Boule Noir and the Bal Nègre, with their black entertainers. She met her famous black lover, Henry Crowder, in Venice, not in Paris, in the Luna Hotel in 1928. In Paris, Nancy's female companions were often the American writers Janet Flanner (who was the Genêt of the *New Yorker* reports) and Solita Solano.

Although Ezra and Nancy had known each other since 1915, they did not become intimate until 1921. That summer, Nancy sent him some poems to judge. A response from Pound, quoted by Anne Chisholm (87), says that during that sweltering summer, he wished that she were there to free him from the predatory American females who were all around him. He signed off in Latin: "Farewell and love me!" Their correspondence continued in 1922 at a rather torrid pace as Nancy kept moving frantically from Paris to the Midi to Venice to England. On September 10 aboard a train heading south, she fervently wished that he was still with her, as he had been during a previous night. From Milan, she said that everyone in the world was "bloody"—except him. On September 13 from Venice, she asked if he would rush down and join her if she took a palazzo. On September 18, she begged him to come at once. She had rented one third of the Ca' Mainella in San Trovaso and missed him very much: "I will watch you after we have bathed together." This letter continues with a frenzy of passion, promising creative and social delights mixed with the erotic.

On September 22, Nancy realized that he could not join her, but told him that the following year they would become "The Lovers of Venice" (in French). She adored the many letters that he was sending her (most of which have disappeared) and sighed: "Now I am beginning to long for you terribly, beginning to find it very hard that you can't be here." Her passion continued throughout the month, despite a plethora of social and cultural events and the arrival of Wyndham Lewis. But Lewis she now found demanding and dreary, like the Sitwells and Robert McAlmon, her other former companions in joy; and so she composed her letters alone, sipping her white vermouth and gazing out over the lonely canal: "I am dull without you."

The correspondence cooled off in November, as Nancy returned to cold and dismal London and Scotland, although she constantly wished that she were with Pound, who was now in Rapallo. In 1923 the letters are less passionate but still warm and friendly, although she is always trying to entice Ezra away from Dorothy, who is seldom mentioned at this time. Back in England again in December, she was abysmally bored, although she would soon begin an affair in Paris with Louis Aragon and then in 1928 with the black pianist from Georgia, Mr. Crowder, who was a good decade older than she was. Through that affair, she finally found a cause, and for the next few years she supported black movements at the same time that she began the Hours Press. She published Henry's musical compositions on her press, and later her own *Negro Anthology* through Wishart and Company of London in 1934, when she had divested herself of her publishing venture. Pound contributed a very short piece on the German anthropologist Leo Frobenius to the latter. She was going to publish Pound's "Probable Music of Beowulf: A Conjecture" after July of 1928 when she bought her printing press from William Bird, but the ill-starred project never materialized. She *did*, however, publish his *Draft of XXX Cantos* in 1930 after many misadventures. Pound was eternally grateful to her for that, even though her poor distribution led to a profit of only about £35 during one time span. She ran her press out of her country house in Réanville, Normandy, to begin with, and then from 15 Rue Guénégaud in Paris. At times she was closely associated with the well-known François Bernouard of elegant editions, who operated out of 71 Rue Saints-Pères when he was not bankrupt.

Pound was always extremely supportive of Nancy, even after she became the subject of notoriety in the late twenties because of her affair with Henry. She was not only gossiped about, but disowned though not disinherited by her mother (although she had long had some money from her father). Olga Rudge remembered that when Pound returned on visits from Rapallo in the late twenties, he and she would frequently go out dancing with Nancy and her lover, or they would go to the Plantation and other clubs where Henry was playing. But then the Depression came and times were bleaker. In the thirties, Pound swung further and further right while Nancy went in the opposite direction, and Henry went home to Washington. In 1937, Nancy sent the poet an anti-Fascist tract concerning the Spanish Civil War, which was of great importance to her. Pound replied in a barbarous way, using the word "kike" both as a noun and a verb, and telling her that her communist friends were all barbarians.

Nancy held her peace, but when Ezra was in St. Elizabeth's and tried to enlist her sympathy, if not her aid, she wrote him on June 11, 1946, from the southern France to which he had introduced her: "I have been wanting to write you this for some time—for some years—but I could not do so because you were with the enemy in Rome, you were the enemy." She went on to excoriate all right-wingers, recalling that in 1935 he had even called the Ethiopians "black Jews." She then noted that when she had first met him back in London, she had thought from his name and his appearance that he was Jewish himself. She thanked him for his criticism of her poetry in 1921, for his lovely Gaudier-Brzeska book (which had made him known to her and her mother), and for the town of Gourdon, from where she was writing. She also thanked him for "your charming and appreciative ways with Henry, my Henry of colour. Do you remember how often we were together? Henry loved you—as did I always, then, and before then and up to the last time I saw you in 1928." She did not drop him, however. She enjoyed the allusions to her in Canto 80/495 and 510 when it appeared in 1948 and to a walking tour that had led her to the place where she now was living: "you will never forget . . . Gourdon (let's call it that) ne-vairr" (9/3/48).

A longer relationship was that with Bride Scratton, which was mentioned in chapter 4. This love affair had begun in 1910 and continued through the war to the Paris period. A traumatic event occurred on October 22, 1923, when Pound was named co-respondent in the divorce proceedings launched by Edward William Howel Blackburn

Scratton against his wife, Evelyn St. Bride Mary Scratton (born Goold-Adams). The divorce was granted that day in Strand, Middlesex County, on the grounds that the defendants, Mrs. Scratton and Ezra Pound, had committed adultery and therefore violated the marriage pact. The charge had a crushing impact on Bride; we do not know how it affected Ezra, since he does not mention it in letters that are available. He was in Paris when the divorce was granted, apparently staying as far away from the field of battle as possible.

We know from the *Cantos* that Bride and he met on the Continent on at least one occasion during this period. Pound mentions being with Thiy (his secret Egyptian name for Bride) in Verona with someone called "il decaduto" (the downfallen one). It has long been known that the latter is T. S. Eliot, whose financial situation and mental health were indeed both in a fallen state at this time. The lines from Canto 78/481 say:

> So we sat there by the arena,
>   outside, Thiy and il decaduto
> the lace cuff fallen over his knuckles
>   considering Rochefoucauld
> but the program (Cafe Dante) a literary program 1920 or
>   thereabouts was neither published nor followed

The Roman Arena at Verona is also mentioned prominently in Cantos 4 and 12. The three writers were drinking at the Cafe Dante, dreaming up a literary plan, probably Bel Esprit to help writers, that never materialized. Eliot had the dark, skeptical look of the Duke of La Rochefoucauld on his face, while his clothes seemed old-fashioned (lace cuff) and ill-fitting. The dating for this meeting used to be questioned, but the recent publication of Eliot's letters reveals it to be early June of 1922, a year before the divorce (and probably part of the grounds for it). Pound at this time was in Venice and hence easily in reach of Verona, while Eliot had been given some money by his wife's father to take a much-needed vacation in Switzerland (his second in a year); he had gone this time to Lugano, very near the Italian border.

After the divorce, Bride fell into bad financial straits. Since she had been the guilty party, her husband was responsible only for supplying support for the children; he remarried shortly after the parting, and he and his new wife took the two smaller children to live with them. Bride was left to support herself suddenly in a variety of ill-paying jobs with department stores or art galleries (as a writer); then when her husband himself died of tuberculosis on May 8, 1926, she was saddled with the children and no money. She explained her predicament to Ezra on April 4, 1927, and on January 14, 1928, she said very openly that she was "desperately in need of money," even forced to sell her clothes. Ezra responded speedily by sending her some cash, which she said she would treat as a loan. Finally an amicable settlement was made when her ex-husband's second wife granted her a small allowance to support the children, which was also sufficient to keep Bride going too. In 1928 she moved to Cambridge (where she died in 1964), often serving as a guide to the local university. Bride remained friendly with Ezra (and even Dorothy in later years) down to her final days. She visited the beleaguered Pounds during the St. Elizabeth's period, and was recommended by them to visitors to Cambridge as a person to look up.

There is no doubt that Bride Scratton was one of the major women in Pound's life. She might even have been *the* major one if she had not been married when he met her in 1910, or if she had been more willing to break free of a marriage that was a fiasco for years. In an "Imaginary Letter" contained among her papers at the Beinecke Library of Yale, Bride expresses her own real-life situation. It is supposedly written from Capri (perhaps with a memory of the real voyage that took her to Verona before the divorce): "I got your letter this morning expressing surprise that I had not made up my mind to settle in Paris. That seemed the obvious thing to do after the divorce. Yes, so obvious that one saw every step of the way one would take, until one was an old woman. That's why I'm not going. You must remember, in spite of my carrying the letter A round my neck, that I've been married fourteen years and had three children. And am in the ambiguous position of having no lover waiting to marry me. My adventures began too late . . . I can face the barrenness of unwinding years in England, but not from a cheap hotel bedroom or café table in Montparnasse." Although from one perspective, Bride might seem a coward, from another she looks very courageous in her determination to cling to her independence.

But Pound's most important love during his Paris years was, of course, Olga Rudge, the violinist. After their first meeting at Natalie Barney's in the winter of 1922–23 (the exact date long forgotten), they were together constantly because of their mutual interests in music. Olga enjoyed the socializing that Dorothy did not care for, and she liked to play tennis; she recalls playing tennis with Ezra in Paris in a closed court run by one of the many deposed Russian nobles of the day who referred to the wrists as "ankles of your hand." Since Dorothy herself was independent, and would increasingly visit her mother more and more after the death of her father and the birth of her son Omar (who lived in England), there were long stretches, especially in the future after Olga moved to Venice in 1929 and then Siena, when she and Ezra could be together. The birth of Mary to Olga in Bressanone (Brixen) on July 9, 1925, also cemented the bond between them.

Olga would be with Pound at his death in 1972, when Dorothy, who was no longer able to tend the sick and often downhearted man after 1961, finally withdrew from his side. One of the positive outcomes of the Paris years was that Pound, the reckless Casanova of London, would now become the loving husband, father, and lover of the last half of his life, and Olga Rudge would be the person most responsible for this transformation.

19

A Paris Diary

> "mi-hine eyes hev"
>   *well yes they* have
> seen a good deal of it
>   —*Canto 80/498*

1921

January 3: (Letter to John Quinn from Kensington) Pound discusses his impending trip to France and asks Quinn to pass on a message to the Japanese actor Michio Ito, who has been in New York since 1916.

January 4: (Letter from William Carlos Williams in Rutherford) The Doctor tells his "Liebes Ezrachen" that he wishes that he were with him in lively and naughty Paris (a familiar motif until Williams's visit in 1924).

January 6: The last of William Atheling's reviews appears in the *New Age;* the journal announces that it can no longer pay for articles; Orage will leave for France in a year to be with Gurdjieff.

January 10: The *Paris Herald* welcomes Pound, who "has just ar-

	rived in Paris from London" and will soon be heading south.
January 13:	The article "Axiomata" appears in the *New Age* as a last farewell with Orage's rejoinder; Pound's translation of Gourmont's "Dust for Sparrows" continues to run in the *Dial*, but his journal output is considerably smaller now that he has left England.
January 21:	(Letter from John Quinn in New York) The lawyer is now in the middle of the *Ulysses* case, defending the *Little Review* and its fractious female editors. Instead of stressing the literary value of *Ulysses*, Quinn is emphasizing its lack of prurience—rather weakly. The angry Quinn resents Pound's request about Ito and doesn't want to hear any more about Joyce or others; he has Old Man Yeats and the perennially sick Symons on his hands, and that's enough: "Please don't answer this letter" (RJQ, 480). He will write when the case is over.
January 30:	(Letter to parents) This is the first letter sent from St. Raphael, the Hotel Terminus. This charming Riviera resort, known to Maud Gonne from the 1890s, lies near St. Tropez, west of Cannes and east of Toulon. Like its neighbor Fréjus, it is an old Roman town that suggests something of a past, unlike Cannes, which Pound thought was an overrated fishing village (PC 578). St. Raphael offered tennis and swimming but no library worth mentioning or any other "Kulchur." The Pounds will stay here until April.

(A long letter to F. S. Flint—their first major correspondence since the imagist debate of 1915) In answer to Flint's proposal to write a new essay on the true history of imagism, Pound agreeably tells "Dear Frank" that he should include the following elements:

1. The cenacle of T. E. Hulme (1909).
2. The collateral existence of Ford, Yeats, and the French symbolists.
3. Pound's arrival on the scene.
4. Hulme's talk about "images" and his propelling Tancred into imitating Herrick.
5. The word "imagism" coined by Pound at Church Walk.
6. Pound's mention of Cavalcanti to Hulme.

7. Hilda, Richard, and the marginal presence of Williams.

Flint accepted these far-ranging sources very amicably, and in a French essay that he wrote for the *Mercure* in 1928 (No. 206, 240), he said unequivocally that the term imagism had been coined and shaped by Ezra Pound, although others were also involved. This effectively closed the six-year argument between Flint and Pound in a sensible way.

February 2: (Letter to Williams; *SL*, 165) Discusses William Brooke Smith, the dedicatee of *A Lume Spento* who died of tuberculosis in 1908. Williams had not known Smith in Philadelphia, even though they both knew artists like Charles Demuth, Charles Sheeler, and Morton Schamberg. This letter is moving, as are the three letters from Smith to Pound in the Beinecke Library, written before the young painter was called "to a world of jade and sapphire" (as Smith wrote on April 4, 1907). Most of what Pound knew about art before meeting Lewis and Gaudier was gleaned from Smith. (Williams was now publishing *Contact* with the help of Robert McAlmon.)

February 13: Robert McAlmon marries Bryher in New York City, with H.D. and Williams at the celebration; all except Williams prepare to leave for London.

February 21: The *Little Review* loses its case over Joyce's "Nausicaa" chapter, despite Quinn's fervent defense. He warns Misses Heap and Anderson not to be publishing any more obscene literature, and Anderson impishly asks him to define obscenity. The two women are fined $50 apiece and are forced to suspend serialization. They immediately make plans to depart for France in the near future.

April 2: (Letter to parents) He and Dorothy plan to be back in Paris next week.

Early April: (Undated postcard to Agnes Bedford) Back in Paris at the Hotel Pas-de-Calais, 59 Rue Saints-Pères (around the corner from Natalie Barney's pavillon). Pound finds Picabia and Cocteau "intelligent," and Joyce's new "Circe" chapter is "enormous—megaloscrumptious—mastodonic" (*SL*, 166). Pound lives in a comfortable two-room studio in this hotel,

	with a view of the nearby Seine River, until December of this year.
April 11:	(Letter to John Quinn) Pound asks the overworked lawyer if he can try to arrange a job for him on the *Century Magazine*. Still depressed from his loss of the Joyce case, Quinn retorts angrily on May 1 that he is not an employment agent. But his better nature takes over, and he does make the inquiry, but is refused (RJQ, 490).
April 20:	(Letter to parents) Joyce's new Circe chapter is "Magnificent, a new Inferno in full sail." The Hotel Pas-de-Calais is comfortable but a bit expensive.
April 24:	(Letter to parents) The *Dial* job runs out on July 1 and prospects are not good. (Pound was retained only as a foreign correspondent, writing a "Paris Letter.") He praises Brancusi, Cocteau, Picabia, Cros, and Morand—the last two to a lesser degree.
April 27:	(Letter to Wyndham Lewis) As printed in the *Selected Letters*, No. 177, Editor D. D. Paige censored a scurrilous poem which begins: "Sound of shit and shitwell is forgot / And Roger's visage overcast with snot" (166), castigating the Sitwells and Roger Fry, old enemies of the two. Pound says that he is resuming duties with the *Little Review*. After discussing modern French painters, Pound concludes: "You ought to get Eliot out of England somehow." Only in May does he give T.S. his exact address.
April:	(Undated letter to Agnes Bedford; *SL*, 167) Pound criticizes Debussy (Rummel's idol), Satie, Auric and other French musicians for being mushy or boring.
	(Undated letter to Marianne Moore; *SL*, 167–68) He asks her help in converting the *Little Review* into a quarterly, seeking American writers. The magazine will do a special issue in honor of Joyce.
April 30:	James Joyce writes to Quinn that Sylvia Beach will be publishing his *Ulysses* as a book. Quinn replies that he will photograph some pages of the manuscript in his possession and send copies to Paris.
May 7:	(Letter from Quinn) Informs Pound about the preceding and asks if he is finally free of the parasitic Joyce and Lewis. A financial crash in November has everyone, including Quinn, very worried.
May 9:	(Letter to parents) The *Little Review* is being reorga-

	nized. Joyce's novel will soon be out, along with the French translation of *Portrait* done by Madame Bloch-Savitsky (actually published March, 1924).
Spring Events:	Pound joins the Dadaists in a mock trial and condemnation of the popular nationalistic author Maurice Barrès; in New York, Kreymborg and Loeb start to found *Broom;* McAlmon appears in Paris with Bryher and Hilda; the ladies move on, while Robert has an unsuccessful interview with Pound; Kitty Cannell divorces Skipwith.
May 31:	(Letter to parents) He wants President Stryker's translation of "Ein feste Burg" from the *Hamilton College Hymnal.* He is glad that Ford was kind to him in *Thus To Revisit.* Rummel just gave a well-received concert, and Rodker is in town.
June 18:	Cocteau's lighthearted *Les Mariés de la Tour Eiffel* is presented. John Quinn writes Pound that he will be in Paris soon; he is now thoroughly fed up with the elder Yeats and Lewis, and he detests Picabia.
June 21:	Pound signs the postscript to his translation of Gourmont's *Natural Philosophy of Love,* although it will not be published until 1922. This famous defense of sexuality was extolled by the translator, who claimed that "the brain itself is, in origin and development, only a sort of great clot of genital fluid held in suspense or reserve" (149). He spoke of man as the "spermatozoide charging" (150) and of woman as "chaos" (see Canto 29/144). In equating the intellective and sexual processes, he said: "The mind is an upspurt of sperm, no, let me alter that . . . the sperm, the form-creator, the substance which compels the ovule to evolve in a given pattern" (152). In conclusion, Pound said: "the brain is thus conceived not as a separate and desiccated organ, but as the very fluid of life itself" (158).
June 25:	John Quinn sails for Europe; in July he sees Pound and Joyce often, sometimes together, and adds more Picassos and Brancusis to his impressive collection. Judging Pound to be needy, Quinn offers him a loan of $200, which Pound rejects, but later he accepts it as a gift through the mail.
June–July:	Pound meets E. E. Cummings through Scofield Thayer, and he introduces Thayer to Gertrude Stein,

but Pound breaks a chair in her salon and soon his friendship with her is ended. Nancy Cunard sends Pound some poems to read. Dorothy is away in England for a time. Pound contributes to the Dadaist publication *Le Pilhaou-Thibaou* (July 10). He reviews the Douglas-Orage *Credit Power and Democracy* for Williams's *Contact*.

July 23: Pound writes Quinn that a musician (Agnes Bedford) will soon be coming over from London to help him on his opera (*Le Testament de Villon*).

August: Sylvia Beach's new shop at 12 Odéon is now open. Pound spends part of every day with Agnes Bedford at Natalie Barney's house, working on her piano. He purchases a bassoon for his composition. The August *Dial* contains Cantos 5, 6, and 7 (but in differing forms from the present versions).

August 15: John Quinn sails for New York, laden with art.

Autumn issue of the *Little Review* contains Pound's essay on Brancusi. September *Dial* contains Pound's translation of Paul Morand's "Turkish Night," and the October issue his "Paris Letter" on Proust and Morand; he commends Natalie Barney for her *Pensées*.

September 18: (Letter to parents) He has rented a lovely new studio but the former tenant has not yet moved, and indeed she clings to the space for some time.

October 11: Arthur Griffith, the founder of the revolutionary Sinn Fein and the current Minister of Foreign Affairs for the self-proclaimed Irish Republic, is delegated by "President" Eamon de Valera to go to London to confer with Prime Minister Lloyd George about Irish independence. Pound goes to London and meets Griffith through his assistant, Desmond FitzGerald, whom he knew well back in 1909: "one of the most illuminating hours of my life was spent in conversation with Griffith, the founder of Sinn Fein. We were in his room to avoid the detectives who infested the hotel. It was the time of the armistice when the Irish delegates had been invited to London. . . . Griffith said: 'All you say is true. But I can't move 'em with a cold thing like economics' " (*CC*, I, 78; see also *SP*, 239). This scene, with a slick detective watching, is described in Canto 19/84–85, and Griffith's words run as a sad refrain from Canto 78/481 on. In *Life and the Dream* (307), Mary

	Colum tells how Pound tried to promote the Social Credit message to Griffith and failed.
October 22:	(Letter to parents) He has come back from his one-week trip to London, where he found Yeats "somnolent" and Eliot on the verge of a nervous breakdown. Eliot, ordered to take a three-month rest, is now on Margate Strand, able to connect nothing with nothing. Of the London crowd, only Wyndham Lewis seemed alive.
October 26:	T. S. Eliot writes a letter to Julian Huxley (*TSEL*, 480) in which he says that Lady Ottoline Morrell has suggested that he go to Lausanne, Switzerland, to seek the care of an excellent psychologist named Roger Vittoz, who had helped her and Huxley greatly in the past. Eliot makes plans to do so after Huxley expresses his approval.
	November *Dial* contains Pound's translations of some "Strophes" by O. W. de Lubicz-Milosz, even though Pound's formal affiliation with that magazine has ended; Pound knows some relatives of the Baltic poet who are living in Paris.
November 18:	T. S. Eliot leaves London for Lausanne; en route, he stops briefly in Paris to visit Pound and to deposit the ailing Vivien, who stays for a time in Pound's hotel and then in another nearby. Eliot shows Pound parts of a "long poem" that he had mentioned to his mother as early as December 18, 1919 (*TSEL*, 351). The original title was "He Do the Police in Different Voices," and its epigraph was from Conrad. The title had been taken from Dickens's *Our Mutual Friend*, but this was dropped at Pound's suggestion with the epigraph, since Pound did not think that either Conrad or Dickens merited the honor.
	Eliot presented Pound with an untidy manuscript that was still not as long as it would be at its maximum, since Eliot had not finished the poem. Pound attacked what he had, marking some passages "Echt" (authentic) and crossing out others. Eliot departed hastily, promising to return with more if his health allowed it; he told Donald Hall in a *Paris Review* interview in 1959: "He was a marvelous critic because he didn't try to turn you into an imitation of himself. He tried to see what you were trying to do" (52–53). By

	late November, Eliot was ensconced (not too happily) in the Hotel Ste. Luce, Lausanne, where, as he later told Quinn, most of the existing poem was written.
December 3:	(Letter to parents) Dorothy and he have finally moved into their new apartment, where he set to work building some furniture. During this period Nancy Cox McCormack, a sculptor from Nashville and later Chicago, who was a friend of Nancy Cunard, did a life mask of him (she later became famous for these masks). With winter upon them, Dorothy and he were comfortable with their warm stove, which delighted many of their guests. When he was not out, Ezra and Dorothy ate his cooking off a Chinese dining table.
December 6:	A treaty between Great Britain and Irish representatives establishes the Irish Free State, but Eamon de Valera does not accept Griffith's work, and the ground is laid for civil war.
December 13:	T. S. Eliot writes to his brother Henry from Lausanne that his condition is not as bad as one might have feared, and he is ready to work on his poetry again. He may send Pound further selections before Christmas.
December 14:	Eliot writes André Gide that he will be leaving Lausanne around Christmas (*TSEL*, 494).
December 19:	Eliot tells Sydney Waterlow that he is leaving on Dec. 24 (*TSEL*, 495) and is "trying to finish a poem—about 800 or 1000 lines," but he is not sure if it will work (*tient* in French).
December 24:	(To T. S. Eliot) This letter about *The Waste Land* (No. 181 of Pound's *Selected Letters*), dated cryptically 24 Saturnus An 1, is often ascribed to this day, but should be dated January 24, 1922. This was clearly too early for Eliot to complete his work and for Pound to edit it so closely; also, although Eliot lingered on a bit longer in Lausanne (he wrote a letter from there to Alfred Knopf on Christmas Day), Pound would certainly have been informed (as were Gide and Waterlow) that Eliot was leaving on the day that Pound wrote the letter.

(To Quinn) Pound says that he is not crying because Sherwood Anderson got the *Dial* Award for the year, and he explains that Editor Thayer fired him for alleged economic reasons, although both he and Quinn know otherwise.

December 28: Ernest Hemingway and his wife Hadley, who arrived six days earlier and are staying at the Hotel Jacob on the recommendation of Sherwood Anderson, browse through Sylvia Beach's store. Beach much enjoys her new customer, who buys a copy of Joyce's *Dubliners* for 22.50 francs and becomes a regular subscriber to her lending library.

1922

January 1: Pound meets Picasso for the first time during the early hours of a New Year's Eve party.

January 2: Eliot arrives back from Lausanne, according to his wife Vivien, who is staying near Pound's old hotel in the Hotel Bon Lafontaine. He is due back in London on Monday, January 16 (*TSEL*, 501). At this point, Pound certainly had all of the first rough draft of Eliot's long poem and could proceed with his excisions and emendations.

January 8: (Letter to parents) Ezra plans to retire in Italy (probably Verona, Venice, or Milan) and tries to persuade Homer, who will retire shortly, to abandon plans for California, as Homer eventually does. Ezra mentions that Eliot has returned to Paris with a new poem, but says little more. Ezra has introduced Eliot to the publisher Horace Liveright (1886–1933), who has been on the scene since Christmas. An anecdote about Ezra and Liveright being entertained in a lower-class bistro by a peg-legged dancer and his 60-year-old hula-dancing girlfriend is recounted in Canto 80/505. Later on June 25, Eliot reports his encounter with Liveright to Quinn (*TSEL*, 530); this meeting was important, since Liveright's firm would publish *The Waste Land* on Dec. 15 of the oncoming year.

January 10: The Boeuf Sur Le Toit nightclub opens with Jean Cocteau presiding.

January 17: Maud Gonne arrives in Paris to represent the Irish Free State at the request of Arthur Griffith at an International Irish Race Convention, which is trying to drum up support for the fledgling nation from its farflung constituents. With her are Eamon de Valera and Yeats.

In her memoir, Mary Colum says: "Ezra, of course, was present escorting Yeats, who knew only English" (308). The director of the convention, Robert Brennan, said that "The Congress was a hotbed of intrigue" in his *Allegiance* (335); others said it was full of warring delegates who were either Republicans (wanting all of Ireland to be Irish) or Free Staters, who supported Arthur Griffith's concessions to the British. In *A Servant of the Queen*, Maud Gonne MacBride spoke of the "sneers and mockery of the reporters of the French newspapers" (173) when they saw the pseudo-royal trappings that the Republicans wanted to adopt. Yeats gave a talk about the Abbey Theater, and Desmond FitzGerald was also present, but the congress achieved little. It did, however, give Pound a chance to renew his ties with Ireland and to introduce Yeats to many friends.

January 24: (dated 24 Saturnus, An 1 p. s. U.): This strange dating of a letter from Pound in Paris to Eliot in London can be explained by the calendar which would appear in the Spring issue of the forthcoming *Little Review*. This was Pound's half-serious attempt to create a new pagan calendar. The year would begin on his birthday, October 30, which he called the Feast of Zagreus, who was a manifestation of the god Dionysus as he appeared in the Eleusinian Mysteries. This was the first year (Annus 1) after the writing of *Ulysses* (*post scriptum Ulixes*), which was ironically enough completed on Pound's birthday. This letter has often been misdated in December (as in the *Selected Letters*, No. 181), but the calendar clearly stipulated that Saturnus is Pound's name for January; December is Zeus.

This is an extremely important letter, for with it Pound returns the typescript with some rough drafts of *The Waste Land* containing his major markings; these can be seen in the facsimile edition published by Valerie Eliot in 1971, after the typescript had disappeared for a time. On Oct. 23 of this year, Eliot sent the typescript as a present to John Quinn for his many kindnesses, and after Quinn's death, it then passed into the hands of heirs who did not know where it was; finally in 1958 it was quietly sold to the Berg Collection of the New York Public Library, where it is

YEAR 1 p. s. U.

And fifty 2 weeks in 4 seasons

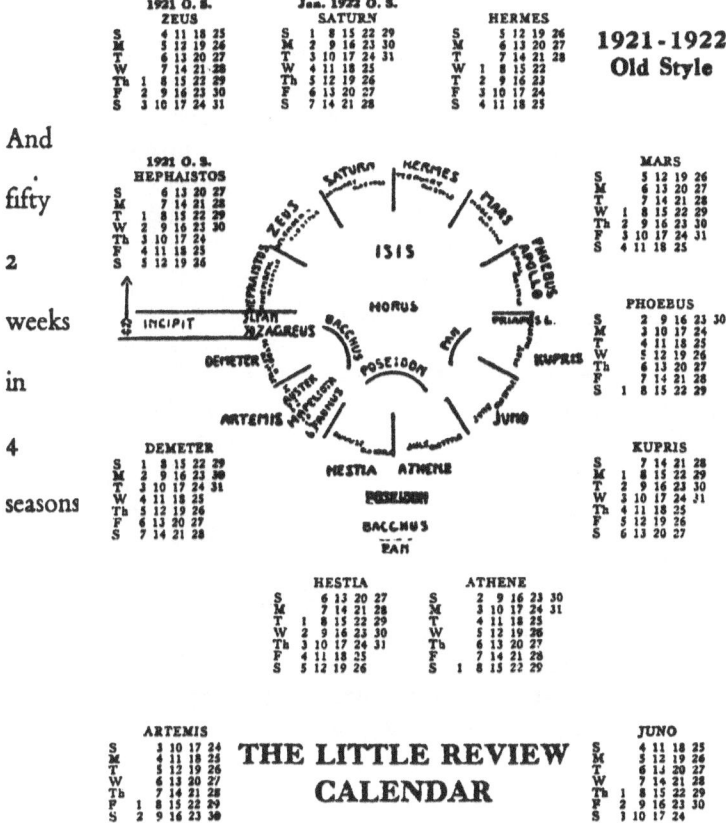

THE LITTLE REVIEW CALENDAR

Note to Calendar

The Christian era came definitely to an END at midnight of the 29-30 of October (1921) old style.

There followed the Feast of ZAGREUS, and a Feast of PAN counted as of no era: the new year thus beginning as on 1st November (old style), now HEPHAISTOS.

The new months, replacing the old months: of cold months HEPHAISTOS (for November), and then in the following order ZEUS, SATURN, HERMES, MARS, PHOEBUS APOLLO; and the warm months; KUPRIS, JUNO, ATHENE, HESTIA, ARTEMIS and DEMETER, the male months being also under ISIS, and the female months, two by two, under PAN, POSEIDON and BACCHUS.

The following feasts are instituted, to ZAGREUS on the 30th Demeter; to PAN on the 31st Demeter; Feast of Figures on the 14th Hermes; Feast of Political Buncomb, ancient feast of fools or feast of the ass, Mort de Caesar, Jules, 15th Mars; PRIAPUS, 1st Kupris; EPITHALAMIUM, ancient Corpus Domini, 15th Juno; FAUNUS 6th Artemis; AUSTER and APELIOTA 14th Artemis.

The year turns upon HORUS.

Pound's new calendar for the Age of *Ulysses* or Uranus, as published in the *Little Review* of the Spring of 1922.

housed today. (See the entry of Feb. 26, 1923, for an explanation of the disappearance.)

Pound says: "The thing now runs from 'April . . .' to 'shantih' without a break. That is 19 pages, and let us say the longest poem in the English langwidge. Don't try to bust all records by prolonging it three pages further." He then excised three shorter poems and expressed his envy of the work: "Complimenti, you bitch. I am wracked by the seven jealousies, and cogitating an excuse for always exuding my deformative secretions in my own stuff, and never getting an outline." Pound was not alone in his envy. Williams said in his *Autobiography:* "Then out of the blue *The Dial* brought out *The Waste Land* and all our hilarity ended. It wiped out our world as if an atom bomb had been dropped upon it and our brave sallies into the unknown were turned into dust" (174). Yet the event had a positive side too; suddenly Pound felt impelled to start imposing an "outline" over his work to bring the chaotic cantos into some kind of recognizable order.

There is no room here to go into an elaborate analysis of Pound's edition of the poem. Most people feel that Pound did an excellent job of deleting many passages that were simply parodic or loose, like the fifty-four-line, prosey narrative that originally opened the poem, describing lower-class life in London. Then there was also a long, forty-three-couplet imitation of Alexander Pope's satires which began Part III. Pound wisely warned, according to Eliot: "Pope has done this so well that you cannot do it better . . . for you cannot parody Pope unless you can write better verse than Pope—and you can't." A three-quatrain description of the life of a sailor at the start of Part IV was also cut.

The most questionable deletion was also in Part IV: a seventy-one-line description of a shipwreck off New England, based in part on one of Eliot's childhood experiences off Cape Ann and owing something to the death of Ulysses in Dante's *Inferno* 26. Some critics feel that this would have fleshed out Part IV, which looks truncated, containing only the death of Phlebas the Phoenician. Eventually Eliot wanted to cancel the whole section, but Pound felt that it was needed for thematic reasons.

In the main, Pound's taste was excellent. Eliot never tried to blame him later for any of the criticisms that were heaped on the poem. He showed his appreciation by finally dedicating the work to his editor, *il miglior fabbro* (the better craftsman), as Guido Guinizelli calls the troubadour Arnaut Daniel in Dante's *Purgatorio* 26. This dedication was first written in by hand in the Boni and Liveright edition of December 15, 1922, and it was made permanent in Eliot's *Poems 1909–1925* in 1925.

Pound ended the formal part of his letter by saying that this was a great literary period; and it was. He then tacked on some comic poetry that said that Eliot had begotten the work through the Uranian Muse (p.s.U. can also mean *post saeculum Urani*, "after the Age of Uranus," the ruler of Aquarius—an astrological allusion that Yeats would understand); but Ezra claimed that he had performed the "Caesarian Operation." He then spoke of himself as a "Vates cum fistula" (poet with a pipe or a cyst)—he was suffering from the latter at the time.

Another letter from Eliot in London answers Pound and accepts most of the criticism; Eliot says: "Complimenti appreciated, as have been excessively depressed" (a new date of about January 28 to February 1 should be assigned to this letter; *TSEL*, 504). He wanted to print Pound's amusing poetic postscript before the poem, but wisely never did.

Pound replied to this letter a few days later, probably from February 6 to 15 (misdated in the first edition of *TSEL*, 505), advising Eliot not to print "Gerontion" as a prologue to the poem, and insisting on keeping Phlebas.

A last letter, from Eliot to Pound, clearly dated March 12, drops the Conrad epigraph for one from Petronius' *Satyricon* (*TSEL*, 506ff.). With the operation completed, Dr. Pound returned to his own work, which was badly in need of attention.

February 2: On this, Joyce's 40th birthday, *Ulysses* was finally published. Copies were rushed from the printer in Dijon to Paris. Sylvia gave one to the author, while displaying the other in her shop from 9 in the morning until closing time. Everyone important showed up then or soon after—except Gertrude Stein, who issued another of her sibylline pronouncements: "People like Joyce because he is incomprehensible and anybody can understand him." Miss Beach generously offered the author 66 percent of all profits, thereby joining Quinn and Weaver in the pantheon of great patrons.

February 3: Joyce cabled Quinn: ULYSSES PUBLISHED. THANKS.

At 7 a.m. of this day Jack Yeats, the poet's father, died in New York, with Quinn having attended him the night before.

(Letter to Grandmother Loomis) To the aged lady, who is back in Philadelphia after sending him postcards from Montana, Pound described Paris, which has more greenery that one might imagine. He will be leaving for Siena in April.

Circa February 9: Pound bumps into Hemingway at Beach's store, and they meet for tea at Pound's studio. Hemingway, who now lives on Rue Cardinal Lemoine, finds Pound pretentious and distasteful at first—but soon changes his mind.

February 19: (Letter to parents) Pound starts reviewing Joyce (see May below). He mentions having seen Desmond FitzGerald, who was one of the 1909 "gang" recently, and speaks about going to Sirmione soon. He tells Ingrid Davies in the 1950s that FitzGerald is the "live man" who is played off against dead material and tawdry imagery (beer bottle on the base of a statue's pediment) in Canto 7, which is occupying his attention now.

February 21: (Letter to Quinn) Pound tells his patron that Eliot has come back from his Lausanne "specialist looking O.K.; and with a damn good poem (19 pages) in his suitcase; same finished up here; and should be out in Dial soon." He adds: "About enough, Eliot's poem, to make the rest of us shut up shop. I haven't done so; have in fact knocked out another Canto (not in the least . . . connected with 'modern life')."

March 10: (Letter to Amy Lowell; *SL*, 172) Another misunderstanding arising over gossip. Pound says that she is

	not getting enough out of life, and since that would end for her in 1925, he was somewhat right.
March 14:	(Letter to Eliot) A tirade in which Pound refuses to have any part of any English journal, including the one that Lady Rothermere wants to back (*The Criterion*).
March 18:	(Letter to Williams; *SL*, 172–74) Eliot, now at his last gasp, desperately needs money, which Pound is trying to raise through his Bel Esprit effort. After Eliot, Ezra plans to subsidize Marianne Moore and even Williams—for trips to Europe. Williams answers cantankerously on March 29: "What the hell do I care about Elliot [*sic*]." But he contributes to the project, as do May Sinclair, Natalie Barney, and others.
March 22:	(Letter to parents; PC 597) The *Dial* has graciously sent him 50 "bones" for Canto 8, and he is more determined than ever to scour Italy for retirement places. He is reading Confucius in a French translation and enjoying it enormously. (Letter to H. L. Mencken; *SL*, 174) "The Christian Era ended at midnight on Oct. 29–30 of last year. You are now in the year 1.p.s.U" (see January 24 above). Pound enlists Mencken's aid in Bel Esprit and invites him to come to Europe, as he does almost every American.
Circa March 23:	(Letter to Kate Buss of Boston, who had written him during the war) He wants her to distribute the Bel Esprit circular printed by Rodker—but privately, in order to protect Eliot's bank job.
March 27:	He and Dorothy leave Paris for Siena.
March 29:	(Genoa; postcard to parents) From the Hotel Royal Aquila, he asks if they stayed here on their trip back in 1902. He is not attending the big economic conference that starts soon, but is leaving for Siena shortly, via Carrara, the marble city.
April:	Hemingway is now in Genoa, attending the conference, where he meets Lincoln Steffens, just back from Russia, and William Bird; he will present both to Pound in the near future. One day he drives to Rapallo to visit the cartoonist Max Beerbohm, and he later raves about this place, where Pound will settle. The *Dial* for this month carries Pound's "Paris Letter," which denounces English journalism, especially his

	new enemy Murry, who attacked Flaubert recently; Pound defends Flaubert ferociously.
April 4:	(Siena; letter to Quinn) Pound plans to visit several sites in Italy, and to be in the Lake Garda region in June; then Dorothy will go to England to visit her parents. Quinn needs Sirmione! Indeed.
April 5:	(Siena; letter to Wyndham Lewis) Pound says that Bel Esprit could do very little more than provide him with a studio, since Lewis has succeeded in supporting himself for years without starving. Lewis's report that Eliot is skeptical about the whole project is dismissed cavalierly by Pound, who continues in his unwanted act of generosity. Pound advises Wyndham to flee England, which is laboring under a curse (*SL*, 176).
April 11:	(Siena; letter to parents) The weather is milder in this hill town than in Sirmione. Pound likes this city, and will like it even more when Olga Rudge assumes a position with the Chigi Musical Academy in the early 1930s. He plans to take the bus to Florence, and then go on to Rome, checking out Perugia at some point. He will be translating Paul Morand shortly.
May:	The *Dial* issue for this month contains his "Paris Letter," which is largely a blurb for *Ulysses*. After having read the novel in bits and pieces, but not consecutively from the start, Pound at last has a chance to survey it in its entirety and is even more impressed with Joyce's performance, although once again he accentuates the satiric aspect perhaps too strongly. There is no doubt that a deeper reading of the way that Joyce used the figure of Ulysses-Leopold Bloom convinced him that he might adapt the same peripatetic figure as an organizing device for his own epic. However, Pound would become Ulysses (as well as other figures) himself, whereas Joyce was never Ulysses-Leopold Bloom.
May 4:	Pound and Dorothy are now in Venice; he tells his parents in a letter written later on the 22nd from the same Hotel Savoia that he has been investigating Cortona, Perugia, Assisi, Spoleto, Ancona, Rimini, and Ravenna as possible retirement places. On studying the beautiful Temple in Rimini built by Sigismundo Malatesta for his mistress and lover Isotta, which contains a blending of Christian and pagan de-

	signs and sculpture, Pound decided to devote a canto in his long poem to this swashbuckling Renaissance strong-man. As we shall see, this canto grew and grew. (Letter to Williams; *SL*, no. 188) Discusses the possibility of his friend's staying in his studio in Paris in July, when Dorothy will be in England. Pound thanks him for the money sent. (Letter to Kate Buss) He thanks her for her efforts in promoting the Bel Esprit cause, and commends her to Natalie Barney and Picabia, since Kate is in Paris. Eliot, ill again, will be in Switzerland in late May.
May 6:	The Pounds are in Perugia, where Ezra continues his Bel Esprit talk in a letter to Quinn. Pound likes this Umbrian hill town and its neighbor, Assisi, but not well enough to settle there.
May 22:	(Letter to parents) Pound is now back in Venice after the Umbrian-Romagnole tour. Clearly Venice and Verona are far up on the list of choices as retirement sites. He says that he has provided for Joyce, but poor Eliot is still on his hands.
Early June:	Pound, Bride Scratton (Thiy), and Eliot (the man fallen on hard times: *il decaduto*) meet in Verona to discuss a "literary program" (obviously Bel Esprit) in the Cafe Dante, but it never gets off the ground (Canto 78/481). Eliot stays only two days (*TSEL*, 535–36), while Bride moves north to Paris. The Pounds go on to Sirmione, where they are visited by the Hemingways. Ernest, touring war sites and the Lake Garda country, interviews Benito Mussolini, editor of the powerful fascist newspaper *Il Popolo d'Italia* in Milan. He describes the future dictator as a "big, brown-faced man with a high forehead, a slow-smiling mouth, and large, expressive hands"; he quotes Benito as bragging that Italy can now overthrow any country that is foolish enough to attack it. Hemingway was impressed by the man, although his foray into his own past seemed disappointing, probably because there was little truly heroic there to support it.
June 9:	(Letter to Quinn from Sirmione) Pound and Aldington have now raised half the money they need to support Eliot. The Earthly Paradise of Sirmione has enabled Pound to block in four new cantos. He has used

	Quinn's anecdote about a sodomitic merchant seaman giving birth to a baby (now in Canto 12), and hopes that he hasn't spoiled the anecdote in the telling. He is also working on his own "Hell" canto (later 14), which is centered in England.
Late June:	Civil war breaks out in Ireland over De Valera's long refusal to accept Griffith's treaty with the English; this goes on for about a year. Pound cites Padraic Colum's poetry in Canto 80/496 for eloquently stating the difficulty of getting soldiers to lay down their arms (in this case after the battle with the British had ended): "Your gunmen tread on my dreams."
July:	There is no government in Italy for several weeks as socialists clash with fascists. Yeats is given an honorary degree by Queen's University, Belfast, and Maud Gonne is infuriated that he would accept such a thing from the Protestant enemy. Wyndham Lewis, in Paris, opens the door to Pound's studio and observes the poet boxing with a splendidly built stranger named Hemingway. The Pounds had returned on July 4.
July 8–9:	(Paris; letter to Professor Felix E. Schelling of Penn) Pound has just recently returned from Italy and is staging a showing of Tami Koume's paintings in his studio on July 11. This long letter (reprinted in *Selected Letters*, no. 189) contains many valuable insights on a variety of topics, but is largely a self-defense by Pound of his poetry written against the Professor's recent review of *Poems 1918–21* and some other work in the *Public Ledger*. Pound says that the four people who have helped him the most are Robert Bridges, who cautioned him against using homophones; Yeats, who told him to ignore adverse criticism; Ford, who told him to use a living language; and Hardy, who wanted *Propertius* titled differently from being an *Homage*. In chapter 11, it was noted that Pound used the same four names, but with some different advice in his interview with Donald Hall.

Pound defends his translation of Propertius as an adaptation and says that his Provençal translations were shots in the dark, perhaps as illuminating as much for what they miss as for what they gain. He again states his own uneasiness about his cantos: "Having the crust to attempt a poem in 100 or 120 cantos long after all mankind has been commanded never again to attempt a poem of any length, I have to stagger as I can" (*SL*, 180). Yet he insists that his first eleven cantos are merely "a preparation of the palette" in which he lays down his basic colors. He also confesses "I am perhaps didactic" (180), but quickly adds that other epic writers like Homer, Dante, and even the lyrical Villon were didactic too, that morality is an inherent part of great literature. Yet he also notes that he is no more Hugh Selwyn Mauberley than Eliot was Prufrock. On a note of attempted accord, Pound apologizes for his youthful ranking of George Bernard Shaw over Shakespeare at Penn (which infuriated Schelling), and says that now the modern playwright strikes him as "fundamentally trivial." He then discusses in detail the Professor's adverse criticisms.

July 13: Dorothy leaves Paris for England for a long stay with her parents, thus enabling Pound to see many other women who are around. Bride Scratton is one of them; Pound took her to Brancusi's studio among other places.

July 14: (Letter to Kate Buss) He has translated two volumes of the work of Paul Morand and has blocked in five more cantos.

July 16: (Letter to Harriet Monroe) He begrudgingly allows her to make a selection of his work for her forthcoming anthology. He recommends Marianne Moore as the next recipient of a Bel Esprit award, and then launches into some strong anti-Judaic, anti-monotheistic statements: "Say that I consider the Writings of Confucius, and Ovid's *Metamorphoses* the only safe guides in religion.... I consider the *Metamorphoses* a sacred book, and the Hebrew scriptures the record of a barbarian tribe, full of evil" (*SL*, 183). This new strain of vitriole seems to derive from his interests in Confucius and Douglas's study of banking.

Circa July 18: (Letter to parents; PC 616, misdated) Pound has helped Koume with his show, and now has 22 pledges for Bel Esprit. He has just run into Frank "Baldy" Bacon, whom he has not seen since 1910, and is using some material from Baldy's life in Canto 10 (now Canto 12). Pound has completed rough drafts of Ur-Cantos 9 to 13, including the Hell Cantos. Probably because so many of his friends are sick (Eliot, Joyce, Quinn), he is interested in a glands specialist named Louis Berman (whom he had once discussed in the *New Age*); Berman is now in Paris and examines Joyce, but is only a fad for Pound. Ezra has taken out a three-year lease on his studio, and is having its mud-green walls painted a deep sea blue.

July 19: (Letter to Amy Lowell) Her lack of cooperation in Bel Esprit causes him to write a brief, derogatory note, where he calls her a "hell-roarer" and a "kuss" (*SL*, 183).

On the same date, Eliot tells Quinn that he will give the lawyer the typescript of *The Waste Land* with Pound's suggested alterations (*TSEL*, 548).

August 1: (Letter to Williams; *SL*, no. 192) Pound informs his friend about the appearance of William Bird (via Hemingway), who wants to publish some prose works, with Ezra as the arbiter. Pound asks Williams what he has, and later accepts *The Great American Novel.*

August 10: *The Natural Philosophy of Love* in Pound's translation of Gourmont is published by Boni and Liveright of New York.

(Letter to Quinn) Fifty-six people were in his studio last week, and maybe even more. He hasn't seen too much of Joyce, whose latest complaint is a case of dental abscesses. Lewis was in town and seemed "more settled." Hemingway, a "good chap" who was buried alive during the war (that old story that made its way into the *Cantos*), has a friend with a printing press who may do some publishing. Pound recalls Old Man Comley of his Jenkintown days, who constantly chewed tobacco but warned the boys away from it; Ezra feels that he is similar—telling people that epics should not be written, and writing one anyway (see 28/136). Yeats is "shut in" by Irish battles, and Desmond FitzGerald writes Pound that he is fortunate to be living in Paris.

August 12: Arthur Griffith dies of a stroke in a nursing home in Dublin, as much a victim of the Irish violence as any soldier.

August 20: (Paige Carbon 619 to parents) "Flood of people"... Lewis, Rodker, Etchells from London... Watson of the *Dial*... Léger doing good painting... Jean de

	Bosschère . . . "everyone in and out of Paris" . . . visited Brancusi . . . Working on the Sigismundo Malatesta material that will become Cantos 8–11.
September 2:	(Letter to parents) "flood of people" . . . Hilda and her mother, Watson of *Dial*, Bishop of *Vanity Fair*. The medium Mlle. Claire de Pratz is now living in Judith Gautier's old apartment with relics from Théophile; the junkhouse effect reminds Pound of Aunt Frank's boardinghouse on East 47th St. in Manhattan around the turn of the century.
September 9:	William T. Cosgrave is elected the new President of the Irish Provisional Government, with FitzGerald as the Minister of External Affairs; the Constitution is ratified in October. The Malatesta Canto is now expanding into two (later four).
September 21:	(Letter to Quinn) Bird, with his press, wants Pound to consider doing a periodical; Ezra is "plugging on" at his cantos.
October 15:	*The Waste Land* is published in *The Criterion* (Eliot's new journal, which is driving the editor to distraction).
October 23:	Eliot mails Quinn the manuscript of *The Waste Land*, which does not reach New York until January 13.
October 28:	Mussolini leads the famous fascist march on Rome and is received by King Victor Emmanuel III, who allows him to put the troubled country into order. This event, which will eventually prove to be so meaningful in Pound's life, seems to pass by totally unnoticed.
October 30:	(Letter to parents) Last night he heard Lincoln Steffens, a "damn good chap" who is a friend of Hemingway's, talk about the Russian Revolution; this event is memorably described by Mary Colum in her autobiography (307): "Ezra insisted on taking us [her and husband Padraic] to a lecture by Lincoln Steffens on Soviet Russia [at Bird's place on the Ile St. Louis], the Russia of Lenin . . . The lecture seemed to me of an appalling dreariness and I hated being dragged to it . . . But Ezra listened to it with rapt attention, his eyes glued to the speaker's face, the very type of a young man in search of an ideology. . . . He seemed to have an intense interest in new political and economic ideas, and after Steffens was finished he rose to his feet and started talking about the Douglas plan, to

which he had tried to convert Arthur Griffith and through him the new Irish state. He had begun the writing of those letters of his to every prime minister in Europe on this subject.... Later I was not surprised to hear of Ezra's attachment [to] Italian fascism, though he was strongly anti-German." At this key point in his life, Pound was desperate for something to believe in, and he was already veering right rather than left, in keeping with the politics of his American ancestors.

In his *Autobiography,* Steffens described Ezra as an American who "was seeing and seizing all the world for his. Pound was a private, professional propagandist, as Gertrude Stein was" (II, 833). But Pound would become much more public a decade later.

Pound tells his parents that Hemingway is back from the Greek and Turkish War, thoroughly disgusted by the indiscriminate sale of munitions. (Clippings concerning the infamous "merchant of cannons" Sir Basil Zaharoff, known in the *Cantos* as Metevsky, begin to appear in Pound's papers at this time.) Eliot's new quarterly is good in an "octogenarian" sort of way. Horace Liveright and the *Dial* are paying Pound's rent.

November issue of the *Dial* contains *The Waste Land* and Pound's "Paris Letter," promoting the Bel Esprit project, but without Eliot's name; Pound also praises Proust and Cocteau, rather lukewarmly, but he quotes with enthusiasm a line from the Italian D'Annunzio's *Notturno:* "In Koré's house there are now only white peacocks" (see Canto 3). Pound also quotes the historian Platina's statement about the topics discussed by intelligent men: "de litteris et de armis, praestantibusque ingeniis" (about literature, arms, and outstanding geniuses), which is applied to Malatesta in Canto 11/51— and later to Jefferson and Adams. He rather severely criticizes modern patrons in a way that infuriates millionaire backer Watson, and his job is in jeopardy.

Mid-November: (Paige Carbon 617, misdated in August) Ezra tells his mother that Ford has arrived in Paris for a month. Ford has been talking with one of Pound's friends, a Russian ex-general named Golijevski. Bill Bird is now promoting Ezra's opera on Villon. Brancusi is very active, and Ford has just finished *The Marsden Case* (published in 1923). Eliot's new magazine has merits, but is dull. Hawley Chester, son of the Wyncote preacher Carlos Tracy Chester, now turned farmer (to whom Pound dedicated *Exultations* back in 1909), has been visiting, offering news about Ezra's mischievous boyhood playmate Tommy Cochran of the haunting smile (78/481, 91/615).

Ford and Stella are staying at the Hotel de Blois on the nearby Rue Vavin near the Metro stop; they will remain here for a month before heading south.

November 16: The *Liverpool Daily Post* publicizes Pound's Bel Esprit program in a way that humiliates Eliot, who is furious and is threatening to sue the newspaper to protect his job and dignity. What began as charity on Pound's part has become an embarrassment.

November 20: Hemingway covers an international conference in Lausanne to settle the Greco-Turkish conflict, along with Lincoln Steffens (who later thinks wrongly that he met Hemingway at this time). Ernest again encounters Mussolini, but this time he calls him "the biggest bluff" in Europe. He describes the Duce in a satiric poem that will appear in the 1923 Spring issue of the *Little Review* as follows:

MUSSOLINI has nigger eyes and a bodyguard and has his
picture taken reading a book upside down. MUSSO-
LINI is
wonderful. Read the Daily Mail.

Pound has no feelings on the subject at all. When Hemingway plans to visit Ezra in Rapallo in 1923, he is very nervous, because Mussolini is aware of his antagonism and has threatened to create problems for him.

December: The *Dial* gives its annual award to T. S. Eliot.

December 6: The Dáil of the Irish Free State formally assembles, and W. B. Yeats is nominated as a Senator. Pound is happy about this, as his letters to Yeats show. Orage is now ready to leave England to study with Gurdjieff at Fontainebleau; he will not return until the thirties.

December 15: *The Waste Land* is published by Boni and Liveright.

December 20: Cocteau's *Antigone* opens with scenery by Picasso and music by Arthur Honegger of The Six, who will do an operatic form in 1927. Pound praises this and Cocteau's other dramatic works in his March "Paris Letter."

December 25: (Christmas greetings to his parents) Pound announces that his three Malatesta cantos are now in good shape. He had a marvelous turkey truffle lunch with Natalie Barney and her friend Romaine Brooks yesterday. It is about this time or later in 1923 that Pound meets Olga Rudge at a Barney reception. See March 25, 1923, for the first occurrence of her name in the Paige Carbons.

Ford is off to Cape Ferrat on the Riviera, where he will stay in Harold Monro's tiny villa. Meanwhile, others have hit town, such as Augustus B. Wadsworth, a wealthy stockbroking relative from New York related to mother Isabel. Scores of people are planning to descend on Dorothy and him soon in Rapallo, and he will attempt to go underground there.

1923

January: Pound's essay "On Criticism in General" in this month's issue of Eliot's *Criterion* enunciates many of the principles later made in "How to Read" (1929); it distinguishes three primary features of poetry: melopoeia, the making of sounds; phanopoeia, the making of imagery; and logopoeia, the "dance of the intellect" or creation of sense or sensibility. These are also mentioned in the later *ABC of Reading* (1934; 37). Pound's "Paris Letter" in the *Dial* praises the art of Léger and mentions Edgar Williams's remarks on sculpture in 1911.

January 16: Now at the Hotel Mignon in Rapallo, Pound writes for Joyce a humorous poem about one of his *Ulysses* characters, Buck Mulligan, who is portrayed as an Irish senator (see *SL*, no. 193).

January 19: (To parents) Pound finds Rapallo pleasant, but wonders about the sea air during the winter. (When he

	and Olga Rudge had the option during the 1960s of spending the winter either in Venice or Rapallo, they chose humid Venice because it was milder.) He has met an affable young Southerner from Princeton named Henry (Mike) Strater, who is interested in doing paintings.
January 23:	The Hemingways write from Chamby, Switzerland, that they intend to join the Pounds soon for a projected walking tour, but Hemingway confesses later that his heart was not in it, and he makes unnecessary delays. He tells Ezra about a horrendous thing that happened in mid-December: Hadley lost all of his early writings—including the carbons—in a train station in Paris as she was preparing to join him in Switzerland. Ernest is devastated—and this event has a strongly negative influence on the future of their marriage.
January 27:	(To Hemingway) Pound urges the "Colonel" to "come on down," and also advises him not to tease Benito further. He and Strater are playing tennis together and might even go over to "Cans" to challenge the lady stars. He comforts Hemingway about his lost writings by saying that one's juvenilia are often dispensable, and so what looks like a loss now might ultimately be a gain. Nancy Cunard is expected shortly. Pound is not interested in touring Calabria, which Hemingway would like to see.
January 29:	Hemingway answers from Chamby that he and Hadley plan to arrive toward the end of February, but this plan changes. He wants to know if Ezra is going to break away south with Cunard, and says that Calabria still interests him more because of its rugged scenery than do the tame historical sites of Tuscany.
February:	The *Dial* this month contains Pound's second-to-last "Paris Letter," and one can understand why the editors might have been unhappy. Instead of giving the reader some idea of what was going on in the city, Pound merely harangues about aesthetic issues.
February 9:	(To William Carlos Williams; *SL*, no. 194) Pound offers details about Bird's printing of Williams's *Great American Novel*. Robert McAlmon has been in Florence for two months after his autumn-long debauch with Nancy Cunard in Venice—along with Wyndham

	Lewis and the Sitwells for a time. Pound expects McAlmon in Rapallo shortly. The Hemingways and the Pounds intend to head south in three days.
February 12:	According to Carlos Baker, Hemingway's first biographer (who received information firsthand), the two couples went to Pisa, Piombino, Orbetello, and Grosseto along the coast, and then swung inland to Siena and the famous battle sites of Sigismundo Malatesta in Tuscany. For about five days, they visited battlefields and picnicked out-of-doors; they especially viewed documented places like Rocca Sorano and other sites carefully chosen by Pound. As Pound read segments of Renaissance history, Hemingway strutted around the battlefields, trying to reconstruct the events as they might have occurred. By the 17th, the Pounds continued south to Rome and the Hemingways returned to Rapallo.
February 17:	(To John Quinn from Rome) The Pounds have just arrived here, and Ezra is filling in his Malatesta cantos with daily immersion in the Vatican Library.
February 20:	(From Nancy Cunard in "not habitable" Florence to Pound in Rome) She has been consorting with McAlmon and Norman Douglas, but Bob is heading for Rapallo, while she is traveling south to Rome, where she very much wants to see Ezra again. She will be staying at 48 Via Margutta with the sculptress Nancy Cox McCormack, who did the life mask of Pound in Paris and who will marry soon.
Circa February 22:	McAlmon appears at Rapallo en route to Paris. After checking in at the Hotel Splendide, he "encountered Ernest Hemingway and his wife, Hadley, and also Henry (Mike) Strater, the painter and his wife. I had never heard of any of them before. Hemingway was a Middle Western American who worked for a Canadian newspaper, and he was a type outside my experience. At times he was deliberately hard-boiled, case-hardened, and old; at other times he was the hurt, sensitive boy, deliberately young and naive, wanting to be brave, and somehow on the defensive, suspicions lurking in his peering analytic glances at the person with whom he was talking. He approached a café with a small-boy, tough-guy swagger, and before strangers of whom he was uncertain

	a potential snarl of scorn played on his large-lipped, rather loose mouth. Mike Strater was a far simpler and direct young American, a Southerner, not only unpretentious but actually modest" (*Being Geniuses Together*, 157). They were all working on their art, but "although the Sitwell trio seemed happy in that environment, Rapallo after the sun goes down struck me as dismal and depressing" (158).
February 24:	(To parents from Rome) Pound detests this teeming, overly busy "tail end" of Europe as much as he did back in 1902. He is immersed in Malatesta history.
February 26:	(From Quinn in New York to Eliot in London) The outspoken patron has just read the marked-up typescript of *The Waste Land* and says that he thinks that Eliot let Pound take too many liberties with the poem. Still, Quinn will see that the emendations and deletions will not reach the public's eye (this letter explains better than any other one why the typescript disappeared for so long).
March 1:	(To parents from Rome) He has not been here for 21 years, and will not hasten to return. He is leaving pronto.
March 2:	(To parents from Florence) Dorothy and he have just arrived, coming via Orvieto, where they spent the night. This letter is written in bad Italian: for example, "Il sua lettera ittaliana recevuta...."
March 6:	(From Nancy Cunard speeding by train to Naples) She missed him again in Rome! What terrible luck! "Ezra dearest, Italy is for us, you know . . . we *should* live in it."
March 9:	Pound signs into the State Archive at Modena to study Malatesta.
March 10:	(From Hemingway in Milan) He liked "Orbitello." (He and Hadley move north to the ski resort of Cortina d'Ampezzo, where they meet Renata Borgatti, Olga Rudge's maligned pianist accompanist. Renata is kind to both until the Hemingways leave for Germany.)
Mid-March:	*Indiscretions* is issued by Three Mountains, dedicated to A. R. Orage "at whose request this fragment was first hitched together." Pound's last "Paris Letter" in the *Dial* distinguishes between his and Coburn's vortographs and Man Ray's rayographs. Pound praises Cocteau as one of the few dramatists worth notice.

March 17:	(From Nancy Cunard in Positano to Pound in Cesena) It will soon be April, and she is reserving that month for Ezra; could they possibly meet, with or without Dorothy, in the North somewhere? Pound is toiling away in the Malatesta Library in this charming Romagnole town, where he has the good fortune to meet the very civilized librarian Manlio Dazzi, whom he praised often later, especially in his essay "Possibilities of Civilization: What the Small Town Can Do" in the *Delphian Quarterly* of Chicago (July, 1936). Cesena of the beautiful columns (Canto 11/50) appealed greatly to the Pounds. Ezra was impressed by the way that Dazzi, who was also a musician, was able to schedule magnificent concerts on a shoestring; this gave him the idea of doing the same thing in Rapallo during the '30s. Later Dazzi moved to assume the directorship of the Quirini Stampalia Library in Venice, and became a close friend.
March 25:	(Florence; to his parents) He is trying to finish a new violin suite for Olga to play in London (this is the first occurrence of her name in the Paige Carbons). He is going to Venice soon and wants his sympathies conveyed to Aunt Florence Foote of North Philadelphia on the death of Grandmother Susan Angevin Loomis, who was living with her.
March 26:	Pound writes Hemingway from the Palace Hotel in Rimini, saying that his next stop is Venice, and then Milan in 10 days. Pound is working in the Gambalunga Library here in Rimini, as well as studying Sigismundo's beautiful Temple. According to Peter d'Epiro's study of the Malatesta cantos, Pound was examining the unpublished chronicle of the life of Sigismundo written by one Gaspare Broglio, which supplied him with a great many new facts that were incorporated in a revised version of the Malatesta cantos that he sent on March 24 to Watson of the *Dial*. During this period Pound also visited libraries and churches in Ravenna and Bologna, and renewed his long acquaintances with Mantua and Ferrara.
March 30:	(Venice; to his parents; PC 633, misdated Mar. 20) He has just found Andreas Divus' Latin translation of Homer's *Iliad*, a companion to the *Odyssey* that he

	had purchased about twelve years ago in Paris. This discovery obviously makes Pound aware again of the other translation, and may help to explain why he, still searching for a way to begin his long poem, finally settled on an English version of Divus' Canto 11.
April:	The "Exiles Number" of the *Little Review* contains selections from Hemingway's *in our time*, as well as work by Stein, Cummings, McAlmon; it also has the score for Antheil's brief "Airplane Sonata," as well as a "Design" by Dorothy Shakespear and Léger's "Aesthetics of the Machine," which is dedicated to Pound. Bird publishes Ford's *Women & Men* this month.
April 24:	(Letter to parents) He is back in Paris, helping Bird to publish his books. He has purchased a new Underwood Portable typewriter and has tons of work to do. Hemingway is back from Germany, Strater from Italy.
May:	Bird publishes Williams's *Great American Novel* and B. C. Windeler's *Elimus*, the story of a young man who can't hold a job in a meaningless society. Next comes Bride's *England*, a collection of four *Dubliners*-like stories that reveal her country as a wasteland.
May 11:	(Letter to parents) When they break up their house on retirement, he wants them to salvage a copy of the How coat of arms, portraits of Isabel's Wadsworth grandmother and his Grandma Weston, and chessmen from his Hamilton College days. Bird plans to do a deluxe edition of his cantos, with Strater creating initial capitals. Walter Rummel has surfaced after the Isadora Duncan affair.
May 12:	(Letter to Kate Buss; *SL*, no. 195) The *Dial* has now cut him off even from writing the "Paris Letter"; all his ties to America are severed; what next? He castigates Frank Crowninshield (whose name is suppressed in the *Selected Letters*) of *Vanity Fair* for wanting him to write commercial fluff. The *Criterion*, like Eliot himself, is as "heavily camouflaged as Westminster Abbey" (he is stealing Wyndham Lewis's famous line). Despite this gloom, Bird will issue his first 16 cantos in a deluxe edition at $25 per copy "and 50 and 100 bones for Vellum and illuminateds." There will only be about 60 copies for sale.
May 19:	(Letter to parents) McAlmon is flourishing as a prose hope, as is Hemingway. Pound has recently had lunch

with the chic and influential Princess Bassiano "with all the stars": Larbaud, Cocteau, etc. Jean was in excellent form. Joyce finally had thirteen rotten teeth pulled and is feeling better, while Brancusi is now sculpting his famous birds. Picabia seems a bit tired, but his current show is quite good.

May 29: (To Quinn) Deep into his Malatesta cantos.

June: A note in Pound's hand in the Beinecke correspondence with Eliot says that T.S. received £20 from Bel Esprit.

June 6: (Letter to parents) Dorothy is going to England to look after her sick father. Hemingway, McAlmon, and Bird are all in Spain, sampling their first bullfights. Rodker was pleased by the way the older Pounds received him in Wyncote on his visit.

June 13: George Antheil and his beloved Boski arrive from Berlin; they take a room in a small hotel near the Sorbonne, but shift to a place above Shakespeare and Company. Soon afterward, Margaret Anderson introduces George to Pound, who excitedly asks him for several violin sonatas for Olga Rudge. Antheil writes his First, and then takes off to North Africa for a month.

June 21: (Letter to parents) Pound is working on the famous Confucius Canto (13), using Pauthier and the Confucian *Odes* translated into Latin. A meeting with Heap and Anderson reveals that the latter has more brains than the former, but he is beginning to share Quinn's doubts about both. Dorothy is off in London and will be gone for quite a while. (Olga Rudge plays tennis to keep him company.) Pound explains that the Princess Bassiano from May 19 is a plain American girl who is married to an Italian count; she gives elegant lunches to artists and men of letters. McAlmon, who was given $70,0000 this year by his father-in-law, is now joining with Bird in publishing; he has established his Contact Co., which is allied with Three Mountains. The trio of bullfight fans has returned from Spain. Pound is very taken with the free-verse novels of Mina Loy.

July: *Criterion* has Cantos 9–12 of a Long Poem (now 8–11, Malatesta); acting in Eliot's place, the assistant editor Aldington censored Pound's calling Pope Pius II

	an "s.o.b.," and Pound transferred the epithet to Aldington himself in a letter.
July 6:	Hemingway leaves for five days of bullfighting in Pamplona; this visit will deeply influence his future work. On this second trip, he goes with Hadley and returns shortly. Henry Hope Shakespear dies; Dorothy will be in England for quite a while helping her mother.
July 8:	(Letter to parents; PC 641) After telling them the bad news above, he notes that Harriet Monroe is in town, and he has finally met her; she is just as spinsterish as he had imagined. He is seeing a lot of Heap and Anderson, even if they are not always sympathetic. George Antheil is the "bright spark" who also likes Pound's orchestration; he is the man to watch.
July 14:	Malcolm Cowley socks the surly owner of the Café Rotonde, is arrested, and is proclaimed a hero by his companions (Loeb, Aragon, and Lawrence Vail, a graphic artist married for a time to Peggy Guggenheim).
July 23:	John Quinn sends T. S. Eliot his first annual payment of $400, with more promised to come. Eliot, with this support and that of Lady Rothermere, is totally disinterested in Bel Esprit, because Pound has handled it poorly. On October 4, Eliot writes Quinn copious thanks.
That summer:	Archibald MacLeish is now visible, but is never close to Pound in Paris. Ezra bumps into Djuna Barnes (whom he soon unsuccessfully tries to seduce, according to her biographer Andrew Field); she is walking with Edmund Wilson, a rising critic, whom Pound totally ignores.
August 17:	Hemingway and his pregnant wife sail for Canada, where he resumes his work on the *Toronto Star*. Ezra warns Hadley (who doesn't like him) not to try to change Ernest after their baby is born; she later views this as an ill omen auguring their future divorce.
August 24:	(Letter to parents) He is deep into his musical research. Antheil plays Stravinsky for "us" (Olga, him, and Barney). He has now finished Cantos 5 to 11, and has thoroughly revised the early part of the poem, which has given him the most trouble. The Joyces have returned from Ireland and are staying at the

	Victoria Palace Hotel. Joyce is already hard at work on his great new epic [*Finnegans Wake*]. Pound, who has not seen it, crows that it is "Cal'lated to take the hide off a few more sons of bitches." He would change his mind drastically when he settled down to actually reading it.
August 30:	(Letter to parents) Pound thanks them for the money but didn't need it. After the death of an aunt, Dorothy, still in England consoling Olivia and helping her settle her father's estate, is now receiving more than the approximately £200 that she had received recently (according to Pound's letter to Quinn on July 4, 1922). Antheil is "very solid." Pound is now moving ahead past Canto 16, studying the Borgias, just as he was already doing advanced work this year on the Estes. Ford is due back soon.
September 3:	Ford and Stella return from the South and take his brother Oliver's rundown rear cottage at 65 Boulevard Arago, later moving to a nearby studio. They give large dancing parties attended by the "London girls" of war days: Nina Hamnett, Mary Butts, Phyllis Reid, and also some Parisians like Olga Rudge. Pound and Ford eat together often—at Emile's, the Closerie, or Ford's preferred Nègre de Toulouse. Ford and Joyce immediately become friends.
September 6:	(Letter to Wyndham Lewis) Pound has complained to Eliot about the dullness of the *Criterion*, but Eliot answers that it is hard to find first-rate people who will contribute to it. The magazine and his bank job are together driving him to a breakdown.
September 12:	(Card to parents) Ford has been reading him parts of *Some Do Not.* . . . Antheil has been going over the Villon opera with him. Bird is in Venice, Williams due to come to Paris that winter.
	(Same day) Quinn sails on the *Paris;* he will spend about three weeks in Paris, after a rest in Brittany, working on a difficult case. Ford and Stella have sold their farm in England for $2000, and Ford is dreaming of starting a new magazine.
October 3:	(Letter to parents) Quinn, now in Paris, has met Ford for the first time, and is interested in his projected review.
	A famous photograph shows these two and Joyce in

the court at Ezra's studio, where Quinn appears often when he is not working on his complicated legal case. Around October 12, Quinn decides to give Ford a $1000 advance to start his magazine, which is first called the *Paris* and then the *Transatlantic Review;* an additional $1000 was added in 1924. Ford was immediately making the same kind of grandiose plans that killed his *English Review*. Quinn tells Joyce (with whom he already has somewhat strained relations) that he will soon be paring down his enormous library, and he plans to sell the manuscript of *Ulysses*. Joyce accepts this news sullenly, appreciating the fact that Quinn offers him half the profit, but when the sale is transacted, he is furious. Quinn's liver is inflamed during the entire trip, and he is often in pain; his disease still has not been diagnosed as cirrhosis.

Lincoln Steffens is back in town and has tea with Pound and Ford.

October 4: Three compositions by Antheil are presented before a performance of the Swedish Ballet. A near-riot ensues, with Man Ray punching somebody; Erik Satie and Ezra Pound, among others, heartily welcome the extreme new music.

October 7: (To Wyndham Lewis) Pound announces that a new review is beginning, but he hesitates to mention the name of the editor, since Lewis detests Ford.

October 10: Around this time Harold Loeb, still much involved with *Broom* in New York, is in Paris and meets Ford Madox Ford for the first time. He says in *The Way It Was:* "His head resembled Humpty-Dumpty's except for the walrus moustache and the rosy complexion of a retired officer of the Indian Army" (188). Loeb (the despicable Robert Cohn of *The Sun Also Rises*) is not a close friend of Pound, whom he nevertheless describes as one of the more colorful male inhabitants of Montparnasse in his memoir (165).

October 22: Ned Scratton wins his divorce suit against his wife Bride and Ezra Pound on grounds of adultery. She is forced to take jobs as a sales clerk or a writer for galleries, while the two youngest Scratton children are awarded to Ned and his new wife. Bride does not accept Pound's invitation to move to Paris.

October 27: A very tired John Quinn sails home on the *Berengaria*,

Three writers and a patron gather next to a statue of Diana in Pound's courtyard: a pensive Joyce, a restless Pound, a magisterial Quinn, and a Ford who, as usual, finds it hard to keep his mouth closed. See Canto 107/761: "Diana crumbles in Notre-Dame des Champs." (Poetry Society of America and Estate of Jeanne Robert Foster)

	after a quick trip to Italy with Mrs. Jeanne Robert Foster. By this time Cummings has also gone back to New York with Elaine, the wife of Scofield Thayer, whom he will marry and then very quickly divorce. Thayer, who fired Pound from the *Dial*, has returned from his psychoanalysis with Freud and is in New York too.
November 9:	Edouard Estaunié's *Appel de la route* (1922) is published by Boni and Liveright as *The Call of the Road*, translated by one Hiram Janus (none other than E.P.). This was part of an agreement made with Liveright on Jan. 4, 1922, by which Pound would be paid a minimum of $500 over a two-year period to do certain translations, but the agreement went nowhere beyond this.

November 14: Yeats's Nobel Prize for 1924 is preannounced; he goes to Stockholm early the next year to receive it.
November 22: (Letter to parents) Pound is very enthusiastic about Antheil, who is now in Berlin, but will be returning to give a concert with Olga on Dec. 11. George is working on a second violin sonata for her, and both will be played. Ezra proudly announces the title of his new opera as *Le Testament*. Dorothy is due back next week.
November 25: Eliot visits Pound and talks about leaving the abominable bank.
December 8: (Letter to parents) Olga and George are making such a racket in Pound's studio preparing for the concert that the Swede upstairs complains bitterly to the police, but the police support the musicians and art. Pound writes a funny account of this to William Bird (*SL*, no. 196).
December 11: The concert goes off as planned at the Salle du Conservatoire.
December 12: Raymond Radiguet, the young novelist and lover of Cocteau, dies of typhoid fever, contracted that summer; his funeral, attended by many celebrities, is interestingly described by Nina Hamnett in her autobiography. Cocteau then goes into a deep funk that brings him to opium and Maritain.
December 25: With Dorothy safely back for some time, Pound has many friends in for the Christmas season.
December 31: Hemingway resigns his job in Canada as of this date; he, Hadley, and their beautiful new son John (familiarly known to all as Bumby) prepare to sail on the Cunard Liner *Antonia* for France again.

1924

January: The first issue of the *Transatlantic Review* appears with Pound's "Two Cantos" brushing shoulders with four poems by E. E. Cummings, McAlmon's story "Elsie," some memoirs of old Luke Ionides of London (a Greek friend of Olivia Shakespear; see Cantos 40/198, 100/714, and 104/743), a Conrad-Ford story from the past, and the first installment of Ford's *Some Do Not*. . . .

As everyone agreed, it was a very mixed issue—possibly too mixed. The title of the magazine was printed in lower-case letters—not out of pretentiousness but because it was too long to fit easily in capitals. Pound's "Two Cantos" were 13 (the Kung Canto) in its current form and 12—minus Quinn's anecdote about the Honest Sailor, which was later moved there.

The magazine was emanating from Bird's establishment on the Ile St. Louis. Very soon Ford declared Thursday an open-house tea day, and he grandly presided over an array of visitors. Since a White Russian "prince," one E. Seménoff, and the wildly elusive poet Basil Bunting (1900–85) had already left the operation before it officially began, Ford was assisted at this time only by Marjorie Reid, his secretary, whom Pound had "discovered" at the Dôme Café, as she sipped an aperitif.

January 2: Jean Cocteau bolts for Monte Carlo, trying to shake off the ghost of Raymond Radiguet.

January 3: Pound is stricken with appendicitis and goes to the American Hospital in Neuilly, but rules out an operation.

January 6: (To his parents) Back from the hospital, Pound is on a strict diet. He thanks them for 600 lire, and has booked a sleeper for Rapallo, where he plans to get some much-needed rest. He leaves shortly thereafter on Tuesday morning.

January 9: William Carlos Williams and his wife Flossie sail on the *Rochambeau* for France, arriving in Le Havre on the 18th, where they are met by Kay Boyle.

January 14: John Quinn auctions off the manuscript of *Ulysses* for $1975 to the bookseller A. S. W. Rosenbach, founder of the Rosenbach Museum in Philadelphia, where it is now housed. Quinn had informed a passive Joyce of this move back in October, but now Joyce indignantly wants to buy the manuscript back. Rosenbach refuses to sell; he is the "Rosy Brook" of Joyce's little poem cited by biographer Ellmann (559):

Rosy Brook he bought a book
Though he didn't know how to spell it.
Such is the lure of literature
To the lad who can buy it and sell it.

1924

January 18: (From Williams's diary as reported in the Mariani biography) Williams and Flossie arrive in Paris, staying at the Lutetia Hotel in a room arranged by McAlmon. The next day, McAlmon introduces them to Brancusi in his cavernous studio and to the delightful Birds. That evening they dine with the Joyces at the Trianon and later drink whisky at the Dingo Bar. McAlmon confesses to Bill that his marriage is a mockery, since H.D. is really Bryher's mate. Williams is confused and upset. McAlmon's Contact Editions has now formally merged with Bird's firm.

January 19: Hemingway and his family sail from New York on the *Antonia*.

January 22: McAlmon throws a party for the Williamses at the Trianon, inviting the Joyces, Fords, Birds, Antheil, Duchamp, Ray, Loy, Beach, Aragon, Kitty Cannell, and her new admirer Loeb. Williams delivers a foolish speech of gratitude, but the party is saved by late drinks at the Dingo. Williams finds Pound's much-touted friend Ford ("a lumbering Britisher") charming and intelligent. The next day, the Doctor has a terrible hangover; he already has the impression that Paris is "enervating."

January 28: On his last night in town before heading south, Williams attends a large dancing party at Ford's place on the Blvd. Arago, where Man Ray's assistant photographer, Berenice Abbott, is punched and knocked to the floor by a man who then lifts her up and dances with her, while the party goes on and on. The Williamses sneak quietly away to the Riviera, where they see Nancy Cunard and Djuna Barnes, and then to Italy and Austria.

January 29: (Hotel Mignon, Rapallo; to his parents) Pound is now recuperating nicely, having avoided all visitors. He reminds them that they met Baldy Bacon of Canto 12 in Wyncote back around 1910; Baldy turned up in Paris during the past year.

The Hemingways arrive in Paris, and Ernest looks up Ford, whom he has heard much about from Ezra; Pound did not introduce them, as they later thought and others have declared. On Pound's previous glowing recommendation, Ford immediately invites the unemployed young man to serve as a manuscript scout for his review; soon he becomes an unpaid subeditor, replacing the irresponsible Bunting, who was jailed for drunkenness after receiving his first paycheck and who then vanished before Christmas.

February: The *Transatlantic Review* has three poems by H.D., an article on Russia by Lincoln Steffens, Antheil's brief "Sonata 3," and William Atheling's "Notes for Performers," as well as more Ionides, a Conrad-Ford collaboration, and Ford's novel installment. "Atheling" has been raised from the dead in a selection of music articles from the *New Age* made by Agnes Bedford, along with some minor notes by Pound on Antheil and other subjects.

February 5: (Rapallo; to his parents) After two years at Fontainebleau, Orage has gone to the United States with the Gurdjieff "gang" to continue his theosophic "kink." Pound did *not* visit Orage at Fontainebleau during his two years there (but he did visit Gurdjieff earlier).

February 10: (To his parents) He is searching for a villa in Rapallo for permanent residence. Estaunié, whom he translated for Liveright, is "bad."

(From Hemingway in Paris to Pound) After an ocean voyage of ten days, Ernest went to Pound's apartment in Paris, but the concierge would not let him have the key, since there were no explicit instructions (despite Ford's saying that all had been arranged). Hemingway soon finds another place up the street, although it is over a noisy sawmill that drives him to the Closerie des Lilas to write. Gilbert Seldes, one of Cummings's friends, has left the *Dial* as editor, being replaced by an "aged virgin," who is Marianne Moore. The recent *Dial* award went to Van Wyck Brooks—such is the way of the world.

February 17: (Hemingway to Stein out in the country) As Ford's talent scout, Ernest has succeeded in persuading the malleable editor to publish the first installment of her *Making of Americans*, although Ford does not seem to understand how long the piece is. (Even after Hemingway's later falling-out with Gertrude, he always claimed that this was her masterpiece.)

March: The *Transatlantic Review* contains Pound's "Treatise on Harmony," along with stories by Mary Butts and by B. M. G. (no hyphen) Adams, alias Bride Scratton,

	the latter one about "Uncle Bertram," a man who committed suicide even though he seemed to have everything he needed. There is also Williams's "Last Words of My Grandmother" (she was bored with trees), as well as an Art Supplement featuring Braque, Ray, and others.
March 12:	(Rapallo; to his parents) Pound feels much better; he has climbed nearby Monte Allegro. The peripatetic Basil Bunting, now living in the hills, has just stopped by for tea. Pound says that Luke Ionides' memoirs were dictated to Olivia Shakespear.
March 17:	(Hemingway to the "Duce" Pound; HSL) Ernest is now writing for Ford; Bunting is in jail in Genoa (apparently before his arrival in Rapallo); Strater has gone back to the United States, McAlmon is in Toulon, and Antheil is on his way to Tunis. *in our time* will be issued by Bird any day. Hemingway compliments Pound greatly, as opposed to that "English country gentleman" named Ford. He does not want Pound's Paris apartment if Ezra decides to give it up.
March 18:	Old Luke Ionides dies, but his memoirs continue into the next fall. He had been born in 1837. Spring Issue of the *Little Review* still has Pound's name on the masthead; it features Dadaists like Huelsenbeck, Arp, and Tzara. Harry and Caresse Crosby arrive in Paris. In an article in the German *Der Querschnitt*, Pound defends the awarding of the Nobel Prize to Yeats and says that Joyce would have been a good second choice—or some other expatriate.
April:	The *Transatlantic Review* has Pound's note on the "death of Arsène Lupin" (the "most famous thief in cheap fiction," PC 678) and the first installment of Stein's *Making*, along with Djuna Barnes's short story "Aller et Retour," concerning a meaningless journey made by a deracinated woman (Pound liked this story very much, but he later became disenchanted with Djuna, writing a scurrilous little verse about her in which he rhymed her first name with "Baboon. Her.")
	A Literary Supplement contained the first installment ever of Joyce's *Finnegans Wake*, under Ford's temporary title, "Work In Progress." Joyce soon dubbed Ford the godfather of the book for this support (Ford was about the only person who was contending for

that honor). There was also a short story that had no title then (later called "Indian Camp") by Hemingway about his Michigan experiences, and there were some notes by René Crevel.

Barrès, who had been mockingly "tried" and condemned to death by the Dadaists, died in actuality, as was noted on page 242 of the review.

April 6: (Florence; to Bird) Pound is sorry that his wife Sally is ill, and he makes some adverse criticisms of Strater's capitals for his forthcoming *Cantos*.

April 9: (From Bird in Paris to Dorothy) Bird is concerned because Ford told him that Ezra had suffered a second attack of appendicitis.

April 10: (Florence; to his parents) He has had lunch with the great art critic Bernard Berenson, a close friend of Natalie Barney, and with Quinn's friend Charles Loeser. Proofs of his *Cantos* have arrived from Bird. Florence still seems uninhabitable. They intend to spend a month in Assisi.

April 17: (Florence; to Bird, *SL*, no. 197) He feels that Strater's art wanders all over the page in a distracting way. The air and noise of Florence are intolerable.

April 21: (Florence; to Bird) He and Dorothy are heading for Perugia; more quibbles over Strater's art.

Circa April 24: (Perugia; to his parents) The next stop is Assisi; then Paris by June 1. He is fascinated by his readings of Thomas Jefferson, the most civilized man who was ever President. (He exempted Lincoln, who was Jesus Christ, and he had not yet studied John Adams, who would later contend for Jefferson's rank.)

May: The *Transatlantic Review* announces through Hemingway's chronicle that Henry Strater has gone home to paint in New York City (355), while Djuna Barnes is in town. Hemingway also states flatly that "Dada is dead" (356), and indeed with André Breton issuing his *First Surrealist Manifesto* this year, he is right. A Music Supplement contains more of Atheling's "Notes for Performers" and some marginalia written in 1918 by Antheil. The magazine is now in deep financial trouble. Ford tries to sell shares, and then decides to go to America for help.

May 2: (Hemingway to Pound; HSL) Cummings has married Elaine Thayer (actual date: March 19) in New York,

	while Lincoln Steffens, aged as he is, has run away to Italy with an obnoxious young Bloomsbury "Jewine" (114). There is much talk against Ford, who is currently publishing trendy French "shit." Margaret Anderson is conspicuous around town with her new flame, the beautiful French actress Georgette LeBlanc, whom she had met back in New York.
May 7:	(Assisi, to Bird; *SL*, no. 198) The title of the book Bird is publishing is to be "A DRAFT of 16 Cantos for a poem of some length"; it is NOT an epic poem; just a long one.
May 8:	(Hotel Windsor, Assisi; to Yeats) Pound is recovering slowly from his appendicitis problems. Are Maud Gonne or Iseult in jail?
	(From Ford in Paris) He asks Ezra, as director of his company, to take action to save his struggling journal; on May 13 Pound scribbles a hasty note on this letter, empowering Ford to act as his proxy. Only Natalie Barney and her friends seem truly sympathetic.
May 9:	(Assisi; to Olga Rudge in Paris) She is preparing for a London concert with Antheil, and Pound says that he cannot instruct her now; she will have to do the best she can on her own. Antheil stayed with Olivia in London and took a surprisingly long bath.
May 16:	(Assisi; to his parents) He and Dorothy like this town, but not for a lifetime. Olga and George have given their London concert, which the audiences liked, but the critics did not. Pound meanwhile is deep in his study of the history of Ferrara, especially the Este family and the Borgias.
	(Assisi; to Olga) To please the critics next time, she should adhere to a classical program.
Circa May 21:	Ford drops off a letter to Conrad in Plymouth Harbor as he sails to America, desperately searching for funds. Quinn will be too sick to see him there, and others will close their doors.
Circa May 26:	Eliot is rumored to be in Paris, seeing no one, appearing in cafés like the Dôme in a top hat and striped trousers.
May 28:	(Rapallo; to his parents) Pound is sorry that he never really knew his Congressman grandfather, T. C. Pound, since he has been reading that man's writings and finds that they have much in common, both in world

outlook and style. He is especially delighted by T.C.'s saying that it is cheaper to educate an Indian than to kill him (see Canto 22). Ezra wants to know how T.C. died and why he was broke. Was his grandmother Susan Angevin Pound (whose name he long thought was Selina) from Anjou? These questions show that he himself did not believe in the Loomis Horse-Thief theory of his origins. He and Dorothy leave shortly hereafter for Paris.

(Williams diary) The Williamses visit Nancy Cunard's place on the Quai d'Orléans in Paris and see the famous *Fawn* sculpted by Gaudier-Brzeska that Pound had popularized. McAlmon and his sometime wife Bryher are in town, somewhat together, so that Williams has a chance to see Hilda again.

June 1: Williams and his wife are eating one of Adrienne Monnier's deliciously cooked chickens at her place near her bookshop—along with Sylvia, H.D., Bryher, and McAlmon—when suddenly they all hear the voice of Ezra Pound calling up from the street. Pound does not want to intrude upon their dinner, but since Williams has not seen him in over a decade, he dashes down the stairs and they have a joyous reunion in the middle of the Rue de l'Odéon.

June 2: The Williamses and some American friends see Cocteau's *Juliet and Romeo* at La Cigale; the Doctor finds it mere fluff, despite Pound's exaggerated praise of Cocteau's talent.

June 3: Williams goes alone to Pound's place, passing Dorothy (whom he can't quite recognize) in the street. He and Ezra talk for hours about Ezra's appendix and his music-writing, which Williams finds hard to accept, since, like Yeats, he believes that Pound is tone-deaf. Later the two wives join them. Flossie admires Dorothy's art. The Williamses dine that night at the Hemingways' place up the street, and then go off to see a prize fight.

June 4: Dr. Williams circumcizes Hemingway's little boy Bumby while the would-be toreador cringes in a corner (Williams, *Selected Letters*, 294). He then lunches with Sally Bird after hearing her sing arias from Mozart and Puccini, and he has a late repast with Pound and McAlmon. At Nancy Cunard's party that

	night, he meets Cocteau for the first time in an atmosphere of drunken revelry.
June 5:	Ezra takes "Bull" to a tea at Natalie Barney's famous salon, and the Doctor is both amused and appalled by the preciosity of the place: the pseudo-Greek temple, the cooing doves in the garden, the obsequious Japanese servants, the mascaraed lesbians dancing with stiffly elegant grace to the latest Argentine tango. Pound is once again condescending about his old friend's social and intellectual standards.
June 9:	McAlmon leaves Paris by taxi, not saying a word to anyone, while Williams spends almost the whole day with Ezra, even eating a meal that Pound prepares in his studio.
June 10:	James Joyce has his fifth eye operation. Pound takes Williams to visit Léger's studio, but Williams does not appreciate the cubist art.
June 11:	After a busy day with Mina Loy, Sylvia Beach, and the Birds, the Williamses visit the Pounds at 10 p.m. and chat till midnight. They leave Paris early the next morning for home. The two college friends will not see each other again until 1939. Williams begins to realize all that he has missed by remaining in America. The Williamses sail on the *Zeeland*.
June 19:	(Paris; to his parents) On July 7 in the Salle Pleyel, Antheil will perform six piano sonatas and a new quartet, while Olga will perform Pound's "fiddle music." He is writing a book about music with an essay on Antheil and harmony.
	(To Yeats in Ireland) Pound would like to arrange a concert for Antheil there; he describes his opera about Villon, which is based on a one-act Greek model with major characters to appear in masks.
June 21:	(To his parents) He continues to find his grandfather's memorabilia fascinating, especially the private money he issued (Canto 22). Poor Tami Koume has been killed in an earthquake in Tokyo.
July issue of the *Transatlantic Review* belatedly announces that Ford is going to America and leaving the magazine in the hands of Hemingway. In his "Chronique," Hemingway criticizes Cocteau, Tzara, and Gilbert Seldes in a way that annoys Ford.	
July 4:	Ford's ship docks back at Cherbourg after his unsuc-

cessful fund-raising tour. He is angry about the way Hemingway handled the review.

July 7: The Rudge-Antheil concert is given at the Salle Pleyel. Olga plays some "Music of the 15th Century" edited by Ezra Pound, as well as his "Fiddle Music: First Suite." Together she and George perform Antheil's "Second Sonata for Violin and Piano," while Antheil's "String Quartet" is also given a debut.

July 10: Pound sends his last letter to John Quinn, saying that he is sorry that his friend is so ill. During the previous year, Pound had constantly tried to tell the lawyer to "take it easy," but to no avail. It was now too late.

July 13: (To his parents) The critics did not like the recent Rudge-Antheil concert. Pound's book on Antheil is completed. He has fallen out completely with Anderson and Heap. Dorothy is off to London, while Ford is back from America. Olga keeps him company during Dorothy's absence.

July 14: Hemingway has spent about two weeks in Pamplona with John Dos Passos, McAlmon, and the Birds, having the time of his life. This trip precedes the more famous one the following year, which will lead to the writing of *The Sun Also Rises*.

July 19: (From Hemingway in Burguette, Spain, to Pound) He adores this remote town and is having a marvelous time in the wilds (which he much prefers to Pound's Kulchur centers). Several of his friends have left, walking over the Pyrenees. He knows that Ford is furious with him, and he will be back in a week.

July 27: Hemingway faces his angry boss, offering a new idea for a backer who may yet save the magazine: an old friend from Chicago named Krebs Friend, who was shell-shocked in the war and married a millionairess much older than he.

July 28: John Quinn dies in New York at 6:30 a.m., looking yellow and emaciated. Maecenas is gone and will be sorely missed.

August issue of the *Transatlantic Review*, assembled by Hemingway, is considered by Ford to have an "unusually large sample of the work of that young America" admired by his sub-editor. One of the contributors is the eccentric Greenwich Village friend of Williams called Elsa, the Baroness von Freytag-Loringhoven (mentioned in Canto 95/646), who wore outlandish clothes

	and constantly tried to seduce the doctor when he was in New York. The Music Supplement contained "VI," a composition by Ezra Pound, and more comments by the reborn Atheling and the thriving Antheil.
August 3:	Joseph Conrad dies.
August 9:	(Hemingway in Paris to Stein in the country) Krebs Friend is the new President of Ford's review. McAlmon has returned to London to try to pry more money out of Mr. Ellerman.
August 12:	(To his father) Lincoln Steffens has just come back from his idyll in San Remo with the Bloomsburyite. Dorothy is in wet Devon with Olivia, and Quinn is in his grave—alas! Ezra has just met an Idahoan named C. E. S. Wood, who knew the pioneer Hailey, a stagecoach driver, for whom his birthplace was named; Wood is himself a poetaster of sorts. The notorious anarchist Emma Goldman, long a friend of Anderson and Heap, is now a fixture at the Dôme Café.
Circa August 27:	(To his parents) He has just returned from a six-day walking tour in the Poitiers area. (He did this with Olga, who says that some days they covered as much as 30 kilometers.) She has gone to a phonograph company to discuss making a record, but the cost is prohibitive. John Rodker is visiting from London.
August 28:	(To Thomas Curtin, Quinn's executor, concerning the dead man) Pound paraphrases Suetonius on Nero's words about his own death: "What an artist has perished!"
	September issue of the *Transatlantic Review* is an English number to offset Hemingway's Americanism. It announces the deaths of Quinn and Conrad, and carries a special Conrad Supplement, where Hemingway needlessly insults Eliot (341).
September 4:	(To his parents) He has played a lot of tennis with Hemingway, and his health is better. Dorothy is due back today.
September 8:	(From Agnes Bedford in London) She is glad that Dorothy, with her adverse comments on music, is gone, but sends her her love.
September 12:	(Hemingway to Edward J. O'Brien, a short-story editor from Boston who is living on Monte Allegro above Rapallo) Dorothy and Ezra will arrive there in November.

(To his parents) James Joyce has recovered from his latest operation; his son Giorgio will sing a bass role in Pound's opera. Picabia and Satie are preparing a ballet together. Antheil continues to write orchestral pieces and Olga works on her Mozart. He is having dinner with Krebs Friend and is now a director of the reorganized review.

Autumn-Winter issue of the *Little Review* no longer had Pound's name on the masthead.

October: *Antheil and the Treatise on Harmony* is published by Bird for 10 francs a copy.

The *Transatlantic Review* contains Natalie Barney's "After Reading Chinese Poems," which has been "arranged" by Ezra Pound (437), as well as fragments from "The Automation" by Nancy Cunard, and more of the endless Stein and Ionides.

October 7: (Letter to parents from Rapallo) The Pounds expect Robert McAlmon and Yeats as guests soon.

October 10: (Hemingway in Paris to Stein in the country) Pound has just gone away to Italy for good. He "contrived" a little nervous breakdown before going, in order to avoid the rigors of packing their many belongings, and had to spend two days in the American Hospital. (This jest merely underscores once again Pound's poor health at this time. In actuality, Pound left a whole trunk of books, letters, and other valuables behind in the safekeeping of Bill Bird, and many of these lay dormant for decades.)

October 15: (To his parents) He and Dorothy are back at the Hotel Mignon, relaxing after the enervations of Paris. Antheil is writing a new violin sonata for Olga, who was fortunately unscathed when the taxi she was riding in recently in Paris collided with a tree.

He is playing tennis now daily in empty, tranquil Rapallo, and his closest neighbors of note are H.D. and Bryher up north in Switzerland. Dorothy's mother is staying with them for a while until they are settled, but they are still exploring other parts of Italy, especially Sicily in the future. Sadakichi Hartmann of London (80/495) has just sent him an interesting but poorly written play called *Confucius*.

October 15: (Hemingway in Paris to Pound) The poet Ralph Cheever Dunning, an upstairs neighbor, was drunk or

	high on opium, cavorting on the roof of Pound's building and had to be escorted to the Santé Prison by McAlmon and the police. (Dunning is like the Elpenor of Homer in Canto 1).
October 22:	(Hemingway to Pound) McAlmon has left for Switzerland to see H.D. and Bryher. Hemingway misses Pound very much: "It is a lousy feeling to know that you are gone for good."
October 25:	(To his parents) He wants to work on some American cantos but can't decide on a subject: Jefferson possibly?
November:	The *Transatlantic Review* contains Ford's apology for Hemingway's insult of Eliot (550), along with 12 poems of Dunning, Barnes's "The Passion," and Hemingway's "The Doctor and the Doctor's Wife." Pound edits the Music Supplement.
November 29:	(To his parents) His Hell cantos are not neatly sorted out the way Dante arranged his Inferno. Pound relies on the reader forming his own plan of the whole. Cantos 18 and 19 are like listening to voices over the radio "letting cats out of bags," asking: who made the war?
November 30:	(To R. P. Blackmur; *SL*, no. 200) Pound defends the price of his *Cantos* and the non-Dantesque order of the poem. He also mentions that his father already has typescripts of Cantos 18 and 19.
December:	This issue of the *Transatlantic* (the last) is extremely weak, containing only Hemingway's "Cross-County Snow" and two minor stories by Jean Rhys (an eccentric Montparnasse drifter from the West Indies, who is Ford's new flame), as well as McAlmon's story "Village." At this point, Hemingway and Ford are scarcely speaking to each other.
December 3:	(To Wyndham Lewis; *SL*, no. 201) Pound has just taken out an old copy of *Blast*, and he is impressed once again with their bravery back in 1914. He tells Lewis that he added fifteen years to his life by leaving London and another ten by leaving Paris. He will be departing for Sicily soon.
December 8:	(From Nancy Cunard in London) She misses Paris, her true home, greatly, and she loves Ezra as much as ever.
December 10:	(From Hemingway in Paris to Robert McAlmon) The *Transatlantic* is through for good, although Ford wants to begin a new review, *Hats Off To France*.

December 21: (Taormina, Sicily; to his parents) The Yeatses are due in nearby Siracusa on Jan. 6. He and Dorothy have taken quarters in the Hotel Naumachie, which has a view of the Greek theater on the hill to the left and snowcapped Mount Etna on the right, with a cerulean sea in between. Dorothy is painting a lot of landscapes. They will be leaving for Siracusa on Dec. 28. Naples was dirty, and this town is rather small. He is devouring Ovid's *Fasti* (see Canto 17).

Late December: (To Bird) He wants two free copies of his cantos sent to Dorothy and Manlio Dazzi; proof sets are to go to his father, Bride Scratton, Agnes Bedford, and himself.

December 30: (From Bird in Paris) The binding of his book will be ready at the end of January; the proof copies are on their way.

1925

January 3: (Hotel Roma, Siracusa; to his parents) This place is too commercial and unattractive to be habitable.

January 16: (Palermo; to his parents) The Yeatses are still here. He and Dorothy have seen the Vale of Enna. He finds it hard to locate a cheap place to play tennis.

January 23: (Pension Suisse, Palermo; to his parents) Taormina was nothing but a British suburb, while Siracusa was a wasteland with Greek ruins. He is very disappointed with Sicily, like Yeats, who has moved on to Naples.

January 25: (Palermo; to Bird; *SL*, no. 204) He has received his proofs of the *Draft of XVI Cantos* and likes the oversized format and art work of Strater, which he had formerly criticized. His final impression of Strater's art is that it was a "bhloody ghood job."

January 28: (Palermo; to his parents) He repeats his dissatisfaction with this city, which is interesting artistically, but only livable for the well-heeled tourist. He begins: "I recon' it'll be Rapallo." And indeed it was.

After stops in Naples and Rome, he was collecting books from America for his residence in Rapallo, and by Feb. 26 was back in that Riviera town, where he would live primarily until his arrest in 1945.

With the first section of his masterwork now in print and his home established, Pound had one other major event to look forward to in this momentous year of his life: the birth of his child, Maria or Mary, by Olga Rudge, who had now driven away all the women of his life except Dorothy. The birth took place in Bressanone in the Italian Tyrol, in a Catholic clinic. When asked why she chose to deliver her child up there in the mountains, Olga replied that she wanted a safe, clean place, and everyone advised her to go to Germany. The choice of this clinic with its Austrian tradition of hygiene was a compromise.

Yet once she got there, Olga was upset by the cold and callous treatment that she received fron the nuns (who were obviously more than aware of the fact that the man with her was neither her legal husband nor a Catholic). Both Ezra and she had decided before the event that neither could take the child with them back home: Pound could not expect Dorothy to rear another woman's baby, and the highly professional Olga could not be expected to maintain her busy career as a violinist and rear a child at the same time.

The solution to the problem came by chance. A woman in a neighboring bed named Frau Marcher from the little town of Gais had lost her own child and was deeply grieving; when she learned of the dilemma of Ezra and Olga, she offered to rear their child as her own, but without adopting her legally. This solution was accepted, and so Mary found herself at birth almost literally between two worlds, although this position would not become clarified until she was older.

After the birth on July 9, Pound returned to Rapallo, where an obviously disturbed Dorothy quietly vowed that she would also have a child, and indeed the next year on September 10 Omar Shakespear Pound was born. But just as Mary grew up in Gais, Omar grew up in England under the tutelage of Grandmother Olivia. Life went on in Rapallo tranquilly, without the distractions and discomforts caused by children.

20

"The Fortieth Year of My Life..." (1925)

> *In the thirtieth year of my age*
> *I have drunk to the dregs of shame—*
> *Not a total fool, not a total sage,*
> *And not without a little pain ...*
> *I mourn the slipping days of youth*
> *That more than other men I supped,*
> *For Age kept mum his awful truth,*
> *Not whispering time would soon be up.*
> *On foot he did not take his fling,*
> *On horseback—no! How did he go?*
> *Whisp!—like that—a burst of wings,*
> *And not one souvenir did he throw.*
> *He's gone. And me—here I sit*
> *Weak in knowledge and poor in sense,*
> *Berry-black-sad and out of it,*
> *With no fixed income, cash, or rents ...*
> *Where are the gentlemen debonair*
> *I chased in the days that now have fled,*
> *Who sang so sweetly, talked so fair,*
> *Charming in all they did and said?*
> *Some are stiff, and some are dead,*
> *And some are almost all bereft;*
> *In Paradise may they find a bed,*
> *And God save all of us who are left!*
> —François Villon, The Testament
> (Translated by J. J. Wilhelm)

Pound's fortieth year and Villon's thirtieth were, Ezra felt, in many ways similar, and that is why he was writing his opera about this fifteenth-century poet. Villon was an outcast who would disappear shortly after the writing of his mock will. Ezra, of course, would go on for another forty-seven years. But their sad economic straits (which Villon in many ways blamed for his life as an outlaw) are in both cases responsible for their developments and ends.

During the course of this book, we have seen some momentous changes come over the young rebel who fled America in 1908, took London by storm, led a revolution against prevailing literary taste, joined in an important artistic cause (vorticism), and then suffered through the long and disheartening war, watching friends disappearing around him. Ezra Pound had developed artistically from a late-Victorian bard to a forger of a new poetic doctrine that led in effect to the liberation of the poem from a fixed diction, fixed rhythm, and (finally) a fixed point of view. Rudyard Kipling hymning the British Empire in a predictable rhetoric and in doggerel rhythm was everything that Ezra Pound despised; yet it is perhaps fitting that Kipling coined the phrase "the tale of the tribe" that Pound excerpted to describe his own masterwork. For by 1925, Pound had changed from a conservative aesthete to a rebellious artist who was no longer interested in aesthetics per se. Economics, history, and politics were now at the center of his vision; poetry was the *medium* for conveying this logopoeia—not an end in itself, as most poets see it. When the *Cantos* finally appeared in their early form in 1925, they were both a break from the conservative past of English literature (thereby joining Eliot's *Waste Land* and Joyce's *Ulysses* as the final third of the three great modernist masterpieces); and they were also a break from Pound's earlier lyric past. Once Pound turned from lyrics to his "long poem," he would never really go back, except in the sense that certain cantos—especially the last Fragments—are little lyrics themselves.

In many ways, the *Cantos* are a continuation of Pound's earlier development. Despite an occasional narrative line, there are still clusters of images that help to crystallize various ideas or pictures. The vorticist heritage can be seen in the way that certain Cantos—the opening of Canto 2, for example—bring together a series of disparate images taken from different cultures and time periods, and place them in a forceful montage or collage. Pound's *Cantos* have to be judged by the same standards that one employs for Picasso or Stravinsky. It is unfair to judge them as if they were contemporary with Tennyson or Milton.

In the following discussion, I am going to emphasize the shiftings of time, which tend to throw many readers off, showing how we move largely back and forth between the Ancient, Medieval, and Modern worlds, with a bit of the Renaissance thrown in for contrast. I am also going to emphasize the intertwining of the themes of love and war—the old Venus-Mars contretemps that figures prominently in ancient mythology. In many ways, the *Cantos* were the product of World War I. They might never have been written, had Pound not had to suffer that event. Indeed Canto 16, which closes this segment, ends there, leaving the reader puzzled, precisely as Pound wanted him to be, by the problem: how did we get into this mess? The next group of *Cantos* would bring in the American dream, along with Douglas's Social Credit and other economic ideas, and the Confucian element would bulk larger as the poem progressed. This was the overall plan, as yet untouched by Italy and Mussolini's fascism, which do not play as large a role in the poem as Pound's enemies would have us believe.

As we proceed, I think it becomes clear how deeply Pound's own life (and educational development) are woven into the fabric of his creation:

Canto 1: Ancient Greece. The figure of Odysseus (who is also Pound) is established as a peripatetic wanderer and judger, going here to a never-never land to speak with the dead (or in other words, to write an epic, since an epic is a discourse with history). Homer's *Odyssey* is translated via the Latin of Andreas Divus (which Pound found in Paris in 1910 or thereabouts, since he often changed the date); Pound's English is itself an imitation of the Anglo-Saxon "Seafarer," thus bringing the great narrative of the European North in touch with the South. Odysseus is fleeing the horrors of the Trojan War. The canto ends with a mention of the beautiful golden goddess Venus-Aphrodite, the lover-enemy of Mars-Ares.

Canto 2: Ancient Rome. The opening brings together Browning's *Sordello* (which Pound read to Yeats at Stone Cottage), Picasso's art, and Homer's Helen of Troy, the human counterpart of Aphrodite, who is the alleged cause of the Trojan War (here the golden woman reflecting the golden goddess is a metaphor for the gold or economic cause of any war). The heart of the canto presents the birth of Bacchus or Liber (the liberating god of wine); we must remember that this canto was written with America in the grip of Prohibition and much of the world in the grip of British imperial prohibitions. Pound now adopts the voice of Acoetes, a common sailor from Ovid's *Metamorphoses*, who tells the story of how Bacchus-Liber took over his ship. The power of an enlightened polytheism or acknowledgment of many forces in the universe is accentuated; we know that in 1924, as in 1904, Pound was devouring Ovid (see the Dec. 21, 1924, entry in the preceding chapter).

Canto 3: Pound as Pound now appears, impoverished in Venice, as he was in 1908 when he fled America after the Wabash College debacle. Then come two brief mentions of the hero of *The Cid*, who is fooling usurers (as Pound is *not* clever or daring enough to do) in order to finance his private but justifiable war against the insensitive king who expelled him. The final lines describe the great palace in Mantua owned by the Gonzagas, with Mantegna's paintings and Isabella d'Este's inscription "Neither with Hope nor Fear"; they suggest a decadent end to glorious action, as the vortex of energy that impels one segment of history declines in another. The Ancient, Medieval, and Modern worlds have now all been cited, pointing toward Renaissance decadence.

Canto 4: The horror of the Trojan War is now emphasized, the archetype for all wars, with Helen the metaphoric cause (beauty or love perverted or gone astray). But the scene soon shifts to the troubadour world of the Middle Ages, with its endless conflicts, but also its dedication to poetry and love. Using vidas that he had edited in the Bibliothèque Nationale in 1911 and at other times, Pound relates Cabestan's murder and his lover's flight out a window to the transformation of Philomela and Procne into birds in Greek myth; thus Provence and Greece "rhyme"—as Pound was later fond of calling this sort of intellectual alignment. The same union is effected with the troubadour Vidal and the ancient Actaeon being set upon by beasts. The canto also contains idyllic scenes from the 1919 walking trip: the church at Poitiers with the fish-scale roof and the wormlike procession in Toulouse by the Garonne. An archetype of the Ideal City forms, with Ecbatan as the base, where Danae is the golden bride of God (human and divine merging). East and West also merge with the mention of Oriental places in nature and myth.

Canto 5:	After a reprise of Ecbatan, the canto moves upward into a paradisal vision that suggests the Neoplatonic mystic Iamblichus and Dante's ascending sparks in *Paradiso* 18.100. The canto then returns to a human marriage: that of the Roman girl Arunculeia, whom Catullus hymned in a poem that Pound studied in his early Penn days. The vision then becomes violent as Pound presents the troubadour Gaubertz de Poicebot (studied with Shepard at Hamilton), who was betrayed by his Helen-like wife. Pound then mentions a "little Trojan War" near Troyes (Troy) in the Auvergne, centered on the troubadour Peire (Pieire) de Maensac. The canto ends in Renaissance violence involving the Borgias of Ferrara, whom Pound had been studying assiduously in 1923.
Canto 6:	Odysseus returns, rhyming now with the earlier mentioned troubadour William of Poitiers, the grandfather of Eleanor of Aquitaine, who, like Helen, was used as a gold-chip-pawn in warmaking. The beauty of Bernart de Ventadorn's love poetry rhymes with that of Sordello, although Sordello's wild love affair with Cunizza da Romano and the actions of the Theseus-like Cairels of Provence bring the canto to a violent end, as lust and brutality (Venus and Mars turned totally negative) run rampant.
Canto 7:	Helen the Destroyer opens this canto, linked with her namesake Eleanor, as Ovid and Dante are again sounded in leitmotif fashion. Soon the medieval pomp and glory descend to a world of matter, the lowest in the Neoplatonic scheme. Most of the canto moves in a late nineteenth-century world, with citations from Flaubert and the "great domed head" referring to the seerlike Henry James. In the center, however, we have the romantic vision of the troubadour Arnaut Daniel, hymning the beauty of a naked woman by candlelight at Bouvilla. Pound wrote to Ingrid Davies, a friend of Brigit Patmore, on December 8, 1954, that the "live man" mentioned toward the end of the canto who is trying to combat the general modern tawdriness is the Irish patriot Desmond FitzGerald. Pound's Flemish poet friend Fritz Vanderpyl, the art critic of *Petit Parisien*, is cited observing a beer bottle on the pediment of a statue.

	Once again, the section ends with Renaissance brutality and violence.
Cantos 8–11:	Pound puts four cantos together for the first time, showing his extended study of the famous Renaissance condottiere Sigismundo Malatesta. Sigismundo was a professional fighter serving on many sides in the bewildering swirl of Renaissance history, but he also built the great Temple of Rimini, subsidized artists and writers, engaged in love affairs, and fiercely struggled against a corrupt Church that was trying to excommunicate him. To Pound, Sigismundo was that rare individual who is able to salvage truth and beauty out of the chaos around him (to paraphrase Canto 13: a man who can keep the blossoms of the apricot from falling).
Canto 12:	This is a tawdry canto, based on the cheap monetary transactions of Baldy Bacon and his buddy Mons Quade (see July 18, 1922, and Jan. 29, 1924, in the preceding diary). Pound had known both men back in the days of Aunt Frank's boarding house and in 1910. John Quinn's playful anecdote about a sodomitic merchant marine being transformed into a saint because he believes that he gave birth to a child reverberates against the stiffness of the unfeeling bankers to whom Lawyer Quinn (alias Jim X) tells the story. The pervading atmosphere here is one of intellectual and moral squalor.
Canto 13:	On this supposedly unlucky number, Pound offers his first true glimpse of the Earthly Paradise, which is what concerns him in this poem. He presents scenes from Confucius's *Analects* (through the French of Pauthier), and creates a world of beauty, sensitivity and truth.
Cantos 14–15:	This is Pound's true Hell, the London before World War I. Here Pound is investigating the causes of that horrendous war, indicting various people whose names have rotted away. In a letter to John Lackay Brown (*SL*, 293), Pound said that the real names of the "rotters" were not worth knowing, and that is why he reduced them to dots. Bill Bird tried to get the number of dots to coincide with real names, but Pound did not encourage him in this. Nevertheless, as the *Companion* indicates, some of the names are Lloyd George and Wilson on the first blanks on page

61; Basil Zaharoff is lashing the financiers, while Winston Churchill is most certainly the "swollen foetus" on page 64, and Lord Northcliffe is a news-owner on 65. Still, in Pound's Hell, light does not penetrate the darkness and total knowledge here is impossible.

Canto 16: As an aftermath and result of the preceding graft and corruption, we have World War I in all of its virulence, where Aphrodite or Love has totally vanished. Here we encounter many of Pound's friends who fought in the debacle, such as Aldington, the tragically slain Gaudier-Brzeska, Hulme, Lewis, B. C. Windeler, old Captain Guy Baker (a close friend of Wyndham's who actually died of flu), one Fletcher (definitely not John Gould, an American), and finally Ernest Hemingway, as Pound buys "Hem's" version of his own heroism. (In the 1925 edition of this canto, Windeler was Vanderberg, Baker was Corcoran, Fletcher was Bimmy, a friend of Nancy Cunard's named Bimbo Tennant, and Hemingway was Cyril Hammerton). The canto presents some stories told to Pound by old Plarr (on Galliffet's ineffectual charge of the French against the Prussians), some more recent horror stories of battle, and finally some of Lincoln Steffens' accounts of the Russian Revolution; it ends with people vainly hoping that a winning offensive under General Haig will get under way. The reader is left hanging, just as the British were left hanging, hoping for a quick, decisive victory that was a long time in coming. In short, there is no real liberation from the horror. One cannot flee, the way Odysseus left a ravaged Troy, and hope for an easy restitution of things. As Pound says often later: "I sing perennial war," and a close look at these first 16 cantos reveals that this is true. All epics concern war to some degree, and in this sense, Pound's is a true one. But the big difference between Pound and many of his predecessors is that he is not glorifying the conflict. He is simply trying to understand it.

We shall leave Ezra Pound at this point, in the fortieth year of his life, having begun the masterwork that would occupy his main attention for the rest of his life. The Ezra Pound we are leaving is essentially a happy man, having found himself a nice apartment atop a seaside building in Rapallo, with a beautiful view of the Gulf of Tigullio; the address from the rear was 12 (now 20) Via Marsala. Here he and Dorothy would live for about twenty years, being joined at the end of the twenties by his retired father and his mother. In 1929, Olga Rudge would accept a house in Venice from her father and later take a position with Count Chigi's Music Foundation in Siena; still later, she would be able to see Ezra often when he arranged a house for her in Sant'Ambrogio, on the top of the southern hill above Rapallo. When Dorothy was off in England visiting her child Omar and her mother, Ezra was free to stay with Olga in Venice, often joined there or elsewhere by their daughter Mary. As a result, intellectually and emotionally, Pound was at last having a small taste of the Earthly Paradise in Rapallo, which Yeats said looked like the Irish Sligo translated to Heaven as the mist rolled in (77/473; 80/507; 114/793).

But as we know, Paradise never lasts very long. Medieval theologians doubted that Adam and Eve tasted perfection for one full day. Pound was luckier. Even as the proverbial storm clouds gathered in the thirties and he immersed himself deeper and deeper into economics, he still was relatively happy, staging musical events (especially of Vivaldi) in the Rapallo Town Hall and elsewhere. But gradually the threat of worldwide destruction and the nightmarish feeling that the world's wealth was being "hogged" by an oligarchy of usurious bankers and moneymen drove him further on the side of Mussolini and fascism, and caused him to attack the Rothschilds and other bankers in a way that sounded as if he were a simplistic anti-Semite. Up to this point in the book, Ezra Pound has shown few traces of any kind of anti-Semitism; in fact, if one carefully peruses his correspondence (where such things tend to show up most clearly), one will find more ethnic slurs in the letters of Quinn, Eliot, and Hemingway than in Pound. But unfortunately the radio broadcasts that he naively made for Benito Mussolini's Italy during wartime would change all that, and Pound would have to bear the scarlet letter of Anti-Semite in a way that would hinder his future fame. After the broadcasts came the fall of Italy, his arrest and detainment in the detention camp at Pisa, his arraignment in Washington, his placement at St. Elizabeth's Hospital for the Insane to prevent a trial for treason, and many years of penitential confinement. These were followed by more years of self-imposed silence until his death in 1972 and burial on the Island of San Michele in Venice.

The Pound we are leaving in 1925 was a different man from that; he was happy and fulfilled. He had established a name for himself as a great lyric poet and what Edgar Jepson had called "a warrior for the arts." Even if Pound's life had stopped here, he would be a man worth remembering. But the Wheel of Fortune turned on, and gradually his happiness turned to torment—albeit a torment that included creativity. Conversely, the story we have just told of Pound in London and Paris is a comedy as Dante would have understood the term, and this has come to an end.

Bibliography

I. Works Cited in the Text

(Note: casual mentions of the voluminous works of Pound's friends are not documented here; they are cited in the text with the date of publication in parentheses. See Abbreviations for his major works in modern editions.)

Ackroyd, Peter. *T. S. Eliot.* New York: Simon and Schuster, 1984.
Adams, B.M.G.-. *England.* Paris: Three Mountains, 1923.
Aldington, Richard. *Life for Life's Sake.* New York: Viking, 1941.
American Writers in Paris, 1920–1939, ed. K. L. Rood. Detroit: Bruccoli-Clark, 1980.
Anderson, David. *Pound's Cavalcanti.* Princeton: Princeton University Press, 1983.
Anderson, Margaret. *My Thirty Years' War.* 1st ed., 1930; New York: Horizon, 1969.
Antheil, George. *Bad Boy of Music.* New York: Doubleday, 1945.
Baigent, Michael, Richard Leigh, and Henry Lincoln. *Holy Blood, Holy Grail.* New York: Delacorte, 1982.
Baker, Carlos. *Ernest Hemingway: A Life Story.* New York: Charles Scribner's Sons, 1969.
Balakian, Anna. *André Breton: Magus of Surrealism.* New York: Oxford University Press, 1971.
Barry, Iris. "The Ezra Pound Period." *Bookman*, 74, 2 (1931), 159–71.
Beach, Sylvia. *Shakespeare and Company.* London: Faber and Faber, 1956.
Bottome, Phyllis. *From the Life.* London: Faber and Faber, 1946.
Brooks, Van Wyck. *Scenes and Portraits.* New York: E. P. Dutton, 1954.
Burger, Nash K. *Confederate Spy: Rose O'Neal Greenhow.* New York: Franklin Watts, 1967.
Bush, Ronald. *The Genesis of Pound's "Cantos."* Princeton: Princeton University Press, 1976; rev. ed. 1989.
"Cantos of Ezra Pound": Some Testimonies by Hemingway, Ford, Eliot, etc. New York: Farrar and Rinehart, 1933.
Cardozo, Nancy. *Lucky Eyes and a High Heart.* Indianapolis: Bobbs-Merrill, 1978.
Charters, James. *This Must Be the Place.* London: Joseph, 1934.
Chisholm, Anne. *Nancy Cunard.* New York: Alfred A. Knopf, 1979.
Colbourne, Maurice. *The Meaning of Social Credit.* Rev. ed. London: Figurehead, 1935.
Colum, Mary. *Life and the Dream.* New York: Doubleday, 1947.
Companion to the "Cantos." See *CC* in Abbreviations.

Cork, Richard. *Vorticism and Abstract Art in the First Machine Age.* 2 vols. Berkeley: University of California Press, 1976.
Cournos, John. *Autobiography.* New York: Putnam, 1935.
Crosby, Caresse. *The Passionate Years.* New York: Dial, 1953.
Daniel, Arnaut. *Poetry,* ed. J. J. Wilhelm. New York: Garland, 1981.
Dasenbrock, R. W. *Literary Vorticism of Ezra Pound and Wyndham Lewis.* Baltimore: Johns Hopkins University Press, 1985.
Davie, Donald. *Ezra Pound: Poet as Sculptor.* New York: Oxford University Press, 1964.
De Rachewiltz, Mary. *Discretions.* Boston: Little, Brown, 1971; *Ezra Pound: Father and Teacher.* New York: New Directions, 1975.
Doolittle, Hilda. *End to Torment.* New York: New Directions, 1979.
Douglas, C. H. *Credit Power and Democracy.* London: Palmer, 1921; rev. ed. London: Nott, 1934.
———. *Economic Democracy.* London: Nott, 1920; rev. 1934; rpt. 1974.
———. *Social Credit.* London: Palmer, 1921; rev. 3rd ed. London: Eyre and Spottiswoode, 1934.
Ede, H. S. *Savage Messiah: Gaudier-Brzeska.* New York: Literary Guild, 1931.
Eliot, T. S. *The Waste Land: A Facsimile and Transcript,* ed. Valerie Eliot. New York: Harcourt Brace Jovanovich, 1971. (See also *TSEL* in Abbreviations.)
Ellmann, Richard. *James Joyce.* New York: Oxford, 1959; rev. 1982.
———. *Yeats: The Man and the Masks.* New York: W. W. Norton, 1978.
Epstein, Jacob. *An Autobiography.* London: Hulton, 1955.
Espey, John. *Ezra Pound's "Mauberley."* Berkeley: University of California Press, 1955.
Field, Andrew. *Djuna: The Life and Times of Djuna Barnes.* New York: Putnam, 1983.
Fitch, Noel Riley. *Sylvia Beach and the Lost Generation.* New York: W. W. Norton, 1983.
FitzGerald, Desmond. *Memoirs . . . 1913–16,* intro. Fergus FitzGerald. London: Routledge and Kegan Paul, 1968.
Fletcher, J. G. See FLMS in Abbreviations.
Flory, Wendy Stallard. *Ezra Pound and "The Cantos": A Record of Struggle.* New Haven: Yale University Press, 1980.
Ford, Ford Madox. *It Was the Nightingale.* Philadelphia: J. B. Lippincott, 1934.
———. *Return to Yesterday; Reminiscences 1894–1914.* London: Gollancz, 1931.
———. *Thus to Revisit: Some Reminiscences.* London, 1921; rpt. New York: Octagon, 1966.
Frost, Robert. See FSL in Abbreviations.
Gallup, Donald. *Ezra Pound: A Bibliography.* Charlottesville: University Press of Virginia, 1983.
Garnett, David. *The Golden Echo.* 2 vols. New York: Harcourt, Brace, 1954.
Goldring, Douglas. *South Lodge.* London: Constable, 1943; rpt. 1977.
Gourmont, Rémy. *Natural Philosophy of Love,* trans. Ezra Pound. New York: Collier, 1960; 1st ed., Boni and Liveright, 1922.
Grover, Philip, ed. *Ezra Pound: The London Years, 1908–1920.* New York: AMS, 1978.
Guest, Barbara. *Herself Defined: The Poet H.D. and Her World.* Garden City: Doubleday, 1984.

Hall, Donald. "Ezra Pound: An Interview." *Paris Review, 28* (1962): 22–51.
———. "T. S. Eliot." *Paris Review, 21* (1959): 47–70; rpt. *Writers at Work*, 2nd Series. New York: Viking, 1963.
Hamnett, Nina. *Laughing Torso*. London: Constable, 1932.
Hemingway, Ernest. *A Moveable Feast*. New York: Charles Scribner's Sons, 1964.
———. *Selected Letters, 1917–1961*, ed. Carlos Baker. New York: Charles Scribner's Sons, 1981. (See also HSL in Abbreviations.)
Hesse, Eva. "Note on Iseult." *Paideuma, 3* (1974): 416.
———. "The Vortex." *Paideuma, 9* (1980): 329.
Homberger, Eric, ed. *Ezra Pound: The Critical Heritage*. London: Routledge and Kegan Paul, 1972.
Hooker, Denise. *Nina Hamnett, Queen of Bohemia*. London: Constable, 1986.
Hopkins, Kenneth. *The Powys Brothers*. London: Phoenix, 1967.
Huddleston, Sisley. *Paris Salons, Cafés, Studios*. Philadelphia, 1928; also called *Bohemian Literary and Social Life in Paris*. London: Harrap, 1928.
Hulme, T. E. *Speculations*, ed. Herbert Read. New York: Harcourt, Brace, 1936.
Hunt, Violet. *The Flurried Years*. New York: Boni and Liveright, 1926.
Hutchins, Patricia. *Ezra Pound's Kensington*. London: Faber and Faber, 1965.
Jepson, Edgar. *Memoirs of an Edwardian and Neo-Georgian*. London: Richards, 1937.
Jones, Alun R. *Life and Opinions of T. E. Hulme*. London: Gollancz, 1960.
Josephson, Matthew. *Life Among the Surrealists*. New York: Holt Rinehart, 1962.
Joyce, James. *Selected Letters*, ed. R. Ellmann. New York: Viking, 1966.
Kennedy, Richard S. *Dreams in the Mirror: A Biography of E. E. Cummings*. New York: Liveright, 1980.
Kenner, Hugh. "D.P. Remembered." *Paideuma, 2* (1973): 485–93.
———. *The Poetry of Ezra Pound*. New York: New Directions, 1952.
———. *The Pound Era*. Berkeley: University of California Press, 1971.
Kreymborg, Alfred. *Troubadour: An Autobiography*. New York: Boni and Liveright, 1925.
Lawrence, D. H. See LL in Abbreviations.
Lewis, Wyndham. *Blasting and Bombardiering*. See LBB in Abbreviations.
———. *Rude Assignment: An Intellectual Biography*, ed. Toby Foshay. Santa Barbara: Black Sparrow, 1984; London, 1950.
———. *Time and Western Man*. New York: Harcourt, Brace, 1928.
Litz, A. Walton. "Pound and Yeats: The Road to Stone Cottage." *Ezra Pound Among the Poets*, ed. G. Bornstein. Chicago: University of Chicago Press, 1985: 128ff.
Loeb, Harold. *The Way It Was*. New York: Criterion, 1959.
Longenbach, James. *Stone Cottage: Pound, Yeats, and Modernism*. New York: Oxford University Press, 1988.
———. "Ezra Pound's 'Canzoni': Toward a Poem Including History." *Paideuma, 13* (1984): 389ff.
———. "Order of the Brothers Minor." *Paideuma, 14* (1985): 395ff.
MacBride, Maud Gonne. *A Servant of the Queen: Reminiscences*. 1st ed., 1938; Woodbridge, England: Boydell, 1983.
Mackenzie, Faith C. *As Much as I Dare*. London: Collins, 1938.

Mairet, Philip. *A. R. Orage: A Memoir.* New Hyde Park, N.Y.: University, 1966.
Mariani, Paul. *William Carlos Williams: A New World Naked.* New York: McGraw-Hill, 1981.
Materer, Timothy. *Vortex: Pound, Eliot, and Lewis.* Ithaca: Cornell University Press, 1979.
McAlmon, Robert. *Being Geniuses Together 1920–1930.* rev. and enl. Kay Boyle. San Francisco: North Point, 1968.
Meyers, Jeffrey. *The Enemy: A Biography of Wyndham Lewis.* London: Routledge and Kegan Paul, 1980.
———. *Hemingway: A Biography.* New York: Harper and Row, 1985.
Mikriammos, Philippe. "Ezra Pound in Paris (1921–1924); a Cure for Youthfulness." *Paideuma, 14* (1985): 385ff.
Mizener, Arthur. *The Saddest Story: A Biography of Ford Madox Ford.* N.Y.-Cleveland: World, 1971.
Monroe, Harriet. See MPL in Abbreviations.
Moody, A. D. "Pound's Allen Upward." *Paideuma, 4* (1975): 55ff.
Moore, Mary. Collection of Letters. Manuscript Collection, Van Pelt Library, University of Pennsylvania.
Mullins, Eustace. *This Difficult Individual Ezra Pound.* New York: Fleet, 1961.
Munson, Gorham. *Aladdin's Lamp.* New York: Creative Age, 1945.
Patmore, Brigit. *My Friends When Young,* ed. and intro. Derek Patmore. London: Heinemann, 1968.
Pound, Ezra. "How I Began." *T.P.'s Weekly* (June 6, 1913): 707.
———. *Patria Mia and the Treatise on Harmony.* Chicago: Seymour, 1950; London: Owen, 1962. (See Abbreviations for major Pound listings).
Read, Herbert. *The Contrary Experience.* London: Faber and Faber, 1963.
Reck, Michael. *Ezra Pound: A Close-Up.* New York: McGraw-Hill, 1973.
Reid, B. L. see RJQ in Abbreviations.
Rhys, Ernest. *Everyman Remembers.* London: Dent, 1931.
Robinson, Fred C. " 'The Might of the North': Pound's Anglo-Saxon Studies and 'The Seafarer.' " *Yale Review* (Winter 1982): 199ff.
Robinson, Janis S. *H. D. The Life and Work of an American Poet.* Boston: Houghton Mifflin, 1982.
Ross, Ishbel. *Rebel Rose: Life of Rose O'Neale Greenhow, Confederate Spy.* New York: Harper, 1954.
Schafer, R. Murray. *Ezra Pound and Music: The Complete Criticism.* New York: New Directions, 1977.
Schneidau, Herbert N. *Ezra Pound: The Image and the Real.* Baton Rouge: Louisiana State University Press, 1969.
Selver, Paul. *Orage and "The New Age" Circle.* London: Allen and Unwin, 1959.
Sieburth, Richard. *Instigations: Ezra Pound and Rémy de Gourmont.* Cambridge, Mass.: Harvard University Press, 1978.
Steegmuller, Francis. *Cocteau: A Biography.* Boston: Little, Brown, 1970.
Steffens, Lincoln. *Autobiography.* 2 vols. New York: Harcourt, Brace, 1931.
Stein, Gertrude. *Autobiography of Alice B. Toklas.* New York: Harcourt, Brace, 1933.
Stock, Noel. *Life of Ezra Pound,* expanded ed. San Francisco: North Point, 1982.
Sullivan, John Patrick. *Ezra Pound and Sextus Propertius: A Study in Creative Translation.* Austin: University of Texas Press, 1964.
Thompson, Lawrance. *Robert Frost: The Early Years, 1874–1915; The Years of*

Triumph, 1915–1938. New York: Holt, Rinehart and Winston, 1966, 1970.
Voorhis, Jerry. *Out of Debt, Out of Danger.* New York: Devin-Adair, 1943.
Wickes, George. *Amazon of Letters: The Life and Loves of Natalie Barney.* New York: Putnam, 1976.
Wilhelm, J. J. *The American Roots of Ezra Pound.* New York: Garland, 1985.
———. *The Poetry of Arnaut Daniel.* New York: Garland, 1981.
Williams, William Carlos. *Autobiography.* New York: Random House, 1948.
———. *Selected Letters,* ed. John C. Thirlwall. New York: McDowell, Obolensky, 1957.
Woolf, Virginia. *Diary.* 4 vols. London: Hogarth, 1977.
Yeats, William B. *Autobiography.* New York: Macmillan, 1965.
———. *Collected Poems.* New York: Macmillan, 1956.
———. *Letters,* ed. Allan Wade. London: Hart-Davis, 1954.
Yip, Wai-Lim. *Ezra Pound's "Cathay."* Princeton: Princeton University Press, 1969.
Zinnes, Harriet, ed. *Ezra Pound and the Visual Arts.* New York: New Directions, 1980.

II. Other Sources, Largely Biographical

Ackroyd, Peter. *Ezra Pound and His World.* London: Thames and Hudson, 1980.
Aiken, Conrad. *Selected Letters,* ed. Joseph Killorin. New Haven: Yale University Press, 1978.
———. *Ushant: An Essay.* 1st ed., 1952; New York: Oxford University Press, 1971.
Allan, Tony. *An American in Paris.* London: Bison, 1977.
Bald, Wambly. *On the Left Bank, 1929–1933.* ed. B. Franklin V. Athens: Ohio University Press, 1987.
Blair, Fredrika. *Isadora.* New York: McGraw-Hill, 1986.
Bornstein, George, ed. *Ezra Pound Among the Poets.* Chicago: University of Chicago Press, 1985.
Boll, Theophilus. *Miss May Sinclair Novelist.* Rutherford, N.J.: Fairleigh-Dickinson, 1973.
Brodzky, Horace. *Henri Gaudier-Brzeska.* London: Faber and Faber, 1933.
Brown, Frederick. *An Impersonation of Angels: A Biography of Jean Cocteau.* New York: Harlow, Longmans, 1969.
Caldwell, Helen. *Michio Itow.* Berkeley: University of California Press, 1977.
Callaghan, Morley. *That Summer in Paris.* Toronto: Macmillan, 1963.
Cannell, Kathleen. *Jam Yesterday.* New York: Morrow, 1945.
Carpenter, Humphrey. *A Serious Character: The Life of Ezra Pound.* London: Faber and Faber, 1988.
———. *Geniuses Together: American Writers in Paris in the 1920s.* London: Unwin Hyman, 1987.
Charters, James. *This Must Be the Place.* London: Joseph, 1934.
Clearfield, Andrew. "Pound, Paris, and Dada," *Paideuma,* 7 (1978): 113ff.
Cole, Roger. *Burning to Speak: The Life and Art of Henri Gaudier-Brzeska.* Oxford: Phaidon, 1978.

Colum, Padraic. *Arthur Griffith*. Dublin: Browne and Nolan, 1959.
Cowley, Malcolm. *Exile's Return*. New York: Norton, 1934.
Cox, Sidney. *A Swinger of Birches: Portrait of Robert Frost*. New York: New York University Press, 1957.
Cunard, Nancy. *These Were the Hours*. Carbondale: Southern Illinois University Press, 1969.
Curran, Joseph M. *Birth of the Irish Free State, 1921–1923*. University: University of Alabama Press, 1980.
Damon, S. Foster. *Amy Lowell: A Chronicle*. Boston: Houghton Mifflin, 1935.
D'Epiro, Peter. *A Touch of Rhetoric: Ezra Pound's Malatesta Cantos*. Ann Arbor: University of Michigan Press, 1983.
Douglas, Charles. *Artist Quarter*, London: Faber and Faber, 1941.
Egan, Margarita. *Vidas of the Troubadours*. New York: Garland, 1984.
Ellmann, Richard. *Eminent Domain*. New York: Oxford, 1967.
Fielding, Daphne. *Emerald and Nancy: Lady Cunard and Her Daughter*. London: Eyre and Spottiswoode, 1968.
FitzGerald, Mary. "Ezra Pound and Irish Politics: An Unpublished Correspondence," *Paideuma*, 12 (1983): 377ff.
Flory, Wendy S. "The 'Tre Donne' of the Pisan Cantos." *Paideuma*, 5 (1976): 45ff.
———. *The American Ezra Pound*. New Haven: Yale, 1989.
Ford, Hugh, ed. *Nancy Cunard*. London: Chilton, 1968.
———. *Four Lives in Paris*. San Francisco: North Point, 1987.
Frost, Robert. *Selected Letters*, ed. L. Thompson. New York: Holt, Rinehart, 1964.
Froula, Christine. *To Write Paradise*. New Haven: Yale University Press, 1984.
Gallup, Donald. *T. S. Eliot & Ezra Pound: Collaborators in Letters*. New Haven: Wenning/Stonehill, 1970.
Generoso, James. "Social Credit 1918–1945: An Essay and Select Bibliography." *Paideuma* (Spring, 1990).
Goldring, Douglas. *The Last Pre-Raphaelite . . . Ford Madox Ford*. London: Macdonald, 1948.
Gordon, Lyndall. *Eliot's Early Years*. Oxford: Oxford University Press, 1977.
———. *Eliot's New Life*. New York: Farrar, Straus, and Giroux, 1988.
Gould, Jean. *Amy: The World of Amy Lowell and the Imagist Movement*. New York: Dodd, Mead, 1975.
Grant, Joy. *Harold Monro and the Poetry Bookshop*. London: Routledge and Kegan Paul, 1967.
Griffin, Peter. *Along With Youth: Hemingway, The Early Years*. New York: Oxford, 1985.
Heymann, C. David. *American Aristocracy: Lives and Times of James Russell, Amy, and Robert Lowell*. New York: Dodd, Mead, 1980.
Holroyd, Michael. *Augustus John*. 2 vols. London: Heinemann, 1974–75.
Huddleston, Sisley. *In and About Paris*. London: Methuen, 1927.
Imbs, Brävig. *Confessions of Another Young Man*. New York: Henkle, 1936.
John, Augustus. *Autobiography*. London: Cape, 1975.
Kenner, Hugh. *A Homemade World*. New York: Alfred A. Knopf, 1975.
———. *The Mechanic Muse*. New York: Oxford University Press, 1987.
———. *Wyndham Lewis*. New York: New Directions, 1954.
Kiki. *Memoirs of Kiki* (of Montparnasse). Intro. E. Hemingway; trans. S. Putnam. London: Tandem, 1964.

Knoll, Robert E. *McAlmon and the Lost Generation: A Self-Portrait.* Lincoln: University of Nebraska Press, 1962.
Knox, Bryant. "Allen Upward and Ezra Pound." *Paideuma*, 3 (1974): 71ff.
Laney, Al. *Paris Herald: The Incredible Newspaper.* Westport, CT: Greenwood, 1947.
Laughlin, James. *Pound Az Wuz.* Port Townsend, WA: Graywolf, 1987.
Levenson, Samuel. *Maud Gonne.* New York: Reader's Digest, 1976.
Lewis, Wyndham. *Letters*, ed. W. K. Rose. London: Methuen, 1963.
Lidderdale, Jane, and Mary Nicholson. *Dear Miss Weaver: Harriet Shaw Weaver, 1876–1961.* London: Faber and Faber, 1970.
Loeb, Harold. *The Way It Was.* New York: Criterion, 1959.
Longenbach, James. *Modernist Poetics of History.* Princeton: Princeton University Press, 1987.
Lowell, Amy. *Fir-Flower Tablets*, trans. with Florence Ayscough. Boston: Houghton Mifflin, 1921.
———, ed. *Some Imagist Poets: An Anthology.* Boston: Houghton Mifflin, 1915; rpt. 1969.
Lynn, Kenneth S. *Hemingway.* New York: Simon and Schuster, 1987.
MacBride, Maud Gonne. *A Servant of the Queen: Reminiscences.* 1st ed. 1938; Woodbridge, England: Boydell, 1983.
MacDougall, Allan Ross. *Isadora: A Revolutionary in Art and Love.* Edinburgh: Nelson, 1960.
MacLeish, Archibald. *Reflections*, ed. B. A. Drabeck and H. E. Ellis. Amherst: University of Massachusetts Press, 1986.
Mackenzie, Faith Compton. *As Much As I Dare.* London: Collins, 1938.
Martin, B. K. "Ezra Pound and T. E. Lawrence: 74/444:472." *Paideuma*, 6 (1977): 167ff.
Marvil, Jonathan, *Frederic Manning: An Unfinished Life.* Durham: Duke University Press, 1988.
Materer, Timothy. "Henri Gaudier's 'Three Ninas.' " *Paideuma*, 4 (1975): 323ff.
McDougal, Stuart Y. *Ezra Pound and the Troubadour Tradition.* Princeton: Princeton University Press, 1972.
Meyers, Jeffrey. "New Light on Iris Barry." *Paideuma*, 13 (1984): 285ff.
Michaels, Walter. "Lincoln Steffens and Pound." *Paideuma*, 2 (1973): 209f.
Monnier, Adrienne. *The Very Rich Hours of Adrienne Monnier*, trans. Richard McDougall. New York: Charles Scribner's Sons, 1976; Paris, 1960.
Monro, Harold. *Some Contemporary Poets (1920).* London: Parsons, 1920.
Moore, Harry T. *The Priest of Love: A Life of D. H. Lawrence.* Carbondale: Southern Illinois University Press, 1954; rev. 1962.
Munson, Gorham. *The Awakening Twenties.* Baton Rouge: Louisiana State University Press, 1985.
Norman, Charles. *Ezra Pound.* New York: Macmillan, 1960.
Perloff, Marjorie. *Dance of the Intellect.* Cambridge, England: Cambridge University Press, 1985.
Poli, Bernard J. *Ford Madox Ford and the "Transatlantic Review."* Syracuse: Syracuse University Press, 1967.
Pritchard, William H. *Frost: A Literary Life Reconsidered.* New York: Oxford University Press, 1984.
Putnam, Samuel. *Paris Was Our Mistress.* New York: Viking, 1947.
Rascoe, Burton. *We Were Interrupted.* Garden City: Doubleday, 1947.
Reynolds, Michael. *The Young Hemingway.* Oxford: Basil Blackwell, 1986.

Richardson, Joanna. *Judith Gautier.* London: Quartet, 1987.
Robinson, Janice S. *H.D.: The Life and Work of an American Poet.* Boston: Houghton Mifflin, 1982.
Sachs, Maurice. *Au temps du Boeuf sur le Toit.* Paris: Nouvelle Revue Critique, 1939.
Sanouillet, Michel. *Picabia.* Paris: L'Oeil du Temps, 1964.
Sieburth, Richard. "Canto 119: François Bernouard." *Paideuma,* 4 (1975): 329ff.
Spender, Stephen. *T. S. Eliot.* New York: Viking, 1975.
Stead, C. K. *Pound, Yeats, Eliot and the Modernist Movement.* London: Macmillan, 1986.
Thomas, R. George. *Edward Thomas.* Oxford: Clarendon Press, 1985.
Tytell, John. *Ezra Pound: The Solitary Volcano.* New York: Doubleday, 1987.
Ullman, Pierre L. "Eugene Paul Ullman and the Paris Expatriates" *Papers on Language and Literature, 20* (Winter, 1984): 99ff.
Wees, William C. *Vorticism and the English Avant-Garde.* Toronto: Toronto University Press, 1972.
West, Martha Ullman. "Lady with a Poet: Margaret Cravens and Ezra Pound." *Helix, 13/14* (1983): 15ff.
Whittemore, Reed. *William Carlos Williams.* Boston: Houghton Mifflin, 1975.
Wickes, George. *Americans in Paris.* New York: Doubleday, 1969.
Witemeyer, Hugh. *The Poetry of Ezra Pound: Forms and Renewal, 1908–1920.* Berkeley: University of California, 1969.
Woolf, Virginia. *Roger Fry: A Biography.* London: Hogarth, 1940.
Yeats, W. B. *Poems: A New Selection.* 1st ed., ed. R. Finneran; 2d ed., ed. A. N. Jeffares. London: Macmillan, 1988.

III. Chronology of Pound's Major Books to 1926

(Taken from Donald Gallup's definitive *Bibliography*, which should be consulted for minor works and pamphlets.)

1908: *A Lume Spento.* Venice: Antonini. *A Quinzaine for This Yule.* London: Pollock & Co.; Elkin Mathews.
1909: *Personae.* London: Elkin Mathews (for the modern use of this title, see 1926). *Exultations,* London: Elkin Mathews.
1910: *The Spirit of Romance.* London: J. M. Dent and Sons. *Provença.* Boston: Small, Maynard.
1911: *Canzoni.* London: Elkin Mathews.
1912: *Ripostes.* London: Swift. *Sonnets and Ballate of Guido Cavalcanti.* Boston: Small, Maynard.
1913: *Hesternae Rosae, Serta II* (with Walter M. Rummel). London: Augener.
1914: *Des Imagistes: Anthology.* February *Glebe.* New York: Albert and Charles Boni. *Blast* (with Wyndham Lewis).
1915: *Cathay* (Fenollosa, Mori, Ariga). London: Elkin Mathews. *Blast 2* (with Wyndham Lewis).
ed. *Poetical Works of Lionel Johnson.* London: Elkin Mathews.
ed. *Catholic Anthology—1914–1915.* London: Elkin Mathews.

1916: *Gaudier-Brzeska: A Memoir*. London: John Lane. *Lustra*. London: Elkin Mathews. *Certain Noble Plays of Japan* (with Fenollosa). Churchtown: Cuala.
1917: *'Noh' or Accomplishment* (with Fenollosa). London: Macmillan. *Dialogues of Fontenelle*. London: Egoist.
1918: *Pavannes and Divisions*. New York: Alfred A. Knopf.
1919: *The Fourth Canto*. London: Ovid. *Quia Pauper Amavi*. London: Egoist.
1920: *Instigations* (essay by Fenollosa). New York: Boni and Liveright. *Hugh Selwyn Mauberley*. London: Ovid. *Umbra*. London: Elkin Mathews.
1921: *Poems 1918-21*. New York: Boni and Liveright.
1922: trans. Rémy de Gourmont: *Natural Philosophy of Love*. New York: Boni and Liveright.
1923: *Indiscretions; or, Une Revue de Deux Mondes*. Paris: Three Mountains. (trans. Edouard Estaunié: *The Call of the Road*. New York: Boni and Liveright.)
1924: *Antheil and the Treatise on Harmony*. Paris: Three Mountains.
1925: *A Draft of XVI Cantos*. Paris: Three Mountains.
1926: *Personae: The Collected Poems of Ezra Pound*. New York: Boni and Liveright. There were many later editions, including that of New Directions in 1949, with subsequent printings.

General Index

Subheads under individual entries are arranged chronologically. Pages with biographical material are listed first.

Abbey Theater, 37, 134, 306
Abbott, Berenice, 333
ABC of Reading, 90, 113, 130–31, 203, 320
ABC Restaurant, 84, 90, 113, 130–31
Abercrombie, Lascelles, 29, 87, 106, 117–18
Adams, Brooks, 220
Adams, John, 216, (in *Cantos*), 235, 318, 336
"Affirmations," 174
Agassiz, Louis, 150 (in *Cantos*)
Aiken, Conrad, 169, 171, 176
Ainley, Henry, 181 (in *Cantos*)
alba, 25–26, 39
Albigensian Crusade, 98, 230–31, 276
Aldington, Richard
  early life, 91–92
  imagist with H.D., Pound, 90–95, 106, 114–15, 117, 121–22, 299
  in *Poetry*, 101
  in *New Age*, 114
  in *Des Imagistes*, 124–25
  criticizes Pound, 124, 162–63, 223
  marriage to H.D., 132–33, 151, 153
  breakup of marriage, 132–33, 222–23
  with *Egoist*, 141, 191
  with vorticists, 156
  with Lowell, 160–63
  in war, 190
  birth of Perdita, 222–23
  enters journalism, 223, 226, 326
  helps Eliot, 226, 313, 326
  later life, 132–33, 223, 264
  letters to, 212
  in *Cantos*, 352
  photo, 137
Alexander the Great, 219 (in *Cantos*)
Allègre, 238 (in *Cantos*)
Altafort (Hautefort), 233
A Lume Spento, xiv, 4–6, 28, 146, 299
"Ancient Music," 178–79
Anderson, Margaret, 194–95, 202, 212–13, 224, 268, 271, 281, 299, 326–27, 337, 340, 341. See also *Little Review*
Anderson, Sherwood, 280, 304
Anglo-Saxon language, 86, 199, 207
Angoulême, 98, 234

Antheil, George, 267–71, 262, 264, 270 (in *Cantos*), 279, 288, 325–29, 331, 333, 334, 335, 337, 339, 340–42
Antheil and the Treatise on Harmony, 268, 339, 342
anti-Semitism, 188, 237, 247–48, 282, 293, 315, 353
Apollinaire, Guillaume, 272, 275
"Apparuit," 105
Appel, Carl, 37
"Approach to Paris," 116
Aragon, Louis, 247, 273, 291, 292, 327, 333
Ariga, Nagao, 130, 175
Arles, 98, 230 (in *Cantos*)
Armenonville, 233 (in *Cantos*) Restaurant, 290
Arnaut Daniel. See Daniel, Arnaut
Arnold, Matthew, 7
Arp, Hans, 272, 335
art, 18, 113, 140–60, 176–77, 197–98, 270–74. See also Brancusi, Constantin; Gaudier-Brzeska, Henri; Lewis, Wyndham; Picabia, Francis; Picasso, Pablo; Pound, Dorothy; Quinn, John; vorticism
Asquith, Herbert H., 157, 181 (in *Cantos*)
Assisi, 336–37
astrology, 41, 309
Atheling, William, 86, 200–201, 205, 211, 249, 297, 334, 336, 341
Athenaeum (magazine), 240, 242, 246, 248
Aubeterre, 235 (in *Cantos*)
Auric, Georges, 300
Awoi No Uye (Noh), 194 (in *Cantos*)
Ayscough, Florence, 175
"Axiomata," 254

Bacchus, 348–49 (in *Cantos*)
Bach, J. S., 229 (in *Cantos*)
Bacon, Francis S. (Baldy)
  in *Cantos*, 62–63, 315, 333, 351
Baigent, Michael, 276
Baker, Carlos, 322
Baker, Guy, 224, 352 (in *Cantos*)
Balakian, Anna, 273

Bal Bullier Dance Hall, 289–90 (in *Cantos*)
Ball, Hugo, 272
"Ballad of the Goodly Fere," 26–27, 39, 52
Ballylee Tower, 201, 226
Bank of England, 215–18
Barbezieux, Richart de, 234
Bariatinsky, Princess Lydia, 59, 89 (in *Cantos*)
Barker, Wharton, 243
Barnard Club, 65
Barnes, Djuna, 58, 284, 327, 333, 335, 336, 343
Barney, Alice, 260
Barney, Natalie, 260–64, 114, 250, 277, 295, 302, 311, 313, 320, 327, 337, 339, 342
  in *Cantos*, 262–64
Barrès, Maurice, 301, 336
Barry, Iris, 185, 207, 208, 210, 212, 225
Bassiano, Princess of, 262, 326
bassoon, 281, 302
Baudelaire, Charles, 35
Baumann, Walter, 90
Baxter Jordan, Viola, 58–59, 151
Beach, Sylvia, 277–80; 246–47, 264, 268, 300, 302, 305, 309–10, 326, 333, 338, 339
Beardsley, Aubrey, 5, 110 (in *Cantos*)
Beardsley, Mabel, 110, 118
Beaucaire, 98, 230 (in *Cantos*)
Beck, Jean, 72
Bedford, Agnes, 210, 246, 249, 253, 299, 300, 302, 334, 341, 344
Beecham, Sir Thomas, 186
Beerbohm, Sir Max, 253, 311
Bel Esprit campaign, 294, 311–13, 315, 316, 318, 319, 326, 327
Bell, Clive and Vanessa, 145
Belloc, Hilaire, 19, 136
Bellotti's Restaurant, 179–80 (in *Cantos*)
Benda, Julien, 246, 247 (in *Cantos*)
Bennett, Arnold, 21, 68–69, 253
Beowulf, music of, 292
Berenson, Bernard, 261–62, 336
Bergson, Henri, 35, 36, 79–80, 146, 156
Berman, Louis, 316
Bernouard, François, 238 (in *Cantos*), 275, 293
Bertran. *See* Born, Bertran de
Beyea, James, xiv, 64
Bible, 115, 315
Biddle, Nicholas, 217 (in *Cantos*)
Binyon, Laurence, 6–8, 19, 46–47
  in *Cantos*, 7, 8, 47
Bion, 253
Bird, Sally, 283, 333, 336, 338–40
Bird, William, 268, 281, 283, 285, 292, 311, 316, 317, 318, 321–325, 326, 328, 331–333, 336, 339, 340, 342, 351. *See also* Three Mountains Press
Bishop, John Peale, 280
Blackmur, R. P., 343
Black Sun Press, 290
Blake, William, 146
"Blandula, Tenulla, Vagula," 53
Blast 1, 97, 142, 147, 154–60, 343
Blast 2, 145, 171, 173, 178–79
Blaye, 234
Bloch-Savitsky. *See* Savitsky
Bloomsbury group, 145, 171, 211
Blunt, Anne, 82 (in *Cantos*)
Blunt, Wilfrid S., 106, 136–38, 138 (in *Cantos*), 154, 137 (photo)
Bodenheim, Maxwell, 180
Boeuf sur le Toit Nightclub, 277, 291, 305
Bologna, 324
Bomberg, David, 145
Borgatti, Renata, 249, 323
Borgia family, 328, 337, 350 (in *Cantos*)
Born, Bertran de, 26, 39, 98, 183, 189, 232, 233, 235
Bornelh (Borneil), Guiraut (Giraut) de, 138, 232
Bosschère, Jean de, 188 (in *Cantos*), 316–17
Bottome, Phyllis, 8
Bowen, Stella, 173, 209, 212, 225, 236, 290, 319, 328
boxing, 280–81, 288, 314
Boyle, Kay, 332
Brancusi, Constantin, 271, 274 (in *Cantos*), 300–302, 315, 317–19, 326, 333
Braque, Georges, 335
Breton, André, 273, 336
Bridges, Robert, 106, 147, 184, 314
Brinkley, Frank, 134
British Empire, decline of, 113, 254
British Museum, 7, 26, 46, 92–93, 177, 248–49
Brive, 98, 232, 234–35
Broglio, Gaspare, 324
Bronner, Milton, 182
Brooke, Rupert, 28–29, 87, 88, 104, 106, 176, 178
Brooks, Romaine, 262, 320
Brooks, Van Wyck, 116, 334
Broom (magazine), 286, 301, 329
Brown, Ford Madox, 22
Brown, John L., 351
Brown, Slater, 285
Browning, Robert, 26, 29, 161, 169, 173, 184, 199
  in *Cantos*, 183, 200, 348
Bryher. *See* Ellerman, Winifred
Bubb, Rev. C. C., 87, 205
Buddhism, 59, 129, 171
Bunting, Basil, 286 (in *Cantos*), 332, 334, 335

Burger, Nash K., 97
Burne-Jones, Sir Edward, 110 (in *Cantos*), 126
Burrows, Louisa, 47
Bush, Ronald, 183
Buss, Kate, 190, 311, 313, 325
Butts, Mary, 173, 188, 225, 277, 328, 334
Byng, Lancelot, 120–21
Bynner, Witter, xiv, 64
Byzantium 40, 114, 188 (in *Cantos*), 218, 227. *See also* Constantinople

Cabaret Club, 108–9, 127, 140, 145, 155, 186
Cabestan, 22, 45, 349 (in *Cantos*)
Cahors, 98, 222 (in *Cantos*), 232
Cairels, Elias, 98, 350 (in *Cantos*)
calendar, pagan, 306, 311, 307 (photo)
Cambridge University, 36, 50, 107, 295
Camoëns, Luis de, 46, 199 (in *Cantos*)
Campbell, Joseph, 32, 34, 52
"Camraderie," 29
Can Grande della Scala, 53
Cannell, Kathleen (Kitty), 115, 277, 301, 333
Cannell, Skipwith, 115, 125, 277, 301
Cantos. See also Index of References to the *Cantos* and specific allusions
 first mentions, 62, 182
 problems with form, 182–84, 314–15
 Browning and, 183–84
 first publications, 195, 198–200, 202, 205, 238, 240, 302, 326
 opening of, 207
 economic base of, 203, 220–21
 difficulty in, 238, 314–15
 final forms of first, 16, 347–52
Canzoni, 44, 64–65, 68–71, 74–76
Capdoil, Pons de, 249
Cardozo, Nancy, 197
Carnevali, Emanuel, 284
Carrara, 54 (in *Cantos*)
Cathay, 172, 174–76, 188, 190
Catholic Anthology, 180
Catullus, Valerius, 53–54, 189
 in *Cantos*, 54, 200, 244, 350
Cavalcanti, Guido, 46, 54, 64, 69–70, 78–79, 86, 95, 107, 240, 298
 in *Cantos*, 200, 229
"Cavalcanti," 79
Cave of the Golden Calf. *See* Cabaret Club
Celtic twilight, 41–42
Cerebralist (magazine), 135
Certain Noble Plays of Japan, 186, 193
Cesena, 324–25
Cézanne, Paul, 69
Chaigneau, Thérèse, 96, 266
Chaise-Dieu, 98 (in *Cantos*)
Chalais, 235 (in *Cantos*)

Chalus, 222 (in *Cantos*)
Chambers, Jessie, 47
Charters, Jimmy (the Barman), 282, 289
Chaucer, Geoffrey, 183, 249
Chavannes, Puvis de, 200 (in *Cantos*)
Chennevière, Georges, 113–14 (in *Cantos*)
Cherbury, Herbert of, 173 (in *Cantos*)
Chester, Carlos Tracy, 39, 319
Chester, Hawley, 319
Chesterton, G. K., 46, 84–85, 249 (in *Cantos*)
Chinese literature, 8, 16, 124–25, 129, 130, 162, 172, 193. *See also* Confucius, *Cathay*, etc.
Chinese written characters, 129–31, 240 (Fenollosa's book)
Chirico, Giorgio di, 273
Chisholm, Anne, 212, 291
Churchill, Winston, 104, 163, 352 (in *Cantos*)
Church Walk, Kensington, 37–38, 76, 81, 92–93, 115–16, 150, 181, 298, 38 (photo)
Cid, El, 37, 46, 199, 349 (in *Cantos*)
classicism, 35–36, 45, 112, 162, 286
clavichord, 154, 201, 288
Clermont, 232
Closerie des Lilas Restaurant, 289, 334
Clowes, William, 187 (in *Cantos*)
Coburn, Alvin L., 132, 172, 197, 323, 159 (photo of vortograph)
Cochran, Tommy, 319 (in *Cantos*)
Cocteau, Jean, 273–77, 238, 262–64, 264 (in *Cantos*), 268, 270, 275–76 (in *Cantos*), 291, 299, 300, 301, 305, 318, 320, 323, 326, 331, 332, 338–39
 photo, 278
 Pound on, 271, 275, 276
 on Pound, 276–77
Coke, William, 150 (in *Cantos*)
Colbourne, Maurice, 217–18
Collignon, Raymonde, 201–2
Collins, Adrian, 236–37
Collins, Churton, 9
Colum, Mary, 302–3, 306, 317–18
Colum, Padraic, 314 (in *Cantos*), 317
Comley, of Jenkintown, 316 (in *Cantos*)
communism, 203–4, 214–15, 281, 293, 317–18
Coney Island, 60–61 (in *Cantos*)
Confucius (Kung-fu-tsu), 59, 86, 120–21, 173, 182, 194
 in *Cantos*, 150, 200, 311, 315, 326, 342, 351
 See also Canto 13 in Index of References
Conrad, Joseph, 21, 22, 190, 197, 282, 303, 309, 331, 337, 341
Constantinople, 179 (in *Cantos*)
Contact (magazine), 284, 299, 302

"Contemporania," 101, 112, 180
Corbière, Tristan, 116, 205, 253
Cork, Richard, 143, 146–47, 156–58
Cournos, John, 91–92, 106–7, 117, 124–25, 127, 132, 150–51, 161–63, 172, 181
Courtney, W. L., 28
Cowley, Malcolm, 327
Crane, Stephen, 22
Cravens, Margaret, 52–53, 56, 65, 67–69, 81, 95–99, 97 (in *Cantos*), 265–66
"Credo," 87
Crevel, René, 336
Criterion (magazine), 271, 273, 311, 317, 318, 320, 325–26, 328
Cros, G. C., 271, 300
Crosby, Caresse, 198, 290–91, 335
Crosby, Harry, 335
Crowder, Henry, 292–93
Crowninshield, Frank, 325
Cuala Press, 186
cubism, 148, 160, 272
Cummings, E. E., 285–87, 58, 286–87 (in *Cantos*), 301, 325, 330, 331, 336
  on Pound, 286
Cunard, Lady Maud, 157, 179, 181, 186, 196, 203, 212
Cunard, Nancy, 291–93, 98, 157, 186, 210, 212, 225, 226, 236, 238, 283, 293 (in *Cantos*), 302, 321, 322, 324, 333, 338–39, 342–43, 352
Cunizza da Romano, 183, 350 (in *Cantos*)

Dadaism, 224, 271–73, 301–2, 335–36
Dahler, Warren, 58 (in *Cantos*)
Daniel, Arnaut, 24, 25, 45, 52, 67–73, 76–78, 86, 98, 138, 205, 234, 236, 240, 309, 350
  in *Cantos*, 72–73, 236, 350
D'Annunzio, Gabriele, 262, 318 (in *Cantos*)
Dante Alighieri
  translation of, 7
  verbal precision in, 22, 77
  Pound's devotion to, 37, 53
  in lectures and *Spirit*, 45–47
  works cited, 51, 70, 98, 219, 308, 309, 350
  compared to Pound, 107, 315
  Eliot and, 168, 170
  and *Cantos* form, 182, 190, 200, 221, 343
  in *Cantos*, 150, 200, 350
Dasenbrock, R. W., 160
Davies, Donald, 160
Davies, Ingrid, 109, 132, 153, 173, 310, 350
Davis, Jefferson, 97 (in *Cantos*)
Davray, Henry, 136
Dazzi, Manlio, 324, 344

Debussy, Claude, 69, 265 (in *Cantos*), 300
De la Mare, Walter, 119
De Lara, Isidore, 180 (in *Cantos*)
Delarue-Mardrus, Lucie, 261
Democritus, 95 (in *Cantos*)
Demuth, Charles, 299
Des Imagistes, 88, 124–25, 161
Deutsch, Babette, 190
Diaghilev, Serge, 275
Dial (magazine), 190, 229, 240, 242, 247, 248, 253, 262, 276, 285, 298, 300, 302–4, 311–12, 318, 320–21, 323–25, 330, 334
Dial Award, 304, 319, 334
Dialogues of Fontenelle, 119
Diana, statue of, 287 (in *Cantos*), 330 (photo)
Dias, B. H., 86, 200, 226, 249
Dickens, Charles, 42 (in *Cantos*), 303
Dieudonné Restaurant, 142, 160–64
  in *Cantos*, 109, 161
Dingo Bar, 289, 333
Dioce, 235 (in *Cantos*)
Dismorr, Jessie, 156–57, 191
Divus Justinopolitanus, Andreas, 99, 207, 324–25, 348 (in *Cantos*)
Dolmetsch, Arnold, 6, 154, 172
Dôme Restaurant, 289, 332, 341
Doolittle, Charles Leander, 57, 80, 114, 132
Doolittle, Hilda (H.D./Aldington)
  early life as Dryad, xiii
  Hilda's Book, 102
  in U.S., 1910, 57–61, 286
  and Williams, 59–60, 80, 338
  and Rummel, 61, 80–82, 94–95, 265
  in London, 20, 80–82
  with Aldington and Pound as imagist, 20, 91–96, 101–2, 114–15, 117, 121–22, 125
  on Flint, 31
  marriage to Aldington, 132–33, 151, 153
  on Pound's marriage, 81–82, 151–54
  defection to Lowell, 160–64, 172
  during war, 163, 172
  breakup of marriage, 132–33
  birth of Perdita, 222–23, 231
  with W. Ellerman (Bryher), 222–23, 284, 299, 333
  in Paris, 301, 338
  End to Torment, 20, 61, 81–82, 93, 102, 151–53, 223
  in *Cantos*, 109
Dordogne, Valley of, 99
"Doria," 105
Dos Passos, John, 285, 340
Doughty, C. M., 173 (in *Cantos*), 184
Douglas, Major C. H.
  life, 213

General Index 369

theories, 213–21, 203, 237, 254, 302, 315, 317–18, 348
 in *Cantos*, 217
Douglas, Norman, 20, 24, 223, 322
Dowson, Ernest, 7
Draft of XVI Cantos, A, 283, 337, 344–45
Draft of XXX Cantos, A, 292
Drogheda, Countess Kathleen of, 212
Dryad. *See* Doolittle, Hilda
Duchamp, Marcel, 272, 333
Duhamel, Georges, 113
Dulac, Edmund, 87, 91, 168 (in *Cantos*), 172, 186, 236
Dulac, P. A., 229 (in *Cantos*)
Duncan, Isadora, 197, 262, 266, 325
Dunning, R. C., 287–88, 342–43

"Early Translators of Homer," 207
Easter Uprising, 32–33, 186, 195
Ecbatan, 349–50 (in *Cantos*)
economics, 213–21, 302–3. *See also* Douglas, C. H.
Ede, H. S., 128
Edel, Leon, 88
Eden, Hotel, 53, 69, 114, 243
Edward VII (England), 180 (in *Cantos*)
Egoist (magazine), 33, 118–21, 123, 133, 136, 139, 141, 146, 176, 184, 191, 200, 207
Eiffel Tower Restaurant, 31–32, 127, 155, 157, 212
Eleanor of Aquitaine, 234, 350 (in *Cantos*)
Eleusinian Mysteries, 120, 122, 231–32, 306
Eliot, Thomas Stearns
 early life, 168–71
 appears in London, 168–69
 at Oxford, 171–72
 Pound promotes, 171, 179, 181, 191, 194, 198, 207
 Pound on, 169–71, 242, 308–11
 on Pound, 79, 126, 169, 171, 190, 198, 242, 253, 303
 compared to Orage, 84
 compared to Pound, 70, 105, 119, 145, 170, 183–84, 211
 with Lewis, 158, 169, 170–71, 211, 226, 245–46, 325
 marriage, 172, 226
 "Prufrock," 171, 181, 200
 in *Blast 2*, 179
 in *Catholic Anthology*, 181
 during war, 186–87, 202
 as banker, 188, 200, 226
 with *Egoist*, 191, 200, 207
 seen by H. Read, 211
 health problems, 226, 235–36, 300, 303–9, 313, 316
 walking tour (1919), 226, 235–36
 and Joyce, 245–46
 and Quinn, 242, 306–7, 310, 313, 316–17, 323, 327
 visits Paris after war, 303, 305, 331, 337
 edits *Criterion*, 311, 317, 318, 320, 326, 328
 wins *Dial* Award, 319
 in Verona, 294, 313
 and Quinn, 242, 306–7, 310, 313, 316-17, 323, 327
 Antheil on, 270
 Hemingway on, 282, 341, 343
 McAlmon on, 285
 Waste Land, (typescript of) 60, 316, 323, 347; (editing of) 303–310; (publication of) 305–9, 317–20
 in *Cantos*, 84, 236, 294, 313
 death, 169–70
 letters to, 304, 306–9, 311
 letters from, 309
 photo of Lewis drawing, 170
Eliot, Valerie, 306
Eliot, Vivien, 171–72, 226, 246, 303, 305
Elizondo, José M. de, 46
Ellerman, Sir John, 133, 284–85, 341
Ellerman, Winifred (Bryher), 133, 222–23, 284–85, 299, 301, 338, 342–43
Ellmann, Richard, 332
Eluard, Paul, 273
Emery, Mrs. Edward. *See* Farr, Florence
English Review (magazine), 21, 24, 26–28, 39, 44, 52, 54, 139, 143, 215
Ennemoser, Joseph, 133, 173 (in *Cantos*)
Epstein, Sir Jacob, 60, 78, 80, 88, 108, 127, 128, 143, 145, 146, 156, 174
Eri(u)gena, John Scotus, 231 (in *Cantos*), 267
Espey, John, 252–53
Estaunié, Edouard, 330, 334
Este, Isabella d', 349 (in *Cantos*)
Este family, 328, 337
Etchells, Frederick, 145, 156–57, 160, 191, 316
Excideuil, 232, 235–36 (in *Cantos*)
Exultations, 26, 39–40, 54, 64, 100, 319

Faber and Faber, 171
Fabian Society, 83
Faidit, 98, 249
Fairfax, J. G., 12, 19, 54
Falange, La, 276 (in *Cantos*)
Farr, Florence, 32, 42, 105
fascism, 314, 317–19, 348, 353
Federal Reserve System, 215–17, 219
Fenollosa, Ernest, 124–25, 129–30, 172, 175, 193, 240
Fenollosa, Mary, 124–25, 129, 131
Ferdinand of Spain, 201
Ferrara, 324, 337, 350 (in *Cantos*)
FitzGerald, Desmond, 54, 71, 306, 310, 316–17
 in *Cantos*, 32–33, 302, 350

FitzGerald, Fergus, 32
Fitzgerald, F. Scott, 282
Five Troubadour Songs, 249
Flanner, Janet, 291
Flaubert, Gustave, 21, 24, 35, 89, 106, 117, 311–12, 350 (in *Cantos*)
Fletcher, J. G., 115–19, 123, 158, 160–63
Flint, F. S., 28, 30–35, 39, 87, 104, 111, 116, 125, 136, 161–63, 176, 298–99, 137 (photo)
Florence, Italy, 323, 336
Flory, Wendy S., 51
Foix, 98, 231–32
Fontanas, André, 246
Fontenelle, Bernard de, 184, 206
Ford, Ford Madox (Hueffer)
  early life, 20–27
  heads *English Review*, 21–28, 44
  affair with Hunt, 23–25, 94
  scandal with Hunt, 24, 94, 109–10, 155
  breakup with Hunt, 101, 154–55, 179–80, 209, 211, 224–25
  promotes Pound, 25–27, 44, 175
  compared to Yeats, 20, 42, 103, 106
  Pound praises, 20–21, 34, 95
  influence on Pound, 24, 34–35, 73–75, 147
  and Lewis, 22, 46–47, 143, 155, 329
  and Lawrence, 47–48
  South Lodge life, 23–24, 47, 52, 73–74, 90–91, 118, 148, 154, 179
  Canzoni and Giessen visit, 67, 73–75
  and James, 21, 88–89, 94
  and Hudson, 21, 90
  The Good Soldier, 24, 155
  other publications, 22, 24, 25, 155, 319
  with imagists, 123, 125, 136, 155, 160–63, 172, 176
  with vorticists, 148, 155
  in war, 173, 179, 183, 190, 200
  after war with Bowen, 224–25
  in *Hugh Selwyn Mauberley*, 225, 252–53
  arrival in Paris (1922), 319, 328
  social life in Paris, 264, 289, 328, 332–43
  and Joyce, 328, 333
  and Quinn, 328–29, 337
  and Hemingway, 281–82, 333–43
  heads *Transatlantic Review*, 329, 331–43
  and Williams, 333, 338
  death, 20–21, 197
  in *Cantos*, 20, 24, 197
  photo, 330
Fort, Paul, 279
Foster, Jeanne R., 330
Fowler, Alfred (Taffy), 12 (in *Cantos*)
Fowler, (Aunt) Eva, 12, 18, 52, 110
France, Anatole, 21
"Francesca," 39–40
Frank, Aunt. *See* Weston, Frances

Fratres Minores, 138, 156 (poem)
free verse, 34, 87, 93, 115, 123, 162, 175–76
Freewoman. See *Egoist*
Freiburg, 72 (in *Cantos*)
Freud, Sigmund, 247 (in *Cantos*), 273, 275, 286, 330
Freytag-Loringhoven, Elsa von, 340–41 (in *Cantos*)
Friend, Krebs, 340–42
Frobenius, Leo, 292
Frost, Robert, 110–12, 117, 119, 123, 176, 179
Fry, Roger, 143–45, 150, 300
Future (magazine), 205
futurism, 93–94, 144, 146, 148, 155

G.-Adams. *See* Scratton, Bride
Gais, 345
Galantière, Lewis, 280–81
Galliffet, charge of, 7, 224 (in *Cantos*)
Gallup, Donald, 205
Galsworthy, John, 21
Galton, Rev. Arthur, 12, 19
"Game of Chess, The" 179
Garda, Lake, 53–54, 243–44 (in *Cantos*)
"Garden, The," 112–13
Gardone, 54 (in *Cantos*)
Garnett, Constance, 21–22
Garnett, David, 21–23, 36
Garonne River, 229, 230
  in *Cantos*, 232, 349
"Garret, The," 112
Gaudier-Brzeska, Henri, 126–28
  with imagists, 128, 161–62
  with vorticists, 128, 145, 147–48, 156, 160–61
  Pound promotes, 136, 174, 176–77, 197–98, 288, 338
  sculpts *Hieratic Head of E.P.*, 148, 150
  in war, 167–68
  death, 176–77
  in *Cantos*, 150, 161, 352
  photo of *Head*, 149
Gaudier-Brzeska: A Memoir, 177, 186, 293
Gaudier-Brzeska, Sophie, 127–28, 167, 176–77, 197–98
Gauthier-Villars, Henri, 229 (in *Cantos*)
Gautier, Judith, 276 (in *Cantos*), 317
Gautier, Théophile, 35, 253, 276 (in *Cantos*), 317
George V (England), 104, 208, 209 (in *Cantos*)
Germany, 73–75, 115, 239, 318
Gershwin, George, 269
Geryon, 219 (in *Cantos*)
Gesell, Silvio, 220
Ghose, Kali Mohan, 106
Gide, André, 247, 262, 275, 304
Giessen, 24, 73–75

Gilchrist-Clark, Maud, 248–49
Giles, H. A., 124, 175
"Gironde," 99
Glebe, 124, 286
Glidden, Carlton, 61
Goddeschalk, 206 (in *Cantos*)
Gogol, Nikolai, 240
Goldman, Emma, 341
Goldring, Douglas, 21, 23–24, 41, 180, 191, 227
Gomme, Laurence, 62, 185
Gonne, Maud. *See* MacBride, Maud Gonne
Gonzaga family, 349 (in *Cantos*)
Goold-Adams, B. *See* Scratton, Bride
Goose, Edmund, 179
Gould, Joe, 286 (in *Cantos*)
Gourdon, 98, 293
Gourmont, Rémy de, 69, 89–90, 113, 114, 116, 176, 180, 206 (in *Cantos*), 240, 247, 260, 261, 298, 301, 316
Gray, Cecil, 223
Great Titchfield Street, 4 (in *Cantos*), 29
Greek art, 114, 132, 162
Greek myth, 45, 199, 349 (in *Cantos*)
Greenhow, Rose, 97 (in *Cantos*)
Gregg, Frances, 58, 80–81, 85, 102
Gregory, Lady Augusta, 41–42, 107, 133, 196, 201
Gregory, Major Robert, 227
Grey, Mary, 240
Griffith, Arthur, 302–6, 302 (in *Cantos*), 314, 316, 318
Grover, Philip, 229–30
Guest, Barbara, 223
Guggenheim, Peggy, 327
Guide to Kulchur, 268, 274
Guillaume, Guilhem of Poitiers, Poitou. *See* William, Duke IX of Aquitaine
Guinizelli (Guinicelli), Guido, 309
Gurdjieff, George, 255, 274, 297, 319, 334

Hagoromo (Noh), 139, 181
haiku, 33–34
Hailey, Idaho, xiii, 250, 280, 341
Hale, W. G., 227–28, 236
Hall, Donald (*Paris Review* interview), 147, 169, 182, 303, 314
Hamilton, Alexander, 216–18 (in *Cantos*)
Hamilton College, xiv, 18, 156–57, 182, 325, 350
Hamnett, Nina, 128, 150 (in *Cantos*), 211, 277, 328, 331
Hardy, Thomas, 21, 106, 147, 239 (in *Cantos*), 254, 314
Harrison, Austin, 24, 215
Hartmann, Sadakichi, 342 (in *Cantos*)
Haw-Haw, Lord, 262
Hawkesby, Mrs., 89 (in *Cantos*)
H.D. *See* Doolittle, Hilda

Heap, Jane, 194–95, 202, 212–13, 224, 271, 299, 326–27, 340–41
Heine, Heinrich, 70, 161
Heinemann, William, 129
Helen of Troy, 234, 348–50 (in *Cantos*)
Hell Cantos. *See* Cantos 14, 15 in Index of References
Helmholtz, Bastien von, 139
Hemingway, Ernest, 280–83
  in World War I, 280–81, 313, 352
  arrival in Paris (1921), 280, 281, 305, 310; (1924) 333–34
  on Pound, 270, 280–82, 310, 343
  Pound on, 270, 280
  life in Paris, 287–88, 314, 318
  and Bird, 281, 283, 285, 311, 316, 326, 335, 340
  in Italy, 311, 321–22
  and Mussolini, 313, 319, 321
  and McAlmon, 282, 284, 285, 322, 326, 340, 343
  in Spain, 281, 285, 326, 327, 340
  and Ford, *Transatlantic Review*, 281–82, 333–43
  and Stein, 263, 281–82, 334, 341, 342
  and Antheil, 270, 271
  and Eliot, 282, 341, 343
  death, 280
  publications, 281, 329, 335, 336, 339, 340, 341, 343
  in *Cantos*, 270, 352
Hemingway, Hadley, 281, 321, 327, 338
Hemingway, John (Bumby), 331, 338
Henderson, Alice Corbin, 100, 195
Henry II (England), 39, 233
"Henry James," 207
Heraclitus, 95 (in *Cantos*)
Hesse, Eva, 146, 197
Hesternae Rosae (with Rummel), 68, 115, 265
Hewlett, Maurice, 12, 19, 82 (in *Cantos*)
Heydon, John, 173 (in *Cantos*)
Heyman, Katherine Ruth (Kitty), xiv, 3, 9–11, 56, 59, 70, 89, 172, 264–66, 10 (photo)
Hidden Nest (Venice), 181, 250
Hieratic Head of E.P. (Gaudier-Brzeska), 148–50, 149 (photo)
Hilda's Book, 102
Hinduism, 83, 120, 133
"History of Imagism" (Flint), 33–34, 176
Hitler, Adolf, 73
Hobart College, 37
Hogarth Press, 226
Holland Place Chambers, 132, 151, 152 (photo)
Hollywood film world, 56, 268–69
Homage to Sextus Propertius. *See* Propertius translations
Homberger, Eric, 228

Homer (*Odyssey*), 54, 99, 112, 315
  in *Cantos* 199, 207, 348
Honegger, Arthur, 320
Honorius, Pope, 133
Hooker, Denise, 277
Hopkins, Kenneth, 102
Hours Press, 292
Housman, A. E., 71
"How I Began," 3–5, 11, 12, 26, 27, 98, 105
"How To Read," 320
Huddleston, Sisley, 269, 289–90
Hudson, W. H., 21, 90 (in *Cantos*)
Hueffer, Elsie M., 22–24, 73, 94, 109
Hueffer, Ford. *See* Ford, Ford Madox
Hueffer, Francis (Franz), 22
Huelsenbeck, Richard, 272, 335
Hugh Selwyn Mauberley, 251–53, 7, 68, 187, 188, 225, 239, 261, 315
Hulme, T. E.
  as imagist, 30–36, 71, 74
  with art world, vorticism, 78–80, 107, 143, 146–48
  in war, 173, 176
  death, 202
  heritage, 209, 240, 298
  in *Cantos*, 202, 352
  "Autumn," 31
Hunt, Alfred, W., 23, 38
Hunt, Mrs. Alfred W., 23, 94
Hunt, Violet
  at South Lodge, 23–25, 47, 52, 88, 91, 108, 118, 154
  at Giessen, 73–74
  scandal with Ford, 24, 94, 109–10, 155
  breakup with Ford, 101, 154–55, 179–80, 209, 211, 225
  loyalty to Pound, 161, 163–64, 180
  death, 164
Hutchins, Patricia, 38
Hutchins, Robert, 247 (in *Cantos*)
Huxley, Julian, 303
Hyde-Lees, Georgie. *See* Yeats, Georgiana

Iamblichus, 350 (in *Cantos*)
Ibbotson, J. D., xiv, 86
ideogram, 130–31
"I Gather the Limbs of Osiris," 86
Image, Selwyn, 6 (in *Cantos*), 7, 19, 30, 32
Imaginary Letters, 198
imagism. *See also* entries for individuals mentioned below, H. Doolittle, Aldington
  Hulme and, 33–36
  Ford and, 74–75
  early tenets of, 87–88
  founding of group, 92–93, 104–5
  Pound's promotion of, 101–5, 124
  Frost and, 111–12
  Fletcher and, 117
  Lowell's usurpation of, 122–23, 141–42, 160–64, 172
  Pound abandons, 162–64
  and Chinese characters, 130–31
  Flint and, 33–36, 176, 298–99
"In a Station of the Metro," 75, 105, 112, 188
"Indiscretions," 242–43
Indiscretions, 283, 323
"In Durance," 28
Instigations, 87, 130, 207, 239–40
Ionides, Luke, 331 (in *Cantos*), 334, 335, 342
Ireland, 32–33, 40–42, 186–87, 195–96, 302, 304–6, 314, 316–19
"Island of Paris," 248
Italy, Pound's trips to. *See also* individual cities
  early, xiii–xiv;
  in 1910, 52–56
  in 1911, 69–72
  in 1912, 98
  in 1913, 113–15
  in 1920, 242–46, 255
  in 1922, 311–13, 317
  in 1923, 320–25
  in 1924, 332–38, 342ff.
Ito(w), Michio, 181 (in *Cantos*), 186, 297
Itys, 45
"I Vecchii," 6

Jackson, Andrew, 217 (in *Cantos*)
Jackson, Holbrook, 83
James, Henry, 88–90, 21–23, 94, 240, 350, 185 (death)
  in *Cantos*, 89, 350
Jammes, Francis, 116
Janus, Hiram (E.P.), 330
Japanese language, literature, 31, 33–34, 40, 124, 129–30, 193
Jefferson, Thomas, 216, 218–19 (in *Cantos*), 318, 336, 343
Jepson, Edgar, 8 (in *Cantos*), 9, 28, 46, 154, 207, 248, 353
Jews, 179, 188–89, 220, 243, 247, 293. *See also* anti-Semitism
Jockey Bar, 291, 278 (photo)
John, Augustus, 109, 143, 209, 212, 291
Johnson, Lionel, 5–7, 15, 74, 182 (*Works* edited by E.P.)
Jones, Alun R., 35–36
Jordan, Viola. *See* Baxter Jordan, V.
Josephson, Matthew, 286, 289
Jouve, J. P., 113, 116
Joyce, Giorgio, 244, 246, 342
Joyce, James
  Pound hears of and promotes, 125, 135–36, 156, 191, 205
  and Yeats, 125, 245
  during war, 179, 201, 223–24

General Index

in *Little Review*, 194, 198, 201, 223–24, 298
Ulysses, 179, 195, 201, 223–24, 230, 244, 245, 247, 279, 280, 298–300, 306, 309–10 (published), 312 (reviewed by E.P.), 329, 332–33 (manuscript)
and Quinn, 195, 201, 224, 245, 279–80, 298, 299, 300, 310, 329, 332–33
and Weaver, 119, 136, 191, 223–24, 245, 280
and Beach, 246–47, 279, 300, 306, 309–10, 333
meets Pound, 243–45
arrives in Paris, 245–47, 279
and Hemingway, 282, 284, 305
and McAlmon, 136, 284–85, 333
and Stein, 310
and Ford, 328–29, 333, 335–36
and Williams, 333
Antheil on, 270
health problems, 201, 316, 326, 339, 342
on Pound as person, 136, 245
Pound on as person, 245
Chamber Music, 5, 245
Dubliners, 136, 305
Portrait of the Artist, 119, 136, 185, 246
Finnegans Wake, 244, 328, 335–36
in *Cantos*, 244
photo, 330
Justinopolitanus. *See* Divus, Andreas
just price, 218

Kabir, 106 (in *Cantos*)
Kagekiyo (Noh), 193 (in *Cantos*)
Kant, Immanuel, 80
Kardomah Restaurants, 85, 215
Kavka, Jerome, 177
Kemp, Harry, 62
Kenner, Hugh, 17–18, 89, 235, 253
Kensington, 37–38, 92–93, 168 (in *Cantos*). *See also* Church Walk
Kensington Gardens, 113
Kerr, Elizabeth, 4
Kibblewhite, Ethel, 80, 148
Kilmer, Joyce, 62, 100
Kinuta (Noh), 139
Kipling, Rudyard, 184, 347
Knopf, Alfred, 185, 190, 193, 195, 206, 226, 304
Komachi (Noh), 194 (in *Cantos*)
Konody, P. G., 202, 211
Koume, Tami, 181, 288, 314–15, 339
Kreymborg, Alfred, 116, 124, 171, 180, 185, 286, 301
Kung. *See* Confucius

Lacock Abbey, 248
Laforgue, Jules, 198, 205 (in *Cantos*), 253

"Lament of the Frontier Guard," 175
Landor, W. S., 11 (in *Cantos*), 184
Lane, John, 5, 155, 177, 180
Langham Street, 4, 26, 39, 172
Langley, Sam, 38
Langley, Mrs. Sam, 38, 132
Lanier, Sidney, 53, 97 (in *Cantos*)
Larbaud, Valéry, 326
larks, 233–34, 238
Laurencin, Marie, 275 (in *Cantos*)
Lawrence, D. H., 46–48, 56, 109, 119, 124, 132, 162–63, 187, 222–23
Lawrence, Frieda, 109, 223
Lawrence, T. E., 107, 204, 224, 242
Lawrence, W. G., 107
LeBlanc, Georgette, 268, 337
Lechmere, Kate, 147–48, 156
L'Effort Libre, 113–14
Léger, Fernand, 271, 316, 320, 325, 339
Lencour, Vail de, 188
Leopardi, Giacomo, 70
Le Puy, 98 (in *Cantos*)
Lévi, Eliphas, 173
Lévy, Emil, 72–73 (in *Cantos*)
Lewis, C. S., 45
Lewis, Froanna, 226
Lewis, Wyndham
early life, 143
meets Pound unsuccessfully, 46–47, 142
and Ford, 22, 47, 143, 155, 281, 329
and Hulme, 80, 143, 146, 147–48
and Cabaret Club, 108, 145
becomes friendly with Pound, 145–48
leads vorticism, 140–48, 151–52, 155–60
Blast 1, 155–60, 273, 343
Blast 2, 145, 173, 178–79
and Aldingtons, 151, 156
with N. Cunard, 157, 210, 212, 226, 292, 321–22
and Eliot, 158, 169–171, 245–46, 300, 312
in war, 167, 173, 190, 200, 202–3 (freed from trenches), 209–11, 225
and Quinn, 174–75, 191, 260
in *Little Review*, 194, 198
described by Read, 209–11
love affairs, 209–12
life after war, 225–26
drawings of Pound, 225, 241
with Joyce, 245–46
Antheil on, 270
with McAlmon, 284, 292, 321–22
with Hemingway, 281, 282, 314
visits Paris, 314, 316
Pound on, 148, 226, 271, 303, 316
on Pound, 156, 158, 202, 245–46
letters from, 198, 202

letters to, 69, 212, 300, 312, 328, 329, 343
death, 158
in *Cantos*, 46–47, 84, 200, 202, 352
photo, 144
photos of drawings, 170 (Eliot), 241 (Pound, 1920)
"L'Homme Moyen Sensuel," 200, 206
Linati, Carlo, 246
Lincoln, Abraham, 217, 336
Lindsay, Vachel, 100, 171
Li Po, 130
Literary Essays of E.P., 48, 79, 87–90, 93, 99, 112, 119, 138, 200, 205–207, 312, 320
Little Review. See also Anderson, Margaret; Heap, Jane
  contacts Pound, 194
  moves to New York with Quinn as advisor, 194–95, 198, 201–2, 208, 213, 224, 273, 281, 298–99
  in Paris, 271, 300, 302, 325, 335, 340, 342
Litz, A. Walton, 16, 138
Liveright, Horace, 305 (in *Cantos*), 318, 330, 334
Lloyd George, David, 302, 351 (in *Cantos*)
Lodge, Drusilla, 97
Loeb, Harold, 277, 286, 301, 327, 329, 333
logopoeia, 113, 320
London
  arrival in, 3ff.
  reasons for leaving, 240, 254–56, 298
  in *Cantos*, 255–56, 351–52
Longenbach, James, 70, 138, 174
Longfellow, H. W., 63
Loomis, Susan A. *See* Pound, Susan Angevin
Loomis family, 11, 338
Louÿs, Pierre, 262
Low, Lady Anne Penelope, 52
Lowell, Amy
  early life, 122
  with Pound, imagists in London (1913), 122–23, 125, 141–42
  second visit (1914), 160–64
  usurps imagism, 117, 123, 124, 142, 151, 160–64, 174, 176, 190, 195, 248
  as Chinese translator, 175
  and *Egoist*, 119, 141–42
  letters from, 122, 141, 172
  letters to, 135, 141–42, 172, 195, 310–11, 316
  in *Cantos*, 161
Lowther, Aimée, 19
Loy, Mina, 326, 333, 339
Lubicz-Milosz, O. W. de, 303
Lupin, Arsène, 335
Lustra, 105, 123, 175, 182, 187–90, 195, 229

McAlmon, Robert, 283–85. *See also* Three Mountains Press; Bird, William
  marriage to Bryher, 284, 299, 301, 338, 343
  with Pound, 284, 289, 322, 325, 338, 342
  in Paris life, 274, 277, 301, 333, 335, 339, 343
  with Bird in publishing, 283–85, 326, 343
  own publications, 284, 325, 331, 343
  and Joyce, 136, 284–85, 333
  and Lewis, 226, 284, 321–22
  and Williams, 277, 283–84, 333, 338–39
  and Hemingway, 282, 283–84, 322, 326, 340, 343
  on Stein, 285
  on Eliot, 285
  with Cunard, 292, 322
  death, 285
MacBride Stuart, Iseult, 186, 196–97, 201, 210, 267, 274, (in *Cantos*), 197
MacBride, John, 186, 196
MacBride, Maud Gonne, 15, 186–87, 195–97, 201, 206, 298, 305–6, 314
MacBride, Seagan, 196
McCormack, Nancy C., 304, 322
machinery and art, 146, 269. *See also* futurism
Mackenzie, Faith, 109
MacLeish, Archibald, 327
Macmillan and Company, 182, 193
Madison Square Presbyterian Church, 250
Maensac, Peire de, 350 (in *Cantos*)
Maent, Lady, 189, 233
Magna Charta, 248–49
Maison Carée, 230 (in *Cantos*)
Maitland, Cecil, 277
Malatesta, Sigismundo, 312–13, 322, 351. *See* Cantos 8–11 in Index of References
Mallarmé, Stéphane, 31
Manicheans, 98. *See also* Albigensian Crusade
Manning, Frederic, 12–13, 17, 19, 70, 74, 136, 224
Mansfield, Katherine, 83, 128
Mantua, 71, 324, 349 (in *Cantos*)
Mapel, Adah and Ida, 68, 228, 236
Marcher, Johanna, 345
Mariani, Paul, 333
Marinetti, F. T., 93–94, 140, 144–45, 155, 273
Maritain, Jacques, 276, 331
  in *Cantos*, 247, 263–64
Marsden, Dora, 118–19, 136, 141, 191
Marsh, Edward, 87, 104–5, 163, 179, 186
Marshall, John, 185
Martial, 189

General Index

Marueil, Arnaut de, 234
Marwood, Arthur, 21
Marx, Karl, 214, 247 (in *Cantos*)
Masefield, John, 5, 46
Massenet, Jules, 186
Masters, E. L., 174, 180
Masterson, C. F. G., 184
Materer, Timothy, 146, 160
Mathews, Elkin, 5, 6, 11(in *Cantos*), 12, 19, 29, 43, 65, 100, 106, 108, 112, 179, 180, 182, 187–88, 208, 237, 239, 255, 279
Mathews Chinese dictionary, 131
Matisse, Henri, 69, 271
Mauberley. See *Hugh Selwyn Mauberley*
Mauléon, Savairic de, 231–32 (in *Cantos*)
Maupassant, Guy de, 21
Mead, G. R. S., 45, 79, 121–22
melopoeia, 113, 131, 320
Mencken, H. L., 136, 188, 311
Mercure de France (magazine), 114, 136, 142, 207 (in *Cantos*), 299
Metevsky. See Zaharoff
Meyers, Jeffrey, 142–43, 147, 158, 209–10
Meynell, Francis, 180
"Middle-Aged," 99
Milan, 72, 246, 324
Milhaud, Darius, 269, 277
Millevoye, Lucien de, 196
Milton, John, 109
Minnesinger, 115
Mizener, Arthur, 20, 74
Mockel, Albert, 206–7 (in *Cantos*), 236
Modena, 323
modernism, 75, 126, 138, 347
Modigliani, Amadeo, 150
"Moeurs Contemporaines," 202
Molay, Jacques de, 231 (in *Cantos*)
Mond, Sir Alfred, 24 (in *Cantos*)
Monnier, Adrienne, 246–47, 279, 338
Monro, Harold, 87–88, 104, 110, 169, 180, 185, 320
Monroe, Harriet. See also *Poetry*
  first meeting with, 327
  letters with, 99–101, 104, 109, 111–12, 117, 122–23, 140–42, 171, 174, 180, 194–95, 202, 207, 248, 315
Montesquiou, Robert de, 275
Montparnasse, 270, 287–89, 295
Montréjeau, 230–32 (in *Cantos*)
Montségur
  in *Cantos*, 230–32, 235
Moody, A. D., 121
Moore, George, 139
Moore, Marianne, 208, 284, 300, 311, 315, 334
Moore, Mary, xiv, 3, 9, 11, 14, 17, 27, 58–59, 94
Moore, Sturge, 41, 46–47, 106–7, 136, 143

in *Cantos*, 47
photo, 137
Morand, Paul, 271, 300, 302, 312, 315
Mori, Kainan, 129–30, 175
Morrell, Lady Ottoline, 157, 303
Morris, William, 133, 173, 184
Morrison Chinese dictionary, 131, 154
Morse, Cornelia, 265
Morse, Samuel F. B., 3, 265
"Mr. Nixon," 68
Muir, Edwin, 83
Munson, Gorham, 220
Murry, J. M., 83, 85, 128, 240, 246, 248, 311–12
music, 42, 52, 56, 62, 65, 67–70, 72–73, 115, 200–201, 205, 213, 249, 260, 264–70, 324–28, 331, 339–40. See also Atheling, William; Antheil, George; Heyman, K. R.,; Rudge, Olga; Rummel, W. M.; troubadours; *Testament de Villon;* bassoon
Mussolini, Benito, 53, 73, 121, 313, 317, 319, 348, 353
  in *Cantos*, 24, 121

Naidu, Sarojini, 129
Na-khi tribes, 193–94 (in *Cantos*)
Napoleon Bonaparte, 235
Nasher Collection, Raymond D., 149–50
Natural Philosophy of Love (trans. of Gourmont's), 206, 316
"Near Périgord," 183, 189
Nègre de Toulouse Restaurant, 290, 328
Neoplatonism, 350
Nevinson, Christopher, 145
New Age (magazine), 174, 200–202, 207, 215, 226, 230, 236–38, 242, 249, 254–55. See also Orage, Alfred R.
Newark Prize, 187
Newbolt, Henry, 74, 106
  in *Cantos*, 82, 286
New Freewoman (magazine), 118–20. See also *Egoist*
New Weston Hotel, xiv, 64
New York City, 57–66, 235
New York City Public Library, 65, 306
Ney, Marshal Michel, 289
Nicoletti, Giachino N.
  in *Cantos*, 32, 54
Nietzsche, Friedrich W., 83, 120
"Night Litany," 11
Nîmes, 98, 230 (in *Cantos*)
Nishikigi (Noh), 131, 139, 193
Nobel Prizes for Literature, 227, 282, 331, 335
"Noh" or Accomplishment, 193–94
Noh plays, 130–31, 134–35, 138–39, 147, 154, 180, 184, 186, 190, 193–94. See also separate titles
noigandres, 72–73

Northcliffe, Lord Alfred C. W., 223, 352 (in *Cantos*)
Norton, Charles Eliot, 244
Norton, Sarah, 244 (in *Cantos*)
Notre Dame de Paris, Cathedral of, 68 (in *Cantos*)
Notre Dame des Champs, Rue, apartment in, 287–88, 304
novel writing, 39
Nutt, David, 111
"N.Y.," 64

O'Brien, Edward J., 341
Ocellus, 150 (in *Cantos*)
Odysseus, *Odyssey*, 99, 199, 207, 308, 312
  in *Cantos*, 324–25, 348, 350, 352
Omakitsu. *See* Wang Wei
Omega Workshops, 145
Orage, Alfred R. For Pound's articles, see *New Age*
  begins *New Age*, 83–86
  Pound meets, 80, 83
  supports Pound with articles, 84–86, 175–76, 228, 230, 237–38, 242
  hires Pound as music and art critic, 200–201
  and Upward, 85, 120–21
  and Major Douglas, 203, 213, 215, 218, 220, 237
  and other friends, 84–86, 207, 210
  farewell to Pound, 254–55, 298
  closes journal, 255
  later life and death, 255, 297, 319, 334
  in *Cantos*, 84
  photo of drawing, 85.
Others (magazine), 171, 286
"Our Contemporaries," 178
Ouspensky, P. D., 255
Outlook (magazine), 238
Ovid (Publius Ovidius Naso), 237, 315, 344
  in *Cantos*, 199, 348–50
Ovid Press, 226, 231, 238, 239, 252
Oxford University, 12, 19, 69, 107, 147, 169, 171

Pagani's Restaurant, 19, 47
"Pagani's, November 8," 187
Paige, D. D., 248, 300
Paige Carbons (letters to family and others), 4, 7, 12, 13, 19, 20, 26, 36–38, 41, 52, 53, 62, 63, 65, 67–69, 71–73, 75, 79, 80, 106, 112, 133, 153, 182, 183, 195, 201, 202, 205, 208–9, 212–13, 224, 226, 228, 230, 232, 237, 238, 242, 243–48, 271, 298–305, 310–21, 331–44
Palgrave *Golden Treasury*, 182 (in *Cantos*)
Paris: early visits, xiii, 3, 52, 67–69, 94, 113, 115, 265
  lure of, 236, 240, 244, 259–60
  highly praised, 248
  final departure for, 253
  arrival in (1921), 254, 297–98
  worlds of, 259–96
  music world, 264–70
  art world, 270–74
  French literary world, 274–77
  English literary world, 277–87
  Pound's social world, 287–96
  events (1921–24), 297–344
  departure from for Italy, 342ff.
Paris, Gaston, 37
Paris Review interview. *See* Hall, Donald
Pas-de-Calais Hotel, 287, 299, 303
passports, 184, 228
"Pastiche: The Regional," 230
Patchin Place, 58 (in *Cantos*), 286
Paterson, William, 216 (in *Cantos*)
Patmore, Brigit, 82, 91–92, 101–2, 132–33, 154, 156, 188–89, 223
Patmore, Coventry, 91
Patmore, Derek, 154
Patmore, Netta, 133
Patria Mia, 65
Pauthier, M. G., 173, 326, 351
Pavannes and Divisions, 205–7
"Peacock" (Yeats), 134 (in *Cantos*)
Pearson, N. H., 163
Pennefeather, Rev., 38, 156
Pennsylvania, University of, xiii, 37, 46, 53, 189, 243, 350
Pennsylvania Railroad Station (N.Y.), 65
Penthesilea, 8
Périgueux, 98, 235 (in *Cantos*)
Personae (1909), xiv, 27, 30, 37, 54, 64, 100, 239
Personae (1926), 6, 7, 26, 27, 31, 40, 53, 68, 69, 97, 99, 112, 113, 124, 156, 175, 178–79, 187, 189, 200, 202, 206, 225, 228, 252–53
Perugia, 313, 336
Petrarch, Francis, 79
Petronius, 309
phanopoeia, 113, 320
Philadelphia, 57, 61–62
Picabia, Francis, 271–74, 273–74 (in *Cantos*), 277, 282, 299, 300, 313, 326, 342
Picasso, Pablo, 60, 147, 154, 200, 259, 270–71, 275, 301, 305 (first meeting), 320, 347–48 (in *Cantos*)
"Piere Vidal Old," 39
"Pierrots," 206
Pirandello, Luigi, 275 (in *Cantos*)
Pius II, Pope, 326–27
Pius XI, Pope, 72 (in *Cantos*)
"Planh for the Young English King," 39
Plarr, Victor, 6–7, 19, 52, 106, 110, 136, 224, 253, 352 (in *Cantos*), 137 (photo)
Plotinus, 146

General Index

Poe, E. A., 115
Poetry (magazine), 99, 101, 106, 109, 111–12, 131, 136, 139, 141, 171, 176, 185, 194, 195, 198, 205, 207. *See also* Monroe, Harriet
  Awards, 124, 154
Poetry and Drama (magazine), 87–88, 185
Poetry Review (magazine), 87
Poetry Society of London, 87
Poets' Club, 19, 30–31, 33, 52
Poicebot, Gaubertz de
  in *Cantos*, 231–32, 350
Poitiers, 98
  in *Cantos*, 234–35, 349
Polignac (Polonhac), 98 (in *Cantos*)
Polignac, Edward de, 262
Polytechnic Institute of London, lectures at, 9, 18–19, 37, 44
Pope, Alexander, 308
"Portrait d'une Femme," 77, 105
"Post Mortem Conspectu," 97
Pougy, Liane de, 261
Poujol's Hotel, Mme.
  in *Cantos*, 232, 235
Pound, Dorothy Shakespear
  meets Ezra, 16–18, 44, 52
  personality, 17–18, 151–52
  compared to Olga Rudge, 18, 51, 251, 295
  compared to Bride Scratton, 50–51
  first visit to Italy, 55–56
  and Hilda Doolittle, 58, 80–82, 115, 151–52
  and *Canzoni*, 69, 71
  and Margaret Cravens, 95, 97–98
  protracted courtship, 94, 102–3
  involvement and removal in London life, 109, 173, 225, 226
  later visits to Italy, 114, 242–46, 311–13, 320ff.
  marriage to Ezra, 139, 153–54, 172
  and cooking, 151, 288
  with imagists, 161, 164
  at Stone Cottage with Yeats, 173–74, 183–84
  finances, 185, 240, 328
  and Pound's amours, 173, 196, 225, 291, 295
  with Eliot on walking trip in Midi, 227–36
  creates art, 55–56, 230, 236, 315, 338, 344
  on Joyce, 244
  and Magna Charta, 248–49
  in Paris, 279, 282–83, 288, 295, 299
  and Nancy Cunard, 291
  visits England, 295–96, 302, 315, 326–31
  son Omar, 295–96, 345, 353
  later years, 296

letters to/from Ezra, 62, 69, 94, 97–98, 114, 115, 118, 123, 129, 133
letters from/to Ezra, 80, 95, 103
photo, 55
Pound, Ezra (*Entries here stress major encounters with major people chronologically; italicized items indicate more details under that entry; see other entries for additional people, places, periods, and ideas, as well as the Index of References to the "Cantos"; poems, essays, and books are listed under titles as separate entries.*) *See also* art; economics; music; calendar, pagan; Rapallo; Venice; Pennsylvania, University of; etc.
  early life and education, xiii–xiv
  arrival in London, 3ff.
  meets *Elkin Mathews* and friends, 5ff.
  first London publications, 5, 11–12, 26–28
  lectures at *Polytechnic Institute*, 9, 18–19, 37, 44
  meets *Olivia Shakespear* and *Dorothy (Pound)*, 14ff.
  early London social life, 18–19, 23–24, 47
  meets *F. M. Ford* and *Violet Hunt* at *South Lodge*, 20ff.
  in *English Review*, 26–28, 44, 52, 54
  meets *F. S. Flint*, *T. E. Hulme* and "School of Images," 30ff.
  meets *W. B. Yeats*, 36ff.
  Exultations published, 39
  meets *Wyndham Lewis*, 46–47
  meets *D. H. Lawrence*, 46–48
  Spirit of Romance published, 44–46
  meets *Bride Scratton*, 48ff., 293–95
  active with Dorothy, 52–56
  with *W. M. Rummel* in Paris, Shakespears in *Italy* (1910), 52ff.
  patronized by *Margaret Cravens*, 52–53
  return to U.S. (1910), 56–66
  in Paris with Rummel and Cravens (1911), 67–69
  Ford and *Canzoni*, 69–75
  Hilda Doolittle (H.D.) arrives in London, 80–82
  work on *Arnaut Daniel* and troubadours, 76ff.
  meets *A. R. Orage* of *New Age*, 83–87
  H.D., *Richard Aldington* and roots of imagism, 91ff.
  meets *Henry James*, 88–90
  Cravens suicide, 96–98
  walking tour in Midi (1912), 98–99
  hears from *Harriet Monroe* and *Poetry*, 99ff.
  Ripostes published, 104–5
  meets *Robert Frost*, 110–12

in Italy (1913), 113ff.
meets *J. G. Fletcher*, 115–17
with *H. S. Weaver* and *Egoist*, 118ff.
meets *Amy Lowell*, 122–24
translates *Chinese* from MS of *Ernest Fenollosa*, 124–25, 129ff.
meets *Henri Gaudier-Brzeska*, 127ff.
with Yeats at *Stone Cottage*, 133–39, 173–74, 184
translates first *Noh* plays, 134–35, 138–39
writes to *James Joyce*, 135–36
with *Wyndham Lewis* and artists of vorticism, 140ff.
abandons *imagism* to *Amy Lowell*, 122–23, 141–42, 160–64
marries Dorothy, 139, 153–54
T. E. Hulme and art world, 143, 147ff.
head sculpted by Gaudier-Brzeska, 148–50, 149 (photo)
Ford-Hunt breakup, 154–55
Blast 1 published, 155–58
World War I begins, 162ff.
meets *T. S. Eliot*, 168ff.
hears from *John Quinn*, 174ff.
Cathay published, 175–76
death of Gaudier-Brzeska, 176–77
Blast 2, 178–79
Catholic Anthology published, 180
begins writing *Cantos*, 182ff.
Gaudier-Brzeska: A Memoir published, 186
Lustra published, 187–90
"*Noh*" or *Accomplishment* published, 193–94
joins *Little Review*, 194ff.
affair with Iseult MacBride, 196–97
vortographs with *A. L. Coburn*, 197
first *Cantos* published, 198–200
music and art critic for *New Age*, 200ff.
interested in *Major C. H. Douglas* and *Social Credit*, 203, 213–21
memorializes *Rémy de Gourmont*, 205–6
end of war, 208–12, 222–27
"translates" Propertius, 227–28, 236–38
walking trip with Eliot in Midi (1919), 228–36
Instigations, 239–40
farewell to London, 240–56
meets *James Joyce at Sirmione*, 244–45
Joyce follows to Paris, 246–47
reviews *Olga Rudge*, 249–51
Hugh Selwyn Mauberley published, 251–53
arrival in Paris (1921), 254, 297–98
with *Natalie Barney*, 260–64
with Paris music world, 264–70
with *W. M. Rummel*, 264–67

with *George Antheil*, 267–70
with *Francis Picabia*, 271–74
with *Jean Cocteau*, 274–77
with writers of English, 277–87
at *Sylvia Beach*'s store, 277–80
with *Ernest Hemingway*, 280ff.
with *William Bird* and *Three Mountains Press*, 283
with *Robert McAlmon*, 283–85
with *E. E. Cummings*, 285–87
social life in Paris, 287–96
with *Nancy Cunard*, 212, 291–93
with *Olga Rudge*, 295–96
events 1921–25, 297–345
edits *Eliot's Waste Land*, 303–9
Joyce's Ulysses published, 309–10
starts *Bel Esprit* for Eliot, 311ff.
Indiscretions published, 323
Ford Madox Ford and *Transatlantic Review*, 319, 328–43
health problems, 65, 131–32, 309, 332–36, 342
permanent departure for Italy, 342
Draft of XVI Cantos, A, 344–45, 347–52
settles in Rapallo, 344–45, 353
birth of daughter *Mary de Rachewiltz*, 345
death, 353
photos, ii, 137, 278, 330
sculpture, 149
vortograph, 159
drawing, 241
Pound, Homer
father in Ezra's childhood, xiii–xiv
supports son, 4, 37, 64, 65, 81, 185, 192, 243, 328, 332
during return of 1910, 56, 57, 61, 62, 65
and Ezra's marriage, 154, 172
as literary reader, 183, 199, 224
and family relations, 242, 337–38
and *Instigations*, 239
retirement in Italy, 305, 311, 313, 325, 353
letters from, 4, 53, 81
letters to: see Paige Carbons
Pound, Isabel. See also Paige Carbons
mother in Ezra's childhood, xiii–xiv
during return of 1910, 57, 61, 62, 63, 65
concern for son's health, 131–32, 332
and Ezra's marriage, 154, 172
retirement in Italy, 353
Pound, Omar, 16, 249, 283, 295, 345, 353
Pound, Susan Angevin Loomis, 310, 324, 338
Pound, Thaddeus C., xiii, 100, 172, 242
in *Cantos*, 337–38, 339
Powys, Llewelyn and John Cowper, 85, 102
Pratz, Claire de, 235, 317
Pré-Catelan Restaurant, 290 (in *Cantos*)

General Index

Predappio, 121 (in *Cantos*)
Pre-Raphaelites, 6, 22, 253
"Prolegomena," 87
Propertius (Sextus) translations, 86, 198, 207, 227–28, 236–37, 254, 314
Prothero, G. W., 99
Proust, Marcel, 35, 223, 247, 275, 302, 318
Provença, 64
Provençal. *See* troubadours
Punch (magazine), 29, 107
Putnam, G. H., 18
Putnam, Samuel, 276

Quade, Mons, 63, 351 (in *Cantos*)
Quia Pauper Amavi, 202, 230, 236–37
Quiller-Couch, Arthur, 103–5
Quinn, James, 191
Quinn, John
 early life, 60, 191
 Pound meets in 1910, 60–61
 friendship begins in 1915, 174–75
 promotes Pound's work, 182, 185, 191–92, 205–6, 212–13, 240, 300–301
 informed of *Cantos*, 182, 190, 238, 310, 314, 317, 326
 in Paris (1921), 301–2; (1924), 328–30
 promotes art, 60, 174–75, 177, 191, 197–98, 301–2
 and J. B. Yeats, 60–61, 298, 301
 and W. B. Yeats, 60, 227, 300
 and Joyce, 119, 195, 201, 224, 280, 298–300, 310, 313–14
 Ulysses manuscript, 247, 300, 329, 332
 and Eliot, 226, 240, 242, 304, 305, 310, 313, 327
 Waste Land manuscript, 306–7, 316–317, 323
 and Lewis, 175, 191, 260, 300, 301
 and Gaudier-Brzeska estate, 174, 176, 197–98
 and Knopf, 185, 193, 195, 205–6, 226
 and Conrad, 190, 197
 and *Little Review*, 194–95, 198, 212–13, 224, 298, 299, 300
 and *Dial*, 240, 248, 304
 and *Transatlantic Review*, Ford, 328–29, 337
 dedication of *Pavannes and Divisions*, 204–7
 letters from Pound, 60, 135, 154, 174, 176, 181, 185, 190, 193, 201, 206, 224, 226, 227, 238, 242–43, 245, 246, 248, 260, 264, 271, 279, 288, 297, 300, 302, 304, 310, 312, 313–14, 316, 317, 322, 326, 340
 letters to Pound, 60, 174, 176–77, 190–92, 242–43, 280, 298, 300, 301
 health problems, 206, 243, 300, 312, 316, 329, 337, 340
 death, 340, 341
 in *Cantos*, 60, 61, 332, 351
 photo, 330
Quinzaine for This Yule, A, 9, 11

Rabelais, François, 224
Rachewiltz, Mary de, 181, 296, 345, 353
Radiguet, Raymond, 263–64, 276, 331–32
Ramperti, Marco, 32 (in *Cantos*)
Rapallo, 38, 311, 320–23, 332–35, 341–44, 352–53 (in *Cantos*)
Ratti, Achille. *See* Pius XI, Pope
Ravel, Maurice, 53
Ravenna, 312, 324
Ray, Man, 124, 194, 269, 272, 323, 329, 333, 335, 278 (photo)
Read, Forrest, 136, 243
Read, Sir Herbert, 35, 83, 209–12, 223, 225
Rebel Art Centre, 148, 158
Reck, Michael, 186
"Redondillas," 70–71
Reid, Marjorie, 332
Reid, Phyllis, 173, 225, 328
Reinach, Salomon, 261
"Religio," 119–20, 206
"Rémy de Gourmont," 89–90, 206
Renaissance, 6, 18, 36, 46, 69, 70, 99, 138, 200, 231, 313, 322, 348–51
"Renaissance, The," 138
Rennert, Hugo, xiv, 46, 243
"Retrospect, A," 87
"Return, The," 105, 285
Rhymers Club, 7
Rhys, Ernest, 6, 8, 19, 32, 37, 46, 52, 81, 106
Rhys, Jean, 343
Ribérac, 234
Ricketts, Charles, 174, 186
Rihaku. *See* Li Po
Rimbaud, Arthur, 116–17, 205, 248
Rimini
 in *Cantos*, 312–13, 324, 351
Ripostes, 31, 34, 64, 93, 94, 104–5
"River Merchant's Wife: A Letter," 175
"River Song," 175
Rives, Amber, 23 (in *Cantos*)
Roberts, William, 145, 156–58, 160, 191
Robinson, Fred C., 86
Robinson, Janice, 222
Rocamadour, 232–34
Rock, Joseph, 193–94 (in *Cantos*)
Rock-Drill (Epstein sculpture), 128 (in *Cantos*)
Rockefeller family, 242
Rodenbach, Georges R., 270
Rodez, 98
Rodker, John, 180, 188, 225–26, 231, 238–39, 246, 252–53, 277, 301, 311, 316, 326, 341

Romains, Jules, 113, 116, 205
  in *Cantos*, 114, 207
romanticism, 36, 40, 45
Rome, 322–23
Rosenbach, A. S. W., 332–33
Ross, Ishbel, 97
Rothermere, Lady Mary Lilian, 311, 327
Rothschild family
  in *Cantos*, 180, 220
Royal Café, 127, 155, 157, 186, 212
Rudel, Jaufre, 234 (in *Cantos*)
Rudge, Olga
  early life, 250
  Pound reviews, 249
  Pound meets, 320, 324
  music affairs, often with Antheil, 250–51, 262, 268–70, 312, 324, 326–27, 331, 337, 339, 340, 342
  in Paris social world, 94, 251, 287–88, 293, 295–96, 320, 328
  on walking tour, 341
  and Hemingway, 283
  in later years, 170, 296, 353
  daughter Mary, 296, 345, 353
  compared to Dorothy Pound, 18, 295–96
  compared to Bride Scratton, 51
  letter to, 337
  photo, 251
Rummel, Frank, 67, 265
Rummel, Walter Morse, xiv, 264–67
  hosts Pound in Paris, 3, 52, 67–69, 94, 113, 115, 265
  visits America, 61–62, 182, 265
  collaborates on music, 62, 65, 67–70, 115, 201, 205, 213, 260, 264–65
  in London, 76
  and H.D., 61, 80–82, 265
  Cravens affair, 96, 265
  Duncan affair, 197, 266, 325
  death, 197, 265, 267, 274
  in *Cantos*, 197, 265, 267
Ruskin, John, 6 (in *Cantos*)
Russell, Ada, D., 123, 161
Russia, 215, 281, 311, 317–18, 334, 352
Rutter, Frank, 209

Sackville, Lady Margaret, 30–31
Sagetrieb, 231 (in *Cantos*)
St. Bertrand de Comminges, 230–31 (in *Cantos*)
St. Elizabeth's Hospital, Pound in, 20, 68, 131, 177, 249, 293, 295, 353
St. George, Adam of, 71
St. Hilaire, Church of, 234 (in *Cantos*)
St. Raphael, 287, 298–99
St. Trophime, Church of, 98, 230 (in *Cantos*)
Salle du Conservatoire, 331
Salle Pleyel, 339–40

Salò, 53
Sandburg, Carl, 100, 171, 180
San Michele, island of, xiii, 353
San Pantaleo, Church of, 38 (in *Cantos*)
San Zeno, Church of, 71–72
Sappho, 34, 112
Satie, Erik, 268–69, 300, 329, 342
Saunders, Helen, 156–57, 202, 211–12
Savitsky, Ludmila Bloch-, 246, 301
Scaliger family, 53
Schafer, Murray, 201
Schaffner, Perdita, 223
Schamberg, Morton, 299
Schelling, Felix, xiv, 177, 189, 243, 253, 314
Schloss, Arthur. *See* Waley, Arthur
Schneidau, Herbert N., 35
Scratton, Bride (Evelyn)
  early life and loves, 48–51, 153, 197
  publications (as G.-Adams), 283, 325, 334
  in Verona, Paris, 294, 313 (in *Cantos*), 315
  divorce and later life, 293–95, 329, 344
  photo, 49
Scratton, Edward (Ned), 50–51, 293–94, 329
Scratton, Michael, 50
"Seafarer, The," 86, 105, 175–76, 199, 348
Seldes, Gilbert, 240, 285, 334, 339
Selver, Paul, 83–85, 236
"Serious Artist, The," 119
"Sestina: Altaforte," 26–27, 32, 233
Shakespear, Henry Hope, 14, 17, 81, 94, 132, 153–54, 249, 327–28
Shakespear, Olivia
  Pound meets, 13–14
  early life, 14–16, 331, 335
  and Yeats, 15–16, 36, 40, 42, 55, 201
  in Italy, 55, 113, 329
  and *Canzoni*, 71
  promotes marriage of Dorothy, 81, 82, 103, 153–54
  and H.D., 82, 95, 231
  promotes arts, 127–28, 150
  cards to from Midi (1919), 229, 231–35
  death of husband, 326–28
  rears Omar Pound, 345
  publications, 14, 133
  death, 153, 223
  photo, 15
Shakespeare, William, 94, 180, 279, 315
Shakespeare and Company. *See* Beach, Sylvia
Shaw, George Bernard, 19, 32, 83, 84, 116, 197, 260, 315
Shepard, W. P., xiv, 46, 231, 350
Sibelius, Jean, 265 (in *Cantos*)
Sicily, 343–44
Sieburth, Richard, 99, 206

General Index

Siena, 296, 298, 312, 353
Sinclair, May, 8, 17, 19, 20, 23, 25, 52, 67, 81, 82, 100, 119, 173, 180, 222, 311
Singer, Paris, 266
Sinistrari, L. M., 134
Sirdar Restaurant, 290 (in *Cantos*)
town, 233 (in *Cantos*)
Sirmione, 53–57, 54 (in *Cantos*), 69, 114, 243–44, 300, 313
Sitalkas, 120–21 (in *Cantos*), 150
Sitwells (Edith, Osbert, Sacheverell), 209, 211, 225, 292, 300, 322–23
Sloan, John, 61
Slonimsky, Henry, 80, 95 (in *Cantos*), 106
Smart Set (magazine), 112, 136
Smith, Justin H., 98
Smith, William Brooke, xiii–xiv, 299
Social Credit, 203, 213–21, 255, 302–3, 348
socialism, 83, 203, 215, 314
Solano, Solita, 291
"Song of the Bowmen of Shu," 175
Sonnets and Ballate of Guido Cavalcanti, 69, 78–79, 95
Sordello (Lo Sordels de Goito), 71, 98, 183, 230, 350 (in *Cantos*)
Sordello (Browning), 173, 183–84, 199, 348 (in *Cantos*)
Soupault, Philippe, 273
South Lodge, 23–24, 47, 73–74, 90, 118, 148, 154, 179, 25 (photo)
Spain, 281, 285, 326–27
Spire, André, 116, 205 (in *Cantos*), 246, 271, 279
Spirit of Romance, 8, 37, 44–46, 52, 54, 71, 79
spiritualism, 40–41, 122, 133, 201, 273
Square Club, 9, 28, 46
Steegmuller, Francis, 276
Steffens, Lincoln, 281, 311, 317–19, 329, 334, 337, 341, 352 (in *Cantos*)
Stein, Gertrude, 8, 259, 263, 281–82, 285, 288, 301–2, 310, 318, 325, 334, 335, 341–42
Stieglitz, Alfred, 272
Stone Cottage
in 1913–14, 133–39
in 1914–15, 173–74
in 1915–16, 184
honeymoon in, 154
Storer, Edward, 33–34
Strachey, Lytton, 145
Strater, Henry (Mike), 321–23, 325, 335–36, 344
Stravinsky, Igor, 126, 269, 275, 327, 347
Strindberg, Frida, 108–9, 140, 145, 155–56
Stryker, M. W., 301
Stuart, Francis, 196–97
Stuart, Iseult. See MacBride, Iseult

Stuart, Mary, 82
"Study in French Poets," 205
Stulik, Rudolph, 155, 157, 212
Sullivan, J. P., 228
surrealism, 273–74, 336
Svevo, Italo, 135
Swarthmore, 57, 61, 265
Swedenborg, Emanuel, 133
Swift and Company, 94, 105
Swinburne, Charles Algernon, 11 (in *Cantos*), 69, 77
symbolism, 38, 206, 298
Symons, Arthur, 38, 41, 116, 135, 182, 298
Synge, J. M., 5, 36–37, 40, 134

Tacitus, 21
Tagore, Rabindranath, 101, 106–7, 156
Tailhade, Laurent, 116, 178, 205, 207 (in *Cantos*)
Talbot, Charles, 248–49 (in *Cantos*)
Talleyrand, 189, 232, 235 (in *Cantos*)
Tancred, F. W., 30, 34, 42 (in *Cantos*), 298
tanka, 34
Tarascon, 230 (in *Cantos*)
Tennyson, Alfred, 126, 174
Testament de Villon (opera), 302, 318, 328, 331, 339, 347
Thayer, Elaine, 285–86, 330, 336
Thayer, Scofield, 240, 263, 285–87, 301–2, 304, 330
This Generation, 185
Thiy, Thij, 51, 294, 313. See Scratton, Bride
Thomas, Edward, 28, 46, 202
Thompson, Francis, 182
Thompson, Lawrance, 111
Three Mountains Press, 283, 285, 323, 325–36, 333–35. See also Bird, William
Three Songs (with Rummel), 68
Tomczyk, Stanislawa, 42 (in *Cantos*)
Tor, Miquel (Miguel) de la, 95, 98
Tosch, 229 (in *Cantos*)
Toulouse, 98, 228–32
in *Cantos*, 229, 232, 349
Tour Eiffel Restaurant. See Eiffel Tower Restaurant
"To Whistler," 99
Transatlantic Review, 225, 281, 283, 287, 316–17, 329, 331, 334–36, 339, 340–43
Translations of E.P., 73, 77–79, 86–87, 106, 138, 193, 229, 247
"Translators of Greek," 99
Tree, Iris, 225
Trianon Restaurant, 285, 290, 333
troubadours, 18, 26, 28, 34, 36–37, 42, 44–46, 67–70, 72–73, 76–78, 98–99,

191–93, 199, 201–2, 205–6, 213, 230–38, 249, 349 (in *Cantos*)
"Troubadours—Their Sorts and Conditions," 99, 206
Tucker, Major Henry Tod, 14–15, 154
Tucker, Saint George, 15
typewriters, 123–24, 154, 288, 325
Tzara, Tristan, 272–73, 335, 339, 278 (photo)

Ullman, Alice Woods, 69
Ullman, Eugene Paul, 69 (in *Cantos*), 97
Ullman, Sigmund, 69
Umbra, 239–40
Untermeyer, Louis, 190
Upward, Allen, 85, 120–22, 125, 146, 150, 161–63, 180, 121 (in *Cantos*)
Ur-Cantos. See *Cantos*, first publications
Ussel, 233 (in *Cantos*)
Usura, usury, 219–20, 232, 242, 252. See also Geryon
in *Cantos*, 234, 349
Uzerche, 98

Valera, Eamon de, 302, 304–5, 314
Valéry, Paul, 247, 262, 271
Van Buren, Martin, 217 (in *Cantos*)
Vance, Fred, xiv, 200, 287
Vanderpyl, Fritz, 236, 247, 350 (in *Cantos*)
Vanity Fair (magazine), 317, 325
Vatican Library, 322–23
Vega, Lope de, 46
Venice, xiii, 56, 58, 114–15, 181, 199–200, 242–44, 250, 291–92, 296, 312–13, 321, 324
in *Cantos*, 349, 353
Ventadorn (Ventadour), Bernart de, 98, 232–35, 238, 350
in *Cantos*, 233, 238, 350
Verlaine, Paul, 6 (in *Cantos*)
Verog. See Plarr, Victor
Verona, 51, 53, 71
in *Cantos*, 294, 313
Victoria, Queen, 208 (in *Cantos*)
Vidal, Peire, 39, 228, 349 (in *Cantos*)
Vienna Café, 27
in *Cantos*, 7–8, 46–47
Vildrac, Charles, 113, 114 (in *Cantos*), 116, 205
Villars, Abbot of Montfaucon de, 133
Villon, François, 46, 315, 339, 346–47. See also *Testament de Villon*
Vittoz, Roger, 303
Vivaldi, Antonio, 250–51
Vivien, Renée, 261–62
Voisin Restaurant, 161 (in *Cantos*), 290
Voltaire, 188
Voorhis, Jerry, 216
vorticism.
See also *Blast 1, 2*

beginnings of, 113, 128–29
first use by Pound of term, 141
Lewis as leader, 142–48, 155–60
source of term, 146
defined by Lewis, 146–47
defined by Gaudier-Brzeska, 147
and literature, 155–60, 174, 179
and *Cantos*, 160, 200
"Vorticism," 174
vortographs, 197, 323, 159 (photo)

Wabash College, xiv, 37, 75
Wadsworth, Augustus B., 320
Wadsworth, Charles D., 63
Wadsworth, Edward, 145, 156–57, 160, 172–73
Wadsworth, William (son of Charles D.), 63
Wadsworth, William B., 63
Wadsworth family, 325
Wagner, Richard, 22, 265
Waley, Arthur, 8, 145, 175, 205
walking trips
(1912), Midi, 95, 98–99
(1919), Midi, 226, 228–38, 349
(1923), Italy, 281, 321–22
(1924), Midi, 341
Wang Wei, 130
Waterlow, Sydney, 304
Watson, J. Sibley, Jr., 240, 285, 316–18, 324
Watts-Dunton, Theodore, 11 (in *Cantos*)
Weaver, Harriet Shaw, 118–19, 136, 141–42, 191, 223–24, 242, 244–45, 280, 284–85, 298
Welfare sisters, 133
Wells, H. G., 21, 83–84, 207, 208 (in *Cantos*)
Wells, Julia, 57–58, 244
Wessells, Sadie, 64
West, Rebecca, 118, 156
Weston, Ezra B., xiii, 64, 65, 111, 250
Weston, Frances, xiii–xiv, 62–65, 118, 250, 262–63 (in *Cantos*), 317, 351
Weston, Mary, 325
Whistler, James, 260, 287
Whitman, Walt, 28, 117, 118
Wilkinson, Louis, 102
William IX, Duke of Aquitaine, 98
in *Cantos*, 234, 350
Williams, Edgar, 71–72 (in *Cantos*), 320
Williams, Florence (Flossie), 59, 332, 333, 338–39
Williams, William Carlos
early life, xiii
in London (1910), 48
during Pound's return of 1910, 59–60, 62, 66
and H.D., 59–60, 80, 284, 299, 333, 338
Ripostes dedication, 104

General Index

promoted by Pound, 112, 180
and imagism, 125, 299
argument with, 207, 248
in Paris (1924), 332–33, 338–40
and Bird, Three Mountains, 283, 316, 333
and McAlmon, 283–84, 299, 333, 338–40
and Eliot, 308, 311
and Ford, *Transatlantic Review*, 333, 335
letters to, 5–6, 19, 36, 146, 224, 248, 292, 311, 316
Wilson, Edmund, 327
Wilson, Woodrow, 246, 279, 351 (in *Cantos*)
Windeler, B. C., 283, 325, 352 (in *Cantos*)
Withey, Ann, 3–4
Woburn Buildings, 41–42, 117, 196, 227
Wood, C. E. S., 341
Wood, Mrs. Derwent, 52
Woolf, Virginia, 92, 145, 170, 226
Wordsworth, William, 117, 173 (in *Cantos*), 184
World War I
outbreak, 163–64
immediate effects of, 167–68, 172–73
Pound's first attitude toward, 174
early deaths, 176–77
central events, 178–79
later deaths, 202 (in *Cantos*)
later effect on Pound, 203
ending of, 204–5, 208–9
Pound's feelings after, 212–13
in *Cantos*, 348, 351–52
Wright, W. H., 112

"Xenia," 28

Yeats, Georgiana Hyde-Lees, 113, 133, 201, 227
Yeats, John B., 60–62, 61 (in *Cantos*), 298, 310
Yeats, Lily, 186, 193
Yeats, William Butler
early life, 7, 15, 38, 40–41
Pound goes to London to meet, 4, 5
affair with Olivia Shakespear, 15–16
Pound meets, 36, 40
Monday night poetry readings, 41, 52, 87

Pound on, 20, 42, 52, 61, 106, 110, 198
on Pound, 41–45, 55, 107
occult activities, 15–16, 41–42, 79, 133–35, 145, 173
and father, 60–61, 310
compared to Pound, 135
compared to Ford, 20, 42, 103, 106
compared to Orage, 84
compared to Gourmont, 90
and *Poetry*, 100–101, 124, 154
Pound edits, 100, 110
influence on Pound, 101, 106, 147, 187, 314
Pound reads to, 103, 110, 133–34, 173–74, 184
and imagism, 106, 123, 172, 298
and Joyce, 125, 135, 179, 245 (comparison)
and Blunt, 138
at Stone Cottage (1913–14), 133–39
at Stone Cottage (1914–15), 173–74
at Stone Cottage (1915–16), 184
interest in Noh plays, 134–35, 181
At the Hawk's Well, 134, 181, 186
and Pound's marriage, 154
his own marriage, 133, 201, 226
and Easter Uprising, 186–87, 195–97
in Ireland and Irish politics, 32, 195–97, 201, 226–27, 305–6, 314, 316, 319, 339
with Maud Gonne and Iseult MacBride, 15, 186–87, 195–97, 201, 305–6, 314, 337
wins Nobel Prize, 227, 335
in Paris (1911), 68
in Paris (1922), 305–6
in Italy, 342, 344, 353
letters to, 319, 337, 339
in *Cantos*, 20, 42, 68, 84, 110, 134, 173, 353
photo, 137
Yellow Book, 5
Yip, Wai-lim, 176
Yorke, Dorothy, 132
Youngstown, Ohio, 250–51

Zagreus, 208, 306
Zaharoff, Sir Basil (Metevsky), 12, 318, 352 (in *Cantos*)
Ziemska, Hela, 249
Zinnes, Harriet 200

Index of References to the *Cantos*

Canto	Page
1	199, 207, 325, 343, 348
2	183, 199, 347, 348–49
3	199, 200, 318, 349
4	22, 45, 153, 199, 228, 229, 232, 234, 238, 242, 294, 349
5	350
6	234, 350
7	89, 310, 350–51
8–11	311, 317, 318, 320, 322, 323, 324, 326, 351
12	60, 63, 294, 314, 315, 332, 333, 351
13	173, 194, 326, 332, 351
14	223, 238, 303, 314, 315, 343, 351–52
15	223, 238, 303, 315, 343, 351–52
16	7, 202, 328, 348, 352
17	344
18	12, 343
19	302, 343
20	72, 73
22	338, 339
23	98
26	233
27	114, 233
28	316
29	236, 301
31	230
38	215
40	331
42	208
45	219, 230, 234
46	216, 217, 219
48	231–32
51	230, 234
52	229
62	216
65	234
71	216
74	8, 23, 32, 54, 82, 89, 121, 219, 232, 233, 270, 286, 289, 290
76	54, 222, 230, 244, 276, 289, 290
77	72, 95, 97, 106, 161, 181, 218, 219, 275, 276, 353
78	51, 207, 294, 302, 313, 319
79	89, 219
80	4, 8, 24, 46–47, 55–56, 58, 60, 69, 72, 82, 110, 114, 168, 180, 207, 229, 235, 239, 243, 249, 254, 256, 263, 264, 265, 274, 275, 276, 286, 293, 297, 305, 314, 342, 353
81	51, 91, 138, 205, 249
82	11, 20, 42, 187
83	68, 134, 173, 184
84	262–63
85	219
86	219, 274
87	7, 173, 231, 273, 275
89	6, 287
90	231, 235
91	247, 319
92	32–33
93	206
95	32, 219, 230, 340–41
96	24, 179, 184, 188, 218, 230
97	90, 273, 274
98	84
100	38, 230, 331
101	235
103	273
104	24, 197, 206, 267, 331
105	209, 235
107	98, 150, 330 (caption)
110	194
113	109
114	353
115	140
116	205
117	238, 275

www.ingramcontent.com/pod-product-compliance
Lightning Source LLC
Chambersburg PA
CBHW031541300426
44111CB00006BA/139